THE ANCHOR COMPANION TO THE ORCHESTRA

THE ANCHOR COMPANION TO THE ORCHESTRA

by Norman Del Mar

Anchor Press/Doubleday
Garden City, New York
1987

Copyright © 1987 by Faber and Faber Limited Publishers
Library of Congress Cataloging in Publication Data
ISBN: 0-385-24082-1

This book was designed and produced by
Faber and Faber Limited Publishers
3 Queen Square, London WC1N 3AU
for Anchor Press/Doubleday
245 Park Avenue, New York 10167

Foreword

A few years ago I wrote a book about the orchestra in response to the promptings of musical colleagues – and most especially a close composer friend, Thea Musgrave – who urged me to publish my researches into the orchestra, the possibilities of its instruments, and the interpreter's/conductor's/performer's problem of correctly understanding the composer's written notation.

This book, which was ultimately called *Anatomy of the Orchestra* (and which was directed primarily at professional musicians), met with such a gratifying success that my publishers – and in particular my editor, Patrick Carnegy – proposed that I might go on to write another work presenting all the essential information about the orchestra and its instruments, as well as much out-of-the-way material, in the ready-reference form of a companion for everyone interested in classical music.

The present volume is the result: to some extent inevitably a kind of offshoot, but it also contains a great deal of new material and covers more than enough territory outside the province of *Anatomy* to warrant its coexistence. Where it covers the same ground there has been no attempt to say identical things in different words, or to omit information or remarks simply because they are already in the earlier book; but at the same time variations in outlook or emphasis have often led me to make important changes, as well as providing the opportunity to correct, improve or bring up to date the places that, even in the partially revised paperback edition (1983), have still remained outstanding.

In the entries for individual instruments the emphasis is on their orchestral characteristics rather than their solo potential. Historical and technical details of their construction and so on have also, as before, lain outside my province and are in any case easily found in numerous books or encyclopaedias. Voices are again included but here, too, it is towards their relationship with the orchestra and orchestral concerts that the entries have been largely orientated.

As ever, I have no illusions about the ultimate correctness of all that I say. Letters or published criticisms of *Anatomy* have already put me to rights on many important issues and these I shall always welcome. It is in the nature of a book such as this that to wait until everything has been proved, checked and counterchecked with every expert on every subject is to be sure of never going into print at all.

In the meantime my hope must be that the selection has been in line with the overall aim of the book and that the reader, whether concert-goer, performer or composer, will find in it something of interest and value.

As a brief explanatory outline of procedure, it may be helpful to add that a word printed entirely in SMALL CAPITALS is intended to encourage one to turn to that entry for more information. When the information centres on a key word within an entry, then for ease of ready reference that word is printed in **bold** type. It must be confessed that it has not always been possible to achieve complete stylistic consistency. With instruments, for example, I have elected to give individual entries for well-known subspecies, such as alto saxophone, which are therefore presented in strict alphabetical order, this example accordingly being found under A for Alto, but borderline cases like the bass saxhorn are left to be described in general articles on – in this case – the saxhorns as a family. The reason for this is based on my determination that practicality should always be the first priority and that in my experience this is the simplest way to find what one is looking for.

Writing in Britain, I have not unnaturally followed English usage for note values (i.e., 'crotchet' instead of 'quarter note', 'quaver' instead of 'eighth note', etc) and other terms (e.g., 'bar' instead of 'measure', 'note' instead of 'tone', etc) but I only do so in the confident knowledge that these will present no problems to my American readers.

My thanks are, as ever, due to the many friends – professional and otherwise – who have helped me on my way: to Patrick Carnegy himself for his affectionate patience and forbearing, and to the composer David Matthews who has taken valuable time off from writing music not only to read and comment on my errors and idiosyncrasies but to suggest the inclusion of additional illustrative examples from the orchestral repertoire; to Barrie Iliffe who, as so often, showed himself a tower of strength in matters of language and style, as well as in the searching out of literals; to Michael Round for a mass of intriguing instrumental discoveries; to my son Jonathan who continues to bombard me with a myriad of fascinating detail of which I was either ignorant or had overlooked; and especially to Dinah Molloy who has been the soul of encouragement and warm enthusiasm at every stage.

Hadley Common, 1986   *N.R.D.M.*

List of books cited in the text

Baines, Anthony, *Woodwind Instruments and their History*, London, 1957

Berlioz, Hector, *A Treatise on the Modern Instrumentation and Orchestration*, Paris, 1843 (translated from the French by Mary Cowden Clarke, London, 1855)

Blades, James, *Percussion Instruments and Their History*, London, 1957, rev.ed., 1984

Forsyth, Cecil, *Orchestration*, London, 1935

Gevaert, François-Auguste, *Nouveau Traité d'Instrumentation*, Paris, Brussels, 1885

Holland, James, *Percussion* (Yehudi Menuhin Music Guides), London, 1978

Piston, Walter, *Orchestration*, London, 1955

Read, Gardner, *Thesaurus of Orchestral Devices*, London, 1953

Rimsky-Korsakov, Nikolay, *Principles of Orchestration*, St Petersburg, 1913 (English trans., 1922)

Scholes, Percy A. *Oxford Companion to Music*, 6th edition, London, 1945

Smith Brindle, Reginald, *Contemporary Percussion*, London, 1970

Terry, Charles Sanford, *Bach's Orchestra*, London, 1932

Grove's Dictionary of Music and Musicians, 5th edition, ed. Eric Blom, London, 1954

The New Grove Dictionary of Music and Musicians, ed. Stanley Sadie, London, 1980

The New Grove Dictionary of Musical Instruments, ed. Stanley Sadie, London, 1984

A

The note to which orchestras conventionally tune. The term 'giving the A' is normally applicable to the first oboist who, by virtue of the penetrating tone quality of this instrument, sounds and sustains the A above middle C (sometimes after checking with a tuning fork) for his colleagues to match and so find a collectively uniform tuning. This is a highly responsible duty and one that many principal oboists find gruelling.

Because of this, perhaps, a custom has been growing, especially on the Continent, of substituting an electronic machine that can be relied on to emit an unvarying band of sound fixed artificially at 440, 442, 445 or however many vibrations per second is the standard norm. Yet it is surprising how inadequate – even irritating – such substitutes are, and indeed how hard they can be to tune to, compared with the living sound of the oboe.

Certain training-minded conductors have at one time been known to require the entire orchestral personnel to file past an A-giving person or apparatus. Sir Henry Wood made a great feature of this form of discipline during his regime with the principal orchestra of the Royal Academy of Music, where it certainly had a usefulness in sharpening the awareness of young players; but such regimentation becomes intolerable when imposed on professional orchestral musicians who know all too well that within minutes of playing, whether at rehearsal or in concert, intonation will be a matter of constant adjustment as instruments warm up and the temperature in the hall itself varies.

The A is usually called for before the entry of the conductor at the beginning of a concert, and again after the interval, by the leader or sometimes the sub-leader before the leader comes on to the platform.

In the event of a concerto some additional routine is necessary. For a piano concerto the same A is usually sounded on the piano as soon as it has been moved into position and while the conductor is fetching the soloist. In the case of any other instrumental soloist the conductor himself will superintend the situation if the artist indicates that he wants to take the A. This is a very personal affair: some soloists far prefer to dispense with the whole paraphernalia of tuning in public, relying on hearing the orchestra while waiting in the wings; others may use the oboe A on the platform to recheck – pitch can sound deceptively flat heard at a distance – and may occasionally make a positive meal of the whole business. I once found myself waiting for many minutes while my solo harpist (a gentleman of considerable international repute) solemnly tuned his entire instrument in full view of the audience.

One important exception to the orchestra taking the A from the oboe arises when a work requires the organ. The orchestra will then tune from the organ since its pitch is an immutable fact of life. This causes a real problem and one that constantly recurs, partly because organs are often tuned to a different A from our conventional orchestral 440, and partly because even if the orchestra and the organ are hypothetically in tune, the organ may sound disconcertingly flat. Many are the occasions when the great C major organ chords of Saint-Saëns's Third Symphony or Strauss's *Also sprach Zarathustra* make one feel as if in a lift that has suddenly dropped a floor and a half. A clever 1st oboe will often help an orchestra to avoid these stomach-churning moments by acting as intermediary, giving a shrewdly judged compromise A even while the organ is pealing its independent version to the consternation of all.

The oboe obviously does not give the A when the programme begins with a work without oboes, such as Mozart's Symphony No. 39 in E♭ (K. 543), or with a work for strings alone. In the former instance the clarinet (or other woodwind in similar parallel cases) and in the latter the leader himself will generally perform the service.

A CAPPELLA

(Sometimes spelt with a single 'p') this is one of those terms the literal meaning of which is now largely relegated to musicology. Originally it signified sacred choral music entirely devoid of instrumental accompaniment, but now no longer carries reference to chapels or indeed to anything to do with religion. Today *a cappella* can be applied to any wholly unaccompanied vocal piece (e.g. Delius's 'To be sung of a summer's night on the water') or to a movement from a choral and orchestral work (the 'Quaerens me' from Berlioz's *Grande Messe des Morts*), or even to a brief section of such a work, like the notoriously tricky *a cappella* passage 'the trumpeters and pipers' from towards the end of Walton's *Belshazzar's Feast.*

A cappella movements can be a very important element in rehearsal planning since there may often be no purpose in wasting valuable orchestral time working with the choir while the players remain totally unoccupied. Hence the relegation of these works or sections to early choir rehearsals (held with only a pianist or the chorus master in attendance) greatly augments the proportion of total time available for eleventh-hour rehearsals with the orchestra. Where the *a cappella* sections dovetail with orchestral passages, some rehearsal time must of course be allocated to fitting the two together, one reason being that although *a cappella* singing is an essential part of choral work and training there is always associated with it the problem of pitch retention. Virtually all large choirs struggle ceaselessly against the inevitable tendency to drop by as much as a tone, depending on the length of the unsupported movement, generally sinking so gradually that only the wretched members with the gift of ABSOLUTE PITCH (who suffer dreadfully in these circumstances) realize what has happened.

Where the movements are separate entities, however, the effect, if undesirable, need not be disastrous; but calamity is unavoidable when an orchestral re-entry reveals a serious drop in pitch with devastating clarity – for example, the wind fanfares that intersperse the latter part of the crucially difficult unaccompanied choral section of Ravel's *Daphnis et Chloé.*

See also: CHORUS, CHORUS MASTER

ABSOLUTE PITCH

A number of people, not all necessarily good musicians, possess a form of memory that enables them to recognize, or to recall at will, any of the twelve notes that make up the chromatic scale on which Western art music is based. This gift, known as 'absolute pitch' or *perfect pitch*, is an obvious boon in the matter of aural training; yet many of the greatest musicians have lacked it and it can even be held of doubtful overall value. It may certainly cause confusion in the reading or playing of parts for TRANSPOSING INSTRUMENTS and it is especially worrying for its possessor when a pitch has to be adopted other than the current standard, the one on which the memory is based. Yet for conductors (especially of choirs) it makes for efficiency at rehearsal through the immediate identification and correction of errors in the most complicated harmonic structures.

Perfect pitch can naturally also be of untold advantage to singers of contemporary atonal or serial compositions where harmonic logic plays no part in note recognition, although – as one international singer confessed to me during rehearsals of Schoenberg's *Erwartung* – it may lead a performer to tap out the seemingly inconsequential rows of notes like a typist instead of finding the natural phrasing in the way one would for a Schubert melody.

Above all, the identification of perfect pitch with superior musicianship is a fallacy that needs to be avoided in assessing the value of this unquestionably impressive gift.

See also: A CAPPELLA, CHORUS

Abstrich (Ger.), down bow; *see* BOWING, 7

ACCORDION

This popular instrument, indigenous to many different folk cultures, is basically a reed-organ contraption worked on the bellows principle. Its strains are so full of familiar associations that, like the mouth organ, it would seem to have no place in the symphony orchestra, even though its most characteristic tonic–dominant squeeze-box effect has been widely imitated in works depicting popular gatherings, such as Vaughan Williams's *London Symphony* or Stravinsky's *Petrouchka*. Yet, unlike its little cousin the concertina, which appears only in a solitary instance (albeit in 'unlimited' (*sic*) quantities) in Holbrooke's Fantasie *Dylan*, the accordion has in fact made sporadic appearances in orchestral literature. Tchaikovsky wrote for two – to be doubled if possible – in the *Scherzo burlesque* of his Second Suite, Op. 55, while in recent years both Roberto Gerhard and Thea Musgrave have found a place for the instrument in various works using it in complex but basically single-strand styles not normally thought to be its natural mode of expression.

The wide-ranged larger instruments, known as *piano accordions*, are equip-

3

ped with a keyboard of three octaves and a third , but this range can be almost doubled to just under six octaves, according to the number of buttons or combination switches that some monsters can boast.

See also: BANDONEON

AD LIB

Literally 'at will', *ad libitum* denotes freedom of choice in anything ranging from the length of a trill to the improvisation of a whole movement, as in one of Handel's organ concertos. It may also prescribe a spontaneous freedom in rubato, as in the cadenzas for two clarinets and two bassoons from Ravel's *Rapsodie espagnole* or the many solos in Rimsky-Korsakov's *Scheherazade*. Perhaps the most elaborate of all orchestral ad libs is in the first movement of Nielsen's Fifth Symphony, where the side drummer is required to play *à toute la fantaisie de son imagination.*

Another use of 'ad lib' concerns instruments (or voices) the composer intends to form part of his score but may not be confident of having at every performance. Vaughan Williams's overture *The Wasps* has a number of instruments marked 'ad lib' in this way and indeed, in an attempt to widen the sphere of their orchestral performances, Vaughan Williams and Holst marked whole areas of extra instruments 'ad lib' throughout their *oeuvres*. Fortunately such economies are hardly ever resorted to in performances by professional orchestras. An even more extreme example can be found in Fauré's *Pavane*, which has nothing short of a full chorus marked 'ad lib', but in the event this work is almost always performed with instruments alone.

Similarly, in both the *Enigma Variations* and the Overture *Cockaigne*, Elgar marked the concluding organ parts 'ad lib', and here too it has to be admitted that in most performances of both works the organ is omitted, although immense stature is added when it is included. On the other hand in his earlier overture, *Froissart*, Elgar had already added 'ad lib' to the surely essential contrabassoon as well as, incredibly, to the climactic cymbal clash. But surely the most bizarre ad lib of this kind is the crucial tam-tam stroke in the finale of Tchaikovsky's *Pathétique* Symphony. It would be impossible to imagine a performance without this magical *coup de théâtre*, yet the indication is clearly present in the composer's manuscript.

AEROPHON

For a brief period about the time of *Josephslegende* and the *Alpine* Symphony (1913–15) Richard Strauss wrote some impossibly long sustained notes for low wind and brass instruments, adding the instruction in the printed score that in order to prolong the breaths required for these passages *Samuel's Aerophon* was to be used.

This short-lived contraption, invented in 1912 by a German flautist, Bernhard Samuel, seems to have been pumped with the foot, a pipe leading up to the player's mouth supplying the extra wind. Hilarious as this must have been to watch, it was not without its hazards. The eminent flautist Robert Murchie used to relate how, when it was tried out at Covent Garden, the foot pump acted like a vacuum cleaner on the floor of the orchestra pit with disastrous effects for the players. Sadly, therefore, Mr Samuel's ingenious Aerophon (sometimes also called Aerophor) has long since vanished without a trace.

Almglocken (Ger.), *see* COWBELLS

ALPHORN

This is not properly an orchestral instrument in any sense, even though Gerard Hoffnung introduced no fewer than two into the first of his famous Festival Hall concerts in 1956, when they were played by a comedy team called The Alberts.

The alphorn is above all a Swiss national instrument, highly spectacular and picturesque to look at, with its abnormal length (some ten to fifteen feet), but it is very limited in range and technique. In their natural setting alphorns are used for calling from mountain to mountain as their deep majestic tone has immense carrying power.

Curiously enough Richard Strauss ostensibly wrote for the instrument to be played on stage in his opera *Daphne*, which is set not in Switzerland but in Ancient Greece. But he wrote passages

for it rising to the high D ![musical notation: bass clef with high D] ,

clearly expecting the effect that would

be obtained on some heavy brass instrument. In fact the true alphorn is made of wood, and can get only a few natural harmonics. Today the part is usually played on two trombones doubling with a Wagner tuba.

It is amusing to note that the famous horn theme from the beginning of the finale of Brahms's First Symphony was inspired by a phrase the composer heard actually played on an alphorn.

ALTHOBOE

The word Wagner used for the COR ANGLAIS at the end of his life when laying out the score of *Parsifal*. This does not imply any change in writing for the instrument, either in notation or range, but merely a kind of rationalization of its curious name.

ALTHORN

A small tuba built in Eb and really a member of the SAXHORN family. Colloquially known as an 'upright grand', its home is principally in military or especially brass bands where it may be used to replace French horns whose range it largely covers.

Orchestrally it corresponds with the Eb saxhorn used in Berlioz's saxhorn ensemble in *Les Troyens* and also that of D'Indy in *Fervaal* although these composers differ in what they call it, Berlioz confusing the issue by actually describing it as a 'saxhorn tenor en Mib'.

ALTO

(1)
The women's lower line in choral writing. Where solo vocal lines are

5

concerned, a female alto may often be called **contralto** and in fact, strictly speaking, the dictionary definition of 'alto' is the falsetto male voice, 'contralto' signifying the female variety; but this has long ceased to be common usage, the four primary vocal lines being always referred to as SATB. In Britain, moreover, the term 'alto' more usually denotes the choral line, 'contralto' being applied specifically to the solo voice, but this is not uniformly the case in French, German or Italian scores.

Solo male altos are today broadly known as 'counter-tenors', but there no longer exists a differentiation of terms in choral genders, knowledge of composers and styles being the only guide in many cases, such as Stravinsky's *Symphony of Psalms* where, although female sopranos and altos are commonly used, it is known that the composer preferred, and always had in mind, boys' voices.

The range of the altos in choral writing usually extends from, at the most, the low Eb to the G above the stave in the treble clef, which in all modern editions is also used for the alto line. In earlier or more scholarly editions, however, including the Breitkopf scores in the Collected Works series of works such as the Beethoven Missa Solemnis, the alto clef is often retained. A most peculiar exception appears in Mendelssohn's choral works, such as the *Lobesgesang* and *Die Erste Walpurgisnacht*, where the altos as well as the sopranos are notated in the soprano clef.

(2)
The French word for the VIOLA.

ALTO CLARINET

Strictly speaking, this is an instrument built in Eb and used exclusively in military bands (although not in Britain). It is, however, analogous to the BASSET HORN, with the chief difference that the basset horn is built in F, sounding a perfect fifth lower than written. Since they serve the same purpose Stravinsky actually calls the basset horn an alto clarinet in F in *Threni*, but this could be thought more confusing than helpful.

ALTO FLUTE

The big brother of the FLUTE family and perhaps better known by the French name **flûte en sol**. As this indicates, the instrument is built in G and sounds a perfect fourth lower than written. Since it was for so long the only lower instrument of its kind in orchestral use, English scores habitually described it as the 'bass flute' (Holst's *Planets*, Vaughan Williams's *Job*, Britten's *Sinfonia da Requiem*, etc.), but since the middle of the twentieth century there has been a general change of viewpoint, based partly on the logic of the instrument's register and partly on the emergence, in works of contemporary composers, of a true BASS FLUTE sounding a whole octave lower than the flute. A confusing situation thus exists with the bass flute of Britten's *Sinfonia da Requiem* and the alto flute of his *Rape of Lucretia* and subsequent works being in fact one and the same instrument.

It is hardly surprising, perhaps, that it is the French who make the most telling use of their *flûte en sol* – one recalls the magical solos in, for example, Ravel's *Daphnis et Chloé*.

Necessarily such solos are always left studiously exposed as the quality of the instrument is predominantly soft, most players accentuating the breathy side of the flute's timbre. Also, since the chief virtue of the alto flute is its downward extension of range, it is exploited mostly in its lower register. Boulez, however, unexpectedly wrote a supremely virtuoso part for it in *Le Marteau sans Maître*, taking it moreover across an astonishingly wide compass of some three octaves.

One exception in orchestral literature to the alto flute being pitched in G cannot go unmentioned. This occurs in Glazunov's Eighth Symphony, where a 'flauto contralto in F' is listed. This instrument has long since disappeared and players today know nothing about it. Rimsky-Korsakov mentioned it in his *Principles of Orchestration*, though only *en passant* as an alternative to that in G, and since Glazunov never used its bottom notes (on the contrary, writing surprisingly high passages for much of the time), it is hard to know why he should have specified the lower instrument. (It is interesting to find that Rimsky-Korsakov already refers to this F instrument as an alto flute.)

Pfitzner, in his opera *Palestrina*, writes for what he calls an Altflöte, but writing for it at pitch he takes it down to ⸢♪⸣ . This would suggest the alto flute in F, with even an extension key to enable it to reach its low B.

ALTO SAXOPHONE

This is the first and still the most common visitor of its clan to the orchestra. It is in E♭ (sounding a minor sixth lower than written) and appears, always in the role of woodwind principal, in isolated works from Bizet's *L'Arlésienne* via Mussorgsky-Ravel's *Pictures from an Exhibition*, Milhaud's *La Création du Monde* and Britten's *Sinfonia da Requiem* and *The Prince of the Pagodas* to Berg's *Der Wein* and *Lulu*.

ALTO TROMBONE

The highest surviving member of the TROMBONE family, although a soprano trombone seems at one time to have been used, especially in some sacred, choral works. By the turn of this century the soprano trombone had long since disappeared and even the alto instrument had come to be regarded as obsolete, especially by orchestral manuals. The alto trombone has nevertheless recently made a spectacular comeback, particularly for works in which it is specified, such as Beethoven's Fifth Symphony or Schumann's *Rhenish* Symphony. These use very high notes, which were always at risk in the days when a tenor trombone was automatically substituted, and Walter Piston in his book *Orchestration* (1955) asserts that these high alto trombone parts are generally taken over by a trumpet, but this is absolutely not the case anywhere in Europe.

Composers continued to write for the alto trombone until the middle of the nineteenth century, using the alto clef. In fact at one time so much was the trio of trombones taken to consist of one each of alto, tenor and bass that the

7

solo parts of Rimsky-Korsakov's *Russian Easter Festival* Overture and *Scheherazade* are given to the 2nd player to ensure that they are played on the tenor trombone, in whose range they most conveniently fall.

Alban Berg contributed substantially to the alto trombone's revival when he wrote a formidable part for it in his *Drei Orchesterstücke*, Op. 6, although even he came to have reservations about the practicability of finding such an instrument and replaced it with a tenor in a subsequent and possibly ill-judged revision. More recently Britten wrote a part for it in *The Burning Fiery Furnace*.

The alto trombone, which is pitched in Eb, is not only less perilous at the extreme upper register but is also of a pure and noble quality. Its return is a most welcome enhancement to the brass choir and is to be encouraged as much as possible.

Altri, gli (It.), the remainder, i.e. the tutti; *see* DIVISI

Am Steg (Ger.), *sul ponticello*; *see* BOWING, 4

Ambosse (Ger.), plural of *Amboss*; *see* ANVIL

ANTIQUE CYMBALS

These are tiny, carefully cast, metal discs with central dome, but unlike ordinary cymbals they are of definite pitch and tuned in pairs. Antique cymbals give off the most delicate ring, not unlike that of a glockenspiel but of the purest quality. To get this high bell-like ring the one should properly be struck against the other, edge to edge, but players often prefer to strike a single cymbal with a soft beater.

Two pairs are often used together, the most familiar examples occurring in Berlioz's 'Queen Mab' Scherzo (tuned in Bb and F) and in the closing bars of Debussy's *Prélude a l'Après-midi d'un Faune* (tuned in E and high B).

In recent years contemporary composers have come to write for antique cymbals as if they were of indefinite pitch, and admittedly it is easy enough to create the illusion by striking together two cymbals of different pitches so that the listener is aware only of the high-pitched 'ting', which has an unexpected degree of carrying power.

See also: CROTALES

ANVIL

The most famous instances in orchestral literature of the use of the anvil are Wagner's in *Das Rheingold* and Verdi's in *Il Trovatore*, although these composers' numerous anvils (Wagner specifies eighteen) really amount to special realistic effects for operas in which they represent actual anvils used by smiths, whether Nibelungs or gypsies, working at their trade on- or offstage.

Nevertheless the anvil does have a place as a percussion effect in the orchestra, where it may feature as **Amboss** (Ger.), **enclume** or **bloc de métal** (Fr.) or **incudino** (It.). Bax uses an anvil stroke in an imaginative way in place of a cymbal clash at one of the main climaxes of his Third Symphony, and Copland, in *his* Third Symphony, introduces it in the climactic closing section as part of a large percussion group to add point to claves and xylophone. Walton's use of the anvil in *Belshazzar's Feast* could, however, be considered programmatic ('Praise ye the god of iron') and Varèse and Orff find places for the anvil in various works employing every percussion effect available to them at the time.

Apart from the operatic instances of massed anvils and Varèse's typical scoring for two in *Ionisation* (one high and one low), it is usually a single anvil that is used, and quantity does not actually add substantially to the effect. On the concert platform something resembling a smithy is not unknown, but commonly players will simply strike an iron bar with a metal hammer (*martello*).

APPLAUSE

The acknowledgement of applause is one of an artist's hardest, yet most important, assignments. Gauchely handled it may even detract from the effect of a performance, yet behaviour too obviously calculated throws doubt on an artist's sincerity.

From the conductor's point of view the problem first arises at the beginning of a concert. Some orchestras will stand as the conductor comes on to the platform, especially as a mark of respect to a distinguished figure. If they do not, the conductor may raise them on arrival at the podium, so that they can join him in receiving the welcoming applause.

If there are several purely orchestral items the conductor will need to consider how often to raise the orchestra during the course of a programme lest the orchestra itself finds it tiresome, if not a trifle ridiculous, to be raised again and again.

At the end of the concert it is customary for the conductor to shake the hand of the leader. On the Continent it is tradition to do this at the beginning of the concert also. With the world growing ever smaller this extension of the courtesy is becoming increasingly prevalent. It could be thought, however, to be somewhat overdoing the formalities.

Potential recalls are largely a matter of fine judgement. Nothing can be more ridiculous than the vision of the conductor advancing from the wings only to retreat at speed as the applause dies before he can reach the rostrum. Moreover, some orchestras expect the conductor to take a solo bow; others are offended if he takes this on himself before being invited to do so by the players.

On the Continent an extraordinary accolade may be bestowed on a conductor by the continuation of the applause after the orchestra has left, the conductor reappearing to take a solo bow on the empty platform. So prestigious has this become, especially in Vienna, that even the most eminent conductors have descended to artifice in order to engineer the situation.

Conversely, a tradition has crept in by which, the conductor having finally left the platform, applause may break out anew for the leader and orchestra as they take their departure. This is bad practice and should not be encouraged, even among amateur, student or youth orchestras, the breeding ground of the new custom. It mistakes the conductor's purpose in acknowledging applause with the orchestra standing; he has, after all, been thanking the audience on their behalf, with the sole exception of his solo bow, so that this renewed clapping after he has gone implies a misunderstanding of all that has gone before.

In concertante items the usual procedure is for the conductor to refer all applause towards any soloist(s) both before and after their performance, the conductor sharing the applause only after receiving encouragement to do so. The orchestra, too, is raised only at the soloist's invitation. A complication may arise if the concert ends with the concerto or some other solo item as it may be awkward for the conductor to manoeuvre himself into the position of shaking hands with the leader. Even so, this courtesy should not be neglected.

Groups of singers, whether the vocal quartet in works such as Beethoven's Missa Solemnis or the eight soloists of Mahler's Eighth Symphony, must all be acknowledged; the chorus must be raised, and if possible the chorus master brought on to the platform and publicly thanked for his preliminary hard work by means of gesture and personal applause. All this can become quite a pantomime and needs prior thought and organization. Sir Malcolm Sargent used to consider its successful accomplishment so important that he made a point of setting aside part of his already severely limited rehearsal time to the stage management of his applause and that of his soloists.

It is often excellent practice to raise individual members or groups of the

orchestra who have had occasion to exhibit unusual virtuosity. Pierre Monteux used to advance into the very ranks of the orchestra and seize the embarrassed 1st bassoon's hand after a performance of Ravel's *Alborada del gracioso*. A showpiece such as Britten's *Young Person's Guide* could well warrant raising the whole orchestra section by section.

Applause between movements, once welcomed by composers as a mark of success, has become so discredited that other members of the audience tend to turn on the offenders and sternly hush them to silence. It is, however, at best a compliment and certainly need not be greeted by a scowl from the podium; full-scale acknowledgement is out of order, but a smile with a half-turned head can treat the situation with well-mannered appreciation that the movement had given so much pleasure as to cause an unconventional burst of premature applause. There are also famous places where audiences are prone to applaud spontaneously, not only in the middle of a symphony such as Tchaikovsky's *Pathétique*, where the march-like third movement almost always provokes an enthusiastic response if properly presented, or (best loved of all by the orchestra) notorious audience pitfalls such as the end of the actual waltz in Weber's *Invitation to the Dance*, where an epilogue follows a misleadingly conclusive full close. There are even delightful instances of an audience breaking into vigorous clapping and shouts of 'bravo' after a *fortissimo* pause on a dominant chord. One conductor recently even abandoned the entire coda of a symphony in these circumstances, having been too disconcerted by the interruption to restart the music. But it can often be possible for this kind of mass *faux pas* to be restrained in time by means of a suitable gesture from the conductor, especially where the danger is known to be at its greatest.

By tradition some works carry with them an embargo on applause. Much against Wagner's expressed wishes *Parsifal* was one of these, although gradually the custom is lapsing. Bach's St Matthew Passion is another instance, especially when given regularly at Easter time. But this suggests that the works concerned are being attended as part of a religious or ceremonial occasion rather than as works of art.

Finally there remains the question of concerts in churches or cathedrals, applause being for long considered to be entirely inappropriate in sacred buildings. Here too, however, the embargo has gradually been eroded, with the present day increase of concert-giving in every kind of venue, and the ghostly reception of an exhilarating performance is at last becoming a thing of the past. Most people welcome this change of heart even though the act of clapping in the awesome ambience of a great cathedral continues to feel slightly incongruous. Yet it is less disconcerting than the frustration of sitting uncomfortably in numbing silence while the sounds of a Mahler symphony or the Berlioz Requiem gradually fade, the conductor discreetly shaking the hand of a seated leader before himself softly and silently vanishing away.

See also: AUDIENCE, ENCORE

Archet (Fr.), bow; *see* ARCO; BOWING, 2

Archi (It.), string section; *see* BOWING, 1; STRINGS, 2

ARCO

As a term of instruction, *arco* – the Italian word for the bow – being the normal method of playing, appears in scores only as a contradiction to other methods of playing: *pizzicato, col legno,* etc. The French 'avec l'archet' is surprisingly rarely seen but the German **Bog.** (short for *Bogen*) is quite common and continues to cause amusement among English-speaking players.

Exceptionally the Italians do not call the violin family 'strings' as in other languages, but *gli archi,* 'the bows'.

See also: BOWING, PIZZICATO

Armonica (It.), *see* HARMONICA

Armonico (It.), *see* HARMONICS, 2

Arpa (It.), *see* HARP

ARPA-LIUTO

This is a mystery instrument written for by Falla in his *El Retablo de Maese Pedro*. Although the part is always played on a harp, the score throughout specifies 'arpa-liuto' or 'arpa laud', a Spanish translation of the same word, which in English would be 'harp-lute'.

Documentation is lacking on what this instrument could have been. There was indeed at one time a true 'harp-lute', details of which, including pictures, can be found in dictionaries such as *Grove*. But, to judge from the way he wrote for the instrument, its range and type are quite different from anything Falla might have intended. Alternatively, there was once a harp-like instrument called the clavi-harp, which had a chromatic keyboard. Given the participation at the first performance of Madam Henri Casadesus, whose husband was the founder and director of the Société des Instruments Anciens in Paris, the instrument played might well have been one or other of these old instruments, belonging perhaps to Henri Casadesus's collection and in which he might have interested the composer.

ARPEGGIANDO

The instruction that a chord should be spread instead of the notes sounding simultaneously. The symbol for this is a vertical wiggly line. It is used mostly for piano or harp parts, but in the case of the harp it is often absent because most harp chords are to some degree automatically spread. The sound of an unspread harp chord is too dry for most circumstances and the indication *not* to spread, as in Mahler's 'nicht arpeggiert', may more often be found if, conversely, the brusque effect is specifically required. There are, as a result, countless instances where it is far from obvious whether or how much harp chords should be spread, and players will frequently look to the conductor for guidance since taste will usually be the ruling factor.

The normal spread in the absence of any indication is from bottom to top; if the contrary is required a downwards arrow is drawn to the left of the wiggly line.

ARRANGEMENT

An arrangement is, in its widest sense, a version for any medium other than that for which the music was originally composed. There are arrangements made for public performance; others for what one might call utilitarian performance, that is, to simplify or to broaden a limited repertoire, perhaps for school orchestras or bands; and, furthermore, before the advent of the radio and the gramophone, in order to make the music more widely known, arrangements were published for purely domestic purposes to be played on one, two or even more pianos, or on other groups of instruments, with no intention of public presentation. Across these categories, however, there are numerous grey areas. The very term 'arrangement' came at one time to carry a derogatory flavour, although it was by no means always merited.

On this basis Ravel's masterly working of Mussorgsky's *Pictures from an Exhibition*, originally for piano solo, comes strictly into the first category of arrangement, standing as work entirely valid in its own right, and is actually designated an 'orchestration', transcending any such stigma. Ravel also orchestrated many of his own piano pieces, such as *Le Tombeau de Couperin* and the *Valses nobles et sentimentales*, which are as much a true part of the *oeuvre* of their creator as the originals from which they spring.

Busoni's fiendishly difficult versions for solo piano of Bach's unaccompanied violin partitas are called not 'arrangements' but 'transcriptions', as their purpose, virtuoso performance, is purely artistic.

On the other hand, belonging clearly to the second category (for utilitarian performance) are Gordon Jacob's arrangements for orchestra of Holst's works for military band. These were originally composed in a medium that, for the greater part, depends for its repertoire on arrangements of orchestral, operatic or solo works. Here it is Gordon Jacob's orchestral versions that are the arrangements, this transference to the orchestra being rather a matter of convenience than an enhancement of the original conception.

Dissimilar only in degree and taste are the once popular 'orchestral series', prepared for publishers by various hacks under such pseudonyms as 'Aubrey Winter', which reinstrumentated a host of well-known orchestral works in such a way that they could be played by virtually any group of players, good or bad, large or small. Mozart's *Don Giovanni* Overture and Mendelssohn's *Italian* Symphony appeared complete with cornet and trombone parts; Dvořák's *New World* Symphony had all the solos for 3rd and 4th horns reallocated to the 1st and 2nd, and cues were added liberally to all the parts so that any missing instrument could be filled in by somebody else, and so on.

For a brief period in their history, just before the Second World War, the great publishing house of Breitkopf & Härtel reissued a few of the standard orchestral works with an arrangement for salon orchestra incorporated in little notes into the score and parts together with the original text, making an unholy muddle in the process. Tchaikovsky's Violin Concerto grew an apocryphal trombone, and the horn parts of Wagner's *Meistersinger* Prelude were bowlderized to the point where reinstatement of the original became impossible.

Mostly, however, the word 'arrangement' refers to the domestic category: the once much used reductions of the classical symphonies, overtures, etc., for piano solo or duet, violin and piano, trio or, even more hilariously, for four pianos sixteen hands. It is highly entertaining to read down the astonishing list of different combinations or varieties of solo instruments for which Elgar's *Pomp and Circumstance Marches* or the *Intermezzo* from Mascagni's *Cavalleria Rusticana* were arranged in their day. Yet at the same time many were of superb craftsmanship: Liszt's arrangements of the Beethoven symphonies for solo piano have an entirely different artistic value (quite apart from their historical interest) from the familiar ones by, for example, E. Pauer, as have other arrangements made by great masters of the works of composers they themselves admired, such as Mahler's piano reduction of Bruckner's Third Symphony.

Moreover, arrangements of their own works were frequently made by the composers themselves: Ravel's excellent arrangement for piano four hands of his second *Daphnis et Chloé* Suite is, in contrast to the orchestral versions of his own piano music, purely functional, with the sole purpose of familiarizing the music at a domestic level.

The words 'arranged by', however, can indicate that a musician has not merely orchestrated a composer's work, but has collected numerous pieces, movements or fragments and redistributed them to form a new composition entirely different from anything the original author could have conceived. The prime motivation for such bastard works, which were often amazingly successful and have withstood the test of time, has generally been the ballet: *Les Sylphides* (a virtually anonymous compilation of pieces by Chopin, so many have been the hands in its genesis and evolution); the numerous Handel–Beecham Suites; the Scarlatti–Tommasini *Les Femmes de bonne humeur*; Lambert's *Les Patineurs*, a mixture of Meyerbeer movements originally written by their creator for different ballets but reshuffled; the Rossini–Respighi *La Boutique fantasque* and many others. Hamilton Harty made two justly famous reorchestrated suites out of movements from Handel's *Water Music* and *Fireworks Music* purely for the concert hall and Casella wrote many pastiches based on collections of pieces by Scarlatti and Paganini, although they are so ingenious that they almost verge on original composition.

See also: EDITING

ARTIFICIAL HARMONICS

Among the labyrinth of harmonics playable by the string group a further range, which is entirely over and above the series of natural HARMONICS, can be obtained by stopping the string at any point along its length with the first finger and simultaneously touching it lightly with the fourth, or little, finger at a point a perfect fourth above. This produces a harmonic that sounds two octaves above the note stopped by the first finger.

The conventional notation for these, which are known as 'artificial harmonics', is for the stopped note to be represented by a real note symbol while the lightly touched note is shown as a diamond. Thus, for example,

 will sound:

which is a note not otherwise possible as a harmonic without retuning the instrument.

There is a second and similar range that is obtained by touching the string a perfect fifth above the note stopped by the first finger. This produces a harmonic sounding a twelfth above the stopped note (or, perhaps more simply, one octave above the lightly touched note). Again the notation is for a real note together with a diamond above showing where the lightly touching finger is to be placed. This form of notation, however, is not universally adopted and many different methods can be found: one need only contrast Ravel, for example, who frequently writes only the diamonds, with Schoenberg, who writes complicated chord-like structures in an attempt to get the best of every world, or even Verdi, who changed his mind in each new work.

ATTACCA

Attacca, or its more insistent variant, *Attacca subito*, is an instruction often put by composers at the end of a section or movement. The implied intention is that there should be no hold up or even any break, the new movement following immediately on the heels of its predecessor. Such an instruction may be indicated by words in either Italian or a German equivalent (e.g. *folgt sofort, ohne jede Pause*) or simply indicated through the use of a thin double-bar.

Although the intention may seem clear enough, it may not always be possible to observe it in practice unless the last bars are so composed as to be totally inconclusive. Mendelssohn and Schumann planned that their respective *Scotch* and Fourth Symphonies should be played non-stop. While this is easy to observe in transitions such as that between the scherzo and finale of Schumann's symphony, it becomes much harder at the end of the first movement, which has so pronounced a final chord, or at the end of the scherzo of Mendelssohn's symphony with its conclusive *pizzicati*, and few conductors feel able to be punctilious about forging straight ahead into the succeeding slow movements.

It may, in fact, be one of the conductor's more important responsibilities to decide whether or not to make a break between movements and if so how long it should be. It may be an exciting dramatic stroke to plunge into a turbulent finale even when the composer has left no such positive instruction, as in Beethoven's Seventh. Conversely, a long pause is necessary before the adagio of the *Choral* Symphony, partly to allow the dust to settle after the storms and tensions of the first two movements and partly to prepare the audience for what is to be a long and deeply introspective experience. Mahler prescribed a break of 'at least five minutes' after the first movement of his *Resurrection* Symphony, but to stand for a full five minutes motionless in front of the assembled forces and the more or less patiently waiting audience generally proves longer than most conductors have the sang-froid to achieve.

See also: COMMA

AUDIENCE

An indispensable part of any orchestra's world.

Some broadcasting orchestras have been formed with the avowed intention of playing exclusively to an invisible audience, which, they are constantly assured, is many hundred – even thousand – times larger than the real-life audience they would be facing in a concert hall. But the pressure of working in a studio to the dehumanized receiving ear of the microphone, their output controlled by a technician, with no more atmosphere of presentation than the switching on and off of a red light, has proved to be demoralizing to a damaging extent unless punctuated by regular concerts given to a live audience.

The presence of an audience creates a sense of occasion, putting an orchestra and conductor on their mettle; just as, conversely, it is an occasion to any member of that audience to be in the presence of a group of artists re-creating the works of the programme. There is an involvement, a participation, that is entirely absent from the idealized listening to a perfected performance on high-fidelity equipment in the luxury of one's own armchair, which is often – misguidedly – extolled as the supreme artistic experience.

The atmosphere of audience receptivity is something that can be felt by every performer and has, even if subconsciously, to be taken into account, whether in the mastering of nerves or in the sheer timing of events (lengths of pauses, silences, etc.). Some of the world's greatest conductors have played on this audience reaction to the point of theatricality and even, at worst, flagrant showmanship, but it is inescapable that to ignore it altogether is to risk turning a praiseworthy aim for integrity into mere dullness, the one failing for which no artist should ever be forgiven.

See also: APPLAUSE, BIS, ENCORES, PROGRAMME BOOKS AND NOTES

Auf dem Holz (Ger.), *see* BOWING, 6

Aufstrich (Ger.), up bow; *see* BOWING, 7

AUGMENTATION

In the orchestral world, 'augmentation' is the term for what one BBC orchestral secretary used to describe as 'lots of lovely extras' – players over and above the contract strength of a permanent orchestra who are employed *ad hoc* to fulfil the requirements of a work or programme.

This is a constantly recurring necessity. The orchestral repertoire is so varied that no organization could possibly afford to keep on its regular roster a player for every instrument or the number of players for each particular group to satisfy every score, since so many of the more rarely used players would hardly earn their keep. It is therefore more practical to engage them as and when required.

See also: CHAMBER ORCHESTRA, FULL ORCHESTRA, ORCHESTRA, PROGRAMME PLANNING

Bacchette di legno (It.), wooden drum sticks; *see* DRUMS, 3; TIMPANI, 12

Bacchette di spugna (It.), sponge-headed drum sticks; *see* TIMPANI, 12

BACH TRUMPET

This is the name by which are known the smallest members of the TRUMPET family, used for very high parts in baroque music and in some present day scores, and especially for works by J. S. Bach himself, such as the Second Brandenburg Concerto and the B Minor Mass. The most familiar of these little trumpets is the one in high F, but a truly tiny one is sometimes used pitched in B♭ *altissimo*, an octave above the usual B♭ trumpet.

Historically, the term was applied originally to a late nineteenth-century invention, which was devised for the purpose but shaped differently: it was a very long straight instrument (actually in B♭ or A), and was widely, though wrongly, believed to be modelled on the trumpet Bach might have used. It was in any case quickly superseded and has long since disappeared.

BACK DESKS

Although widely derided as the lowest-ranking members of the string section, the back desks not only have a skill and responsibility that is insufficiently recognized but they are sometimes made the specific objects of a composer's attention. Strauss, in *Don Quixote*, uses the back two desks of the 1st violins to accompany the very quiet oboe solo depicting the vision of the Lady Dulcinea as she first appears in the mind of the romancing old Don, whereas Elgar specifies the back desk of each string section in the reminiscences of his motto theme in the First Symphony. Britten extended this idea by using only back players in the closing bars of his Passacaglia from *Peter Grimes*, though here the purpose is to create a mysterious background by requiring each of the last four players in the lower strings to contribute a different but close-lying harmonic.

The truth of the matter is that it can be just as hard to sit at the back of a string section as at the front, and a very special mental alertness, not to mention devotion and enthusiasm for orchestral work, is needed to be so far from the source of decision-making yet still to be able to participate accurately and punctually in the virtuoso string writing of the symphonic repertoire.

See also: PLATFORM ARRANGEMENT, RANK AND FILE, STRINGS

BAGPIPES

Strictly speaking, it could be maintained that the bagpipes, for all their trappings and paraphernalia, are constitutionally a reed instrument of the wind family and could therefore, *ipso facto*, claim membership of the orchestra. There are, however, very real practical objections to their incorporation into the symphonic world in any but the most specialized capacity, as can be deduced from the fact that they play no part in the orchestration of the one work in which they might most be expected to appear – Weinberger's *Schwanda the Bagpiper*. As it happens, there is another Czech opera of much the same period that does incorporate the bagpipes: *The Excursions of Mr Brouček*, in which Janáček writes for them as if they were a kind of weird oboe with a strong folky flavour. But here they constitute a special effect and are played on stage, following to some degree Verdi's incorporation of the Italian equivalent, the **cornamuse**, in *Otello*, as part of a stage group of musicians. In *Otello*, however, this is rarely carried out in practice, a likelihood that Verdi recognized by suggesting that his cornamuse might be replaced by two oboes. In neither case are the bagpipes really integrated into the orchestra, and the reasons for the instrument's non-admission to the orchestral world remain inviolate despite these examples of special pleading.

In the first place the bagpipes must be played standing, or better still striding to and fro – which in terms of the concert platform would mean in front of the orchestra if not in the very body of the auditorium, thus introducing an element of histrionics into the proceedings. In this country, moreover, they are so bound up with a

17

military nationalistic tradition that they are always played in the colourful Scottish uniform with kilt, sporran, etc., and so occupy the centre of all attention – both visually and aurally, for the bapipes are unable to make the slightest variation in their dynamics, which remain a relentless *fortissimo*. Indeed the all-pervading penetration of sheer volume given by the addition of the drones to the chanter, which supplies the melodic part, is so great that it dominates the entire orchestra from the moment it starts to play. And when the instrument stops there is no way of avoiding the formidable *glissando* dip of the drones as the air collapses in the bag.

But perhaps equally important is the fact that the bagpipes are limited to a seven-note scale whose intonation does not conform to that of the symphony orchestra. Hence any attempt to integrate it with orchestral textures could be made only on its own terms, with devastating results.

However, Scottish composers have been known to introduce the 'pipes' into symphonic works, though always as a highlighted soloist featured in apposition to the main body of the orchestra, as in Ian Whyte's *Donald of the Burthens*.

Baguettes de bois (Fr.), wooden drum sticks; *see* DRUMS, 3; TIMPANI, 12

Baguettes d'éponge (Fr.), sponge-headed drum sticks; *see* TIMPANI, 12

Balancier (Fr.), *see* METRONOME

Balzato, *see* BOWING, 11

BANDONEON

A large chromatic version of the once popular concertina invented by one Heinrich Band (1821–1860), to whom it owes its name. Although it is supposed to have found greatest favour in South America, it was for its evocation of the Berlin dance music of the 1920s that Kurt Weill introduced the bandoneon into his unconventional orchestra for *Mahagonny* and the *Dreigroschenoper*.

BANDS

Although used colloquially for any large group of players (students at the London music conservatoires will speak of 'First Band', 'Chamber Band', etc., and members of the larger professional orchestras may lightly refer to their organization as a 'band' and their copies as 'band parts'), the word 'band' properly signifies any such formation that excludes the string group. Hence there are MILITARY BANDS, BRASS BANDS, dance bands, etc. Of these, military bands might occasionally employ double-basses especially when performing indoors, and dance bands might further add one or more violins, but the essence of the definition remains that the string body, which is the primary essential of a symphony orchestra, is absent.

BANJO

A popular strumming instrument, the banjo originated in the American Negro slave music of the cotton plantations but became a widely used folk-style instrument and was soon introduced into jazz and other dance bands. In fact its dry twangy voice generally conjures up memories of many a popular folky act.

The banjo has a fretted neck and a circular, single-sided body, not unlike a large tambourine. It normally has five strings played either with the fingers or with a plectrum, and is notated in the treble clef an octave above pitch (except for a short period in the instrument's very early life when it was a transposing instrument in A). Variants of the banjo exist, such as bass and piccolo, while tenor banjos as well as that other popular instrument, the UKELELE, have made sporadic appearances in works of contemporary composers such as Hans Werner Henze.

The banjo's rare appearance in orchestral music is largely for local or specialized colour, such as in Delius's adaption of 'La Calinda' in the opera *Koanga* and in Kurt Weill's *Mahagonny*. Ernst Křenek, on the other hand, actually integrates two banjos into the unusual orchestration of his *Kleine Symphonie*, Op. 50.

BARITONE

(1)

Vocally, the baritone is the high lyric solo bass with a range somewhat above that of a true bass, so that he can reach a top G, or even A, but lacks the lower range characteristic of a genuine *basso profundo*. The baritone is essentially a soloist and the term is never used for a choral line. There is, of course, a sliding scale of such voices, and on the one hand many of the higher

baritones have gradually turned into the most successful *Heldentenors*, as did the most famous interpreter of Siegfried, Lauritz Melchior, whereas on the other hand many operatic baritone roles require a stronger low register giving rise to the hybrid bass-baritone.

There was once a baritone clef, 𝄢, i.e., the F clef on the middle line, but this is now completely obsolete. Baritone parts are instead notated, confusingly enough, either in the bass clef or an octave above pitch in the treble clef, as in Stanford's *Songs of the Sea* and *Songs of the Fleet*. Stranger still, Strauss in his two *Gesänge*, Op. 44, for baritone and orchestra, wrote the first song in the treble clef and the second in the bass, even though the range is low in the first (*Notturno*) and very high in the second (*Nächtlicher Gang*).

(2)

Instrumentally, this is one of the lower and more flexible members of the SAXHORN family. It is pitched in Bb and has a range exactly like that of the EUPHONIUM and the TENOR TUBA, but is slenderer and hence lighter in character, so that it is no real substitute for either of the others in the highly important solo parts written for them in the military band or orchestra respectively. It is significant, however, that in Schoenberg's *Variations for Wind Band*, which includes parts for both baritone and euphonium, it is the former that enjoys the more agile and responsible solos. Like the euphonium, the baritone is normally written at concert pitch in the bass clef.

Regrettably, the baritone makes no

appearance in the symphony orchestra; nevertheless it corresponds with the continental *Baryton*, which was virtually the same as Mahler's so-called 'Tenorhorn in B' in the first movement of the Seventh Symphony. It is therefore the baritone that should always be used for this work instead of the heavier and thus far less suitable euphonium or tenor tuba which are commonly (and often disastrously) pressed into service in Britain.

(3)
There was also once a stringed instrument of this name (also called *viola di bordone*), which survives at least historically on account of the numerous chamber works composed for it by Haydn. It never, however, made any appearance in the orchestra.

BARITONE SAXOPHONE

One of the lowest members of the family, notated in E♭ in the treble clef like the E♭ alto, but sounding an octave lower, i.e., an octave and a sixth below the written notes. It is a very rare visitor to the orchestra, the outstanding examples being Gershwin's *An American in Paris* (his trio of saxophones being a soloistic feature of the scoring) and Karlheinz Stockhausen's *Gruppen für drei Orchester*. David Matthews uses it in his Violin Concerto as a doubling instrument to the bass clarinet.

BASS

(1)
The lower male voice, so designated for soloists and chorus alike and uni-

formly notated in the bass clef. In choruses there may be first and second basses covering the higher and lower parts of their range respectively but the first basses of a chorus are never described as BARITONES.

The basses will usually sit in the rear centre of a chorus but if – as is sometimes done these days – the chorus is grouped in blocks of descending pitch order they may find themselves on the far right.

The basses of a chorus can be expected to cover as wide a compass as  , although the extremes are comparatively rarely used. However, Mahler writes down to low D♭ in the Eighth Symphony and there are numerous low Cs in Schoenberg's *Gurrelieder*, while at the upper end top Es are fairly common.

The extremes are even rarer in solo writing but it has to be remembered that the word 'bass' can be used to describe vastly different voices. Wagner calls both Wotan and Hunding basses although properly Wotan is a bass-baritone and Hunding – like Hagen or King Mark – a *tiefer Bass* or *basso profundo*. Many very deep bass roles are *buffo* parts and the lowest notes can be used for comic effect, as with Osmin in Mozart's *Entführung* or Baron Ochs in Strauss's *Rosenkavalier*.

(2)
See DOUBLE-BASS

BASS CLARINET

The second lowest member of the clarinet family (the very lowest is the

CONTRABASS CLARINET), the bass clarinet is called **clarone** by Italian composers such as Verdi, or earlier Puccini until *La Bohème*, and also (unexpectedly) by Delius in *An Arabesque*. The instrument is now always built in B♭ but over a long period it was the A instrument that was the most widely used (even in as late a work as Messiaen's *Turangalîla-Symphonie* of 1948) – an inconvenient fact for presentday players who spend their lives transposing. There must once have been a bass clarinet in C as Liszt wrote a part for it in *Mazeppa*, but this vanished rapidly.

The bottom note of the bass clarinet was for long its low E, like that of the B♭ and A clarinets though sounding an octave lower. In fact its overall range is roughly an octave below the clarinet. With the unfortunate disappearance of the bass clarinet in A, however, this standard situation was of necessity complemented by an extension key providing the low E♭. In Russia, however, a larger species of bass clarinet with an extended range down to low C long existed, creating insoluble problems when composers such as Shostakovich automatically took these very low notes for granted. As a result, during the last few decades this larger instrument has wholly replaced the conventional bass clarinet in most other countries.

The speciality of the bass clarinet is its soft quality, especially in the low register. Played loudly it is hard to control and is somewhat inclined to squawk. But its sinuous *pianissimo* can be immensely sinister – for example, when impersonating the Noonday Witch in Dvořák's symphonic poem.

In view of this particular quality it is often substituted for the bassoon in the notorious *pppppp* solo of Tchaikovsky's *Pathétique* Symphony.

The notation for the bass clarinet is fraught with confusion. Essentially there are two quite distinct notations: the 'French' in the treble clef transposing a ninth down (or a tenth for the A instrument), and the 'German' in bass clef transposing a tone (or a third) down. The terms 'French' and 'German' appear in quotes because by no means all the composers using either notation are in fact French or German nationals and may indeed even use the 'foreign' method of notation. César Franck and Mahler, for instance, used respectively 'German' and 'French' notation. Moreover, composers using the 'German' notation are liable to extend the range upwards into the treble clef, whereupon they may continue to transpose as before, or may on the contrary suddenly jump the octave and transpose as in the 'French' system, thereby creating a third and hybrid notation. This last may be hard to detect except by knowledge of a composer's practice or by internal evidence, although sometimes even this may be equivocal, as in the first version of Webern's *Sechs Orchesterstücke*, Op. 6.

BASS DRUM

One of the principal instruments of the PERCUSSION department. Bass drums come in all sizes, from the little Scout Band or Salvation Army type capable of being hoisted on to the chest for playing on the march, to the large drum laid on its side and played by two drummers, as is required in Berlioz's *Symphonie fantastique*. Toscanini used to place his enormous bass drum the same way for the 'Dies Irae' in the Verdi Requiem.

Names for the bass drum include **gran cassa** or **tamburo grande** (It.), **grosse-caisse** (Fr.) and **Grosse Trommel** (Ger.); particularly graphic and attractive is the Spanish term, **bombo**. In this country the military bass drum used to be known as the 'big drum', but this term is never used orchestrally, even when it is the smaller drum with cymbal attached that Mahler stipulated in his First, Fifth, and Seventh Symphonies, or the similar circus drum of *Petrouchka*.

It is an illusion to imagine that the size of the drum necessarily relates to the volume or even the depth of its sound. A simply vast instrument was manoeuvred into London's Festival Hall for the first of Gerard Hoffnung's famous Festivals but it proved to have no voice at all, being purely an advertising stunt.

The bass drum is of indefinite pitch, though some small variation can be achieved by slackening the cords holding the head. It is normally placed upright or tilted and struck on one side; there are in fact bass drums, less common now than they used to be, that have only one head and are called **gong drums**.

Two-headed drums can be struck on both sides and some composers, such as Balakirev, specify this in their scores, emulating the military or Turkish style evoked in classical works such as Haydn's *Military* Symphony. An al-ternative method of beating a bass drum on both sides used to be for one hand to hold a **birch** (or clutch of twigs) instead of a second drumstick. Mahler took over the idea of the birch (**Ruthe**) but generally instructed that it should be used on the rim of the bass drum.

Of the alternative beaters used for the bass drum the most common are the **mailloche** – the large round soft-headed stick – and felt-headed timpani sticks, but side-drum sticks are also occasionally specified. The double-headed bass-drum stick is now out of favour with players who prefer to play a roll with a stick in each hand.

The bass drum was once among the more climactic, even spectacular, members of the percussion section but, disappointingly, players tend more and more to play seated with consequent loss of both aural and visual effect.

See also: CYMBALS, 8

BASS FLUTE

This was for long the accepted term for the instrument now generally called the ALTO FLUTE – i.e., the *flûte en sol*. The true bass flute, pitched an octave below the ordinary flute, has only recently begun to appear in the scores of a few contemporary composers such as Toru Takemitsu in, for example, his Marimba Concerto. It is still therefore very much of a rare visitor to the symphony orchestra.

BASS OBOE

The lowest member of the oboe family and as such the English equivalent of the HECKELPHONE. Specialists will speak vehemently of the difference between the two instruments to the disadvantage of the heckelphone, which they regard as far less refined in character, but for all intents and purposes they are interchangeable except that the bass oboe lacks the bottom notes below B natural that are available on the heckelphone.

Like the heckelphone, the bass oboe is generally notated in the treble clef sounding an octave lower, but Delius writes for it at pitch using both treble and bass clefs.

The bass oboe came into brief favour in the present century and has important solos in Holst's *The Planets*, in many works by Delius, and in Bax's First Symphony. Because of its necessity for these, e.g. Delius's *Mass of Life*, Dance Rhapsody No. 1, etc., the bass oboe – rare as it is, and good instruments are to this day few and far between – has remained an essential, regular visitor to the orchestra.

Tippett has recently given the bass oboe a new lease of life, introducing it magically into his Triple Concerto. As did his predecessors, he employs it largely in a soloistic role, as it has to be acknowledged that, with its highly characterful, rather honky quality, the bass oboe blends uncomfortably with other sections, even with that of its own kin.

Bass saxhorn, *see* SAXHORNS

BASS SAXOPHONE

Pitched in B♭, this is the largest and lowest member of the family and perhaps the rarest in orchestral literature.

Strauss uses a bass saxophone as one of his quartet in *Symphonia Domestica* but this is an early instrument in C, long since extinct. Philip Bate states that it is this same C instrument that Schoenberg calls for in the opera *Von Heute auf Morgen* but since all the instruments in the entire score are notated in C it is more probable that his so-called 'Bass Saxophon' actually represents the conventional B♭ instrument.

Bass trombone, *see* TROMBONE

BASS TRUMPET

Invented by Wagner for *The Ring*, this majestic but somewhat unwieldy instrument has since been used by so many composers of the first rank, such as Strauss, Stravinsky and Janáček, that it has become a regular and indispensable visitor to the brass section of every major symphony orchestra.

The standard instrument in use today is the bass trumpet in C, although composers have written for it in numerous CROOKS. Strauss in particular did so and often allowed no time for change, like the old-fashioned notation for valve technique used by Wagner for the horn parts in *Lohengrin*. (*See* Horn, 8.)

Although theoretically the bass trumpet sounds an octave lower than the trumpet with the same harmonic series, in practice the lower range is barely practicable and few composers have written lower for the bass trumpet than for the trumpet itself. Perhaps the outstanding use of the lowest possible register is Stravinsky's grisly writing for a muted E♭ bass trumpet in *Le Sacre du Printemps*.

The main purpose of the instrument is, however, its pronouncedly fuller, richer tone in which respect it unquestionably makes a real contribution to the brass ensemble.

BASS TUBA

Broadly speaking this is the lowest supporting voice of the symphony orchestra's BRASS choir, generally seated beside the bass trombone and in printed scores often sharing a stave with that instrument.

But there is virtually no uniformity in what it is called. Many composers simply say 'tuba' while others specify 'bass tuba' and a few even say 'CONTRABASS TUBA'. Neither are there instructions for which instrument the player should actually use. The Italian CIMBASSO, as stipulated by Verdi for example, may well fall into this context, being specifically identified by Anthony Baines in *Grove 5* as 'the narrow-bore Italian Tuba in B♭ as used at La Scala, Milan'. More recent scholarly opinion has, however, swung against this view.

Unlike the tenor tuba, the bass tuba is hardly ever a transposing instrument. (Bax's tuba in B♭ in the *Overture to a Picaresque Comedy* is a very rare example.) Hence it is academic what key it is built in, this being very much a matter of taste and fashion. For long the bass tuba in F was the standard orchestral instrument, and tubas in E♭ and double B♭ (also known as the BOMBARDON) were the especial property of military and brass bands. But today

instruments in E♭ and most commonly C have become widely favoured for orchestral use.

Perhaps because composers are unsure exactly what instrument they are writing for, and perhaps also because tubas have evolved in different ways in various countries, the ranges required for tuba parts in the orchestral repertoire are too wide to be satisfactorily accomplished by any one instrument and this explains the extraordinary diversity of tubas seen on the concert platform. At the same time it has to be acknowledged that present-day players have developed such an astonishing degree of virtuosity that this recourse to numerous different-sized tubas is becoming more a matter of convenience than necessity.

See also: TUBA

BASSET CLARINET

It has long been known that the solo parts of Mozart's Clarinet Concerto and Clarinet Quintet are, as we have them, mere bowdlerizations of infinitely superior original versions written for an extinct clarinet in A, which had an extended compass down not to low E but to C (written notes). A further example, this time for B♭ clarinet, can be seen in the aria 'Parto, parto, ma tu ben mio' from the opera *La Clemenza di Tito*.

Of the clarinet family none but the basset horn and the larger form of the bass clarinet – prevalent only in more recent years – still possess this extra range; the extended instrument for which Mozart wrote quickly became obsolete.

However, examples of these extra-long and unwieldy clarinets have begun to be constructed for specialists anxious to bring back the original texts of Mozart's great masterpieces. Such extended-range instruments have been christened 'basset clarinets' to distinguish them from the conventional instruments. They remain rare, and it is no doubt the undeniable clumsiness of their undue length, which had after all caused them to disappear in the first place, that has prevented them from coming back into general use.

Unlike the basset horn, the basset clarinet was always written in the treble clef with extra ledger lines for the lower notes, as comparison of the two relevant arias for the two instruments, both in *Tito*, will reveal.

BASSET HORN

This is the orchestral alto clarinet and so designated by Stravinsky in *Threni*. It is built in F (unlike the military band alto clarinet which is in E♭) and transposes a fifth down except in the bass clef, where, like old notation for the horns, it jumps an octave and thus transposes a fourth up.

It is peculiar in the clarinet family in that it has always had the extra bottom

range taking it down to C: 𝄢

sounding 𝄢 ; a feature the

bass clarinet only gradually acquired and the A and B♭ clarinets lost very early in their existence, except in the rather special case of the so-called BASSET CLARINETS.

The basset horn was once well on the road to becoming extinct despite the essential role it played in many Mozart works – such as the Serenade in B♭ (K. 361) and the Requiem – as well as, unexpectedly, in Beethoven's ballet music to *Prometheus*. It was, however, rescued from limbo by Richard Strauss, who from 1906 onwards incorporated it regularly in his wind ensemble. Indeed in *Elektra* and the orchestral *Lieder* for bass voice, Op. 51, he used a pair of basset horns. Hence, although it is still a comparatively rare visitor to the orchestral woodwind, the fact that so popular a repertoire work as *Rosenkavalier* contains an essential part for the basset horn means that it can no longer rank as a ghost from the past.

Bassi, eighteenth-century terminology for cellos and basses; or abbreviation for *contrabassi*

Basso continuo, *see* CONTINUO

Basson (Fr.), *see* BASSOON

BASSOON

The primary member of the woodwind department's fourth and lowest family, and conventionally the bass of the ensemble, the bassoon is – like the oboe – a double-reed instrument. It possesses a highly individual tone quality, which sometimes makes it less satisfactory as a supporting colour for larger wind groups since it is relatively lacking in weight and power. It has, on the other hand, valuable and indeed beautiful characteristics, whether of lugubrious melancholy, or alternatively

25

of the comic or grotesque – which makes it the obvious choice for roles such as the Grandfather in Prokofiev's *Peter and the Wolf* or the broomsticks of Dukas's *l'Apprenti Sorcier*.

1 Names

The English genus name corresponds with the French **basson** but both the Italian and German names describe the instrument's appearance and wooden construction: *fagotto* and *Fagott*. Curiously *basun* is the Scandinavian for TROMBONE.

2 Range

The bassoon has a very extensive range, which is written at pitch in all of three clefs: treble, tenor and bass. At the upper end its quality has a subtle, plaintive character unforgettably exploited by Stravinsky in the opening of *Le Sacre du Printemps*. Yet this, with its top Ds, does not reach the upper limit, which is probably the high F written in Jean Françaix's *Serenade* for small orchestra, contradicting Anthony Baines's remark to the effect that 'mercifully nothing above E has been written in an orchestral part'.

At the other extreme the standard lowest note of the bassoon is B♭ but composers abound who write low A. Where this is not followed by the B♭ it is common practice for the player (amid a certain amount of hilarity) to extend his bell by sticking in at the top a roll of cardboard whose origin is often only too obvious. Like the flute extensions of the same kind this works perfectly and can be quickly and easily inserted and removed. But Delius, Sibelius and Balakirev all write chro-

matically down to the low A, and A♭s exist in both Strauss's *Rosenkavalier* and Berg's *Drei Orchesterstücke*, Op. 6, allowing for no such simple contrivance but requiring rather the substitution of a contrabassoon.

3 Family

Of all the woodwind instruments the bassoon is the one with the fewest number of varieties. The smaller teneroon has never had more than a shadowy existence and has made no appearance in the orchestra at all. Thus only the CONTRABASSOON survives as a regular associated family member.

4 Character

The bassoon family has the narrowest dynamic range of the whole woodwind department. If it is normally uncompetitive in matters of extreme loudness, so the ultimate refinements of *pianissimo* are extremely difficult, especially in the lower register. In this, of course, bassoons are similar to their double-reed colleagues, the oboes, but since they lie at the bottom of the ensemble, this failing provides one of the main reasons for the bassoon's unsuitability as an all-purpose bass instrument for the woodwind group. Where bassoons lack the roundness and solidity for supporting lines their place is often taken by horns, but the debt is repaid in many scores because in soft playing bassoons blend particularly well with horns and are therefore used together with them as in, for example, the overture to *Hansel and Gretel* or the introduction to the third act of *Die Meistersinger*.

This association, it must be admitted, can have the effect of stirring up the latent resentment sometimes felt by bassoonists at their colleagues in the horn department. For the question of how much sheer tone the bassoons can muster is a thorny one and close to the heart of every player. Yet this was not always so. The purist conductor who today restores in unadulterated form the return of the fanfare on bassoons in the first movement of Beethoven's Fifth Symphony may find himself rubbing salt into the wound, for our noble if over-refined instruments are not the strong raucous bassoons of Beethoven's day and can nowadays make the passage sound no more than a feeble wheezy imitation of the horns' heroic gesture. Tchaikovsky was another who clearly expected his bassoons to sound heroic, as in the opening of the *Manfred* Symphony; yet here, strangely enough, the many reorchestrations for horns *et alia* by well-meaning conductors (including even Toscanini) sound positively crude.

5 Continuo

Curious, perhaps improbable instrument as the bassoon may seem, its primary role as part of the continuo in classical and baroque music has led to its inviolate position in the orchestras of all periods. Indeed in eighteenth-century orchestras it was taken so much for granted that composers often failed to specify where, or even if, the bassoons should play. It would be assumed automatically that one or more would double the cellos and basses unless they should have something better to do in the form of an individual contribution.

In Bach's B Minor Mass, for instance, where the 'Gratias agimus tibi' and the 'Dona nobis pacem' are set to identical music, the bassoons are specified in the one (although they have no individual line) but not in the other, and it is apparent that Bach took it for granted that they would play equally in both. Again, in the ballet music to Mozart's *Idomeneo* the opening Chaconne makes no mention of bassoons, but when the identical music recurs a little later, by which time some solo bassoon parts have made their appearance, the instruments are shown to be playing in unison with the cellos and basses and it is clear that, as in all the early Haydn symphonies, they should have been doubling the bass line from the start, presenting an area of decision-making to the interpreter of today.

6 Hazards

Being, in a way, a kind of double-bass oboe, the bassoon shares many of its occupational hazards, from the question of reed production and titivation (bassoon, and especially contra, REEDS are elaborate and expensive affairs and the number of reeds that must be bought or made before a good one is found can be a ruinous business) to that of stamina and breath control, though in respect of the latter the sheer physical strain is somewhat less acute. Endurance tests for bassoonists are, however, not unknown, such as the 'Deuxième Variation' of the Gavotte from Stravinsky's *Pulcinella*. Very quick tonguing is generally less fluent on the bassoon, though it can be an accomplishment good players pride themselves on acquiring and exhibiting in solos such as the famous virtuoso passage at the reprise in the finale of Beethoven's Fourth Symphony.

Bassus generalis, *see* CONTINUO

Basun (Scand.), trombone; *see* TROMBONE, 1

BATON

The wooden stick used by conductors to improve the clarity and precision of the beat. The skill that goes into making this stick is usually an additional accomplishment of violin-makers, bowmakers or similar craftsmen, as it needs considerable care and attention to achieve a stick of the requisite fineness and balance. 'Built like a rapier . . .' the advertisement of a once well-known firm of baton-makers used to begin, but over the years most conductors have come to prefer ever shorter and lighter batons. Nevertheless this insignia of the *métier* still preserves its aura in publicity and popular image even though many world famous figures have followed the pioneering example of Stokowski in not using a baton at all, substituting an accordingly extra sensitive use of the fingers and hands.

The conductor's baton (curiously pronounced with the accent on the first syllable in Britain and on the second in America) is of immense flexibility both in shape and use. Its build and type are to an overriding degree a matter of personal taste, and a conductor may get so used to the feel, as well as the weight and balance of a particular kind of baton that he may find himself quite ill at ease at having (perhaps in some emergency) to use another and may well prefer to manage without. Baton-less conducting is, however, a skill apart and needs considerable imagination and resourcefulness in compensating for the precision a baton can automatically provide or the immediacy of contact it gives to singers or players at more remote distances from the podium.

Batteria (It.), *see* PERCUSSION, 1

Batterie (Fr.), *see* PERCUSSION, 1

BATTUTE

(1)
  See BOWING, 6

(2)
The plural of the Italian for bar (*battuta*). It will be seen in scores with reference to phrasings across a given number of bars, as at the well-known place in the Scherzo of Beethoven's Ninth Symphony where he writes *ritmo di tre* (later *quattro*) *battute*. The German equivalent is *-taktig – Dreitaktig, Viertaktig* (i.e. 3-barish, 4-barish, etc.), which appears in Strauss's *Don Juan* and countless other works.

Becken (Ger.), *see* CYMBALS

BELL PLATES

These are flat rectangular sheets of heavy metal suspended on a frame and struck like gongs; various types of such **metal plates** have come into prominence comparatively recently to cope with the situation presented by scores requiring bells such as Berlioz's *Symphonie Fantastique* or Mahler's Second, Sixth, Seventh and Ninth Symphonies but for which conventional tubular bells are inadequate, being too high and specific in pitch and lightweight in colour. Berlioz requires bells actually in C and G but Mahler generally wants metal plates of indefinite pitch giving more of an impression of deep bells. Certainly these should in principle be far deeper than can be emulated by conventional tubular bells of whatever size.

Like tubular bells themselves, bell plates are ultimately no more than an artificial contrivance. Yet they fill a real need. Although, unfortunately they are still very much a rarity, orchestras possessing a good set being justifiably unwilling to part with them. At the same time they are so large and unwieldy that they cause a great many practical problems, as James Holland amusingly describes in his admirable manual, *Percussion* (p. 59).

BELL TREE

This is one of an assortment of exotic-looking contraptions known variously as **jingling johnnie**, **pavillon chinois**, **sistrum**, **Turkish crescent**, etc. See also JINGLES.

The actual term 'bell tree' first made its appearance in scores of the works of contemporary composers such as Elisabeth Lutyens or Peter Maxwell Davies (e.g. *Stone Litany*), where it is, however, intended to signify the **Chinese bell tree**, a somewhat different affair. This, to quote James Holland in *Percussion*, 'consists of some 25–30 cup-shaped bells of different pitch, suspended on a cord or rod. When a light metal beater is passed over the edges, a distinctive shimmering *glissando* effect is obtained.'

BELLS

Generally speaking, orchestras are equipped with a double row of not particularly large **tubular bells** with a chromatic range of one and a half octaves from (actual pitch).

This means that any perfectly ordinary phrase of more than this range causes a problem and extra tubes, which may or may not be available, are sent for. Moreover, if additional ones should be obtained, they always turn out to be higher, and it is unbelievably hard to find a tubular bell with notes of a lower octave.

Tubular bells can never be anything but a compromise at best, but nevertheless of necessity they have to be considered acceptable for most circumstances. (However, see BELL PLATES.) The 'ring of chimes' (as they are also called, particularly in American scores) is moreover an awkward contraption, making it virtually impracticable to read the part from a music stand. It is therefore quite usual to see the player, who is trying to keep an eye on the conductor, take the music with him as he goes over to the bells and, with mallet in one hand, hold the music up with the other before him as he plays. As there is only one spot on each bell that gives the pure tone instead of a disagreeable

29

metallic clang, the hazardous nature of the enterprise can well be imagined.

Other terminology for the bells in orchestral scores is: **campane** (It.); **cloches** (Fr.); **Glocken**, or very occasionally **Röhrenglocken** (Ger.). Schoenberg actually cites a metal tube (**Metallrohr**) in *Die glückliche Hand* with a footnote in which oddly he thought it necessary to stipulate that it should sound like a bell. Sibelius writes for 'Glocken' in his Fourth Symphony but this is a *cause célèbre* as there is considerable doubt as to what he meant. From the evidence he left, which is itself far from clear, the probability is that he had in mind a ring of small (not tubular) bells sounding at pitch.

Bells always constitute a special effect and present the strange problem that they give off so many overtones that there are times when it can be quite hard to determine not only which octave is playing, but even what note. Yet the choice of an inept pitch can be more disconcerting than some composers take into account – as with the many operatic clocks that strike to an unprescribed note (e.g. in the third act of *Rigoletto*). The great tolling in Wagner's *Parsifal* is, of course, notorious and has been a matter of continual experimentation, even at Bayreuth where a variety of quite different and many-coloured effects has been used in the search for Wagner's ideal.

The most usual notation for the bells is in the treble clef at pitch, but when composers (such as Bartók in his *Deux Images*) specify deep sounds they do also write in the bass clef (though still usually at pitch). This can also apply when a composer is using both campane and campanella (glockenspiel), in order to make a clear differentiation.

Tubular bells are normally struck with a small wooden hammer covered on one face with felt. But occasionally special beaters are prescribed, such as the metal beater in 'Saturn' from Holst's *The Planets*. It is not uncommon to encounter opposition to this from a percussionist anxious about damage to the bells, but the required effect – however (deliberately) disagreeable – is perfectly practicable.

BELLS UP

This is an enormously dramatic style of playing, which applies in the woodwind to the oboes and clarinets, to the horns, and in the heavy brass to the trumpets and trombones. The player is instructed to raise the instrument so that the sound is projected directly towards the audience.

In the case of the woodwind, although it is repeatedly called for, by Mahler in particular with typical exclamation marks, it can be difficult to induce the players to co-operate fully. No doubt it makes them feel foolish; certainly it is uncomfortable (even verging on the impossible if the stands are too near as they are in some halls) and robs the tone of the refinement they normally strive so hard to cultivate. As a result they tend to make fun of it at rehearsals and often conveniently forget it at the performance. Yet it is generally required only for short passages and it is extraordinary what a strident and arresting effect it produces if the instruments really are stretched out horizontally.

For horns 'bells up' is a much more usual technique, introduced throughout the repertoire by a variety of composers using terms such as **pavillons en l'air** (Fr.) or **Schalltrichter in der Höhe** (Ger.). Nevertheless the instruction is no less unpopular with players; not only is the embouchure disturbed, increasing the risk of cracked notes, but intonation is hard to control and there is a tendency to play sharp. Nevertheless good players have to come to terms with it, however much they may try to compromise with half-measures. There is no substitute for the sheer riotous hilarity of Chabrier's *Joyeuse Marche*, or the true furore of a horn section playing bells up in Stravinsky's *Le Sacre du Printemps*, or in the eagerly awaited climax to Mahler's First Symphony, where he enjoins the players to stand up as well as raising the bells. The effect – visual as well as aural – is unforgettable.

Trumpets and trombones are, by their very nature, normally played with the bells pointing more or less towards the audience, so the instruction for these instruments is less fundamental and rather a question of degree. Nevertheless it can have a real purpose in terms of sheer decibels if carried out punctiliously, and hence is again often used by Mahler with considerable success. One other instance worthy of especial mention is for the trombones in Strauss's *Tod und Verklärung*. In depicting the death struggles of the sufferer who is the subject of the tone poem, Strauss adds a footnote: 'Here . . . the trombone passages must be presented in a horrifyingly biting manner, maybe by blowing with the bells pointed straight at the audience!' The overwhelming blatancy of this can hardly be exaggerated.

See also: EMBOUCHURE

Birch, *see* BASS DRUM

BIS

This French word, meaning 'a second time', is used in connection with the orchestral world in various ways. It may appear in scores and parts over one or more bars to indicate that they are played twice. An outstanding example of this occurs in the first movement of Tchaikovsky's *Serenade for Strings* where in the original edition (taken over identically in the Eulenburg miniature score) one particular phrase is so marked when it first occurs. It is sufficiently rare in scores (although less so in parts, where it creeps in mostly to correct a copyist's mistake) for one to wonder if it was Tchaikovsky's own shorthand notation that came to be carried over into the printed material.

Another way 'bis' may appear in scores is attached to an opus number, where the same work appears in a number of different guises. Hence Brahms's Sonata for Two Pianos, which first saw life as a string quintet and found its final form as a quintet for piano and strings, is described as 'Op. 34 *bis*' in the original Rieter–Biedermann edition.

But perhaps an even more familiar use of the word is by enthusiastic French audiences who shout 'Bis' when demanding an encore.

31

Bisbigliando (It.), murmuring; *see* HARP, 8

Bläser (Ger.), *see* WOODWIND, 1

Blech, Blechbläser (Ger.), *see* BRASS, 1

Bloc de bois (Fr.), *see* WOODBLOCK

Bloc de métal (Fr.), *see* ANVIL

Blockflöte (Ger.), *see* RECORDER

Bog., Bogen (Ger.), bow; *see* ARCO, BOWING

Bois, les (Fr.), *see* WOODWIND, 1

BOMBARDON

This is English band vernacular for the great double Bb TUBA, the lowest member of a noble family and an oversized instrument corresponding to the German equivalent indicated by Wagner's CONTRABASS TUBA. The actual term 'bombardon' is, however, purely colloquial and never appears in scores, even of brass or military band music.

Bombo (Sp.), *see* BASS DRUM

BONGOS

These are not unlike African tom-toms though appreciably smaller. Bongos always come in pairs, one a little larger than the other; they are of indefinite pitch and are properly played with fingers or the flat of the hands. Although a comparatively recent importation into the percussion section of the symphony orchestra, they have come to be very commonly used in contemporary music, where they may be combined with tom-toms and played with sticks.

BOUCHÉ

The term *bouché* indicates a hard, 'buzzy' way of muting with the right hand in the bell, applicable primarily to horns. The French word is the most usual but corresponds with the German **gestopft** (as opposed to *gedämpft*) or the Italian *chiuso* (as opposed to *con sordino*). Stravinsky uses the word 'plugged' in the closing bars of his *Symphonies of Wind Instruments*, but this is purely idiosyncratic.

In the days of hand horns the manoeuvring of the player's hand in the bell was to obtain otherwise impossible notes and the distortions of tone that resulted had of necessity to be accepted. But when valves had made the complete chromatic range possible, the same technique remained available as a way of changing the tone quality of these stopped notes. The conventional notation is a cross placed over the note or notes, contradicted by an 'o' to represent *naturale* or open, as can be seen in the quick $\frac{6}{8}$ section of Borodin's Dances from *Prince Igor*, a particularly good example of the effect.

The strange technical complication of this manner of playing is that as the hand is inserted into the bell the sound at first becomes muffled while the pitch gradually *drops*, and it is only when the hand is firmly pressed in to the utmost, and the tone is – and has to be – produced with an abruptly tongued accent, that the pitch quite suddenly becomes edged and buzzy as well as a semitone *higher*. The F horn player (for example) accordingly now has to transpose for horn in E.

This *bouché* technique becomes increasingly difficult in lower notes until (roughly) G below the treble clef. At this register it also begins to lose the snarling quality that is its strongest characteristic and often its *raison d'être*.

It may, however, be the woolly hushed sound that the composer requires. In this case the player need not strive to reach that degree of pressure with the hand in the bell since less hand pressure produces more of a muffled – even an echo – quality. But the player then needs to transpose the other way – i.e., a semitone *higher* to compensate for the initial lowering of the pitch. Composers do not normally prescribe this second style of muting, so it has no name; but Dukas, for instance, marked in his scores that the player should use the alternative transposition (*prenez le doigté un* ½ *ton au dessus* as he writes in *L'Apprenti Sorcier.*)

Trumpets are also sometimes required to play *bouché* but in their case the indication often arouses troubles and arguments. Few players understand how the sounds are intended to differ from those produced by mutes or, more important, just how they are to be obtained. The very shape of the instrument is an impediment to muting through putting the hand effectively into the bell with manipulation of the wrist as in horn hand-stopping. Often enough, therefore, the players' efforts are apt to sound merely fuzzy and out of tune and, believing that this cannot

possibly be the composer's intention, they all too often fall back on mutes. However, I have encountered conscientious trumpeters who have mastered the skill to excellent effect.

Applied to the trombone, the instruction *bouché* is a different story. The one instance occurs in Debussy's *Fantaisie* for piano and orchestra, an early work. It is hard to know whether to regard this as a genuine piece of experimentation or a mistake on the part of the young and inexperienced Debussy; it is even more impracticable than on the trumpet since, apart from the trombone's equally unsuitable bell, the player has no hand free for the purpose.

See also: CUIVRÉ

Bouteillophone, *see* GLASS HARMONICA

BOWING

1 The Bow

It is axiomatic that all the instruments of the orchestra's string group are played conventionally with a bow. In fact, in Italian, unlike all other languages, the string section is referred to as **gli archi** ('the bows'). These bows all conform essentially to the same basic design although they vary progressively in length and width from the long slender violin bow to the very short high bow of the bass. The hair is generally from white horses' tails, but as this source is becoming scarce even plastic hair has been tried, though with indifferent success. Bass bows are sometimes fitted with black hair, which is beginning to appear in the other bows as well. To make the bow grip the strings, a player periodically rubs the hair with resin.

2 Parts of the Bow

The English word in orchestral scores for the near end of the bow held by the hand is generally **heel**; the Germans use **Frosch**, which corresponds to the English **frog**, but this and yet another English term, **nut**, are rarely used by composers as they are applicable more specifically to the mechanism located at this same end to adjust the tension of the hair. The French and Italians share the word **talon** (**talone**), while the far end is universally known as the **point** (Fr. **pointe**; It. **punta**; Ger. **Spitze** – the direct translation), although *at the end of the bow* (Fr. *au bout de l'***archet**) does also appear.

These terms appear in scores where composers have definite ideas on styles that need to be executed at one or other end of the bow. For example, heavy, rough, or emphatic passages are played with the lower half nearest the heel, while the upper half of the bow – i.e, towards the point – is asked for in pursuance of lightness, delicacy or extreme softness.

3 Arco

ARCO is the normal method of drawing the bow, with the hair passing across the strings at a point midway between the bridge and the end of the fingerboard; it allows the full quality of the instrument to speak and can be taken for granted if no contrary instruction appears. It may, however, need to be specified as a cancellation after some other style of playing has been called for and will then be termed **in modo ordinario** or **naturale** (abbreviated to **nat.**) or even plain *arco*. The Germans use **gewöhnlich** and the French **jeu ordinaire**.

4 Sul ponticello

The instruction **sul ponticello** (It.), i.e., 'on the bridge', if taken literally would produce virtually no sound at all; yet most of the translations are close to this meaning: **am Steg** (Ger.) or *sur le* **chevalet** (Fr.) (although the French do also say **près du chevalet**). In any case it is as well that the terms constitute exaggeration because it is extraordinarily difficult to make orchestral string players observe the instruction meticulously, especially as it is to some extent possible to emulate the required thin glassy sound in other ways without struggling to play in this rather uncomfortable and unnatural position. *Ponticello* is mostly prescribed for the eerie, sometimes magical, atmosphere it conjures up in *pianissimo*; yet it can be excitingly effective in a *forte* or *fortissimo*. Britten instructs the 1st violins and violas to play *forte* towards the bridge (*poco sul ponticello*) in order to get a nasal, strident quality in the opening fanfares of *Les Illuminations*, one of the many brilliantly imaginative strokes with which this work abounds. Falla also introduces a ferocious use of *ponticello* in his ballet *The Three-cornered Hat*, where, apart from its exotic timbre, the edgy texture has the additional advantage of transparency, allowing the woodwind to penetrate the otherwise dense mass of string sound. *Legato* passages can also be played *sul ponticello*, though the result is generally rather unreliable, as the upper frequencies tend to predominate over the actual note intended.

5 Sul tasto

The opposite effect to *ponticello* is achieved by playing with the bow over the fingerboard (It. **sul tasto** – though also sometimes **tastiera** and exceptionally even **cordiera**, as in the full score of Puccini's *La Bohème*; Fr. *sur* **la touche**; Ger. *am* **Griffbrett**). This takes the richness out of the tone – whitens it, one might say. *Sul tasto* is, in the nature of things, an ethereal style and is therefore largely used in soft slower-moving passage work.

It is possible to draw the bow across the strings on the wrong side of the bridge, towards the tailpiece. But this, used as it has been by contemporary composers such as Karl-Birger Blomdahl, is, needless to say, contrary to the design of the instrument and is thus not so much a musical as a sonic effect. Another unconventional, though less rare, device is to draw the bow across the strings with the bow turned upside-down so that the strings are stroked with the wood instead of the hair. This produces very little tone (and thus is generally derided by players) but has, nevertheless, a genuine colouristic validity. When required it is generally prescribed in specific detail, as in Mahler's splendid injunction in the First Symphony: *Kein Irrtum: mit dem Holz zu streichen* ('No mistake: stroke with the wood').

6 Col legno

The simple unqualified term **col legno** (Ger. **auf dem Holz**) automatically assumes a vertical use of the back of the bow, the wood being struck against the strings with percussive effect. This technique, common as it is and widely encountered in the repertoire, is much dreaded by players as it does no good at all to the varnish on their valuable bows. It is true that if executed honestly with only the wood of the bow very little actual note is heard, and when composers write important note formations *col legno*, such as Berlioz in the Witches' Sabbath movement of his *Symphonie Fantastique*, the players will generally cheat by turning the bows sideways so that a little of the hair also comes into play. If they cheat too much, only the hair being brought into contact with the strings, this creates a quite different device, which is found constantly in Rossini under the term **battute** and is another effect much beloved of Mahler who termed it **mit dem Bogen geschlagen** (struck with the bow) as in his Seventh Symphony. None of these vertical techniques produces any enormous volume, especially in view of the cautious attitude of the musicians, but all are prescribed in dynamics of up to *fortissimo* and, in fact, with insistence, a notably percussive sound can be obtained.

Apart from the hair or the wooden back, other parts of the bow have in recent years come to be designated as striking implements: the nut itself, with which one can tap the belly of the instrument, the tailpiece, etc., even, dare one say, the back, as requested by Xenakis, again instructions not especially beloved of players. Conversely the wood or the hair of the bow can be used to strike some object other than the instrument, such as the desks in Rossini's *Il Signor Bruschino*. In modern scores this is humourlessly indicated by cross-headed notes and *col legno*, although Rossini's intention is well known. Of course it never occurred to him that the solid wooden desks of his day would give place to flimsy metal collapsible affairs quite unsuitable for his splendid idea.

7 Part Marking

In addition to composers' specific instructions, agreement is desirable over how the bowing in the orchestra should be organized in the search for unanimity both within and between the sections as far as instrumental character and the orchestration of the music will allow.

Down bow (beginning at the nut and travelling towards the point) and up bow (beginning at the point) provide differences of character in phrasing, and the amount of bow length used will materially affect style and technique. Not even in warm melodic passages is the full length of the bow necessarily required, and it is sometimes important to arrive at the right part of the bow ready for what lies ahead: e.g. for a quick change to PIZZICATO (needing to be at the heel); for a passage to be played off the string (near the middle of the bow) or for a sudden drop to *pianissimo* (best effected at the point). An orchestral player normally follows certain principles when bowing a passage; for instance a *crescendo* is more naturally phrased on an up bow, a feminine ending on a down, and so on.

This organizational work, with its appropriate knowledge and skill, falls properly to the LEADER's responsibility and through him or her to the principals of the other string sections. But both composers and conductors, in order to clarify their requirements and save rehearsal time, sometimes – either themselves or through the agency of the orchestral LIBRARIAN – mark scores and parts with bowing indications using the standard symbols ⊓ and ⋁ to represent down and up bow respectively. These signs may be inverted for use below the notes, viz. ⊔ and ⋀ , but are then often confusing, and can be mistaken for other symbols. The translations are **Abstrich** and **Aufstrich** (Ger.); **tirez** and **poussez** (Fr.); **giù** and **su** (It.).

Conductors in particular know all too well that many of the marks representing hours of painstaking labour and thought may need to be changed on the spur of the moment during rehearsal as the result of the individual views, style and specialist understanding of the orchestra's leader. Nevertheless it is usually found that the time and trouble has been well spent, since a few changes and disagreements with well-thought-out marks can always be solved quickly by a good section, often without even stopping the rehearsal.

Orchestral parts of the classical and romantic repertoire are sometimes already printed with editors' bowings. Such parts all too often conflict with the scores of the selfsame editions and, moreover, may be out of step with each other. Another hazard is that the greatly increased cost of printing means that publishers are becoming more and more reluctant to produce ORCHESTRAL MATERIAL for sale, and the hired parts that constitute the vast majority of materials in circulation are mostly full of contradictory bowings, the legacy of countless previous hirings.

8 Détaché Bowing

In most of these markings the length of the bow used is not specified, on the assumption that it will vary according to the character and intensity of the music. Should normal bowing require special mention it is referred to as **détaché** or (Ger.) **Strich für Strich** (literally 'stroke for stroke') as Mahler puts in his scores. Sibelius, in the opening of the Third Symphony writes *mit liegendem Bogen* (with 'lying bow', i.e., on the string), which actually underlines the firm nature of *détaché* playing in order to avoid the semi-staccato, half-off-the-string technique often adopted in such passages.

9 Long Bowing

However, if, for example, longer strokes are wanted, the notes may be capped with lines, although this symbol can have the side effect of separating the notes; for the line is also a form of stress even if less sharp than the different accent symbols > or ʌ . It was to prevent this kind of ambiguity that Mahler characteristically added verbal injunctions to convey his wishes, such as **lang gestrichen** ('with long strokes'), **viel Bogenwechsel** ('many changes of bow') or the passionate exhortation 'TON!!' Long bows have a particular validity in soft passage work where, if executed with a light bow arm, they give a lucidity to the texture. This style is sometimes known as **portato** (not to be confused with *portamento*) or **louré**, and is particularly appropriate for classical works on account of its origin in viol playing. The whole length of the bow is drawn smoothly and swiftly across the strings with very little weight – e.g. for accompaniment figures in Bach. This is not dissimilar to the technique for **flautato** – as the name suggests, a style producing a pale flute-like quality – also achieved by a fast-travelling bow but with even lighter pressure and used for making a special atmospheric effect in the pursuit of which the bow will be towards the fingerboard.

10 Short Bowing

Where short on-the-string bowing styles are concerned, in **marcato** the sound of each note is stopped by the bow before the next is initiated. The edge of the new note is then sharply attacked, irrespective of whether it is taken with a change of direction or not. *Marcato* may be indicated by means of symbols (lines, accents or arrowheads denoting increasing degrees of intensity) or even by the word itself: the French is **marqué** and the German **markiert**. A true *marcato* should always be interpreted on the string, although the situation is often confused through the appearance of dots – properly the sign for staccato – over the notes. The same confusion arises with the extreme form of *marcato*, **martellato** ('hammered'; the French use the same word, **martelé**, but neither English nor German has a word of its own).

11 Off the String

Conversely, **staccato** should properly be taken off the string though *marcato* or *martellato* at the upper half of the bow is often a safer method for difficult passage work. As with *marcato*, there are different degrees of *staccato*, ranging from what players understand as 'half-off' (normally used in stronger rapid passages where a *détaché* style might become too heavy in quality) to the **spiccato**. Outside English-speaking countries *spiccato* is the general term used for all off-the-string playing regardless of degree, but we tend to use it for the separately bowed, harder, more brittle form of *staccato* referred to abroad as *spiccato assai* or in Italy itself as **balzato**. Any off-the-string *staccato* is usually played near the middle of the bow or towards the heel, where it becomes increasingly easy to control, as well as gruffer and more aggressive. At the point it is generally considered to be impracticable but Sibelius actually prescribes it in his *Valse triste*, as does Roussel in the ballet *Le Festin de l'Araignée*.

There is rarely any guidance in scores to indicate whether a passage is to be played on or off the string, and most players will either make their own decisions or discuss the matter with the conductor.

Shorter and lighter even than *spiccato* is **saltato** (or *saltando*) (Fr. **sautillé**; Ger. **Springbogen**), in which the bow is bounced near the middle, more vertically than laterally, and necessarily with some speed, which in turn becomes an integral part of the effect. This can be executed up- or down-bow, and on one string or across the strings. **Ricochet** or **jeté** are also used for this technique, where the length of the bow is made to travel across the string in a succession of bouncing down bows.

12 Slurs and Phrase Marks
A serious hazard in the adoption of one out of the many possible bowings for a given passage is the fact that the **slur** sign serves both for bowing and phrasing, and it is not always clear which the composer had in mind. Admittedly the inordinately long slurs at the beginning of Wagner's *Siegfried Idyll* are palpably phrasing and give no possible indication of bowing, but many a long-slurred passage is far from obvious, being theoretically feasible in a single bow but in practice making the players feel too cramped. Some suitable point may need to be found for a bow change where the break in phrasing will least disturb smoothness of continuity. Sometimes this is done by having players of the section change bow on different notes, but such FREE BOWING is the exception rather than the rule.

See also: EDITING, ORCHESTRAL MATERIAL, REHEARSALS

BRASS
1 Families
The brass section proper consists of members of the TRUMPET, TROMBONE and TUBA families as well as – like the woodwind – some rare or more exotic visitors, which may also be co-opted as required, such as CORNETS, SAXHORNS, EUPHONIUM, ZINKE, etc. It does not, however, include HORNS, even though these do also logically belong since they are indeed made of brass. Yet however much some composers as well as conductors prefer to consider them as brass, they really have an identity of their own with a foot in both the woodwind and brass camps.

The name translates directly as

cuivres (Fr.) or **Blech** (Ger.), while the Italian **ottoni** can be seen in some recent Russian editions as well as more specifically in scores such as Puccini's *Turandot* to denote a brass band.

2 Section Formations I: Trumpets

The widest definition of the standard brass section is based on the formula seen in catalogues of orchestral works: 4.2.3.1, in which the horn quartet is included and represented by the '4' and the '2' refers to the trumpets, leaving the '3.1.' for the trombones and tuba. There are, however, endless variations: Bach, for example, habitually used a 3-trumpet section for his larger choral movements, while Handel added horns to a similar 3-trumpet ensemble in the *Fireworks Music*. But, thereafter, a pair of trumpets for long became the standard section, lasting for the classical and romantic eras with only a few exceptions. Only for special purposes was a 3rd trumpet sometimes added, as it is by Berlioz in his overture to *Les Francs Juges*, by Mendelssohn in the coda only to the Overture *Calm Sea and Prosperous Voyage*, by Schumann in the *Manfred* Overture and by Liszt in several of the symphonic poems. Berlioz was, however, quick to add to his pair of trumpets a companion pair of the newly invented cornets, taking advantage of their pistons; and French operatic composers soon developed a regular practice of enlarging the brass section to include four players, with two each of trumpets and cornets, the latter being played by the 3rd and 4th trumpet players even though they tend to have much the more interesting and important parts and may even be placed in the score above the first and second trumpets.

This double-pair formation was later adopted by composers in other countries such as, for example, Vaughan Williams in his *London* Symphony and Sibelius in *Pohjola's Daughter*. This is not to say that 4-trumpet sections invariably consist of two trumpets and two cornets; Strauss wrote for four actual trumpets in *Also sprach Zarathustra*, as did Bartók in his *Deux Images*, Op. 10, and numerous other instances abound.

Larger sections continue to remain somewhat exceptional. Berlioz's six players in the Overture *Benvenuto Cellini*, with four trumpets in addition to the two cornets, would seem to be pioneer; but their specific role is to provide all the notes of the big tune when this is declaimed *en masse* at the climax of the piece, since Berlioz was writing for natural valveless instruments, which he pitched in all sorts of different CROOKS for the purpose. However, since the introduction of chromatic instruments this overture has always been played by a total of four trumpets with the melodic notes more practically reallocated.

Debussy in *La Mer* uses three trumpets plus two cornets, an enlargement of the French tradition that he inherited from César Franck and his followers. Strauss writes for five trumpets in *Heldenleben*, three B♭ trumpets plus two in E♭, the first E♭ trumpet being hardly less than a principal player in his own right; Kodály uses six B♭ trumpets in *Háry János*. The record was long held to be Janáček's nine extra trumpets for the *Sinfonietta*

39

(making a total of twelve including the three in the orchestra proper) but Khachaturian actually uses no fewer than eighteen in his Third Symphony.

Opera, too, provides numerous instances of extra trumpets being required off-stage for fanfares, as in the third act of Verdi's *Otello*, or Britten's *Gloriana* where no limit to their number is specified – merely that they must be 'in multiples of three'.

A single trumpet in the wind ensemble of an orchestra – other than as a soloist in such works as Bach's Second Brandenburg Concerto – hardly exists until the mid-twentieth century, the short appearance in Wagner's *Siegfried Idyll* being an isolated and very special instance. But as soon as the Schreker *Kammersymphonie* and Stravinsky's Suite No. 1 for small orchestra had blazed the trail, further instances of writing for a single trumpet were quickly added by Milhaud, Respighi, Tippett and others.

3 Section Formations II: Trombones

Where the brass ensemble carries two or three trumpets it is usually balanced by the 3-trombone section, consisting in the normal way of two tenors and a bass. Yet Berlioz wrote in the *Symphonie Fantastique* for an alto and two tenors, and the classical combination, which continued well into the romantic era, was a trio consisting of one each of alto, tenor and bass. Beethoven, however, used only two in the *Pastoral* Symphony and in *Fidelio* (an alto and tenor in the one and a tenor and bass in the other) but the fact that such combinations are generally considered unsatisfactory is shown by their sub-sequent disappearance.

The use of a single trombone is rare but has a classical tradition, especially in *opéra comique*. Hence Rossini, for example, expected three trombones to be available for *opera seria* but knew that he could count on only a single instrument for *opera buffa*. This accounts for the different scorings of the two main versions of the overture originally written for the comedy *Aureliano in Palmira* and subsequently for the drama *Elisabetta, Regina d'Inghilterra*, but which we know so well as *The Barber of Seville*.

From this tradition may indeed come the symphonic use in the full orchestra of a single bass trombone, as in Weber's *Konzertstück*, the two Chopin Piano Concertos, and Glinka's little wedding scena, *Kamarinskaya*.

The single trombone, though no longer specifically a bass instrument, reappears in the twentieth century as a feature of the chamber orchestra, as does the single horn and the single trumpet. It plays a striking part in numerous Stravinsky pieces for small orchestra, such as the two Suites (the first of which has one each of horn, trumpet, trombone and tuba), *Pulcinella* and the *Danses Concertantes*, in which he was followed by other composers in works for small orchestra, such as Lennox Berkeley's *Divertimento*.

In classical times, from well before Gluck's day, the trombones were confined largely to sacred and ceremonial music, but a century before their symphonic appearance they occupied an important niche in opera, being used predominantly for special occasions such as supernatural, *deus-ex-machina* or religious manifestations.

4 Section Formations III: Tubas

The most normal and basic brass ensemble on contract with presentday symphony orchestras has already been defined above as using the tuba to support the 3-trombone group, this being the standard requirement of most full orchestral works in the mid-nineteenth to mid-twentieth century era. There are, however, two main exceptions to this. Firstly, works exist – and considerable pieces at that – in which the tuba is not scored for at all. Brahms by no means always added the instrument to his brass; the Second Symphony is the only one of the four with a tuba, and Dvořák added it to the *New World* Symphony only as an afterthought, even then using it only for the brass chords at the beginning and end of the slow movement. Perhaps, however, the most surprising reticence is that of Richard Strauss, who found no need for a tuba in his *Aus Italien*, while a striking contemporary instance of the same economy is Tippett's *Midsummer Marriage*.

The other exception is the substitution of a 4th trombone for the tuba. Wagner was certainly not alone in considering the ponderous and round-toned tuba an unsatisfactory fundamental timbre to the trombone group. Its establishment in this capacity came about for no other reason than that it was the nearest available equivalent to the OPHICLEIDE, which it automatically superseded as this became obsolete during the second and third decades of the nineteenth century. Among the many composers who sought some

other replacement was Verdi, who came to abandon the CIMBASSO in favour of a quartet of trombones, i.e., three tenors and a bass, in which he was followed by Puccini. D'Indy was another of the curiously few composers who followed Wagner in writing for the contrabass trombone, using it as a substitute for the tuba in his Second Symphony.

The use of more than one tuba in the brass section remains exceptional, and a second tuba is never carried on the strength. Where two are used they may be either a pair of bass tubas (as in Berlioz's *Symphonie Fantastique* and Strauss's *Also sprach Zarathustra*) or one tenor tuba and one bass tuba (as in both Strauss's *Don Quixote* and *Heldenleben* as well as Holst's *Planets*). Indeed, apart from the quartet of WAGNER TUBAS, which belongs properly to the horn ensemble, no more than two tubas are ever used, with the exception of works with additional brass bands such as Berlioz's *Grande Messe des Morts* or Walton's *Belshazzar's Feast*.

There are occasional instances of a bass tuba being used without trombones – for example, Prokofiev's Violin Concerto, Op. 19 – but the most famous is undoubtedly Mendelssohn's Overture *A Midsummer Night's Dream*, although it has to be borne in mind that the instrument Mendelssohn actually intended was the rougher and more grotesque bass ophicleide. Shostakovich's First Violin Concerto goes still further in that it has a tuba but no other heavy brass at all, not even trumpets, the tuba acting as fundamental to the four horns alone.

5 Brass Ensembles

Wind bands of any size that include no brass at all are unusual, but there are certainly BRASS BANDS that are composed exclusively of brass instruments.

6 Character

Apart from its enormous power, one of the principal qualities of the brass is rhythmic incisiveness, which can have the edge on the entire orchestra. At the same time, this very virtue can be a problem in itself; in many halls (especially radio or recording studios) the brass may tend to sound behind the beat – and this often leads to acrimony, since, while the weight of the brass can hold back the tempo beyond recovery, nothing is more upsetting for the players than to be asked to anticipate, especially in syncopated passage work.

On the other hand the brass section possesses the ability to complement its extreme reserves of volume with a magical *pianissimo*, and it is noteworthy that the brass can more easily produce a sudden drop to a hushed echo quality, as well as a background of velvety softness, than the woodwind as a body can ever achieve.

See also: AEROPHON, EMBOUCHURE, FULL ORCHESTRA, GLISSANDO, HARMONIE, MUTES, PLATFORM ARRANGEMENT, SCORE LAYOUT

Another strange difference is the extraordinary layout of brass-band scores, which are written entirely in the treble clef (including the deepest BOMBARDON) with the single exception of the bass trombone. The appearance of such scores is entirely unfamiliar and perplexing to even the most adept orchestral score reader. These bands are, however, a world of their own and do not impinge on the orchestral scene even for their seeming importations into scores. For Walton's *Belshazzar's Feast*, Respighi's *Pines of Rome* and especially, of course, the four brass bands of Berlioz's *Grande Messe des Morts*, for example, groups of brass players are invariably co-opted individually from among the orchestral profession, whereas for Tchaikovsky's *1812* and especially for trumpet fanfares such as those of Strauss's *Festliches Praeludium* groups of instrumentalists from one of the Guards Bands or military academies are co-opted.

See also: HARMONIE, MILITARY BAND

Bratsche (Ger.), *see* VIOLA

Buccini, Roman brass-band instruments; *see* LITUI, SAXHORNS

Buckelgongs, Javanese gongs; *see* GONGS AND TAM-TAMS

BRASS BAND

A group consisting only of brass instruments, abounding particularly in the North of England. Theirs is, however, a highly specialized outlook in many respects, the most important of which is their exclusively amateur status, which is jealously preserved.

BUGLE

Of all the subspecies of the TRUMPET family perhaps the bugle is the best known, even though it never appears in the BRASS section of the orchestra. Mention of bugles inescapably calls to mind images of either the military or Boy Scouts, in whose province the instrument properly belongs.

The name itself is not free of confusion: although no one has the least doubt over what a bugle is in normal British usage, textbooks refer to different species (including so-called 'keyed bugles'), which apply the word 'bugle' in an altogether wider sense. Moreover the Continental terms are incredibly muddling: the French do possess the word 'bugle' but apply it to the FLÜGELHORN and SAXHORNS. D'Indy writes for two so-called 'bugles' in his opera *Fervaal*, but these are certainly small members of the saxhorn family, the one a *Petit bugle en Mi b* the other a *bugle en Si b*. This last is also the Italian *flicorno* – the equivalent of our Flügelhorn – which the French confusingly call a contralto bugle and is therefore the instrument Stravinsky writes for in *Threni*. The French term for the military bugle is **clairon** and the German **Signalhorn** (which creates further confusion when one thinks of Haydn's Symphony No. 31, subtitled 'Mit dem Hornsignal', but which is certainly written for horns).

The most familiar kind of bugle is a natural instrument without valves, pitched in Bb and having a severely limited compass – indeed only five or, at the most, six notes. The top note, the flattened seventh harmonic, is even more unreliable in intonation than the others.

Another limitation, making the military bugle unsuitable for normal orchestral use, is its potential dynamic range, which is very restricted, since, although it can be played very loudly indeed, it can hardly be made to speak at less than a *mezzo forte*. This is of course consistent with its primary purpose as an open-air instrument.

Bugles generally play together in bands, and Britten writes for a boys' bugle band in *Noye's Fludde*, a work that makes a feature of co-opting non-professional groups. He uses all six notes, writing unusually in concert pitch – the familiar military bugle calls being conventionally notated in C major, i.e., a tone higher than they sound.

Britten allows the leading bugler some solo notes, which is in accordance with the best traditions, and he also writes for mutes, which is not. There are in fact no such things as authentic bugle mutes and these have to be improvised or hired from the publishers, who have prepared suitable objects especially for Britten's purpose.

BULL ROARER

This American Indian native 'instrument' makes only very rare appearances in the orchestra, as in Ronald Stevenson's Second Piano Concerto, a work evoking the folk idioms and textures of different cultures all over the world. The bull roarer is a device consisting of a long flexible object attached to a string. The task of playing it, however, is not readily undertaken by percussionists, since the danger to life and limb is considerable as the player whirls it about his head. It emits an eerie roar that rises in pitch as the whirling increases in speed.

BUMPER

The constitution and seating formation of the HORN section is, from the viewpoint of the layman observer, confused to some extent by the prevalent figure of a supernumary player, seated alongside the 1st horn. This extra musician is known as the bumper (the word coined from the verb 'to bump up', meaning to 'support' and nothing worse). The function of the bumper is to share the burden of the heavier passage work in order to relieve the strain on the 1st horn and keep his lip fresh for solos. He will play either instead of, or even sometimes together with, his principal as the nature of the music allows. Such doubling is left entirely to the discretion of the players and does not properly enter the jurisdiction of the conductor at all.

Comparatively rare until some twenty-five to thirty years ago, the engagement of a bumper for the 1st horn (and incidentally even more recently for the 1st trumpet as well) has gradually grown into something of a status symbol, although it is conceded that many programmes are undeniably heavy for the first players of these sections, especially in view of today's rigorous standards of execution.

CADENZA

Free virtuoso sections for the soloist in concertante works, cadenzas of the classical period are for the greater part not included in the printed score and hence can cause anxiety for the conductor waiting to bring in the orchestra at the conclusion. Since many conventional cadenza endings consist of a trill and the cadenza is not normally played intact at rehearsal, it is not unknown to see conductor and players getting themselves ready to re-enter at the sound of such a trill only to relax once more, looking slightly foolish, as the soloist plunges into further passage work.

Cadenzas may be provided by the composers (as sometimes by Mozart or Beethoven and, after them by Schumann, Tchaikovsky, Sibelius, Rachmaninoff, etc.) and these are so familiar that they rarely cause difficulties, whether the score enables the conductor to follow their course or not. Where no authentic cadenzas exist, soloists usually play traditional cadenzas composed by earlier eminent virtuosi such as Joachim for Mozart's A major Violin Concerto and Kreisler for the Beethoven and Brahms. But often too they may play ones of their own devising, and in such cases the joins to the ensuing **tutti**s can be fraught unless the conductor has had the opportunity of meeting the soloist beforehand, either to obtain a copy or to write out the final linking phrases into his score. Even then, however, there remains an element of skill in obtaining unanimity of attack at the moment of hand over, and this requires collaboration on the part of the soloist as well as quick-witted awareness from the conductor.

The word 'cadenza' is also used by composers for written-out free solo passages within the orchestra. Rimsky-Korsakov's *Capriccio Espagnol* has particularly noteworthy examples of these, while Ernest Bloch actually marks one dazzlingly virtuoso passage for the whole orchestra in his *Schelomo* as *quasi una Cadenza*.

See also: AD LIB, CONCERTO

Caisse claire (Fr.), *see* DRUMS, 1

Caisse roulante (Fr.), *see* DRUMS, 1

Cambia in (It.), change to; *see* TIMPANI, 9

Campane (It.), *see* BELLS

Campanelli (It.), *see* GLOCKENSPIEL, 2

Campanelli a tastiera (It.), keyboard glockenspiel; *see* GLOCKENSPIEL, 2

Capello cinese (It.), *see* JINGLES

Caraxá, *see* RATTLE

Carillon, *see* GLOCKENSPIEL, 2

Carraca, *see* RATTLE

Cassa rullante (It.), *see* DRUMS, 1

CASTANETS

Pairs of small shallow cup-shaped wooden objects, castanets are strongly associated with the folk dancing of Spain, this being indeed their country of origin, which is accordingly evoked in such works as Debussy's *Ibéria* or Chabrier's *España*. It is therefore surprising how much more widely they have been used, they abound in fact in the scores of composers of every country and school, from Wagner (the 'Bacchanale' in the first act of *Tannhäuser*) via Sibelius (*Festivo*) and Dohnányi (Suite in F sharp minor, Op. 19) to contemporary composers such as Stravinsky (*Agon*).

It is normally taken for granted that castanets are wooden, but Saint-Saëns also wrote for iron ones in *Samson and Delilah* (*castagnettes de bois et de fer*) and his example was followed by Milhaud (*Les Choéphores*, etc.). It is sometimes claimed that *castagnettes de fer* are virtually the same as CROTALES but this is an over-simplification, even though crotales are sometimes used as a substitute in emergency.

The general term for castanets is broadly the same in most languages, allowing for small spelling changes. The Italians, however, including, for example, Respighi and Casella, also use **nacchere**.

Usually featured in strong rhythmic passages, following the typical Spanish dance, the most commonly used are the orchestral type, in which the castanets are fixed on a board or manipulated with a handle, and composers often write elaborate passage work that would be hardly practicable with the true Spanish loose castanets held in the palm of the hand. Sometimes they are given isolated clicks, where they act as a kind of substitute for claves or even a very light variety of wood block. For this purpose they can be struck, instead of on each other, with an independent object such as the **legno** (wooden stick) of Stravinsky in the 'Bransle Gay' from *Agon*, though the purpose here is less clear since the usual technique (also wood against wood) gives a virtually identical sound.

CELESTA

Shaped like a little upright pianino with shorter keyboard and, curiously, a single pedal, the celesta is a contraption of metal plates gently struck by hammers with an action not unlike that of a piano and softly sustained by means of resonating chambers. The name of the instrument is universal, even the French form being *celesta*. Strange to say 'celeste', given by Percy Scholes as an alternative and always used in orchestral parlance, is in fact no more than an organ stop.

The range of the celesta is usually cited as being the four octaves of the original, and still most commonly found, Mustel instrument:

(sounding 8va higher) but the five-octave Schiedmayer is a strong competitor and it is this instrument, with its fifth octave extending the range downwards to the lower C, that is necessary for many works, including Mahler's Sixth Symphony. Mahler indeed asks for two instruments, as does Strauss in *Die Frau ohne Schatten*, but such extravagance in celesta writing is extremely rare. When faced with the need for the wider compass, players tend to adapt the music to fit the available keyboard as best they may with octave transpositions; nor is this expedience uncommon since even as standard a score as Ravel's *Ma Mère l'Oye* goes down to B.

In the 'Carillon féerique' from Stravinsky's *Firebird* the celesta is instructed to play *con moderatore*, which can refer only to its single pedal. This, which is known misleadingly as the 'damper pedal', is supposed on the contrary to increase the celesta's sustaining power but it has to be admitted that its effect is imperceptible and (perhaps for this reason) instructions for its application are excessively rare. Moreover, many celesta parts lack any dynamic marks, for the range of dynamics available to the player using the strongest wrist action hardly exceeds a *mezzo piano*.

The conventional notation of the celesta is on two bracketed staves as for the harp and piano but an octave lower than it sounds. There is, however, the additional complication that not all composers, or conductors for that matter, are any too sure either which octave is required or even which octave is actually being played. The limpid bell-like tones are oddly deceptive and the deep notes of the weak register turn out to be unexpectedly high when checked against the piano. Many features of the celesta part of *The Planets* strongly suggest that it should sound at pitch, but Holst's own recording gives it sounding the octave higher throughout. Bax certainly writes the celesta at actual pitch in his *Overture to a Picaresque Comedy*.

The technique of the celesta corresponds broadly (within obvious limitations) to that of the piano, having equal capacity for tremolos, trills, scales, arpeggios, telling chords, glissandi and the like, all of which can add touches of enchantment to a sensitively laid-out orchestral tapestry, and have been widely exploited by composers. Debussy in *La Mer* suggested it as an alternative to the glockenspiel in the second movement 'Jeu de vagues'. It is certainly more suitable here than the over-bright glockenspiel, which is then held in reserve for greater effect in the succeeding 'Dialogue du vent et de la mer'.

This exceptional instance may explain why the celesta is sometimes wrongly listed among the percussion, and the part even sometimes coupled with those of the kitchen department, which can cause total confusion in rehearsal. Properly the celesta lies within the specialized field of a keyboard player and is only very rarely doubled by a member of the percussion group.

Tchaikovsky is generally credited with having introduced the celesta into the orchestra, which he did within ten years of the instrument's invention – not, curiously enough, in the famous 'Dance of the Sugar Plum Fairy' from the *Nutcracker* ballet, but in his symphonic poem *The Voyevode*, which was composed the previous year (1891) but published only posthumously. In this excellent but largely unknown work he was still unsure of the style and dynamic possibilities of the instrument, for he wrote an elaborate pianistic part that he then completely swamped with surging tutti orchestration. But by the time he came to *Nutcracker* he had the full measure of its potential, although he again wrote the part at actual pitch, allowing for the substitution of a piano.

CELLO

The fourth member, in descending order, of the five groups that make up the orchestral STRING section. The cello is very much larger than its immediate neighbour, the viola, and is always played seated, even in solo work, not to mention in performances of the National Anthem. Cellos are equipped with metal spikes that have to be indented into the floor in front of the player, who selects a suitable place on the platform with some care to ensure that the instrument will not slip away during playing. If the floor is made of marble or other totally unsuitable material long wooden contraptions may have to be used. Fixed at one end round a leg of the cellist's chair, these will solve the problem.

Owing to the importance of the angle of the body to the instrument, cellists are highly selective about their chairs and it is not unusual to find the cello section of an orchestra favoured in this respect above all the rest of the players.

The disproportionate size of the cello *vis-à-vis* the violins and violas is reflected in its name, which is short for **violoncello**. The abbreviation 'cello' is in fact simply a general diminutive, as in 'vermicelli', just as the suffix '–one' is an augmentation (e.g. 'padrone'). Thus 'violoncello' literally means a 'little violone' – i.e. a little big viol. Occasionally the howler 'violincello' still makes an appearance.

The strings of the cello are tuned, like those of the viola but sounding an octave lower, in fifths from the low C upwards:

This gives the cello a range from to at least , (as in the first movement of Elgar's A♭ Symphony). Cello parts are thus written in both treble and bass clefs and, moreover, the tenor clef 𝄡 is equally common in moderately high cello writing.

The use of the treble clef sometimes creates uncertainty as some late-romantic composers retain the old cello notation with passages in the treble clef being written an octave higher than they sound. Many a passage in Bruckner's symphonies looks far more formidable than it really is (though the hazard here is less the high range than the need to transpose). While the old notation is still widely found in standard editions of classical chamber music, in the orchestral repertoire many of the parts have been rearranged to avoid the treble clef altogether (generally in favour of the tenor clef) or with the clef retained but the passage transposed to read at pitch. Octave transposition of cello treble-clef notation is to some extent analogous to horn notation in the bass clef, although it has not survived to the same degree, nor is it similarly defended by the players themselves, who on the contrary find it misleading.

At full strength a symphony orchestra will carry five desks of cellos (i.e. ten players) even though some works, such as Strauss's *Also sprach Zarathustra*, specify six desks and write separate notes for each of the twelve players. On tour, or for smaller platforms, four desks or even three are not uncommon.

If according to the PLATFORM ARRANGEMENT the cellos are on the conductor's right and nearest to the audience, as is most usual today, the leading cellist will then generally be on the outside, i.e., the left player of the front desk and nearest to the platform edge, thus mirroring the leader of the orchestra. A few principal cellists, however, object to this seat on the grounds that they find it hard to follow the conductor's beat from so wide an angle. In such cases they will then sit on the inside of the front desk, although the first players of all the subsequent desks continue to sit on the outside, giving rise to certain anomalies in *divisi* passages.

In view of the cello's exceptional power of evocation – its more impassioned utterances can seem at times on the verge of articulate speech, as in Bloch's *Schelomo* – the principal player of the orchestral cello section comes in for a very substantial share of extended solos across the classical and romantic repertoire. Rossini's Overture *William Tell* further provides soloistic opportunities for several cellos in ensemble, as does the first act of Wagner's *Die Walküre* as well as Puccini's *Tosca*. From these it is then a short step to Strauss's *Don Quixote* where the Don himself is characterized largely by the leading cello; in practice this is generally given to a soloist but Strauss's original plan was for the part to be performed within the orchestra, and in several places more than one cello is concerned with the characterization. It is hard to think of any other instrument that could have handled this assignment with such extraordinary success.

See also: ARCO, ARTIFICIAL HARMONICS, BACK DESKS, BOWING, DIVISI, DOUBLE STOPPING, EARLY STRINGED INSTRUMENTS, GLISSANDO, HARMONICS, MUTES,

PIZZICATO, RANK AND FILE, SCORDATURA, STRINGS

Cembalo (It.), *see* HARPSICHORD

Cencerros (Mex.), *see* COWBELLS

CHAINS

It is only natural that chains should appear in opera to represent, for example, the chained prisoners in Janáček's *From the House of the Dead*, but typically Varèse includes an abstract part for 'chaines' in *Intégrales*.

The *locus classicus*, however, of the scoring for chains as a colour in the orchestral spectrum is in Schoenberg's *Gurrelieder* where they are described as *einige grosse eiserne* **Ketten** (some large iron chains) for which he writes rolls, trills, etc. Yet it is difficult to know how the composer intended them to be executed and like so many of these extra-musical effects no hard and fast rule exists, the percussionist usually rattling the chains on some large inverted metal tray or gong.

CHAMBER ORCHESTRA

There is no precise constitution for a chamber orchestra, although it is generally assumed to be in the region of some thirty-five players. There will commonly be four desks of 1st violins with the other strings proportionately disposed, but there could perhaps be fewer according to the programme policy of the organization. Similarly there will often be a pair of each woodwind and two horns, but trumpets and timpani may well be co-opted as required.

Such a group commands a wider repertoire than might be thought. Apart from the very extensive choice of classical seventeenth-, eighteenth- and even early nineteenth-century music, only slight increase in the number of musicians (harp, percussion, a single trombone, etc.) brings a rich repertoire of romantic and twentieth-century works into the standard literature of an established chamber orchestra.

It is therefore often thought logical, where lack of large-scale venues or economical considerations demand, to replace a resident symphony orchestra with a chamber-sized ensemble. Two essential factors are all too easily overlooked when such a proposal is being considered. In the first place it is by definition far harder to fill a hall with such a body. Not only does it lack the superficial glamour that brings mass audiences to orchestral concerts, but the repertoire – wide as it is – omits a large part of the gamut of popular works. Box-office favourites such as Beethoven's Fifth, Tchaikovsky's B♭ minor Piano Concerto, Bizet's *L'Arlésienne* or *Carmen* Suites, Ravel's *Bolero*, all lack their counterparts in the delicate, tasteful world of the chamber orchestra where the most popular items might be perhaps Mozart's *Eine kleine Nachtmusik* or Wagner's *Siegfried Idyll*. Financial problems are thus by no means solved at a blow, and there is also a fallacy in thinking that a small orchestra is *ipso facto* cheaper than a full-sized one, since a chamber group may consist entirely of more highly paid virtuosi.

Second, and central to the success of

49

the chamber orchestra, is the axiom that the smaller the ensemble the greater must be the individual level of proficiency. Blemishes that pass unnoticed in the huge conglomerate of the Mahlerian orchestra simply sound ragged in the fine give-and-take of a chamber group. Moreover, when a heavy concert schedule is undertaken by a chamber orchestra, any casualties or sickness, especially at short notice and where a programme is repeated identically in different locations, can have extremely serious consequences.

When the players really are of a uniform excellence, the joy of belonging to a small specialized ensemble can be infinitely rewarding, with its far greater and more good-humoured camaraderie and its potential for taking real care over artistic detail and problems of technique. As a result many of the finest musicians have come to eschew the grander symphonic repertoire in favour of working regularly with one of the ever increasing number of chamber orchestras of the highest calibre that are springing up all over the world.

See also: ENSEMBLE, FULL ORCHESTRA, ORCHESTRA, PROGRAMME PLANNING

Changez en (Fr.), change to; *see* TIMPANI, 9

Cheese grater, *see* GOURDS

Chef d'attaque (Fr.), *see* LEADER

Chevalet (Fr.), bridge; *see* BOWING, 4

Chimes, *see* BELLS

Chimes, Wind, *see* WIND CHIMES

Chinese bell tree, *see* BELL TREE

Chinese block, *see* WOODBLOCK

Chinese cymbals, *see* CYMBALS, 9

CHINESE TOM-TOMS

The Chinese variety are markedly smaller than all other TOM-TOMS, even allowing for their various size ranges, have curved sides, and are narrower from top to bottom than the African species (although these are in turn narrower than dance-band tom-toms). Chinese tom-toms are also beautifully decorated with a dragon on the playing head. In view of this it will be no surprise to learn that sticks would be a quite unsuitable medium and that they are always played with fingers or the flat of the hands. Chinese tom-toms are never produced by percussion groups unless especially stipulated by composers such as Copland (in his Piano Concerto) or Roberto Gerhard, who possessed his own set of which he was inordinately proud.

Chittara, alla, *see* PIZZICATO, 3

CHORUS

It may seem odd to include an entry on the chorus in a book that is concerned essentially with the orchestra, and indeed there is no intention of treating voices in their function as soloists or even of discussing the wider aspects of choruses or choral writing. Yet the chorus is by far the most important adjunct to the orchestra in the whole of symphonic concert-giving. Indeed, apart from its essentially imposing visual impact, the very power of associations conjured up by human voices is such that it focuses the attention unremittingly on itself – whether it is designed as the centre of attraction in a major choral work or used as an additional colour in a kaleidoscopic score, such as in Ravel's *Daphnis et Chloé*.

Whereas the customary use of the human voice is in the articulation of words using texts in all languages and of all ages, the semi-orchestral role of choruses merely vocalizing has become a prominent feature of late-romantic and contemporary music since Debussy's pioneering introduction of a wordless female chorus into the third of his *Nocturnes* of 1897. Admittedly his purpose in *Sirènes* might be considered special pleading, suggesting as it does the perilously seductive beauties of nautical legend. The chorus often sings the languorous phrases seated, to preserve the elusive distant character of impressionist tone painting, and this is only one of the many practical decisions that has to be taken in planning the presentation not only of this particular work but of any concert that features a chorus.

In 'Neptune', the last of the *Planets*, Holst took over Debussy's wordless female chorus, though he places it off-stage and as far away as practicable, allowing for a final dying away to total inaudibility for the conclusion of the work through the closing of some distant door. Vaughan Williams introduces a wordless chorus of both men and women into his *Old King Cole* as well as *Flos Campi*; and the full chorus is again used as an orchestral colour in Scriabin's *Prometheus* as well

as Bartók's *Miraculous Mandarin* and Suk's *Zrání*. In *The Song of the High Hills* Delius uses the voices' wordless vocalizing very elaborately in his evocation of Norway, with two solo singers, soprano and tenor, as well as full chorus divided into all of eleven parts.

Singers normally vocalize to some vowel sound such as 'ah' or 'la' unless, as for example in *Sirènes*, the instruction is given for closed lips. It is rare, however, to find syllables specified in the score although in *Prometheus* certain passages are marked 'o . . . ho . . . e . . . a', etc.

The standard layout for the chorus is in four parts: SATB, i.e., two lines for soprano and alto, and two for tenor and bass. Sometimes a more complicated work will subdivide the lines into five (usually with 1st and 2nd sopranos), six or even eight parts. The four standard voices are still generally retained in their designation; mezzo-sopranos are rarely found in choral writing and baritones hardly at all. The upper or lower register of each voice is thus given to the firsts or seconds of the respective group, the line dividing for the purpose.

The range for the voices used chorally is astonishingly wide:

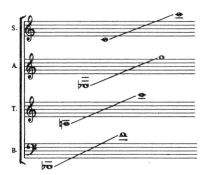

but the outermost extreme ranges are generally avoided where the chorus is introduced wordlessly as an additional sound effect in the orchestral spectrum.

Rehearsal difficulties are often encountered where publishers treat the chorus as part of the orchestra and print the vocal lines individually exactly as they would orchestral parts, with bars rest and no more indication of what is going on around than any instrumentalist is used to having. This practice may appear logical, but it certainly lacks imagination. It not only cuts directly against the way choruses operate, but ignores the sheer difficulty for the singers of how they are to pick out of the blue the notes of their entry.

In the full score the voice or voices are normally placed immediately above the strings. The chorus may be notated either in open score, i.e. with a separate stave for each of the standard voice parts, or in some scores, if there are not many subdivisions, they can be condensed on to two staves. This, however, entails combining the tenors with the basses, both notated in the bass clef at pitch, and as a result the tenor line will be at variance with the individual part.

See also: SOPRANO, ALTO, TENOR, BASS, ABSOLUTE PITCH, A CAPPELLA, CHORUS MASTER

CHORUS MASTER

The *métier* of chorus master needs special skills quite distinct from those possessed by orchestral conductors. In the first place the expert choral trainer must be a keyboard player; he may be an organist, but will always be adept at the piano; he will indeed frequently himself preside at this instrument when rehearsing his singers. An acute sense of pitch is essential for his efficiency and most chorus masters have or soon develop ABSOLUTE PITCH. A knowledge of voice production, different techniques and their terminology is of primary importance as should be an understanding of several languages and their pronunciation; the way in which vowels and consonants are formed is as much part of the chorus master's expertise as are the finer points of musicianship.

So much are words and singing built into his conducting style that it is unusual for a chorus master to use a baton, as the hands and fingers are more flexible in this respect. Nor does he beat the bar structures in so stylized a manner as does the orchestral conductor, since for the greater part his singers are working from scores containing all the vocal lines – unlike instrumentalists who play from individual parts and are therefore dependent on a clear structure-forming beat showing the shape and nature of the bars as they appear in the score. Not all chorus masters aspire to become conductors in the widest orchestral and operatic fields, but make their work with choruses large and small into much respected careers. Others, however, use the opportunities given by increasingly important posts, in opera houses and in key provincial festivals, to aim towards a broader range of conducting activities. This, however, entails a change in technique as well as in mental approach, for there is a marked difference between the style of the chorus master, however accomplished, and the fully fledged orchestral maestro. This difference is indeed radical enough for orchestras to find working under a purely choral conductor all too often a dispiriting affair.

Much as the conductors of choruses may be expected to take over important assignments *ex officio* on many occasions, as in local festivals when their choir works with a major symphony orchestra, a substantial part of their function in performances of large-scale choral and orchestral works will be in the preparation of the chorus for a visiting orchestral conductor to whom the reins will be handed over for the final combined rehearsals and concert. The chorus master may nevertheless also invite the guest conductor to take one of the earlier choir rehearsals with piano, and indeed a close co-operation between chorus master and conductor in preparing a choral and orchestral work is of the utmost importance. It is not unusual for the two to meet as colleagues to discuss points of detail and interpretation so that the chorus master's preparation will be in line with the conductor's later requirements. The PLATFORM ARRANGEMENT of the chorus, as well as when the singers should stand and sit during the music, will all come into these discussions.

The chorus master will contribute an intimate knowledge of the individuals in his choir and this will enable him to make valuable suggestions of disposition and balance. Sometimes he can make use of tricks and devices of various kinds to surmount problems that may arise, such as the subtle doubling of lines (2nd altos with tenors in the cruel Berlioz Requiem, for example), which is unperceived but vastly effective, or the under-stressing of over-prominent consonants such as 'S's (which hiss interminably) or 'T's (which are so seldom together and come across like castanets).

Then, when it comes to the final rehearsals, the chorus master may prefer to take the chorus for a brief warm-up before the conductor takes over, and will frequently run the singers through a quick routine of exercises, which the orchestra listens to with high admiration, interest and possibly amusement. The presence of the chorus master at the conductor's rehearsals, both piano and orchestra, is thus patently of the utmost practical and advisory value.

For these and innumerable other reasons it is therefore customary for the conductor to acknowledge their collaboration by bringing the chorus master on to the platform for a solo bow in front of his chorus at the end of the performance.

Choucalha, *see* GOURDS

CIMBALOM

The cimbalom is a popular Hungarian instrument, still played by virtuosi in every Budapest café and restaurant. It is a table-like affair, usually beautifully carved and decorated, at which the player sits as if at supper but, instead of a knife and fork, he holds a pair of thin wooden sticks covered at their ends with cotton-wool.

Musicological confusion is caused by

one of the Italian terms for the cimbalom being *cembalo*, which has misled even Gardner Read, in his *Thesaurus of Orchestral Devices*, into mixing up the instruments. Although it is as the 'cimbalom' that the instrument is known in orchestral circles, it is closely related to the biblical psaltery and also to the **dulcimer**, under which name it tends to be hidden in reference books or textbooks of orchestration.

Its first appearance in orchestral music is in Liszt's Hungarian Rhapsody No. 3 in D, but by far the most famous example of its exploitation is Kodály's *Háry János* Suite. During the 1920s Stravinsky used the cimbalom briefly for a cluster of works, notably *Renard*, *Ragtime* and the pre-1923 orchestral version of *Les Noces*.

Hungarian cimbalom players do not normally use music at all, improvising around well-established formulae, but for orchestral purposes the cimbalom is notated much like a piano, with which it used to be replaced on occasions when the popular *Háry János* was programmed without a cimbalom being available. A recording with piano was once issued but the substitution proved a travesty for two important reasons. In the first place the cimbalom has a peculiarly individual timbre all its own, more jangling than the piano's, and yet totally different from the harpsichord's, with which instrument the word 'jangling' is more often associated. This arises from the method of playing, which consists of striking, one stick in each hand, the piano-like wire strings directly. As a result of this technique the tremolo has developed into a peculiarly individual

method by which Hungarian folk musicians sustain the long notes of a melody. These are notated either conventionally: (♪ *trem.*) or as a kind of shake: (♪). Such a style of playing patently has more in common with glockenspiel or xylophone technique than the piano or harpsichord, and yet its effect is far removed from these too.

Furthermore, the strings of the cimbalom are oddly arranged, so that the highest and lowest registers lie adjacent, with the middle registers lying to one side. Thus the *glissando* that is sometimes written from top to bottom of the instrument does not represent a continuous descending row of notes such as it would on a piano, but involves a sudden jump in pitch as the sticks pass from one group of strings to the other. Moreover, the *glissando* is executed by continuous hammering with the two sticks and not by sliding as on glockenspiels or xylophones.

The cimbalom is notated at actual pitch but variably on either one stave or two, as dictated by the style of the music, using treble and bass clefs. Stravinsky, however, adds a third stave for isolated notes in more complicated places in his *Ragtime*. He also writes for the cimbalom (which he unusually spells with a 'y') to be played *près du chevalet* (near the bridge) and even *derrière le chevalet*, some strings being stretched over indeed not one but two bridges. The effect, of course, bears no relationship to *sul ponticello* as applied to the violin family, but produces a hard, even vicious sound.

Modern instruments are fitted with a damping pedal, which is prescribed by Bartók in his First Violin Rhapsody. Bartók also writes *pizz.*, meaning that the player should pluck the strings with the fingertips instead of striking them with the sticks, and in addition instructs that the wooden ends of the sticks should be used. In *Renard*, Stravinsky calls for leather sticks in alternation with wood sticks.

The range of the modern Hungarian cimbalom is usually the four octaves from ![notation] but Stravinsky adds ossias in his *Ragtime* and *Renard* making provision for *l'instrument qui a la Ré grave*. The instrument to which he referred was one that, although descending chromatically to E, also had the isolated D string – i.e., it had no Eb. The 'Song' in *Háry János* also uses this D, and in the *Kálló Folk Dances* (which is actually scored for two **Zimbalon** *ungharese*) Kodály writes down to the low C – this is because Hungarian makers are forever building bigger and better instruments. None, however, has ever gone as low as the G below this, which Debussy wrote in his 1912 instrumentation of his own waltz *La plus que lente*. This includes a part for cimbalom, but it needs some adaptation to become playable. Perhaps Debussy misunderstood something he was told by a Hungarian virtuoso.

Cinelli (It.), *see* CYMBALS

CIMBASSO

This could best be described less as an instrument than a function, analogous perhaps to CONTINUO, which can also be played by any one of several possible candidates. Although until recently accepted as having been the prerogative of a BASS TUBA, the role of cimbasso is now thought by scholars to have been originally undertaken by some deep member of the trombone family. In either event the word is used mainly by Italian operatic composers to denote the lowest voice of the brass choir, irrespective of any single and irreplaceable instrument. The Ricordi material of some Rossini overtures, such as *Semiramide* and *William Tell*, includes *ad lib.* parts variably marked cimbasso, tuba, bombardo, etc., not included in the full scores, and in addition to the trombones scored for by Rossini himself.

It is intriguing, therefore, to record that in the past decade actual hybrid instruments have been constructed corresponding roughly with a valved double-bass trombone, though played with a tuba mouthpiece. The designs for them have been based conjecturally on the kind of sonority Verdi may have intended when using the word 'cimbasso'.

Clairon (Fr.), military bugle; *see* BUGLE

CLARINET

1 Members

The clarinet family is the third in descending order of the four main groups in the WOODWIND section. A single REED cylindrical instrument, it is an invention of comparatively recent origin, appearing for the first time in the mid-eighteenth century and hence only gradually taking its place in the Haydn–Mozart orchestra.

Designed from the first in a whole range of different sizes, the clarinet is generally a TRANSPOSING INSTRUMENT, the clarinets in B♭ and A (sounding respectively a tone and a minor third lower than written) having quickly become the twin standard members of the conventional orchestral woodwind group. The clarinet in C, the only non-transposing member of the family, was for much of the nineteenth century an associate standard member. Because of the relative roughness of its tone, however, it became more and more of a rarity, its parts habitually played on the B♭ instrument (the player usually transposing at sight) even though parts for it abounded not only in Beethoven and Schubert but in romantic composers such as Liszt and Smetana.

But Strauss and Mahler used the C clarinet in its own right, specifically for its individual coarser quality, Strauss in particular writing for it in later life as a substitute for the E♭ or D as the top instrument of the group. The *Potpourri* (Overture) to the opera *Die schweigsame Frau* gives a good example of the virtuosity, range and reliability of intonation Strauss already took for granted from players of this relatively unfamiliar and treacherous member of the family.

As a result good instruments and players have once again reappeared and contemporary composers, such as Alexander Goehr, have taken advantage of this and written characteristic and grateful parts for this Cinderella of the clarinet family.

Of the little clarinets the most regularly used is the clarinet in E♭, which sounds a minor third higher than written. There can be no doubt that its supremacy became established because of its individual tonal character, its shrill hard quality giving pronounced drama and incisiveness to the wind band, as in the 'Sunday Morning' opening to the second act of Britten's *Peter Grimes*. But Mahler regularly used the E♭ clarinet to suggest parody, for which its cheeky tone (*keck* – one of the composer's favourite instructions) makes it eminently suitable. It also excels in depicting the Loved One's transformation into a witch in Berlioz's *Symphonie Fantastique*.

On the other hand, the D clarinet, despite the particularly successful and humorous solos Strauss wrote for it in *Till Eulenspiegel*, has largely disappeared and its numerous lines are generally taken and transposed by the perkier E♭ in a way analogous to contemporary practice *vis-à-vis* the C clarinet.

As for the still smaller F clarinet and tiny high A♭ clarinet, these were once known in Continental military bands but never formed any part of the symphony orchestra with the sole exception of Bartók's insertion of a line for the little A♭ – albeit purely in a doubling capacity – into his very early Scherzo for Piano and Orchestra, Op. 2.

It is already clear that there are far more varieties of clarinet than of any other woodwind instrument, and to those already cited must be added the ALTO CLARINET (in E♭ and F, the latter usually called the BASSET HORN), the BASSET CLARINET, the BASS CLARINET and the CONTRABASS CLARINET.

However much the name 'clarinet' may seem obviously to be derived from CLARINO (the English 'clarion'), a kind of trumpet, the instrument has never been anything but woodwind. Curiously, one may still encounter the corresponding English derivative 'clarionet' in early editions and old-fashioned tutors, but it is essentially archaic. Versions of the name in other languages are all very close to one another, although very unusually it is actually called 'clarino' in the full score of Puccini's *La Bohème*.

2 Range

The written E is the standard bottom note of all clarinets (with the exception of the basset horn). This sounds D or C♯ on the B♭ and A instruments respectively, or F♯ and G on the D and E♭ clarinets. However, composers have been wayward enough to write the low E♭ though only for the B♭ or C instruments (even so traditionally minded a composer as Brahms wrote a low E♭ for the C clarinet in the revised version of the Fourth Symphony). In fact B♭ clarinets do also exist today with an extra key in order to provide this extension, for the ability to produce the low concert C♯ is, of course, essential for the many players who prefer to dispense with the A instrument as, in particular, in Latin American countries.

Similarly one might have thought that before long the A clarinet too would have come to be fitted with an extra key, thus providing composers with the bottom C♮. But so far this has not happened, nor have composers optimistically written this note, with the exception of Stravinsky who, in *The Song of the Nightingale* adds a footnote instructing the player to *introduire un cornet de carton souple dans la pavillon de l'instrument*. Furthermore, where the smaller clarinets (E♭ and D) are concerned, the standard low E has also remained their bottom note.

At the upper end of the compass the clarinet is to some extent flexible in potential range, although composers rarely write above G or G♯. Nevertheless top As can be found in the repertoire and Ginastera in his *Variationes Concertantes* continues a solo scale right up to the top B for the B♭ clarinet; Elgar in *Falstaff* goes even further, taking the instrument to the very top C, though admittedly in a tutti passage. The famous death squeal in Strauss's *Till Eulenspiegel*, in which the D clarinet rushes up to seemingly alarming heights, in fact goes up only to its top A♭, which becomes no more than a top G when played, as so often, on the E♭ clarinet.

3 Characteristics

Although much less angular in tone than the oboe, the clarinet can achieve a far greater degree of sheer volume, especially in the upper register where its *fff* becomes incredibly shrill and piercing. At the same time its *ppp* has the potential of achieving a sound at the very edge of audibility, and it can therefore boast the widest contrast of volume in the woodwind section. The extremely soft effect is often known as 'ghosting', although it is not so designated in orchestral scores where it appears as 'echo tone'. Mahler calls for this in an exquisite passage in the first movement of his Second Symphony, as does Copland in the closing bars of *Appalachian Spring*, describing it as 'white tone'. Clarinets can also match the flutes in agility and Stravinsky allocated a splendidly virtuoso *arpeggiando* obbligato to two clarinets in Jocasta's aria 'Ne probentur oracula' from *Oedipus Rex*. Tippett also very cleverly exploited the slinky liquid flexibility of clarinets in the second of his Ritual Dances from *The Midsummer Marriage*, 'The Otter Chases the Fish', in which they brilliantly illustrate the fish's darting movements.

The bottom register of the clarinet has a character all its own, which is even graced by a special term, 'chalumeau' – actually the name of an old forerunner of the family, now long deceased. The chalumeau register is not only particularly beautiful in quality but is also the easiest to control in the handling of very soft effects. This is so much beloved of composers that they often write long passages for two clarinets playing in unison at this register, as at the opening of Dvořák's Cello Concerto or the entire slow introduction to Tchaikovsky's Fifth Symphony.

The upper octave on the other hand has the opposite characteristic, being penetrating and strident and the intonation hard to control; indeed the flutes and oboes, sitting immediately in front, all too often find the top register of their clarinet colleagues, especially those of the Eb, a hazard in the pursuit of perfect blend of tone and pitch.

Another problem indigenous to clarinets is the phenomenon of the 'break' half-way up their compass – i.e. between 𝄞 and 𝄞 – (Ab and B) written notes, where the tone tends to be weak and watery as well as sharp in pitch. It is also hard to alternate notes rapidly on either side of the break.

Trills and shakes, other than those lying across the break, present no problem to the clarinet and are exploited with colouristic imagination by Alban Berg to accompany the lyrical solo violin in the second movement of his *Chamber Concerto* together with FLUTTER-TONGUING, an effect also used by, for example, Strauss and Mahler.

A particular speciality of the clarinet is the GLISSANDO – as anyone who has ever heard the opening bars of Gershwin's *Rhapsody in Blue* will immediately recall.

See also: BELLS UP, DOUBLE-TONGUING, EMBOUCHURE

CLARINO

In many older scores the trumpets are designated by the archaic term *clarini*. Mozart's autographs show that he habitually wrote *clarini* rather than *trombe*, and in the Schott first edition of Beethoven's Choral Symphony *clarini* also appear – although oddly in apparently meaningless alternation with *trombe* in the different movements.

Strictly speaking, however, the term *clarino* referred originally to the higher register of the trumpet rather than to the instrument itself and, with the ever increasing popularity of baroque music in our presentday orchestral life, the 'clarino' playing of Bach's time has once again become a required accomplishment for trumpeters.

Nevertheless opinions differ over exactly what instruments Bach and his contemporaries expected for their 'clarino' parts, such as the familiar solo of the Second Brandenburg Concerto. Arturo Toscanini threw the musical world into confusion when he performed the work using an Eb clarinet. Yet he had more historical justification for so doing, whatever the artistic merits, than was generally recognized at the time – justification that is indeed linked to the very choice of the original Italian name for the newly invented 'clarinetto', which is patently the diminutive of 'clarino'.

At all events the range of clarino writing was characterized not only by its extreme altitude but by the narrow limits within which it was confined, since its purpose lay in using the octave at which the harmonics lay close together so that melodic or motivic passages could be played as readily by horns and trumpets as by woodwind and strings. The avoidance of the low compass (Bach wrote no lower than middle C) then favoured a special mouthpiece and a technique that could be thought enviable by present-day players.

Clarone (It.), *see* BASS CLARINET

Clavecin (Fr.), *see* HARPSICHORD

CLAVES

These are instruments giving an effect of resonant clicking not unlike that of super-castanets but emanating from Latin America instead of Spain. Claves are pairs of short pieces of very hard wood struck together; generally speaking they can make only one kind of sound but composers sometimes try to obtain more variety. Roberto Gerhard in his Concerto for Orchestra suggests different pitches through striking in different places, while Elisabeth Lutyens writes for no fewer than four different sets played simultaneously in her *Essence of our Happinesses*.

A pioneering use of claves – among numerous other special or localized devices – appears with detailed description and instructions in Varèse's *Ionisation* of 1934, but thereafter they were for a time used rarely in symphonic scores. They have, however, rapidly regained orchestral status, partly owing to the influence of Spanish and Latin American composers, such as Carlos Chavez who writes rhythmic passages for them in many serious symphonic works, and partly in the ever growing variety of percussion effects in the areas of contemporary composition.

Claviatur (Ger.) (keyboard), *see* GLOCKENSPIEL, 2

Clavicembalo (It.), *see* HARPSICHORD

Clavichord, *see* HARPSICHORD

Clavier, *see* HARPSICHORD, PIANO, 1

59

Cloches (Fr.), *see* BELLS

COCONUTS

Believe it or not, coconuts – real or imitation – are actually used as part of the percussion department, primarily to imitate the sound of horses' hoofs. However, Varèse uses them in *Arcana*, under the alternative designation of **coques**, as an abstract percussive effect and goes to great lengths to describe how, in the absence of the real fruit, they should be constructed, giving dimensions to the nearest half-inch. From his account it would seem that the two scooped-out half-nuts or their substitutes (which in the event percussionists greatly prefer for being more effective and reliable) are held one in each hand and struck, open end down, on to a wooden board covered with various thicknesses of felt.

Col legno (It.), *see* BOWING, 6

COLOUR ORGAN

This mysterious instrument has in recent years occasionally been revived for performances of one of the only works scored for it, Scriabin's *Prometheus*, where it appears at the head of each page as **Luce** with the clear intention that a constantly changing variety of colour formations would be projected by the machine on to a screen behind the vast orchestra and chorus during the course of the symphonic poem.

The word 'organ' appears by courtesy only since it emits no sound but is, on the contrary, an elaborate kind of kaleidoscopic magic lantern. Curiously enough the question is further confused through the invention in later years of a theatrical lighting system built absolutely on the lines of a cinema organ. One such was installed by a German firm in the opera house in Ankara although to little effect at the time I was there since no one knew how to operate it.

As for Scriabin's *luce*, the choice of which colours of the spectrum were to have been represented by the music on the stave (notated incidentally in the treble clef) can only ever have been conjectured through knowledge of Scriabin's personal associations between colour and sound as outlined in A. B. Klein's *Colour Music*. That this was a strong preoccupation of the period is shown by other such examples of the connection between music and colours shown by Schoenberg's *Die glückliche Hand*, Bliss's *Colour Symphony* and many others. It is known that some composers connected certain keys with colours – Wagner is said to have associated D♭ major with purple, Tchaikovsky F♯ with magenta and so on. But Scriabin's and Schoenberg's incorporation of an actual instrument into the orchestra with the colours represented in musical notation remains purely experimental, probably linked to the invention of exactly such a contraption in 1911, by a certain Professor A. Wallace Rimington.

COMMA

The significance of commas placed variously at the ends of phrases or at the top of the score as a whole is often a matter for controversy. There is a fundamental difference between the implication of Stravinsky's use of commas (which does not hold up the pulse but merely curtails the preceding notes) and their meaning in the sense of the breaks in, for example, Sibelius's First Symphony. Moreover, there are no hard and fast rules even for composers who can normally be taken to intend something quite specific. There is at least one comma in Stravinsky himself (actually in the ballet *Orpheus*) where the composer, when conducting the work, habitually made a pronounced hold up.

So while there are undoubtedly extreme instances that are more generally known and understood, in the works of many composers it can be uncertain whether a **Luftpause** (one of Mahler's favourite words, denoting a definite gap in the sound and pulse) is intended and if so to what degree.

See also: ATTACCA

CONCERT HALLS

As gradually our heritage of splendid halls – the Queen's Hall in London, St Andrew's Hall in Glasgow, the old Free Trade Hall in Manchester and many others – has fallen in ashes due either to air raids or to the hazards associated with wrestling and boxing matches, so they have been replaced by new-style buildings fashioned not in stone, brick and wood but in modern materials such as steel and concrete, and designed according to the latest acoustic theories. The thorny science of acoustics has over the past half-century gained ascendancy over the pursuit of purely artistic considerations, replacing subjective quality of sound with a precisely measured reverberation period tested by firing revolvers.

It has often seemed to musicians that the last people to be consulted have been those who are involved in giving the concerts for which purpose the halls are primarily built. Such expert opinion, it is held, could have prevented absurd blunders – such as the Concert Hall at Broadcasting House, built for the BBC Symphony Orchestra but far too small to accommodate more than a chamber orchestra, or the débâcle of the Sydney Opera House, conceived with performances of Wagner's *Ring* and similar large-scale operas in mind but constructed with an orchestra pit suitable really only for Mozart. Even the Lincoln Center in New York is notorious for the acoustic teething problems of its concert hall, despite thorough prior research into the sound phenomena of all the most successful European auditoria. London's Royal Festival Hall itself, splendid as it is, cannot be counted faultless, and has for long been known widely among orchestral players as 'the dissecting table', as the sound is so clear and yet ungenerous that a string section – for example – may be mercilessly exposed without bloom being added to the tone by the hall itself. Some artificial improvement has, however, been made by the skilful use of ELECTRICAL AMPLIFICATION, which is also being discreetly incorporated into new halls as they are built. Any older building, such as the Royal Albert Hall for all its obvious demerits, can be actually more grateful for the performers where sheer quality of natural sound is concerned.

Acoustics are, however, only one aspect of the problem. Back-stage facilities are another area where, often for reasons of economy, architects are briefed to create halls giving only the barest accommodation for orchestra and soloists alike. Inadequate provision is often made for seating large choirs, which feature so prominently in concert life; an ORGAN is dispensed with as an unwarrantable extra expense; or little flexibility is allowed for the placing of the many OFF-STAGE EFFECTS that abound in the concert repertoire.

While regretting the guarded and qualified praise that has to be expressed over a new building that may have cost millions to erect, it has until very recently been hard to be more enthusiastic both from the musicians' and the concert-going public's points of view. Moreover many of the recent additions to concert venues are no more than adaptations of school halls, deconsecrated churches, sports or community arenas or, perhaps worst of all acoustically, conference centres.

Fortunately, there have been signs that lessons are being learned from the misfortunes of the recent past. For example, within certain planned limitations, and admittedly composite in purpose as its deep CONCERT PLATFORM may be, Snape Maltings is an example of what can be achieved if the correct priorities are kept ever in view and the highest artistic advice sought at every point. Admittedly slightly bass-heavy and with restricted audience amenities, it is a joy to work or listen in and remains a monument of clear thinking by artistic planners in a medium bedevilled by prejudice as well as economic handicaps of every kind. Apart from acute difficulties of sheer access, the new St David's Hall in Cardiff is another new hall where a more enlightened attitude has been allowed to prevail, and there are hopeful signs that others may be on the way.

Concert Master, *see* LEADER

CONCERT PLATFORM

Platforms are, with all their countless variations, essentially of two different kinds: those that have been designed purely for concert purposes, and those conceived for multi-purpose activities. The finest concert halls all over the world have always been those devoted solely to concert-giving, with the orchestra rising towards the majestic, centrally placed organ and with a spacious but not overwide flat area to the front for the string group and solo performers. Between orchestra and organ, and also surrounding the organ, a properly designed concert platform will in addition provide generous accommodation for a large chorus.

There is naturally every kind of variation from hall to hall, but as a general principle no platform intended to serve also for stage productions or other entertainment activities can be without serious drawbacks in the presentation of symphony concerts. This is partly because of the lack of tiering for, in turn, the wind, brass, percussion and chorus, but more because a proscenium arch with its attendant flies, wings, curtains, etc., are all ruinous to sound projection.

When planning a concert, conductors and concert managers have to assess each different hall for the best orchestral layout, bearing in mind acoustic phenomena as well as platform shape and sheer size. Nothing can be more galling than to discover, five minutes before the beginning of the rehearsal on the day of the concert, that the players cannot all see the conductor or, worse still, that there is physically no space for the string strength as ordered, with the disaster looming of musicians having to be paid off and sent home.

See also: CONCERT HALLS, PLATFORM ARRANGEMENT

CONCERTO

In English this is applied purely to a musical form, generally but by no means always including a solo performer set in apposition to the orchestra. In its original Italian, however, the word stands equally for the very concert itself. The same is true of all languages other than our own: the French *concert* or the German **Konzert**, for example, apply equally to the work and to the concert at which it is played.

In works described as 'Concerto for Orchestra' or the like, the conductor retains control of the overall interpretation and decision making, even though sections of the orchestra may at times be treated soloistically. But when a soloist is involved this responsibility may be shared, or even in some circumstances abrogated altogether (however unwillingly).

Much, of course, depends on the relative artistic stature of conductor and soloist. Conflicts have undoubtedly been known to occur with dire consequences to rehearsal atmosphere and even to the performances themselves, but it is rare to find irreconcilable differences between artists of high international prestige. Most distinguished virtuosi will respond to a conductor whom they respect so that the collaboration becomes a rewarding partnership, even if compromise becomes inevitable over divergent points of view with regard either to detail or to something as fundamental as the choice of tempi.

Ultimately the conductor's role in a concerto is to set the soloist at ease so that he will be able to give of his best in what must always be a nerve- and soul-racking exercise. It can therefore be unfortunate if in a desire to retain authority or prestige the conductor over-reacts to the discomfort of the soloist. An additional nervous strain is caused if the conductor insists on performing the accompaniment without a score.

A reversal of the normal bias may occur when the soloist is young or inexperienced. Here the role of the conductor may take on something of the guide or mentor, in the course of which he may legitimately make suggestions, in respect of both artistic considerations and platform behaviour. It is astonishing how little preparation young artists receive at music academies in the art of self-presentation or of receiving applause graciously with the requisite gestures in the direction of the orchestra and conductor. An experienced virtuoso will know, for instance, that the orchestra's first oboe needs acknowledgement after the Brahms Violin Concerto, the solo cello after the same composer's Second Piano Concerto. Failure to shake hands with the conductor and leader or the omission of an invitation for the orchestra to stand either appears gauche or implies lack of cordiality in the relationship. Such details are less easy to negotiate than the layman might realize and constitute a not inconsiderable factor in a concerto performer's popularity with the audience and his colleagues on the platform alike.

See also: APPLAUSE, CADENZA, PLATFORM ARRANGEMENT, PROGRAMME PLANNING

CONDUCTOR

The central controlling figure at any symphony concert. The gibe is often made that the conductor is the one person on the platform who makes no sound, indeed whose mistakes alone are generally imperceptible. Although in a sense such a view is demonstrably valid, the very opposite contains the real truth: i.e., that no sound is made by any player that has not been prethought and willed into being by a projection of mind from the conductor. Moreover, any hesitation or lack of positive confidence – let alone a blunder – is instantly reflected in the response and performance of the players, so finely attuned are they to his or her slightest gesture.

Few things so frustrate orchestras as the necessity to take over the responsibility of ENSEMBLE, attack or interpretation from an inadequate or untrustworthy conductor, although all are perfectly able to cope and save the performance should an emergency arise that the players realize will not be dealt with satisfactorily by the man at the helm. Conversely, much as the players may resent 'saving' a poor conductor, so equally do they react unwillingly to one who allows no recognition of their own artistic judgement. A good conductor will have enough sense of psychology to know how far to insist and when to compromise on practical and musical matters when working with artists who are likely to be as much experts in their own field as he is in his.

To a certain degree it is theoretically possible for orchestras to perform some works or movements without a conductor at all, but the musicians all readily acknowledge that the exercise is unsatisfactory. Apart from the waste of time in REHEARSALS run on too democratic principles, the final outcome is always negative and characterless. However socially outmoded the autocratic relationship between conductor and orchestra may be it remains essential and built into the structure of orchestral life and work.

The conductor is not only the mainspring of all music heard at a concert, he is also to some degree the master of ceremonies. The very character of the event as well as the atmosphere of many of its dramatic moments is inescapably in his hands. If he tries to evade this responsibility – perhaps in all sincerity believing theatricality to be the antithesis of serious musicianship – he may project himself to orchestra and audience alike as a dull fellow and his concert as a tedious affair despite the hardest endeavours of his players. If, on the contrary, he allows his emotions to take command until he overreacts to the music, he may irritate and emerge as an idiosyncratic charlatan bent only on focusing all attention on his own antics, although this may not necessarily have been his intention.

There are of course occasions, such as in accompanying work, where some degree of self-effacement is no more nor less than correct platform manners. Furthermore, in directing smaller and even chamber ensembles a conductor may even choose to perform seated or to control the individual virtuoso artists under his command without a baton, recognizing that his function here is less that of maestro than of director or guide for the ensemble.

One further permutation deserves mention: this is the soloist–conductor syndrome, which has become increasingly prevalent. Such well-known conductors as Bruno Walter or Wilhelm Furtwängler, both accomplished keyboard executants, used to delight in being their own soloist in a Mozart concerto, or in giving performances of Bach with themselves fulfilling the function of continuo player or as solo cembalist in the Fifth Brandenburg Concerto. More recently Leonard Bernstein extended this virtuosity to more complicated feats, such as simultaneously playing and conducting concertos such as those of Ravel and Shostakovich. Yet despite the brilliance of these acrobatics it is impossible to repress a feeling of doubt over whether the resulting performances might not

have gained had the artist concentrated on one or other activity rather than having to divide his attention between both. Nowadays, however, eminent virtuosi have often found the temptation of taking over the conductorship of whole concerts irresistible. Here, too, it is possible to regret the absence of an artist in overall single-minded control, with the specialized experience, background and training of a professional conductor.

See also: APPLAUSE, BATON, BOWING, CONCERTO, EDITING

CONGAS

Although totally different in appearance from bongos or tom-toms, a pair of conga drums belongs essentially to the same family and is played in much the same way, with the bare hands or occasionally with small sticks.

Rarely prescribed in scores, congas are used in such pieces as Bliss's *Miracle in the Gorbals* where native drumming is emulated. For this the congas' very shape makes them eminently suitable: standing over two feet high from the ground, they look splendidly African with their curved, striped, polished sides.

They are sometimes called **tumbas** and appear in this guise in avant-garde works such as Stockhausen's *Gruppen*.

CONTINUO

Although continuo playing has come to be closely associated with the HARPSICHORD in particular, the word itself does not strictly specify any one instrument rather than any other. Piano, harp, harpsichord, organ, even harmonium could theoretically all be used, for the purpose is to support and fill out the harmonies of the musical texture. The bass line itself – in Monteverdi called **bassus generalis**, in baroque music **basso continuo**, and often doubled by a solo cello and/or bass – is usually supplemented by figures printed beneath it in the score; these serve to indicate to the keyboard player which harmonies he is expected to supply. Where none is required the words **tasto solo** are substituted for the figures and he then plays merely the printed bass line.

A skilled continuo player needs no individual part to work from, using for preference a full score identical with that of the conductor. But many editions contain 'realizations' of the figured bass in order to enable the function to be reliably accomplished by an artist who, however skilled, may be less than expert in this somewhat specialized field. These fully worked-out keyboard parts, though no more than conjectural versions prepared for the publisher by some musicologist, are even incorporated into the scores of what are described as *Urtext* editions of Bach and Handel (for example), which correctly should contain nothing beyond the original work.

See also: BASSOON, 5; ORGAN, 3

CONTRABASS CLARINET

Sometimes known as the **pedal clarinet** (though never so termed in scores) this is the deepest in the long gamut of orchestral CLARINETS. It is built to sound an octave lower again than the bass clarinet, and like that instrument it is written in Bb or A (the latter, for example, in Schoenberg's *Fünf Orchesterstücke*, Op. 16), though it seems doubtful whether an instrument in A has ever actually existed. The notation for the pedal clarinet has always been in the bass clef but sounding an octave lower – i.e., a ninth (or tenth) lower than written.

Its appearance in the orchestral repertoire is extremely rare. Schoenberg, in addition to the *Fünf Orchesterstücke*, introduced it into his *Vier Orchesterlieder*, Op. 22, but not, as one might have expected, into his mammoth *Gurre-lieder*, even though this is scored for no fewer than seven members of the clarinet family. D'Indy wrote a part for it in his opera *Fervaal* and Strauss gave it a short passage in *Josephslegende* but so little expected it to be used that he wrote an *ossia* for contrabassoon.

The opinion has often been expressed that the pedal clarinet is so obviously more suited than any member of the bassoon family to supply the bass to the woodwind ensemble that it can be only a matter of time before it sweeps all before it. Yet so far, in spite of a certain amount of experimentation, this has proved an illusion, as the instrument has proved clumsy and often unreliable.

Unlike the other members of the family the contrabass clarinet is always made of metal and so tends to cause raised eyebrows as it looks rather like some obscure saxophone or sarrusophone.

CONTRABASS TROMBONE

This unwieldy creature, pitched in deep Bb, is yet another of Wagner's importations into the orchestral brass choir. It is rarely used – and then only as a supplementary member to the normal group of three.

Wagner in *The Ring* writes down to the low E: 𝄢 . Other composers, such d'Indy and Puccini (in *Turandot*), have also used the instrument, seeking to profit by its virtues of extra weight and downward compass.

CONTRABASS TUBA

Essentially the largest and deepest member of the TUBA family, corresponding to the giant double Bb instrument also known in band vernacular as the BOMBARDON. 'Contrabass tuba' is actually a term invented by Wagner, not so much to indicate just such an oversize instrument, but rather to differentiate between this and his bass tubas, by which he meant the lower pair of what we now call the WAGNER TUBAS.

As with all other bass tubas, orchestrally its part is written at concert pitch and there is no uniformity over what specific instrument a player may choose to interpret the part. For even this mammoth object does not extend the range as low as might be expected, its purpose being primarily extra weight and power. Wagner himself takes it no lower than Eb 𝄢 although theoretically it can go lower down still, an example of, for instance, the low C appearing in Alban Berg's Violin Con-

certo (although with the wistful addition of the words 'if possible').

Contrabasso (It.), *see* DOUBLE BASS

CONTRABASSOON

Strictly speaking, the only subsidiary member of the BASSOON family is really called the **double bassoon** but it is colloquially known as the 'contra' since all other languages give the instrument that prefix: French, *contre–*; German, *Kontra–*; Italian, *contra–*. The Italians, however, also use the spelling **contraffagotto**, as does Beethoven in *Fidelio*, recalling the corresponding Italian spelling for string basses: *contrabbassi*.

The contra is normally written in the bass clef, but sounding an octave lower. Some French composers, however, such as d'Indy, Dukas or Debussy (though not Ravel), write for the instrument at pitch usually adding *octave réelle* to avoid ambiguity. Wagner too, using it for the first time in *Parsifal*, notated it in this way as if it were merely a bassoon with extended compass.

Indeed the contra did at one time look simply like an oversize bassoon, but this somewhat limited older instrument – which even lacked some bottom notes – is rapidly becoming extinct in favour of the larger, serpentine German instrument that supplies the extra two semitones down to the bottom Bb, the standard range required by the orchestral repertoire and with the distinction of being the lowest note obtainable in the entire orchestra. This is not to say that contras have never in earlier times possessed the extended

67

range. Beethoven repeatedly wrote the bottom B♭ for contra both in the Choral Symphony and in the Missa Solemnis, where in the 'Gloria' the contra takes a spectacular leap from the topmost G to the bottom B♭.

The contra does occasionally find itself taken into quite high regions, though usually with the purpose of continuing a doubling of the bass line in preference to omitting a few high notes with the player fitting in fragments of a distorted passage. Nevertheless, while exposed high notes are rare in orchestral writing, a striking instance of a solo high B♭ above the stave does occur in Ravel's inspired use of the contra to depict La Bête in *Ma Mère l'Oye*. In the upper register the contra sometimes goes – like the bassoon – into the tenor clef, but never into the treble.

The contrabassoon is usually thought of as primarily a modern adjunct to the post-romantic super-woodwind sections, and it may come as something of a surprise to meet it in such classical works as Mozart's *Masonic Funeral Music*, where it is the sole member of the bassoon family. As a result of Beethoven's importation of the contra from the theatre for his Fifth and Ninth Symphonies, in which he was followed by Brahms, it entered the standard full orchestral strength ahead of both the cor anglais and the bass clarinet. Its highly individual tones are, however, not as ubiquitous in romantic scores as this might suggest. The French composers in particular, for all their habitual use of four bassoons, more frequently omit the contra prior to the Debussy–Ravel era. Berlioz used it only in *Les Francs Juges* among all his overtures and it makes no appearance in the *Symphonie Fantastique*, despite the presence there of two ophicleides.

The contra naturally accentuates the lugubrious side of the bassoon in the lower register, the bottom notes degenerating into hardly more than a rumble. Nevertheless even here the contra may be required to make a genuinely musical contribution: the beginning of Ravel's Left-Hand Piano Concerto is a particularly famous instance, presenting a long, tortuous melody emerging from these cavernous depths.

Contraffagotto (It.), *see* CONTRABASSOON

Contralto, *see* ALTO

Contralto Bugle, *see* BUGLE

CONTRALTO TRUMPET

This is a larger TRUMPET (though not as big as Wagner's bass trumpet) invented by Rimsky-Korsakov and described by him as a **tromba contralta in F**. It appears not only in his own scores (such as *Coq d'Or*) but also in that of the Russian school that followed him, from the earliest Stravinsky (*Scherzo Fantastique*) to Shostakovich (Symphony No. 1) and Rachmaninoff (Symphony No. 3) generally listed, perhaps confusingly, as 'C-alta tromba – in F'.

The contralto trumpet, being built in F, is naturally a TRANSPOSING INSTRUMENT; but instead of sounding a fourth higher than written, like the old F trumpet with which it corresponds exactly in the length of tubing and hence in the distribution of its harmonics, it sounds – like the horn in F – a fifth lower, which misleadingly suggests to the eye that it really does fulfil its original primary purpose, which was to solve the problem of the low trumpet notes for which Rimsky-Korsakov constantly found the need. But in the event his brainchild did no more than put the clock back to the classical F trumpet from which it was only marginally different, and possessed no more extra notes at the lower end of its compass than that noble instrument, whose unfortunate limitations of range had led to its demise. Moreover, the composer himself wrote a footnote in his *Principles of Orchestration* stating that 'in order to avoid the difficulties of finding a contralto trumpet in ordinary opera houses or concert halls I have refrained from using the bottom notes. The parts can therefore be taken by the normal trumpets in Bb and A.' This self-defeating policy was then followed dutifully by all other Russian composers using the great master's splendid 'new invention', whose usefulness accordingly became confined to providing a slightly fuller tone quality for the 3rd player to support the trumpet timbre in three-part writing. It is thus hardly surprising that it failed to establish itself and quickly became obsolete outside Russia.

Contrebasse (Fr.), *see* DOUBLE-BASS

Contrebasson (Fr.), *see* CONTRA-BASSOON

Coperti, *see* MUTES, 6

COPYISTS

This fraternity is becoming ever more important in the orchestral world now that music engraving is rapidly becoming a thing of the past. While the basic classical and romantic repertoire is played largely from printed material, contemporary music – often in itself hard to decipher – is always prepared from manuscript.

Copyists working for publishing houses or radio stations are of all kinds and of the widest range of musical education and experience. Where a prestige score is in preparation copyists may be employed who are so skilled that the result can look astonishingly like engraving. But it can be seriously disconcerting how regularly orchestral players find themselves working from parts that are barely decipherable and have all kinds of other serious disadvantages.

One obvious way in which copyists fail to understand the requirements of orchestral players is in the matter of page turns. Leaving aside the self-explanatory hazard of turns for solo players in the middle of an extended passage where no hand can possibly be free for the purpose (this occurs more often than one might believe), copyists are prone either to cram too many notes on to a line or, by contrast, too few bars to a page causing over-frequent turning, especially in string parts (arising all too understandably when the copyist is paid by the page). Some copyists, unable to find a suitable place for page turning, spread a part out over three pages with instructions to open up the third page as a flap, forgetting that music stands make no provision for such an exercise. Publishers have been known to send out parts in which, as an extension of this practice, the pages are not bound or stapled, but will open out indefinitely so that an inexpert or hurried page-turn will send the pile concertina-like all over the platform.

But perhaps the most insidious way in which copyists' practice sabotages the economical use of orchestral time is in the question of REHEARSAL LETTERS OR FIGURES. The frequent placing of these at musical or readily identifiable places is a primary element in efficient orchestral work, yet it is often hard to persuade copyists of this.

See also: LIBRARIAN, ORCHESTRAL MATERIAL

Coques, *see* COCONUTS

Cor (Fr.), *see* HORN

COR ANGLAIS

This is the most familiar of all the subspecies of the OBOE family and the third member in descending order. In a way it could therefore lay claim to being the tenor of the group. In fact the original tenor was called the **taille** – a term used for example by Purcell – but since the true alto oboe, the OBOE D'AMORE, has remained something of a stranger in the orchestra, the cor anglais has come to supplant it as the regular alto member of the family.

For all the controversy over its curious name, translations of cor anglais agree in preserving the literal meaning of **English horn**: **corno inglese** (It.); **Englisches Horn** (Ger.). Wagner tried to break the established usage by changing its name to ALTHOBOE in *Parsifal*, but he had few followers, Prokofiev's 'oboe contralto' being the best-known example. In English-speaking countries, however, it is oddly enough the French version that persists and colloquially the instrument is always referred to as the 'cor'.

Pitched a fifth below the oboe, the cor anglais is normally notated in the treble clef as a transposing instrument in F. However, Bach wrote for it – under the name of **oboe da caccia** (strictly speaking its historical predecessor) – at actual pitch in the alto clef, another example imitated by Prokofiev. Gevaert, in his *Treatise of Instrumentation*, cites two other notations of earlier days, an 'Ancienne notation française' and an 'Ancienne notation italienne'. The former, used by French operatic composers up to Halévy, was an ingenious device that, but using the C clef on the second line, managed to combine the actual pitch with the traditional position of the notes on the stave for the sake of the player's convenience. The Italian notation, however, again an operatic tradition, was wholly absurd (as Gevaert frankly admits) since the notes are given an octave below the actual sound. Nevertheless this notation survives in as popular a work as the overture to Rossini's *William Tell*.

Unlike the oboe, which normally goes down to its low Bb: ,

cors anglais with this bottom note are

rare in Britain and the lowest that can be relied on is the B natural, sounding E natural. Occasionally players produce a home-made cardboard extension to get round the difficulty of the several important parts requiring the low Bb, since Continental instruments do indeed abound with the built-in extension. In Schoenberg's *Gurrelieder* there is even a footnote in the score insisting that it must not be taken up the octave, thus revealing that even in Vienna the note could not be relied on as a matter of course. For a famous passage in *Das Lied von der Erde*, Mahler wrote (again in a footnote) that he was prepared to accept B natural as an emergency substitute, although this produces a different – and very interesting – harmony. Dvořák in the *Scherzo Capriccioso* actually wrote low As for the cor anglais, although it seems unlikely that this further extension ever existed, and the Czech complete edition of Dvořák's works bowdlerizes the relevant passages.

Where the top range is concerned, the high E is normally regarded as the upper limit and although it can be found in, for instance, Britten's *Nocturne*, such high cor anglais notes are often considered unmanageable and better given to the oboe; yet in the hands of a virtuoso player their poignancy can be unforgettable.

Although the cor anglais to a large extent shares the penetrating quality of the oboe, there is certainly a marked reduction in stridency, as Wagner discovered to his cost when he wanted his melancholy piper in the third act of *Tristan* to play a jubilant fanfare when Isolde's ship is at last sighted. It was of the utmost importance that this should dominate the orchestra and he therefore inserted a long footnote into the score describing his attempts to create a new instrument for the purpose. His efforts, however, failed to reach the universal acceptance of his other inventions, the bass trumpet and the Wagner tubas, and on such occasions when the cor anglais itself has not been used hybrid instruments such as the Hungarian **tárogató** (a kind of conical wooden clarinet) have been pressed into service, or occasionally – worst of all – a trumpet.

The cor anglais is played generally by the 3rd, or sometimes the 2nd, member of the oboe section, but scores occasionally show a composer expecting it to be played by the principal oboist, e.g. Dvořák in his G major and *New World* Symphonies. There are also works with two cors anglais (and no oboe), which may cause the orchestra's principal player to 'double on cor'. Haydn's early Symphony No. 22 ('The Philosopher') provides an example of this, followed in recent times by Gordon Crosse in his *Ceremony* for cello and orchestra.

Cordes, les (Fr.), *see* STRINGS, 2

Cordiera (It.), *see* BOWING, 5

Cornamuse (It.), *see* BAGPIPES

CORNETS

Perhaps the most important doubling instrument of the TRUMPET family, a *cornet-à-pistons* appears regularly in scores between the early 1830s and the first decade of the present century. French operatic composers in particular made a habit of enlarging the brass section to include four players, two trumpets and two cornets, the latter being played by the 3rd and 4th trumpet players even though they tend to have much the more interesting and important parts and may be placed in the score above the 1st and 2nd trumpets.

Cornets have rarely been specified since then, however, as the instrument's overriding advantage of a complete chromatic range has long been matched by the introduction of pistons or valves to all other members of the trumpet family. The cornet is, however, still used in orchestras, though the striking squat individual shape is not always discernible in modern instruments, which much more nearly resemble trumpets. This may lead to the discomfort of meticulous conductors on the alert for players using trumpets for cornet parts, since the smooth mellower tone quality of the cornet has also come to have less identity in the present refinement of orchestral brass playing, and it has to be conceded that today few people can tell the difference. It is hard, nevertheless, to justify the printed substitution of trumpets for a composer's *cornets-à-pistons* as, for example, in the unfortunate recent 'scholarly' Alkor edition of Bizet's *Carmen*.

Cornetti (It.), *see* ZINKE; CORNET

Corno (It.), *see* HORN

Corno di bassetto (It.), *see* BASSETHORN

Corno di posta (It.), *see* POSTHORN

Corno inglese (It.), *see* COR ANGLAIS

COWBELLS

These are Mahler's **Herdenglocken** of the Sixth and Seventh Symphonies, taken over by Webern in his *Fünf Orchesterstücke*, Op. 10 and by Strauss as **Herdengeläute** in his *Alpine* Symphony. They are, of course, broadly naturalistic effects, as Mahler himself overtly acknowledged; but Webern and his many successors have developed the instruments into a purely abstract colour. They are sometimes referred to as **Almglocken**, as in Henze's *Antifone*.

Although cowbells undoubtedly do have definite pitch, they are normally written without pitch specification since this is supposed to be haphazard, to obtain (as Mahler put it) 'the realistic imitation of the tinkling bells of a grazing herd'. The bells should therefore be gently and intermittently shaken, but players are sometimes tempted to strike them randomly with beaters.

The notation is an extended trill over long notes either in the bass clef (Mahler) or treble (Strauss). Delius writes a precisely rhythmical passage for the similar camel bells in the closing scene of *Hassan*, while the one small cowbell stipulated by Lambert in both *The Rio Grande* and *Summer's Last Will and Testament*, having had its clapper removed (as he instructs) can be played only with a beater. In *Et exspecto*

Messiaen uses a Mexican variety of cowbells called **cencerros** which he writes with definite pitch in treble and bass clefs giving no fewer than three separate ranges, covering in all a compass of three octaves and a sixth. Unlike the cowbells of romantic composers, the cencerros are written with precise notation and thus have to be struck with beaters instead of shaken, for which purpose they always have their clappers removed. Cencerros are hard to come by since they are not yet standard equipment, even though they are used in important works of the contemporary avant-garde.

COWHORN

This rare visitor to the brass ensemble might perhaps properly be allocated to the effects department. The **Stierhörner** in Wagner's *Die Walküre* and *Götterdämmerung*, and the Night Watchman's horn in *Die Meistersinger*, were specially made instruments each playing only a single note (their fundamental). These are respectively ♪ (*Die Walküre*); ♪ and ♪ (*Götterdämmerung*); and ♪ (*Die Meistersinger*). Written as shown here (including clefs), the notes represent the sounding pitch – i.e., the *Walküre* C Stierhorn really does sound an octave lower than the one in *Götterdämmerung*. Usually they are played by trombonists.

Britten also wrote for a cowhorn in C in his *Spring* Symphony and again this had to be made to order. He wrote two

calls 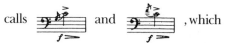 and ♪, which meant that his instrument had to have two keys added to make the extra notes possible.

Crécelle, crécelle à manivelle (Fr.), *see* RATTLE

CROOK

In earlier years the crook used to be a detachable part of a HORN or TRUMPET, the size of the crook determining the pitch of the instrument, which would accordingly be called a 'horn in F' 'trumpet in D', etc., the key being that of the HARMONIC SERIES resulting from playing the open notes. Since there was a wide range of crooks the individual parts were always written in C, horns and trumpets thus being TRANSPOSING INSTRUMENTS.

Gradually, however, with the introduction of valves or pistons the instruments became standardized and the crooks built in as an integral part, making the cumbersome business of changing crooks unnecessary and, indeed, no longer possible (other than by a simple valve mechanism that survives in the case of some double horns incorporating two sets of tubing within the corpus of a single instrument). The terminology of crooks and crook-changing has nevertheless survived, even though it now applies only to mental adjustments by the players in different transpositions, skill in which has become basic and indispensable.

One other instrument, the bassoon, is also said to have a crook, but this is an entirely different case, the crook not being interchangeable, nor having any bearing on the pitch. It is the piece of tubing, shaped like a shepherd's crook, that leads to the reed.

CROTALES

These are, and yet are not, synonymous with ANTIQUE CYMBALS; the paradox is based to a large extent on what composers understand by these terms. Whereas, in the strictest possible sense, there are some small differences, broadly speaking the word 'crotales' is considered little more than an alternative name. There is a further and typical confusion in that the dictionary definition of crotales – including Larousse, which claims to be based on ancient historical evidence – is 'rattle, or the CASTANETS of the Priestesses of Cybele', so they could correspond to Saint-Saëns's *castagnettes de fer* played by the priestesses of Dagon in his *Samson and Delilah*, even though crotales are never made of iron. Perhaps this is why Percy Scholes's *Oxford Companion* describes crotales as a variety of castanets, which is, however, far too loose to stand as an orchestral definition.

Essentially both crotales and antique cymbals consist of brass or bronze discs with central dome, giving off a delicate ring of definite pitch similar to that of a glockenspiel, but crotales are thicker and less finely wrought. Nor are they always suspended freely like antique cymbals but can even be seen laid out in fixed rows of pitches in the same way as the bars of the glockenspiel, where they may be struck not only by other crotales but by various beaters for more complicated passages. They

have a range of some two octaves upwards from middle C, sounding two octaves higher.

Composers make no clear differentiation between the two species but tend to treat them as if they were identical. Following Berlioz, Debussy in 1894 still calls them *cymbales antiques*, but Ravel twenty years later writes 'crotales'; Stravinsky gives *cymbales antiques* in *Le Sacre du Printemps* but changes to 'crotales' for *Les Noces*, and so on. Contemporary composers now virtually always say 'crotales', using them in complete chromatic range on the one hand or, strangely enough, as instruments of indefinite pitch on the other. Certainly the high crystal-clear *ting* can be thought of in terms of pure colour and the illusion of indefinite pitch is easy to obtain by striking together two crotales of slightly different notes. Boulez writes for two sets in this way in *Le Visage nuptial*, differentiating them merely as *aigu* and *grave*.

Cuica, *see* LION'S ROAR

CUIVRÉ

This is an effect used especially for horns but sometimes also for trumpets and trombones signifying 'brassy', i.e., with an exaggerated, overblown quality. The German equivalent, much exploited by Mahler, is **schmetternd** (= 'blaring' or 'blazing'). In the case of the horns, *cuivré* is all too often taken to be synonymous with BOUCHÉ, which, although also brassy and overblown, is a different and muted sound, whereas *cuivré* is an effect in its own right for the open instrument. There is a place, for example, in the *Prélude à l'Après-midi d'un Faune* where Debussy writes the one immediately followed by the other. *Schmetternd*, on the other hand, is never confused with muting in any form or on any instrument.

Cuivres (Fr.), *see* BRASS, 1

Cymbales (Fr.), *see* CYMBALS

Cymbales antiques (Fr.), *see* ANTIQUE CYMBALS

Cymbalom, *see* CIMBALOM

CYMBALS

1 Names
Like the bass drum, with which they are often closely associated, these constitute one of the principal instruments of the PERCUSSION group. Cymbals come in a wide variety of sizes, which are not usually specified except where particularly small ones are required. Normal orchestral cymbals vary between 14 inches and the oversize 24 inch. Naturally the largest make a splendid sound but are inclined to be unwieldy and are therefore reserved mostly for tremendous isolated clashes.

The French term **cymbales** is similar to the English, but in Italian there are both **cinelli** (used by Breitkopf in the Berlioz Gesamtausgabe, for example, and also by Bartók) and – the more usual term – **piatti**, i.e., plates. The standard German word for the cymbals is **Becken**, but composers such as Hindemith do use **Zymbal** though primarily for the smaller dance-band

variety; this, being rarely clashed in symphonic works, is accordingly always in the singular, *Becken* being (like *piatti*) a plural term for the pair of cymbals.

2 Playing Styles I: The Clash
The basic method of playing is the clash with the two cymbals, the term for which – if one is needed at all – is **naturale** or the German **gewöhnlich** (i.e. 'in the usual manner'). The Germans also write '*mit* **Teller (n)**' which, meaning 'with the plates', is used only for 'clashed', the usual English equivalent. Another commonly seen term is *à 2* although this can be ambiguous when more than one pair is used for a single stroke.

It can often be a matter of individual taste or preference whether or not to interpret a cymbal strike as a clash, especially as composers tend to retain the plural even when only one cymbal is to be used, e.g. Holst in *The Perfect Fool*. Debussy's instructions – in *La Mer* among other works – are far from comprehensive, and a particularly well-known instance of uncertainty is the isolated cymbal entry in the last movement of Dvořák's *New World* Symphony. This used always to be played with the stick, but recent custom is changing and the more normally accepted effect has become a gentle clash. This can be produced either by using the whole of both plates, or by sweeping the one half-way up with the tip of the other. The latter method is usually employed in very delicate strokes, e.g. the ending of Debussy's *Fêtes*, while the former may be thought more suitable for *pianissimo* clashes, e.g. the 'Saraband of the Sons of God' from Vaughan Williams's *Job*. The Russians sometimes insert a phrase (in Cyrillic characters) into their scores that denotes 'strike the one against the other'. Strauss in the 'critics' section of *Ein Heldenleben*, marks the cymbal strokes *pp zischend* (an onomatopoeic word indicating the use of the whole plates). Prokofiev, on the other hand, interchanges the effects of clashing and striking very frequently and uses the two signs 'o' and '+' to indicate the pair and the stick respectively. Martinů in his Third Symphony unusually employs ♩, which presumably signifies a suspended cymbal since it is for a sustained *p* roll.

Few orchestral effects are so dramatic—visually as well as sonically—as the sustained clash ('allow to vibrate'; French, **laisser vibrer**; German, **klingen lassen**; Italian, *lasciare vibrare*), the cymbals often held flamboyantly aloft after striking. Yet it is not by any means always shown in the score when this is intended, and indeed the very duration of a clash can be a matter of individual interpretation. Composers' notation can be curiously lax, and a short-value note (crotchet or quaver) should not necessarily be taken to mean that the sound must be damped at the end of its precise value. The clashes at the climaxes of Wagner's *Meistersinger* Prelude, or the crest of the music at Octavian's entrance for the presentation of the silver rose in Strauss's *Rosenkavalier*, would be greatly reduced in their splendid effect if the cold printed text were to be followed pedantically. It is, however, an equally valid effect to stifle the sound of the clashed pair against the body: French, *sec* (dry); German, *schnell abdämpfen* ('damp quickly').

3 Playing Styles II: The Stick

The second most common method of playing is with a drum stick on a single suspended cymbal. The English term for this can be 'struck' (as opposed to 'clashed') but the Germans use the more precise *mit Schlägel*, the French translation being *avec la baguette*, and the Italian *colla bacchetta*.

When a stick is used the cymbal can be suspended by its leather thong in one hand and struck with the other, or it can be hung from a stand, in which case its duration and intensity can be controlled immediately by the hand.

4 Playing Styles III: The Roll

Cymbal rolls can also be effected most easily with either one or two sticks (if the stand is in use) in order to obtain a smooth shimmer.

Another kind of roll consists of rubbing the two cymbals together. The climax of the *Tannhäuser* 'Venusberg' music gives a prolonged two-plate roll; Liszt's *Christus* and Janáček's *Glagolitic Mass* both provide further examples. Yet unless especially instructed by the conductor to the contrary, players tend automatically to use sticks on a single cymbal, regarding the two-plate roll as crude and unsatisfactory, whereas skilfully handled it can be very dramatic. Indeed, in many instances it is specifically prescribed, especially by Bartók. Roussel's *Suite en Fa* has the somewhat equivocal term *roulée*, but Ravel's *2 cymbales frottées* is particularly explicit. D'Indy says *à main* in *La Forêt enchantée*, while Vaughan Williams also states 'rubbed together' in his *London* Symphony.

5 Beaters

When, from among the numerous sticks that can be used to strike a cymbal, composers merely indicate 'hard' or 'soft', it can usually be taken to mean one of the grades of timpani stick; and where, for example in Vaughan Williams's *Pastoral* Symphony, no more specific instruction than the single word 'struck' is given, a hard felt stick is normally intended. Wooden sticks should generally be used only when specially demanded and are moreover not synonymous with side-drum sticks – which players all too easily take for granted in all circumstances. Side-drum sticks are of course also wooden, but they are lighter in character and thus give a much shallower, more clattery effect.

A slender metal stick such as a triangle beater (*Stab* is an alternative word used in German) provides another cymbal colour; and Walton in *Façade* goes still further by requiring the cymbal to be struck by the triangle itself, thus getting the best of both worlds.

Elgar further prescribes a heavy metal beater in the *Enigma Variations* at the climax of the finale, but in practice this is rarely obeyed for fear of causing damage to the cymbal.

The wire brush, though borrowed from the dance-band world, can occasionally be found in symphonic literature, especially in American or English scores where the name gives no problem. But there is as yet no standard translation and cases occur where a wire brush is not necessarily what the composer intended, as in 'The March of the Huntsmen' in Prokofiev's *Peter and the Wolf*, where the word VERGHE is added to the cymbal part.

6 Other Effects

The striking of more than one cymbal is also a real effect in its own right. Janáček provides examples of this in the repeated alternations of tails up and down in *Taras Bulba*, taken to be illustrative of clashing swords. Different cymbal effects are sometimes dramatically combined, i.e. one with stick simultaneously with a pair clashed by another player.

Of course more than one pair of cymbals may be clashed simultaneously: Mahler in his Third Symphony reinforces the already magnificent effect near the beginning of the work by asking for no fewer than three pairs for the return of the passage at the reprise. Extravagant as it may seem in theory, in performance it proves to be marvellously calculated.

The shimmer of a softly struck cymbal contains within it a bell-like resonance, which, although always of indefinite pitch, can vary in height and depth to a certain extent. Nor will a larger cymbal always give off a deeper ring; passages such as the opening of Nono's *Y su Sangre*, in which high, medium and low cymbal strokes are set in apposition, require much experimentation with different cymbals to get the correct effect.

A curious quality can be produced if the cymbal is struck on the dome, the shimmer in this case being largely excluded. Bartók, ever the pioneer, was among the first to exploit this new colour, and in his Violin Concerto (1938) he also experimented with all kinds of unlikely beaters such as knitting needles and penknives. His example was later followed by Roberto Gerhard, who even contrived a set of screw rods (metal rods screw-threaded along their length) that he used extensively in his Concerto for Orchestra; this, however, does the cymbals no good at all and players are prone to bring out their most inferior equipment for such harsh treatment.

Another effect dear to Gerhard's heart is the use of a cello bow drawn across the edge of the cymbal. This device was first exploited by Schoenberg, both in the fourth of his 5 *Orchesterstücke*, Op. 16, and in *Erwartung*, although in the latter he oddly enough changes to a double-bass bow. Well-rosined, the bows will conjure up a penetrating ring, but it is hard to keep the cymbal in position for long. Schoenberg used the effect only in isolated single places in each work, whereas Gerhard maintains it over long periods with several players dovetailing their strokes to ensure its continuity.

7 Characteristics

It has been said with much wisdom that the effect of the cymbal clash is in inverse proportion to its frequency. Although undoubtedly the single climactic explosion, such as marks the high moment of intensity in the first movement of Sibelius's First Symphony, creates tremendous exaltation by its unique position, this is only one side of the cymbals' role and is of com-

paratively recent and romantic origin.

Tiresome as the rhythmic patter of clashed cymbals may become, especially in such extended loud passages as the last pages of Tchaikovsky's *Little Russian* Symphony, it is this that was the original function of the cymbals in Turkish music (used invariably together with triangle and bass drum) and is thus historically authentic; while the cymbals are certainly often used separately, there is a wide area in which the bass drum and cymbals belong positively together. Indeed, in many Italian operas it is extremely difficult to know when or if the cymbals should play, as scores may merely cite *gran cassa*, which by tradition includes *piatti*, the player being expected to know where to add cymbal strokes. It can be as much a howler to leave the cymbals out, on the purist grounds that they are not mentioned in the score, as to put them in on every bass-drum stroke, as one sometimes hears. In grand opera such as Verdi's *Aida* or *opera seria* such as Rossini's *Semiramide* they have to be added, but with knowledge and taste. In *opera buffa* it is even more uncertain whether they are indeed required at all, as composers like Rossini would have had a smaller orchestra with perhaps only one percussionist. Nor should it be assumed in such cases that the bass drum and cymbals are always to be used, even if played in conjunction by the single player, and it remains possible that, on the contrary, the composer may have reserved the use of cymbals for his more lavishly scored operas.

8 Combined with Bass Drum

Indeed the very fact that bass drum

and cymbals can technically be played by one person raises a controversial issue. For either a single suspended cymbal can be struck, thus sacrificing the proper sonority of the clash, as in many pit and small orchestras, or one of the two clashed cymbals can be attached to the head of the bass drum, as is normal today only in military or jazz bands. The loss of tone resulting from screwing down one of the cymbals in this way is only half the problem, as the sound has a particularly characteristic 'tubby' quality that immediately evokes associations with army bands, popular circus music, Salvation Army meetings and so forth. It is specifically for these associations that, ever since Mahler initiated the precedent in his First Symphony, the composite unit of bass drum and cymbals played together by one musician has been prescribed as a special effect by other composers in addition even to a separate bass drum and pair of cymbals played by two other members of the percussion section. However, unless specially stipulated, the combined one-man bass drum and cymbals should never in any circumstances be resorted to, even in cases where finance restricts the employment of all the desired percussionists, so evocative are its cruder associations. Tchaikovsky, in the march of the *Pathétique* Symphony, even inserts a long phrase (fortunately also given in German translation) to insist that 'the cymbals should not be fixed [to the bass drum]'.

9 Exotic Types

Cymbals are primarily Turkish (although the main branch of the famous Zildjian family of makers now operates from the USA), but there is also an important variant that comes from China and is occasionally specified. **Chinese cymbals**, instead of slanting evenly after the central dome, have a pronounced curve outwards at the rim giving them a characteristic, less refined 'clangy' quality of their own, resulting in some limitations on their use and technique. They are therefore never employed unless asked for, as in works by Messiaen and Gerhard. For the greater part they are simply clashed – usually fairly strongly – with far cruder and less controlled effect than is possible with the Turkish variety. They may, however, be called into service for the bowed effect as their outward curve is particularly suitable for this operation.

Jazz-minded contemporary composers have occasionally used other more exotic forms of cymbals such as the sizzle-cymbal (always suspended); this has holes punched at intervals round its surface with inset jingle-like bits of metal that vibrate when the cymbal is struck. 'Hi-hats' – also imported from the jazz world – have also been written for, e.g. in *Pastorals* by Alexander Goehr. These are cymbals with damping pads added, an upper cymbal being brought down on to a fixed lower one by a pedal mechanism.

Cytharra, *see* ZITHER

DAIRA

Scored for by Khachaturian in the ballet *Gayaneh*, daira (or **doira**, according to some authorities) are an oriental-

Russian form of HAND DRUMS not un-like Indian tabla but with jingles so that they somewhat resemble large tam-bourines. They are, however, played like tabla – Khachaturian marking them *colla dite* and *colla mano* for the notes with tails up and down, explain-ing in a footnote that this signifies with the fingers and the palm of the hand respectively.

Dämpfer (Ger.), *see* MUTES, 1

DARBOUKKA

This Arabian HAND DRUM is incorpor-ated by Ibert into his *Suite Symphonique*, describing Parisian scenes, in order to introduce an oriental flavour for the movement depicting the Paris Mosque. A German subheading describes the instrument as a *Fell tom-tom* which is adequate as a rough and ready defini-tion, as the head is usually of sheepskin. Otherwise the darboukka is vase-shaped and made of earthenware, but the material as well as the size can be almost anything so long as it can be held under the arm. It is then played with the fingers and knuckles of both hands.

The name too is infinitely variable and this is the same instrument as the **tarbuka** used by Berlioz for the 'Dance of the Nubian Slaves' in *Les Troyens à Carthage*.

Détaché (Fr.), separate bowing; *see* BOWING, 8

DIVISI

Although found occasionally among woodwind lines in scores, *divisi* is pri-marily a term applied to the orchestral string group.

The German equivalent to the stan-dard Italian term is **geteilt**, but while the abbreviation *div.* is clear enough, the German *geth.*, short for the old German form **getheilt** found especi-ally in Wagner, is not always under-stood by players. The German contra-diction *Alle* corresponds with the Italian TUTTI, while *zusammen* is the equivalent of **unisoni**.

Each string section is frequently re-quired to be divided into numerous different parts and this can be carried out in various ways. It is rare to find one or other form of *divisi* actually speci-fied in scores but the Germans do have the indication **Pultweise geteilt**. Un-fortunately this, meaning literally 'deskwise', is misleading since it is in fact used to signify *divisi* at the desk. Even the simplest *divisi à 2* can be executed either at the desk or by desks. *Divisi* at the desk means that the file of outer players takes the upper line, that of the inner players the lower; this is the manner normally adopted by play-ers for any twofold division unless instructed otherwise. *Divisi* by desks, on the other hand, denotes that the two players at each desk play in unison, the odd-numbered desks taking the top, and the even-numbered the bottom part. This is a very convenient method for music with impossible page turns where, in the absence of rests for example, the outside player can keep the line going while the inside player turns.

A third method of *divisi à 2* is by blocks, front and back. Some works, especially those of composers such as

Strauss and Smetana, create the necessity for this method since different parts are printed carrying the music for only the front or back desks. Although this form of dividing may naturally be applied to any section it often has special relevance to the cellos, whose lower line is frequently in unison with the basses, and so is best played by the back desks who sit nearest to them. The cello parts of Smetana's *Má Vlast*, for example, are printed in this way.

It cannot be said that any of these methods is the best in all contexts. Each is freely used and the different forms of *divisi* may replace each other even within the span of a single work or movement. The choice will depend on various practical considerations arising from the musical layout, or in response to specific instructions in the score.

One outstanding example of such a choice arises when only half the section is required to play. This may be indicated by the Italian *la* **metà**, or by the German *die Hälfte*. (The French equivalent *la moitié* is more rarely seen.) Except in the few instances where the score stipulates the front desks, it is usual for the file of outside players to take the passage by themselves. The virtue of this is not just to reduce the weight of tone but to thin out the actual quality.

Divisi à 3 (en trois parties, dreifach geteilt) can also be handled in different ways. Left to themselves the players for simplicity's sake generally take a desk a line, thus: $\aleph_1$ $\aleph_2$ $\aleph_3$ $\aleph_1$ $\aleph_2$ $\aleph_3$ *etc.*

But this places the players of the third line very far back, as well as keeping each of the desks with the same line to play

almost out of earshot of one another. If therefore the musical context is one of harmonic or chordal textures a better method is effected with a *divisi* by players: $_2\aleph_1$ $_3\aleph_1$ $_3\aleph_2$ $\aleph_1$ $\aleph_1$ *etc.*

Fourfold *divisi* (*à 4, vierfach*, etc.) is on the face of it, a simpler affair since it is an obvious derivative of *divisi à 2* by desks, each line of which is then subdivided again. Looked at from this point of view it can be seen to equate with a *divisi à 4* by players:

$_2\aleph_1$ $_4\aleph_3$ $_2\aleph_1$ $_4\aleph_3$ = $^{(ii)}_1\aleph_1$ $^{(ii)}_2\aleph_1$ $^{(ii)}_1\aleph_1$ $^{(ii)}_2\aleph_1$ *etc.*

This is especially clear when the part is printed on two staves, each bearing a pair of lines, but is less obvious when the publisher has been conscientious enough to lay out the whole scheme on four staves.

Some of the most perplexing situations arise when the composer keeps changing the *divisi* between two, three, four, five and even six or more lines, often within the space of a few bars, causing players to search out their way amid a maze of shifting parts, as in the 'Am Kamin' interlude from Richard Strauss's opera *Intermezzo*. Nor is this the only *divisi* headache here for, having fixed on viola and cello sections comprising five players each, Strauss writes for the three desks in different ways, as if it were alternately the first and the back desk that had the single player, so that the only way to carry out his instructions to the letter is to carry six players with either the second or the sixth remaining silent.

Over the whole repertoire every kind of *divisi* will of course arise, ranging from the simplest block divisions, equal or unequal (e.g. the first movement of Bartók's *Divertimento*), to the elaborate desk-by-desk layouts of Schoenberg's *Gurrelieder* or the ultimate extreme of Ligeti's and Xenakis's compositions, in some of which every single player has a different line to play.

Doira, *see* DAIRA

Donnermaschine, *see* THUNDER MACHINE

DOUBLE BASS

1 Description and Names

The fifth and lowest member of the orchestral string family, the double-bass is the only one to retain in its shape and methods of playing some features of the viol family (the precursors of our violins, violas and cellos), such as the curvature of the shoulders and the so-called Dragonetti bow, held from below instead of above. The ancestor of our modern bass was the violone (literally 'large viol'), which, strictly speaking, was the double-bass viol used by Bach and other early composers.

Where nomenclature is concerned, the Italian *basso* or **contrabasso** (or even – strangely enough – *contrabbasso*) converts naturally into **contrebasse** (Fr.) or *Kontrabass* (Ger., spelt either with a 'C' or a 'K'). In English, in addition to the usual 'bass' or 'double-bass', the term 'string bass' is sometimes used, especially in groups, like dance or military bands, in which string instruments are a minority.

2 Tuning

The tuning of the bass is different from that of all the other strings and is in fourths. This is due to the much wider stretch between the notes of this instrument, intervals of a fourth and upwards being beyond the range of the normal hand. Standard bass tuning is, then, as follows:

IV   III   II   I

sounding an octave lower than written, this being customary notation for the basses.

In consequence, when tuning their instruments bass players adopt a different procedure, which is indeed even more radical than one might expect, because the sound of the open strings is so low that an accurate tuning at pitch would be impossibly hard to recognize, and in fact bass players tune by means of matching high-sounding harmonics.

From the above it would appear that the bottom note of the bass is the low E of the lowest open string, but this is by no means standard. Notes below E occur frequently in music by Bach and Mozart, who were able to take these fundamentals for granted in Germany and Austria, even though when they travelled to Italy and, above all to Britain (where a small three-string bass had come into general favour, surviving well into the twentieth century) they were forced by local conditions to make compromises. Cherubini in *Medée*, composed in 1797, wrote down to low C in circumstances that are unequivocal since the basses are given an individual line – i.e., not merely in unison with the cellos – and he was followed by Beethoven, who commonly used the low notes for important bass passages. No doubt players using more restricted instruments have always been adept at taking it on themselves to transpose up an octave either whole passages or even isolated notes in the middle of a phrase in order to obviate the nuisance and hazards of tuning down, should instruments of the necessary range not be available. The great edition of the classical repertoire, Breitkopf & Härtel, actually went so far as to doctor its published bass parts so that no note below E appears at all, the opening bars of Schubert's *Unfinished* Symphony, for instance, being bowdlerized for the purpose though the score – like the manuscript – clearly shows the low notes for the basses on a separate stave.

Composers of the romantic and later eras generally assume the existence of at least some basses in every orchestra capable of producing the low notes down to C. These instruments are actually a subspecies carrying a fifth string originally tuned not in fourths like the other strings but specifically to C: . Even Walter Piston, writing in the mid-1950s states that this is the tuning of the five-string bass, but the truth is that these days players find it more practical to preserve uniformity of technique by tuning the extra bottom string to B. Many, however, insist that the bigger five-stringer is clumsier as well as less resonant than the conventional four-string bass and for this reason a compromise can often be seen in the form of a finger-board extension fitted to the neck of the four-string instrument.

This always has the lowest string tuned to C and thus, lacking the open E as well as the overall tuning in fourths, is at best no more than a half-measure.

It remains very rare for a large bass section to be made up entirely of five-string or extended instruments and many composers prescribe special low-lying notes or phrases to be played only by those having the extra range, and include insistent instructions that they are not to be played at the upper octave by the other members of the section. Indeed, even today, the five-string bass has by no means become the universal standard instrument one might have expected, and has failed to render the four-stringer obsolete as this in its turn once did the three-stringer. On the contrary, there are orchestras everywhere that do not possess a single bass capable of playing below E without retuning, and the struggle continues unabated when conductors may try to insist on the low notes in, for example, Britten's *Serenade* (Eb) or Strauss's *Die Liebe der Danae* (D), to quote only two among the myriad scores in which the bottom double-bass notes are isolated and are thus particularly indispensable.

Nor is it to be supposed that composers have been satisfied with C as the ultimate fundamental tone. Reger, for instance, specifically instructs his five-string basses to tune the C down to B in his *Hiller Variations*, while Strauss (*Panathenäenzug*) writes as low as Bb.

3 Notation
Where the upper range is concerned, basses need to be at home, as are the cellos, in the tenor and treble clefs, but

they are understandably less frequently used, although Berg writes for the basses as high as C above the treble clef in his *Drei Orchesterstücke*, Op. 6. The treble clef, however, occasionally brings problems as composers are not always consistent over which octave they intend, especially in respect of harmonics, which are sometimes written to sound at pitch as opposed to the conventional double-bass octave drop.

The custom of treating the basses as transposing instruments is bound up with the character of their tone, which in turn reacts on the visual appearance of their line in the score, which is often combined in unison and on a single stave with that of the cellos, even though in fact the basses are sounding an octave lower. For the technical reality of high positions on the bass, which would be necessary to produce a true acoustic unison with the cellos, fails to take into account their timbre at such a register. As a result it turns out to be far more a scientific than a truly musical unison of sonority, a truth revealed disconcertingly when, in consequence of the bias in recent years against the use of transposing instruments in the conductor's score, many composers write for basses at actual pitch – thereby misjudging this aspect of timbre and technique, the players finding themselves endlessly clambering about in uncongenial and ineffectual registers.

4 Characteristics
The strange truth is that the quality of the double-bass is entirely at odds with its noble appearance and continually gives surprise with its usually thin wheezy voice when heard in isolation in any but the lower register where its function is best served.

The standard symphonic strength is for four desks of basses, although for normal purposes three desks will often be thought sufficient especially if there is a space problem on the platform, as basses occupy an inordinate amount of room. Bass players are a proud fraternity and take it ill when – as so often – conductors pay them little attention or reveal an inability to hear whether they are playing correctly or not. They are also loath to play with MUTES, although the indication appears as frequently for them as for the other strings.

See also: ARCO, BOWING, DIVISI, GLISSANDO, HARMONICS, MUTES, PIZZICATO, SCORDATURA, STRINGS

Double Bassoon, *see* CONTRABASSOON

Double-bass Clarinet, *see* CONTRABASS CLARINET

Double-bass Trombone, *see* CONTRA-BASS TROMBONE

Double-bass Tuba, . *see* CONTRABASS TUBA

DOUBLE STOPPING

The device of sounding two notes simultaneously, known as double stopping, properly lies in the province of the string group where, in order to increase the volume of tone, or for some strongly dramatic gesture, use is commonly made of double, triple or even quadruple stopping, in both *arco* and *pizzicato*. In scores this is rarely referred to by the English term, the most normal being the Italian *non divisi* (the German correspondingly *nicht get(h)eilt* or simply a square bracket thus: [♪], but the Germans do also use *Doppelgriff* and the French *double corde*).

In classical scores or the orchestral parts of standard works, square brackets and verbal indications are on the whole rare and it is often a matter of decision for players or conductor whether, or to what extent, chords should be divided in the conflicting interests of tonal weight, panache, dramatic intensity or ensemble, not to mention intonation where the chords lie awkwardly. The most usual way of actually prescribing that a chord should be spread is for the lower notes to be shown with shorter note values indicating that these are to be released while the upper note is held: [♪]. This is, however, less of an expediency than an effect in its own right, as in the first movements of Beethoven's First and Fifth Symphonies.

On violins and violas it is possible for a three-note or conceivably a four-note chord to be played virtually unspread, although hardly in anything less than a *forte*. Even in Mozart some such chords often tend to sound rough, and when players find their execution inconvenient or in the case of some later composers – frankly impossible – they are adept at dividing in such a way as to give a realistic impression of the desired effect. This may be done by various kinds of overlapping so that the compromise is barely perceptible. The overlap will usually be of two and two in three-note chords [♪] but not in four-note ones which are taken three and three: [♪]

Where chords are directed to be spread this is mostly taken to mean from bottom to top and no specific indication is marked. But when the equally possible reverse is required it is notated either by a vertical arrow to the left of the chord or by spelling out the notes as appoggiaturas.

A favourite device often used by Mozart is the rich sound produced by the combining of stopped and open strings, such as the double stopping in unison of the open D string sounded simultaneously with the same note stopped on the G string, as in the opening of his D major Violin Concerto (K. 218). The combining of one or more open strings with other stopped notes above produces a particularly splendid resonance, much exploited by, for example, Rimsky-Korsakov in *Scheherazade*, the *Capriccio Espagnol* and other orchestral showpieces.

Although the fuller harmonic texture that chords supply remains the principal purpose of double stopping, it can also be introduced for contrapuntal writing. This is, however, so exacting that it is rarely used for a whole section; indeed it is mostly written for a single player; the famous extended violin solo from Strauss's *Ein*

Heldenleben, which abounds in double stopping of all kinds, is an outstanding example.

Berg, by an ingenious combination of *arco* and left-hand *pizzicato*, contrived a two-part tutti passage for violas in his Violin Concerto, but felt it wise to add an optional indication (*eventuell geteilt*, i.e. *divisi* if necessary) condoning the sharing of the lines. If acted on, however, this last-resort alternative largely spoils the effect.

Double stopping is equally effective on violins, violas and cellos, but basses are far less often enjoined to double stop with the rest, partly because of the impracticability of the very wide stretches, and partly as it dissipates the tone instead of strengthening it as it does with the higher strings. It is, however, occasionally encountered as in Brahms's *Tragic Overture*.

Some wind instruments, such as oboes and even horns, are occasionally known to 'double stop' (so to speak) with more or less disagreeable results; but these are primarily soloistic parlour tricks and have no place in orchestral writing.

DOUBLE- AND TRIPLE-TONGUING

Rapid tonguing techniques fall most rapidly into the province of the flutes among the woodwind, and of the horns and trumpets among the brass.

Certainly in this respect flutes far outstrip their woodwind colleagues, double-tonguing ('t–k–') and even triple tonguing ('t–d–k–' or occasionally 't–k–t–' as in Stravinsky's 'Dance of the Firebird') being frequently introduced into flute passage work. It is,

however, a rarity in clarinet writing and even more so for oboes and bassoons, though there is a notorious passage of double-tonguing for all the woodwind in the third movement of Hindemith's *Mathis der Maler* Symphony and the ultra-quick *staccato* passage for the oboes in Kodály's *Dances of Galanta* is also often taken in double-tonguing by players who pride themselves on this accomplishment. It is indeed by no means every executant who can boast this as part of his technical equipment.

In the case of the horns and trumpets it is rare to find double-tonguing actually prescribed in scores, and players normally adopt it, as they would also adopt triple-tonguing, according to the speed or style of a specific passage. Rimsky-Korsakov's *Scheherazade* (last movement) or Ravel's *Alborado del Gracioso* both supply excellent examples of passages where the composer clearly assumed that they would be double- or triple-tongued. While trombones and, where necessary, tubas can if pressed produce these effects, the heavier instruments and their larger mouthpieces cause them to be proportionately less successful in agile and spectacular techniques of the kind.

DOUBLING

The term 'to double' in the orchestra has two quite separate and distinct definitions. The first is the natural and straightforward meaning of an extra player executing the same part as another, although the line is written for only a single instrument. Hence 'doubling' has no application to the string group where the players of each department always do play the same parts as one another. But in the wood-wind, brass and very occasionally percussion, players are sometimes asked to 'double up' for special purposes, or extra players may be engaged to double – generally in tutti work – for the whole of a piece or programme.

One of the most regular forms of doubling, and one that is the conductor's responsibility to decide, is for powerful symphonic works such as Beethoven's Seventh Symphony, which are nevertheless scored for only two horns. It had for many years become conventional to use four horns for many such scores, especially where the two horns are combined with trombones as well as trumpets, e.g. for the last movements of Beethoven's Fifth and *Pastoral* Symphonies or Schubert's *Great C major*. The purpose of such reinforcements is patently in the interests of better balance with the increased weight of today's larger string sections, the extra sheer power of four horns being beyond dispute. However, there is a corresponding sacrifice in refinement as well as, curiously enough, brilliance – four horns blazing away have a thicker, 'tubbier' quality than two – and many horn pairs have more recently expressed their preference for coping without this gratuitous doubling.

By extension, four-horn works on a very large scale are sometimes played with eight instruments. Mahler himself used eight horns for Beethoven's Choral Symphony, and conceived the ingenious idea of creating an overwhelming *crescendo* in the 'an die Freude' melody by requiring the first four players to enunciate their parts *ff* while the second quartet played *crescendo molto poco a poco*. Such doublings still survive when the *Eroica*, Bruckner's Fifth or Walton's First Symphonies, all scored for surprisingly modest forces, are played by gargantuan wind and brass groups, either for some special occasion or possibly to underline the prestige of a star conductor.

Another customary 'doubler' in the orchestra is the supernumary horn or trumpet player known as the BUMPER whose purpose is to relieve the strain on the principal player and keep his lip fresh for solos.

Composers themselves very often double solo lines, either to allow for breathing or to create a thicker quality of sound. Dvořák was very fond of the lovely rich effect of two clarinets playing together in *pianissimo*, and Tchaikovsky used the same colour all through the opening statement of the motto theme in the first movement of his Fifth Symphony. Tchaikovsky was also especially addicted to low unison flutes, sometimes using three at a time. Mahler typically takes this to the limit in the second (*Ländler*) movement of his Ninth Symphony, where large groups of each instrument wail out in unison successive phrases of a wide-spanned melody with calculatedly grotesque effect.

Occasionally composers will ask or even insist that, although only a single instrument has been scored for, the entire part should be doubled. Mahler asks that the celesta should be doubled in all the *forte* passages of his Sixth

Symphony. In fact Mahler and Strauss repeatedly asked that their harp parts should be doubled if possible, and Shostakovich goes a step further, stipulating in the Fifth Symphony and Second Cello Concerto, for example, that the single harp must be played in unison throughout by two players and certainly the effect is entirely different if this is obeyed. In many of Elgar's works the second harp part is only marginally different from the first, and in all Rachmaninoff's last orchestral works, including the *Paganini Rhapsody*, he writes the plural 'arpe' against the single harp part; indeed in the Third Symphony he was so keen that the harp part should be doubled that he even added a note in the score to the effect that in the absence of a second harp a small upright piano could be substituted, although it is hard to imagine Rachmaninoff, the great piano virtuoso, seriously contemplating this awful possibility when it came to the point. (Perhaps it was forced on him by his American publishing house.) The extreme case is d'Indy, who took a section of no fewer than eight harps as his norm although in practice he never wrote more than two individual parts for them.

Composers also sometimes ask for the wind and brass to be doubled at special points in a work. Elgar invites such augmentation for his splendid trombone parts at the more rumbustious moments of the *Cockaigne* Overture, and Strauss asks for wind doubling in several places in the *Alpine* Symphony. But these exhortations are in the event rarely acted on for obvious economic reasons.

The second meaning of 'doubling' is when an orchestral musician plays not the same part, but a quite different instrument. A flute player, thus, may 'double' on piccolo, a clarinettist on saxophone, a trumpeter on cornet, a trombonist on bass trumpet or a timpanist on xylophone, etc. Unless especially provided for in the player's contract, where he or she is a member of a permanent full-time orchestra, this kind of 'doubling' is always rewarded by *ad hoc* extra payment. Sometimes all sorts of doubling can be seen to take place in an orchestra – a violinist doubling on celesta, for example – according to the qualifications or varied expertise of the different members. Strauss's *Elektra* asks for part of his violin body to alternate with violas. Varèse actually instructs a 2nd violin player to take up a tambourine in *Arcana* (but it is unlikely that any orchestral percussion section will allow this to happen).

Some instruments are conventionally doubled in this way: in many scores the indication 'one player' will be bracketed, for example, across the piano and celesta parts of a work. This still counts professionally as doubling, however, as does the interchange between many of the countless different instruments handled by the percussion fraternity.

See also: AUGMENTATION

DRESS

Despite the current trend for reduced formality and changing fashion, orchestral wear at concerts has varied little over the years. The conventional wear for a top-class symphony orchestra remains 'white tie and tails' for the men (only the stiff shirt-front and white waistcoat having for practical reasons given way to a soft shirt and the wellnigh ubiquitous cummerbund) and 'long black' for the women.

There are, however, a number of variations to this, the most important of which consists of DJs (dinnerjackets) with black tie and sometimes 'short black' as the female counterpart. This is often seen in provincial orchestras and also in the big London orchestras for less prestigious venues or occasions including, in view of their purposely informal atmosphere, the Henry Wood Proms.

Until comparatively recently sacred buildings were considered unsuitable for what is sometimes labelled 'full fig' and dark suits were prescribed, but over the years this air of disapproval has been relaxed and dark suits are now worn only for afternoon concerts together with short black for women.

Black dresses, however, often look so drab that colours are sometimes encouraged for women for DJ concerts, though still only as a rarity when the men are in tails. It is hard to avert the danger of some colours or designs being chosen of an over-brilliant eye-catching variety; and bare arms, especially bowing arms, can also make an uneasy visual impression.

Morning tailcoats, grey waistcoats and the rest, once not uncommon for conductors at afternoon concerts, or evenings in cathedrals, have now totally disappeared from the concert world. On the other hand the 'white tuxedo', as the Americans call the white dinner jacket, imported from the light-music world by go-ahead conductors for warm summer wear during the last decade or so, are beginning to be adopted by whole orchestras, especially during hot weather, in preference to that other concession to climatic hardship, the shedding of jackets altogether. Indeed, the Royal Philharmonic Orchestra has recently appeared throughout the whole summer season in white.

Isolated attempts by some international artists to relax the stereotypes have resulted in, for instance, the wearing of white poloneck sweaters with tailcoats. Some resident conductors or managers with a penchant for vigorous public relations have thrown the entire orchestra into various types of exotic evening wear. Leonard Bernstein's controversial step with the New York Philharmonic Symphony (red tuxedos) or the London Sinfonietta (variously coloured polo necks or shirts) are noted examples of what are ultimately no more than experimental departures from the continuing sober formality of the mainstream of international concerts.

DRUMS

1 Names and Species

Apart from the TIMPANI (kettle-drums) and the BASS DRUM, the orchestra boasts a variety of drums, of which the most familiar is the family of snare drums, consisting primarily, in descending order of pitch, of the **side drum**, the **military drum** and the **tenor drum**.

It is, however, necessary to stress the

word *orchestra*, because in the drum world – military, civilian and dance band – it is easy to get caught up in the morass of specialist detail, which is, admittedly, both important and interesting but without immediate relevance to the orchestral scene. So interlocked indeed is the situation that the different drums become entangled in their very nomenclature, and one often has only the most general idea of what instrument the composer really meant, coupled with the suspicion that he may himself have had no very positive views.

The term 'snare drum' is sometimes, as in Copland, used to mean the side drum specifically, but in view of the existence of the other snared drums this is clearly a dangerously ambiguous practice. French composers call the side drum either *caisse claire* (its real unequivocal name) or *tambour militaire*. Yet this produces another ambiguity, for *tambour militaire* might also really mean 'military drum', though for this they may very well simply say **tambour**. Delius uses a **military tambour** in *Eventyr* and a 'military drum' in the Dance Rhapsody No. 2, which are presumably both intended for the same side drum. Even the fifth edition of *Grove's Dictionary* gives the one as a straight translation for the other with, it has to be admitted, an element of historical and geographical truth. Yet again, 'tambour' might possibly mean 'tenor drum', for which the real name is **caisse roulante**, a term on the whole less frequently found in orchestral scores.

Turning to the German, a parallel situation exists: **kleine Trommel** is clear enough, but some composers put **Militärtrommel** when they palpably

mean a simple side drum, making things difficult for others like Hans Werner Henze, who when he puts *Militärtrommel* really does mean what he says. At the same time this kind of specialist terminology can cause the kind of confusion created by Strauss when he writes **kleine Militärtrommel** in *Rosenkavalier*. This is actually deeper both in appearance and quality than the side drum (*kleine Trommel*), which is what he calls for in, for example, *Salome*, and it is more than likely what he meant here too.

The German for tenor drum (*Rührtrommel*) is fortunately clear enough and in common use throughout the literature. These also come in different sizes so that Wagner was able to specify a **grosse Rührtrommel** in the *Ring* (where it often supplants the bass drum – a curious touch).

Italian terminology corresponds more or less with a combination of the French and German. Side drum is **tamburo piccolo**, not, it should be stressed, to be confused with the 'tamburi piccoli' of Berlioz's *Carnaval Romain* Overture, which are – maddeningly enough – tambourines. The tenor drum may be **cassa rullante** or **tamburo rullante**, though again the latter is less often found and may be what the composer means by *tamburo*, which in its turn may also signify the military drum (otherwise **tamburo militare**). Rimsky-Korsakov, for instance, plainly regards *tamburo, tamburo piccolo, caisse claire* and *tambour militaire* as all synonymous with the side drum. One has only to consult his book on orchestration to confirm this, let alone his scores, in which the terms may be mixed up in quite a random manner. (In *Scheherazade*, the 'tamburo' of the third movement becomes the 'tamburo piccolo' in the list of instruments that heads the fourth, though thereafter the word 'piccolo' vanishes once more.) For Balakirev there is no differentiation either, the 'tamburo' of the First Symphony becoming 'tamburo militare' of *Thamar*. Walton's Cello Concerto is notorious for alternating side drum, *caisse claire* and *tambour militaire* all within the space of a few pages.

The trouble arises because the many borderline instruments came relatively late to the orchestral scene and by the time the military drum, for instance, appeared with an existence of its own, its name had already been introduced for reasons of differentiation.

Although all these drums are of indefinite pitch, the deeper varieties without snares – such as some tenor drums and even bass drums – can have their heads tightened or slackened to emulate specific pitches. Thus Puccini, in the second act of *La Bohème*, actually calls for *6 tamburi accordati in Si* ♭. They also vary in depth to sufficient extent to be used by composers as a kind of semi-tuned substitute for timpani when scoring for small or unconventional groups. For this purpose snare drums can also be co-opted, pitch difference becoming more adaptable when played without the snares (German, **Saiten**). These are quickly and easily fixed by a kind of clasp, but are left on for normal playing. Nevertheless it is often necessary to ask drummers to slacken the snares when the drum is silent, to prevent them vibrating in sympathy or, worse still, rattling in passages where the timpani or other neighbouring instruments are in loud action. 'Snares off' is also sometimes regarded as a method of MUTING.

2 Styles of Beating

Like timpani, other drums can be played at different places on the head, producing variations of pitch and quality. Bartók exploits all these colours (together with the snares on and off) as a major feature of the slow movement of his First Piano Concerto, placing his percussion section unconventionally near to the solo piano for the purpose.

The frequently met instruction 'on the rim' constitutes a problem as it presupposes that the rim is wooden, whereas in modern drums it is generally of thin metal and gives a very different – and far less resonant – effect, so that players use their ingenuity to imitate the desired sound in other ways. A **rim-shot** however, remains an absolute reality of the most galvanizing nature (always in *fortissimo*) the whole stick being slapped over the side drum, rim and head, creating a crack like a pistol shot – in specific imitation of which Tchaikovsky uses it in his symphonic poem *The Voyevode*, as does Copland for the gunfight in *Billy the Kid*.

3 Sticks

Wooden sticks (Italian, **bacchette di legno**; German, **Holzschlägel**; French, **baguettes de bois**) are the standard implements for the drum family, and 'side-drum sticks' the generic term establishing the conventional shape. This is not to say that other beaters, such as timpani sticks, etc., are not required.

91

4 Other Effects

Drum rolls and figures can be produced across the widest imaginable range of dynamics. Janáček in *Taras Bulba* uses both extremes with startling effect, the murmur in the first movement being no less dramatic than the crashes in the third. Ravel, ever on the lookout for variations of effect, hit on the riotous idea of reducing a side-drum *pianissimo* even further in his Left Hand Piano Concerto by making the drummer continue the rhythm with the sticks no longer on the drum but on each other. In the overture *La Gazza Ladra*, Rossini uses two side drums placed on either side of the orchestra, playing rolls alternately before uniting in a joint *crescendo*.

Many of the figures and rhythms used and practised by drummers and forming the backbone of their technique are known by names such as 'paradiddle', 'flam', etc., but these have not entered the orchestral vernacular. They are numerous and varied enough, however, for Nielsen to instruct his side drummer in the Fifth Symphony to improvise freely on them (see AD LIB).

Side drummers need great stamina and control as well as an iron inflexibility of pulse. Hence works such as Ravel's *Bolero* or Shostakovich's *Leningrad* Symphony (No. 7), both containing some fifteen minutes' non-stop repetition of a rhythmic figure, are examples of the capital composers have made of this accomplishment.

5 Tambourin

One further species of drum needs to be added; this is the old English **tabor** used in morris dancing. Though occasionally found in orchestral scores it is sufficient of a rarity to present a problem when, for example, Elgar calls for it in *Falstaff*. In a preliminary note the composer suggests substituting a military drum, but the nearest equivalent is certainly the Provençal long drum or **tambourin**.

The tabor has no snares and the tambourin only one – so the usual custom of substituting a drum without snares for both is not wholly correct. The tambourin is found in many French scores (notably in Bizet, but also in twentieth-century composers such as Milhaud) and is generally given straightforward rhythmic patterns. Its name gives rise to confusion and, being essentially a French instrument, no translations appear to exist. Furthermore it is very rarely found in any other than French scores, coming into the category of 'local colour'. However Copland unexpectedly writes for 'tabor (long drum)' (*sic*) in *Appalachian Spring*.

The French **tarole** (or **tarolle**) should perhaps also be mentioned, being a local variant of the side drum, though without snares. Poulenc uses it in two of his concertos, as does Varèse in *Ionisation*.

See also: BONGOS, CONGAS, HAND DRUMS, PICCOLI TIMPANI ORIENTALI, TOM-TOMS

Dulcimer, *see* CIMBALOM

DULCITONE

This is a kind of small and gently magical keyboard instrument of great purity of sound in which a set of tuning forks is struck with hammers. The French name for this is **typophone** and it is used by a few French composers such as D'Indy and especially Duparc, in whose beautiful song *L'Invitation au Voyage* it is featured. It was however shortlived and D'Indy already makes the provision in the score that as an *ossia* one might substitute the CELESTA, of which instrument, the *typophone* was in fact the predecessor. It seems indeed to have been the brainchild of the father of the well-known Mustel, who was soon after to invent the more successful and hence enduring celesta.

EARLY STRINGED INSTRUMENTS

A few of the more interesting historical string instruments may sometimes be encountered in the symphony orchestra, though these are never in sections, only as solo players. The most familiar are the **viola d'amore** and the **viola da gamba**, the latter principally introduced as a continuo instrument or for purist performances of Monteverdi, Schütz or other early music. Perhaps its chief claim to a repertoire status in the orchestra derives from the parts in Bach's Sixth Brandenburg Concerto, in the Passions and in some of the cantatas. Bach's notation for it is generally similar to that of the cello, but in Cantata No. 106, 'Gottes Zeit ist die allerbeste Zeit', the first of the gambas is notated in the alto clef and the second in the tenor and bass clefs.

The viola da gamba has six strings and unlike the cello has no spike being gripped between the knees. Moreover, as with all viols, the bow is held from beneath, much like the Dragonetti bass bow. A disconcerting feature of this gamba bow style is that the bow strokes work the opposite way to the regular strings – i.e. the down bow travels from point to heel.

The gamba has not been revived in nineteenth- and twentieth-century music, unlike the viola d'amore which makes periodic reappearances, such as the obbligato at the beginning of Raoul's aria from the first act of Meyerbeer's *Les Huguenots*, the off-stage solo in the second act of Puccini's *Madam Butterfly*, or Pfitzner's inclusion of it in *Palestrina*. Yet even in *Palestrina* it appears, oddly, only briefly in a not particularly exposed passage, whereas the many obbligatos that portray a sixteenth-century instrument in the hands of one of the characters on the stage are taken by one – or at times two – ordinary violas. This is perhaps because players of the extraordinary viola d'amore, with its seven strings plus a further seven sympathetic strings, are extremely rare. In practice all such solos are usually played by the conventional viola, which is even given as an ossia in the 'Parting of Romeo and Juliet' from Prokofiev's ballet. In the case of the Puccini example at least, it must be admitted that the imaginative subtlety in the composer's choice of viola d'amore for Butterfly's touching night vigil largely goes for nothing, played as it is behind the scene in unison with the off-stage chorus.

None of the other ancestors of the violin family have sufficient status orchestrally to warrant inclusion here, despite their appearance in scores by Schütz or other baroque composers. The **violino piccolo** of Bach's First Brandenburg Concerto, Schütz's **violetta** and the numerous other instruments listed and described by Charles Sanford Terry in his book on Bach's orchestra belong wholly to the specialists in authenticity and to history.

EDITING

This involves the decisions taken on what extra marks should or should not be added to the composer's manuscript when preparing music for publication or with a view to performance. These marks may be tempo indications, slurs, phrasings, dynamics – including hairpins (◁===▷) showing subtleties of rise and fall – bowings, breath marks, and so on. Even purist editions of the present day generally require some editorial emendations of this sort, while in the past a text unadulterated to a considerable degree could be hard to find.

While many distinguished solo singers and instrumentalists have over the years published idiosyncratic versions of the works in which they have become famous, with editings based on their interpretations, this is comparatively rare in the case of orchestral scores and materials, any textual emendations being largely the work of scholars or musicologists.

Nevertheless, a few conductors have been tempted in this direction. Sir Thomas Beecham, for example, was persuaded by Boosey & Hawkes to publish many of his edited materials of Mozart symphonies, complete with his notorious hairpins, as well as additional dynamic and phrase marks. Beecham also embarked on a series of completely revised Delius scores, although the edition was destined to be no more than a fragment of the huge corpus that was planned. This was a more valid undertaking since it was Beecham's instinctive understanding of Delius's musical thought and realization of the inadequacy of the composer's own markings that led to the wide appreciation of his *oeuvre*.

On the whole, it tends to be music of the sixteenth to eighteenth centuries that receives most editing at conductors' hands. The music of this period is scantily marked, unlike that of the nineteenth and twentieth centuries, in which the composers themselves usually indicate the necessary phrasings and dynamics. Little more, therefore, needs to be added to such later scores other than BOWINGS, which are in any case generally considered to be the especial responsibility of the leader.

In the classics, however, essential as editing may be, it is always a heart-searching occupation and fraught with pitfalls. Any form of perpetuation such as committing the results to print can be self-defeating. Editions such as Beecham's of the Mozart symphonies were from the first too personal to be of enduring quality, and in any case the rapid changes in taste and aesthetic views as decade follows decade tend always to invalidate the editings of performers, however much sympathy with period styles they set out to have. Thus, Walter Goehr's immensely praiseworthy editions of

Monteverdi, once thought to be models of enlightenment, were all too soon cast aside, and those by Raymond Leppard, which succeeded them, are now suffering a similar fate.

Many conductors, however, wisely believe that at least for their own performances – especially of the classics – some editorial marks are indispensable both as time-savers in rehearsal and to ensure a performance from an orchestra in which the players are restrained from merely repeating their own familiar interpretations instead of adopting the style and readings required by the person actually on the rostrum. The purchase and marking of orchestral parts is an expensive and laborious undertaking, but it almost always pays immense dividends and even fully bowed parts, if presented tactfully and without undue inflexibility to an experienced orchestra, may be warmly accepted by all but the most intransigent leaders of the string sections.

See also: ARRANGEMENT

EDITIONS

It might be thought that a knowledge of music publishing lay in the province primarily of the orchestral LIBRARIAN, but it can be of the utmost importance for a conductor to know where to turn for a reliable text when preparing his score, and sometimes the players' material, before facing the orchestra at rehearsal. He may otherwise all too easily be confronted by a morass of conflicting versions and ideas without the time, or worse still, the *savoir-faire*, to cope with the situation.

If, for example, he has left it to the orchestra to provide the material and he is playing Bach or Handel, say, he should know that the Bach Gesellschaft scores and parts both published by Breitkopf & Härtel in no way correspond, the latter having been substantially edited – and often bowdlerized *en route* – by one Max Seiffert. The conductor is far safer with Peters, even though in these more enlightened days Breitkopf has gone some way towards replacing the offending materials with cleaned-up editions closer to what is today (sometimes over-optimistically) described as *Urtext*. The most up-to-date edition is, however, often Bärenreiter, yet this is by no means universally in circulation, primarily because, being mostly available only on hire, it is not in the orchestras' libraries.

Where Haydn is concerned, the researches of the American scholar H. C. Robbins Landon have for the greater part discredited the previously accepted Breitkopf materials, although the far less well-prepared substitutes are distinctly unpopular with orchestras and need re-marking with the necessary bowings, phrasings and dynamics, all carefully removed by the new publishers, the so-called *Haydn–Mozart Presse*, in pursuit of authenticity. In the case of Mozart, a huge voluminous and vastly expensive Neue Mozart Ausgabe, published once again by Bärenreiter, has, for the last thirty years, been slowly building with the aim of replacing the standard Gesamtausgabe (also Breitkopf). This latter, beautifully prepared during the last decades of the nineteenth century, but still ubiquitous, is sadly unreliable and – as with Bach – subject to wholesale editorial emendations in the parts to the point where they no longer correspond with their own scores.

Beethoven, Schubert and Schumann are less of a problem, although the once very cheap Peters scores differ in many textual respects from the standard Breitkopf. These differences are also reflected in the various editions of miniature scores, primarily Eulenburg and Philharmonia. Schumann and Brahms, too, are normally played from Breitkopf materials, the latter especially so, since for part of the period of their publication, Brahms served on Breitkopf's editorial staff and was thus able to incorporate some revisions of the original Simrock texts. Even so, it is necessary to have some knowledge of the Simrock scores as there are occasionally places where the Breitkopf version proves to be doubtful or even plainly in error.

The Dvořák situation has been broadly resolved since the appearance of the Czech Artia complete edition, but many original materials are still in wide circulation complete with countless errors and questionable readings. Most of Dvořák was published originally – thanks to Brahms's intercession – by Simrock, but odd works were given to other publishers such as Bote & Bock (*Scherzo Capriccioso*) and, unexpectedly, our own Novello (Symphony No. 4, now known as No. 8).

One might expect a parallel state of affairs with Tchaikovsky, but the Russian complete edition – exclusively in Russian with Cyrillic characters – has naturally failed to reach so wide a market. As is the case with all Soviet publications its availability has also been distinctly sporadic. Nor has the bowdlerization for political reasons of works such as *1812* or the *March Slav* endeared the edition to Western orchestras. Most of Tchaikovsky was published originally by Jurgensen, or their Western associates such as Rahter (in Hamburg) or Forberg (in Leipzig) and it is these names that are often to be seen on Tchaikovsky materials. Breitkopf did publish several popular orchestral works in later years as they came out of copyright but unfortunately experimented with, for example, the *Pathétique* Symphony, Smetana's *Vltava*, etc., by giving simultaneously incorporated versions for salon orchestra superimposed on the originals (see ARRANGEMENT).

Mahler's symphonies also present hosts of problems, mainly on account of the revisions to which they were repeatedly subjected. The situation is less bad than it used to be since the appearance of the collected edition edited by Ratz (though this is less reliably authentic than is widely supposed), but many of the works are distributed in reprints by the American Kalmus edition, which, while often invaluable, unfortunately fails to ensure that the text it is reproducing is the correct one, frequently with disastrous results.

Kalmus offers an enormous catalogue of orchestral materials, which are becoming internationally ever more prevalent, but it is always necessary to be alert for unexpected shortcomings. Horn parts may be no more than rough hand-written substitutes; the strings parts may be of one version of a work, the wind of another, and so on.

French and Italian materials are notorious for their waywardness, the orchestral parts differing from the scores to which they belong in a mass of important detail. Many of the repertoire works controlled by such publishers as Durand and Salabert in France (the latter having since the last war swallowed up a variety of smaller publishers such as Rouart Lerolle, Deiss and many others), or Ricordi and Sanzogno in Italy are still in copyright and can be obtained only on hire. In Europe works remain the copyright possession of their publishers until fifty years after the death of the composer; America has quite different laws, but scores and parts imported into Europe of works still protected here are in fact illegal and can be liable to seizure and destruction if detected.

Of necessity this has been no more than a brief survey of an enormous subject, the intricacies of which could be recounted at interminable length: the thorny question of Bruckner's symphonies in *Urfassung*; Sibelius abandoning Breitkopf for Lienau and then Hansen, yet frequently returning for short periods; the great dispute between Universal and Boosey & Hawkes after the war, with its effect on composers such as Delius and Kodály; Strauss's move to Fürstner after a long period with Joseph Aibl, a small publishing house which was subsequently taken over by Universal, although curiously enough most of his tone-poems were bought by Peters; the unique case of the three versions of Stravinsky's *Firebird* Suite, and so on.

Some knowledge of editions is thus not only essential but endlessly fascinating, especially perhaps as the scene is ever changing, ever developing.

ELECTRIC GUITAR

This is a modern species of guitar imported from the popular-music world. It appears in contemporary works as widely differing in character as Stockhausen's *Gruppen* and Tippett's *Knot Garden* together with its parergon, *Songs for Dov*.

The feature of the electric – as distinct from the classical – guitar is that there is no pretence of natural resonance; the belly of the instrument is not hollow but a solid block. The sound of the plucked strings is conveyed entirely by ELECTRICAL AMPLIFICATION, which can reach formidable proportions in the hands of an over-enthusiastic performer. As a result its artificial sonorities tend to be over-obtrusive and this, together with the inescapable evocation of its origins in 'pop', have so far restricted its adoption as a valid addition to the orchestral spectrum in art music.

Like the classical guitar the electric instrument normally has six strings, but an immense number and variety of machines are in circulation including monsters with as many as twelve strings on a double body. The notation is also unchanged, sounding an octave lower than written in the treble clef.

ELECTRICAL AMPLIFICATION

This artificial method of bringing into favourable balance very soft-voiced instruments is not without its perils and disadvantages. It is most usually assumed to be necessary for harpsichord or guitar concertos, now that these are readily put into programmes with symphony orchestras in the largest concert halls. Yet, apart from the unnatural quality electrification lends to the tone of these instruments, such boosting destroys their true delicate quality and belies the intimate chamber-music element that is integral to their very nature.

It is perhaps relevant that, even though electrification of the guitar has led to the invention of an instrument that simply has no independent unamplified existence whatever, the acoustic or classical guitar is still not normally amplified when used as an orchestral colour (as in the second *Notturno* of Mahler's Seventh Symphony), since electronic interference always invites associations or comparisons with the ELECTRIC GUITAR, which is in fact a different animal with a character of its own.

One highly interesting and successful example of electrical amplification as a means of artificially controlling balance occurs in Harrison Birtwistle's *The Triumph of Time*, in which both the solo saxophone and vibraphones are instructed to use an 'air-microphone, the volume being controlled by the player'. Properly handled this produces a truly terrifying effect.

The reciters in Walton's *Façade* are also customarily boosted electrically today, although this has proved somewhat less satisfactory and more prone to disastrous distortion than the original intention of projecting the voices through a megaphone or loudhailer.

In principle, however, the aim with amplification is to introduce it so subtly that the listener is unaware of it, and it is with this pious intention that CONCERT HALLS themselves are now sometimes equipped with electronic devices in order artificially to improve their resonance. Indeed it has become generally accepted that whenever major problems of balance occur, whether with single instruments such as the harpsichord in large concert halls or with whole orchestras in open air venues such as Kenwood or the Hollywood Bowl, electrical amplification of some sort is an unavoidable evil.

Electronic pitch machine, *see* A

EMBOUCHURE

This is the word wind players use when referring to the mouth formations of different types required for blowing. Embouchures can be endlessly varied according to the person's thickness of lips, sensitivity of the muscles, especially at the corners of the mouth, and the regularity – or otherwise – of the front teeth. Thus a musician may occasionally be seen playing with the instrument off-centre, in extreme cases even right over at the corner of the mouth. Brass players will frequently adjust their embouchure according to the register of a passage, and for extremely low notes play well inset – that is, with the mouthpiece actually inserted into the flesh of the lower lip. But for some players a slightly inset embouchure is a normal style of application.

In the course of developing an expertise on a wind instrument a player establishes his embouchure within quite narrow margins. Hence if he has the misfortune to have a sore at that place, or otherwise cut or damage the part of his mouth where he is accustomed to apply the instrument he cannot simply transfer the instrument to another place on the lips and carry on as before. Equally, players are loath to comply with requests to play in exotic styles (such as BELLS UP) that interfere with their normal embouchure, even though within a certain margin such styles need not be totally incapacitating.

See also: LIP TRILLS, PEDAL NOTES

Enclume (Fr.), *see* ANVIL

ENCORES

Unlike the unprogrammed encores that by tradition constitute a major part of solo vocal or instrumental recitals, orchestral encores remain essentially restricted to the special occasion: a visiting orchestra, particularly one travelling from abroad; the eagerly awaited appearance of an international celebrity conductor; perhaps the first or last night of a season. On these or similar festive occasions the conductor may turn again to the orchestra and launch them into an extra, generally unannounced, item, which – it should be remembered – cannot be spontaneous or impromptu as with a solo performer, but will need to have been pre-rehearsed and the material put into the players' folders in the calculated expectation of such an eventuality. However, the skill (it should go without saying) lies in making it seem unpremeditated, and this involves shrewd calculation in timing, for an encore given too soon is unearned and contrived.

The choice of a suitable encore for a full orchestra at the end of a fully fledged symphony concert is, of course, another matter for the exercise of careful judgement. It should be substantial enough to be worth adding to the already completed programme, but by no means long; it can be a brilliant display piece, but a magical soft encore can make a most moving effect; it may be familiar, but may be the more successful if it is wholly unknown, particularly if it is of outstanding interest. Beecham was for a time, especially during his latter years, a master in this field, playing encores of all types and descriptions on the most unlikely occasions, and thus introducing unsuspecting audiences to some of his favourite 'lollipops', culled from the minor works of composers as disparate as Gretry, Delius, Sibelius, Berlioz, Massenet and countless others.

The encore can, of course, be a simple repetition of the last-played item, or the last movement of such an item. If the last work is suitable this can serve well enough to satisfy the unexpected demands of an audience so enthusiastic that last-minute arrangements to play again could hardly in all courtesy by avoided. But Leopold

Stokowski's replaying the entire choral 'Resurrection' section of Mahler's Second Symphony was always thought an outrageous eccentricity.

One further encore element within the ethos of the symphony concert needs to be added: this is the additional solo item or items played *ad hoc* by a concerto soloist, again usually if he is a popular favourite or a visiting international star performer. Such encores are nearly always played unaccompanied (movements from the Bach solo sonatas are common encore pieces for string players) and are also usually short, no doubt out of consideration for the orchestra – and sometimes for the conductor if he allows himself to be caught – who have to remain as still as waxworks while the encore is in progress.

See also: APPLAUSE, AUDIENCE, NATIONAL ANTHEM

Englisches Horn (Ger.), *see* COR ANGLAIS

English horn, *see* COR ANGLAIS

ENSEMBLE

(1)

This is a rather loose term generally taken to signify a smallish group of instrumentalists of too diverse and irregular a character to be categorized as one of the standard formations. The five assorted players required for Schoenberg's *Pierrot Lunaire*; the seven for Stravinsky's *L'Histoire du Soldat*; the percussion group of Varèse's *Intégrales*; these can be classified only as 'ensembles'. It could, of course, be argued that a string octet or the wind groups of Mozart's serenades can equally be described as ensembles, but the fact is that the word is rarely used in title headings and never when a more conventional formation description can be used instead.

Moreover, the larger the group the less applicable the term becomes. The chamber group of Stravinsky's *Dumbarton Oaks* Concerto might just qualify but not a fully fledged chamber orchestra, let alone a symphony orchestra of whatever size.

(2)

The word ensemble is also used in orchestral rehearsing to denote 'together-ness'. Thus bad ensemble playing among the strings of an orchestra, or between strings and wind, wind and percussion, etc., simply means lack of precision in playing together. It should not be supposed, however, that this necessarily reflects on the concentration or quality of the musicians. Perfect ensemble may be the result of an orchestra working constantly together, or repeatedly under the same conductor, until a kind of sixth sense is developed that results in miracles of ensemble playing; wind chording, precision in string *pizzicati*, flexibility in the niceties of rubato, and so on. The players learn to sense one another's timing as well as how to react to the conductor's beat, which may not always be a paragon of clarity. The legion of tales surrounding Furtwängler, for instance, one of the most profound of interpreters but with a proverbially shaky beat, is evidence of an orchestra's ability to achieve an incredible unanimity of ensemble through training over a period with a consistent personnel in circumstances that might seem improbable to say the least. One of the most curious and widely commented upon aspects of corporate behaviour is the tendency among some of the best-trained international orchestras to achieve unanimity of ensemble while playing consistently behind the conductor's beat; yet any attempt on the part of a visiting maestro, with other ideas and style, to interfere with this often disturbing but irrevocably ingrained method of response, can have only disastrous consequences.

The truth is that fine ensemble work remains an elusive art, sought after by every orchestra and every conductor yet either achieved instinctively or equally inexplicably sought in vain. Exasperated leaders deride the wind players, saying, 'Why can't they simply play at the bottom of the beat?'; the wind justifiably blame the strings for always playing late; the percussion and the brass attack each other for faulty rhythm and so on; but when as so often the miracle happens and the orchestra is playing as a single integrated unit, there can suddenly seem no reason why it is not always so easy; for true ensemble playing is, above all, effortless and intuitive.

Éoliphone (Fr.), *see* WIND MACHINE

Etouffez le son (Fr.), damp the strings; *see* HARP, 7

EUPHONIUM

The Chappell reprint of the score of Bax's tone poem *Tintagel*, which inexplicably converts all the names of the instruments into English, oddly translates tuba as 'euphonium'. This further confuses an already highly complicated issue, for there is a school of thought among BRASS *cognoscenti* that virtually equates the terms 'euphonium' and 'tuba'. Common parlance, on the contrary, specifically identifies the euphonium as the heavy, warm-toned B♭ TENOR TUBA whose sonorous voice has earned it a place of solo rank in the military band. For orchestral purposes it is a little too clumsy, especially in the upper register, to serve for the occasional tenor tuba parts that appear in the orchestral repertoire, such as in Strauss's *Don Quixote* or Holst's *The Planets*. Schoenberg's *Variations*, Op. 43, for wind band, which has parts for both euphonium and BARITONE (one of the other alternative instruments of comparable range and size, and also built in B♭) gives all the more athletic work to the baritone. The euphonium is thus not really an orchestral instrument at all – its substitution in Britain for Mahler's Tenorhorn in the Seventh Symphony is always an uncomfortable experience – but it reigns in glory in the worlds of the military or brass bands.

Fiatia (It.), *see* WOODWIND, 1

FIDDLE

This is a secondary English term for the violin, being either purely colloquial or having connotations of folk-song or country dancing, but in any case being outside official orchestral vernacular. Nor does it find any place in printed scores other than in the highly idiosyncratic works of Percy Grainger. Grainger made a strong bid for anglicizing all orchestral terminology (*crescendo molto* being rendered as 'louden lots') as part of which the violas in his scores were even called 'middle fiddles'. The undeniable quirkiness of this, however, meant that he was to have no followers.

Orchestral players do, nevertheless, refer to the first and second fiddles in discussion among themselves, and the term is therefore in this sense by no means archaic.

The word is obviously derived from the German *Fiedel* but this is even more specifically folky (as in Mahler's *wie eine Fiedel* to describe the macabre country fiddler in the scherzo of his Fourth Symphony). The colloquial German term is rather *Geige*, and it is the latter that can occasionally be seen in scores, especially those by Schoenberg.

Fiedel (Ger.), *see* FIDDLE

Flageolet (Fr.), *see* HARMONICS, 2

Flautato (It.), *see* BOWING, 9

Flauto (It.), *see* FLUTE

Flauto dolce (It.), *see* RECORDER

Flauto piccolo (It.), *see* PICCOLO

Flautone (It.), *see* ALTO FLUTE

FISARMONICA

Although normally Fisarmonica is usually the standard Italian word for the ACCORDION, or equally its little cousin the CONCERTINA, the term is widely used in Italian opera houses to signify a very small HARMONIUM used to give the pitch to offstage singers or choruses. Its tone is so small that the instrument can be used without fear of being heard in the auditorium.

One example of its being specified in a score can be found in the 'Prologo in Cielo' (Prologue in Heaven) from Boito's *Mefistofele* where it supports a chorus of cherubs. It is specifically marked 'to sustain the boys' intonation', undoubtedly a wise precaution.

FLEXATONE

This funny little gadget would hardly come within the orbit of even the wide-flung orchestral kitchen department but for the important repertoire works that contain parts for it – works as disparate as Schoenberg's *Variations for Orchestra*, Op. 31, the Khachaturian Piano Concerto and Křenek's jazz opera *Jonny spielt auf.*

While hardly extensive in either scope or range, within these limitations it is none the less irreplaceable. The curious penetrating whine it produces is created by rapid oscillation of two little wooden knobs at the end of thin flexible strips against the broad curving metal plate, whose curvature – and hence pitch – is controlled by the thumb. This effect cannot be simulated by any other means except possibly by the Ondes Martenot or the musical saw; but the latter is orchestrally unknown, and the Ondes, being electronic, bring a new element into the sound pattern that is an ethic apart.

The flexatone is notated at pitch: Khachaturian's solo is melodic in style

and ranges from

Schoenberg takes it a third higher to top B natural. Schoenberg also writes somewhat unrealistically with bursts of widely spaced sounds that are hardly obtainable to any degree of accuracy with such abruptness.

FLICORNI

These are Italian band intruments roughly corresponding to the SAXHORN range. They have no true orchestral existence, but make brief appearances in Italian works such as Respighi's *Pines of Rome*, which add such supernumerary brass to an already generous instrumentation. Respighi calls for six flicorni to act as replacements for ancient Roman **Buccini**, specifying soprano, tenor and bass flicorni.

This is no more than one among many examples of national variation in the evolution of brass instruments, the conventional instruments closest to Respighi's stated requirements being the FLÜGELHORN and SAXHORNS of different pitches and sizes, although their tone quality would surely be too mellow and 'tubby' for the brilliant brass instruments of the Roman Consular Army that Respighi is trying to conjure up from the mists of antiquity.

Flöte (Ger.), *see* FLUTE

Flügel (Ger.), grand piano; *see* PIANO, 1

FLÜGELHORN

This is a kind of super-cornet, also pitched in B♭ (like the standard cornet) and with a still mellower tone. It is sometimes grouped among the saxhorns, but whether or not it originated from this family it has only a limited relationship with them today. The Italian equivalent for the Flügelhorn is *flicorno soprano*, while the French, rather confusingly, is *contralto bugle*; indeed this is what Stravinsky calls the instrument, only adding 'Fluegelhorn' in brackets, when scoring for it in *Threni*. He had, moreover, already intended to use '2 bugles' in the original (abandoned) orchestral version of *Les Noces*, presumably intending Flügelhorns here as well. D'Indy writes for two so-called 'bugles' in his opera *Fervaal* and these are certainly small members of the saxhorn family. The English use of the word BUGLE, however, conjures up quite different associations; in fact our name for the Flügelhorn is palpably of German origin – hence the F and the umlaut, which is always used in scores, contrary to the expressed view in *Grove 5* that it is obsolete.

In Britain the Flügelhorn is primarily a brass-band instrument, where the player is a soloist; on the Continent, on the other hand, it is a standard military-band instrument corresponding to our band use of cornets. The Flügelhorn has nevertheless made a few striking guest appearances in the symphonic field: in Vaughan Williams's Ninth Symphony, Tippett's Third and in particular Mahler's Third where, even though the revised score oddly renames it 'Posthorn', the long off-stage solo passages continue to be regularly played on a Flügelhorn

Stravinsky, in a footnote to *Threni*, cites the range of the Flügelhorn as

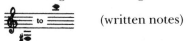 (written notes)

although in the event he only uses

 . Actually it covers

much the same compass as the cornet. Vaughan Williams uses most of this range, although he is cautious enough to use the upper notes only in fully orchestrated passages. The totally ex-posed Mahler Third solo is easily the most elaborate of symphonic Flügel-horn solos and takes the very exacting part up to top B, which for this instru-ment, much more than for either cornet or trumpet, is – and sounds – a very high note.

The Flügelhorn is not used muted, nor are rapid figurations written for it; it is essentially a melodic instrument and is imported into the orchestra purely on account of its mellow singing tone.

FLUTE

The flutes are the uppermost in the WOODWIND department and unique in that they are not reed instruments but blown across a hole in the head-joint. This belies the popular fallacy that the term 'woodwind' refers to the reed itself.

There are three members of the family in common use in the orchestra of which the flute itself is the central figure. Of the others the PICCOLO is

much smaller and higher, while the larger, deeper variety is variously known as the BASS FLUTE OR ALTO FLUTE.

Apart from some older military band instruments, the flute has never been a transposing instrument and is always notated at concert pitch. It also uses only one clef, the G–treble clef, apart from a few early scores in which – as in the famous Bach aria 'Sheep may safely graze' – a different and now obsolete G

clef is sometimes used (🎼).

The names of the flute are similar in the different languages (French, **flûte**; German, **Flöte**, Italian, **flauto**) al-though there are a few variations in those of the subsidiary instruments.

Where range is concerned, this is

normally given as 🎼, but this is

by no means the plain and simple fact of the matter. In earlier years composers rarely wrote higher than top A even if it meant distorting a melodic phrase, but in due course the upper limit came increasingly to be extended not merely to C, as stipulated in so many or-chestration manuals, but to top D. Prokofiev's repeated use of that note in his *Classical* Symphony, being notorious (though it is not a particu-larly difficult note). Officially middle C remains the flute's bottom note, but at the same time a very important part of the repertoire takes the low B for granted and players are usually avail-able who possess instruments bearing the special foot-joint necessary to supply this extra note, even though some make a stand against it on the grounds that it puts the rest of the flute out of tune.

The low B makes its appearance in scores as early as the Intermezzo from Mendelssohn's *A Midsummer Night's Dream*, while in the late romantics it is so common that it can be distinctly awkward to encounter a flute section in which not one has the necessary extension. There are even low B♭s in the repertoire, as in Balakirev's First and Mahler's Fifth Symphonies; but important as these particular examples are, low B♭s are rare, fortunately since this note is impossible on present day instruments and the only way to ensure it is for a member of the section to carry an alto flute for the purpose.

As the only reedless woodwind instrument, the flute has a gentle purity of sound that, especially in the lower register, can err on the side of breathiness. There are strongly opposed schools of thought on the 'right' quality of flute sound, ranging from a firm but slender tone to a warm, rich – even 'fat' – sonority. The slender style of flute tone is often thought to belong to the French school of playing, and one recalls the kind of lithe quality inherent in the extended solo from the Second Suite of Ravel's *Daphnis et Chloé*. Yet even so essentially French a passage as the opening of Debussy's *Prélude à l'Après-midi d'un Faune* is far from unsuitable for the rich tone at one time characteristic of flute playing in Britain, a sound derived from the German school.

In the lower register variety of flute tone is shown to particularly good advantage and can actually come surprisingly close to the timbre of the trumpet, though of course it lacks the power of the brass instrument. The Russian school reveals a penchant for this orchestral colour and Tchaikovsky, for example, often writes for two or even three flutes in unison at their low register, as in the 'Valse mélancolique' from the Suite No. 3, Op. 55, which has a long solo passage for the three flutes treated in this way with remarkable and individual effect.

One outstanding characteristic of the flute is its astonishing agility. The repertoire is full of dazzling cascades of scales and arabesques that exploit this virtue – such as in Strauss's *Till Eulenspiegel*, or Janáček's *Sinfonietta*, whose third movement contains a particularly breathtaking exhibition of virtuosity for a group of unison flutes.

See also: DOUBLE-TONGUING, FLUTTER-TONGUING, GLISSANDO

Flûte (Fr.), *see* FLUTE

Flûte-a-bec (Fr.), *see* RECORDER

Flûte en sol (Fr.), *see* ALTO FLUTE

Flute in G, see ALTO FLUTE

FLUTTER TONGUING

The technique of trilling by rolling the tongue (i.e., pronouncing a continuous series of Rs) is one of the most vivid and spectacular effects of all wind and brass playing. Among the woodwind it is possible for all the instruments but is somewhat less comfortable for the reeds and is therefore on the whole more often prescribed for the flutes, of whom it has become a speciality (except for some players who, distinguished artists among them, happen not to be able to roll their Rs), so that it is one of the commonest colouristic effects written for that family.

Although the normal German translation is the straightforward *Flatterzunge* (abbreviated to *Flz.*), Mahler in the finale of his Second Symphony makes the upper woodwind perform what he describes as *Zungenstoss*—literally 'tongue-attack'. But in the circumstances and the way it is notated, this is indistinguishable from the *Flatterzunge* in Mahler's other works. A parallel term is also used by Strauss for the sheep imitations in Variation 2 of *Don Quixote*. Here, in a footnote, he directs that the wind tremolos must be executed by means of *Zungenschlag* ('tongue-stroke'). Elsewhere in the work, however, he too uses the conventional *Flatterzunge*.

Yet, whereas it does not seem likely that Strauss and Mahler seriously intended any differentiation of technique by the use of these various terms, that may not always be true of other composers. The Romanian composer Anatol Vieru in his Cello Concerto has written both flutter-tonguing and tremolo for the flutes as separate and contrasting effects, although it remains doubtful exactly what he had in mind when he prescribed *tremolo non frullato* for a passage shortly to recur identically but now marked **frullato**. In double-reed instruments the effect is produced at the back of the throat.

Frullato is indeed the Italian equivalent of flutter-tongue, while the French is usually **trémolo dental**, though Ravel describes it as *vibrato* in the Prelude to the ballet version of *Ma Mère l'Oye*. Tippett indicates *Flatterzunge* for the flute at the beginning of the *Adagio* of his Second Symphony, but in the tempo given at the head of the movement this is actually too slow for a true flutter-tongue and there are subsequent indications that the repeated notes are intended to be measured, and hence separately tongued.

Flutter-tonguing is also common practice among the horns and heavy brass. The second movement of Janáček's *Taras Bulba* gives a striking instance of trumpets flutter-tonguing over a sustained period, while Strauss used four trombones flutter-tonguing to horrific effect at the moment Barak's wife sells her shadow in *Die Frau ohne Schatten*. Milhaud even provides a rare example of a solo tuba flutter-tonguing (*enroulant la langue*, he writes) in his formidable *La Mort d'un Tyran*. But perhaps the most extreme instance is where Britten, in the 'Dies Irae' section of his *Sinfonia da Requiem*, makes all the wind and brass flutter-tongue together *fortissimo*.

See also: DOUBLE-TONGUING, LIP TRILLS

Fouet (Fr.), *see* WHIP

FREE BOWING

Free bowing can be a device in its own right, usually in the pursuit of greater intensity of tone, but also for notes or phrases to be sustained beyond the possibility of a single bow.

However, so interested did Leopold Stokowski become in the effects of encouraging every player to give the fullest possible tone that he took the step of training the strings of his Philadelphia Symphony Orchestra to change the bow whenever it best suited each player's personal style. In doing so he deliberately turned a blind eye to the resultant drop in unity and discipline of phrasing, as well as to the untidiness of appearance on the platform, which is of course partially linked with unanimity of ensemble. For this reason Stokowski encountered considerable opposition when he tried to enforce this total freedom of individual bowing on players of other orchestras not accustomed to such unusual methods. It may not be a satisfactory general principle, yet its occasional adoption can still benefit many places in the orchestral repertoire – as, for example, in long melodic passages where the illusion would be created of one single unbroken phrase.

French horn, *see* HORN

Frog, heel of bow; *see* BOWING, 2

Frosch (Ger.), heel of bow; *see* BOWING, 2

Frullato (It.), *see* FLUTTER-TONGUING

Frusta (It.), *see* WHIP

FULL ORCHESTRA

This is a term generally taken to denote the complete array of string players with double or triple woodwind, some four horns plus an impressive array of brass including trombones and tuba, a timpani with extra percussion of assorted species, harp(s), and so on. It corresponds broadly with the French *grande orchestre* or the German **grosses Orchester** – but with the German term serious problems arise.

During the nineteenth century *grosses Orchester* came to signify something far more specific than even Beethoven understood when he for the first time used the term for his Ninth Symphony with its trombones and Turkish percussion ensemble. By the time of Brahms, as Donald Tovey pointed out in one of his celebrated *Essays in Musical Analysis*, it required no more than a pair of trumpets and timpani for an orchestra to qualify as *gross* and hence Brahms described his First Serenade in D, Op. 11, as being for *grosses Orchester* and his Second in A, Op. 16, for *kleines*, since the latter lacked these particular instruments.

Normally, however, it is assumed that *grosses Orchester* indicates the addition of, at least, trombones and tuba, even though strictly speaking one might expect no more than the trombones for the term to qualify, as the symphonies of Schumann and Dvořák show. Hence it is surprising to find the smallest of Mahler's giant symphonies, No. 4, which alone eschews altogether the use of trombones (although it is expensive in extra woodwind), still described as being for *grosses Orchester*.

See also: AUGMENTATION, CHAMBER ORCHESTRA, ENSEMBLE, ORCHESTRA

FULL SCORE

This is the complete chart of what every instrument plays in an orchestral work, the term 'full score' corresponding with the German *Partitur* or the French *partition* (the Italian is similar: *partitura*). Scores are usually laid out either according to the convention of the time, or the views of the composer, or even sometimes the house style of the publisher. There are thus innumerable variations, but broadly speaking the most common format is for the woodwind to be placed at the top of the page, followed, in descending order, by the horns, brass, percussion, harp and/or piano, etc., soloists (vocal or instrumental), and with the strings at the bottom.

The full score is, apart from being a documentation of the composer's work in comprehensive form, above all the working equipment of the conductor in preparation for performance, laying out clearly what each individual player or singer contributes via his orchestral part or vocal score. It can come in all dimensions, from monster scores of very opulently orchestrated works, through the more usual quarto size, exemplified by the familiar Breitkopf & Härtel editions, to quite modest octavo scores, in which form many works by, for example, Dvořák and Tchaikovsky first saw the light of day.

There are also 'miniature scores', known as 'pocket scores' especially on the Continent: *Taschenpartituren* or *partitions de poche*, although the French also frequently call them *partitions en 16*. It is often thought that one of the main differences between miniature and full scores is that in a miniature score the instruments not participating on any single page are omitted altogether, instead of being shown with rests, thereby allowing longer stretches of the music to appear laid out in 'systems' above and below one another. Even as experienced a musicologist as Percy Scholes was sufficiently misled to castigate miniature scores on this count. In fact the same is equally true of most full scores, even though there are undoubtedly a few editions that do print the whole orchestral layout throughout, such as the Peters full scores of the Beethoven symphonies, and including, curiously enough, some early miniature scores. Many in the Donajowski range, precursors of Eulenburg, were printed in this way. Moreover, some pocket scores made by various publishers of their copyright works have always been straight reductions of the full scores.

There has never been a hard and fast custom in this respect even with the composers themselves: Beethoven, Brahms, Tchaikovsky, Dvořák, Strauss all laid out their scores in full, whereas Wagner – a most meticulous autographer – never included in each system more instruments than he expected to need. The remarkable feature here was that when Cosima came to prepare the lined pages of score paper for her Richard to fill in the orchestrations of the *Ring* and *Parsifal*, he knew ahead so exactly what his intentions would be that he was able to tell her how many staves to include in each system, page by page.

Since the score represents to the conductor the precise appearance of each player's printed part, as already described, scores were once always laid out with TRANSPOSING INSTRUMENTS shown unaltered, that is, as the player would read them, the Bb clarinet parts being in Bb, the horns in F, etc. Prokofiev was one of the first composers to rebel against this, writing – and insisting on his publishers printing – all his scores entirely in concert pitch, with a brief note at the beginning to say how the players' own parts are transposed. Thus the horns representing the wolf in *Peter and the Wolf* appear to be growling away in the bass clef until one realizes that in reality they are reading a fifth higher in their comfortable middle register.

With the coming of Schoenberg and the atonal schools the adoption of this new system of score presentation quickly gathered pace. Schoenberg himself was an ardent reformer in this respect, taking the first plunge with a vengeance in his *Vier Orchesterlieder*, Op. 22, which appeared in a so-called 'simplified study and performance score'. This was in fact no more than a glorified 'particell' – a composer's working short score – with all the instruments grouped together on only a very few staves crowded with identification symbols. Rather than 'simplified', however, this proved virtually indecipherable and Schoenberg then expanded his idea in an attempt to standardize a format in which wind and strings were separated but still grouped together within their own families on only three staves each for the upper, middle and lower members. The published scores of both the Violin Concerto and the opera *Moses und Aron* were laid out in this way but it too was a failure for practical reasons of quick legibility in complex structures, as well as impeding the subtlety of the composer's own orchestral colouring. Another misguided venture in score 'simplification' lay in introducing only

fragments of the staves themselves and largely dispensing with clefs as instruments appear and disappear. Most of Stravinsky's latest works were printed in this maddening way (much against the better judgement of his publishers) as is Hans Werner Henze's opera *Elegy for Young Lovers*, but fortunately this utterly confusing experiment has also fallen into disuse.

The fashion for casting the score entirely at concert pitch has, however, continued to gain a firm universal foothold among contemporary composers, even though some of the arguments in its favour might be considered tenuous. But so far, the full scores of the vast bulk of repertoire orchestral music continue to be published in the old familiar conventional form on which the conductor depends for quick and efficient working with his orchestra.

See also: COPYISTS, EDITIONS, LIBRARIANS, ORCHESTRAL MATERIAL, PARTICELL, SCORE LAYOUT.

Geige (Ger.), *see* VIOLIN

GEOPHONE

Unlike the scientific instrument of the same name, this is an object belonging to the effects department designed purely to evoke the sound of the sea and is used by Messiaen in *Des Canyons aux Étoiles*. While it is curiously realistic, it consists of no more than a drum shell containing lead pellets that revolve as the player rotates the horizontally held container.

Gestopft (Ger.), *see* BOUCHÉ

Geteilt, Geth., Getheilt (Ger.), *see* DIVISI

Gewöhnlich (Ger.), ordinary; *see* BOWING, 3; CYMBALS, 2; TIMPANI, 12

Giù (It.), down bow; *see* BOWING, 7

Glass balls, glasses, *see* GLASS HARMONICA

GLASS HARMONICA

Glass Balls, Glasses, and Other Vitreous Instruments

The glass harmonica is the 'instrument' for which Mozart wrote his *Adagio* and *Adagio and Rondo* shortly before his death. This was in all essentials the **musical glasses** that have in recent years returned to the concert scene through the virtuosity of Bruno Hoffman who performed on a row of glasses variably filled with, or immersed in, water and rubbed with the moistened fingers. This homespun device was resurrected in 1973 by Peter Maxwell Davies in his *Stone Litany*, writing for **wine glasses** in Eb and C.

This, however, is not at all what is required for scores specifying the *Glasharmonika*, or HARMONICA as it is often more briefly described (confusingly in view of its current application to the mouth organ). So many different contraptions have been created to serve the purpose that it is no longer at all certain what composers such as Saint-Saëns or Strauss expected or intended when they wrote for the instrument in the *Carnival of the Animals* and *Die Frau ohne Schatten*

respectively. Glinka wrote an elaborate part for it in *Russlan and Ludmila* that strongly suggests the necessity of a keyboard, and in performance today a CELESTA is usually substituted. This would hardly do for Strauss's opera, which is already scored for no fewer than two celestas in addition to his *Glasharmonika*.

Instruments that either are or have been in existence are widely varied – such as harmonicas consisting of glasses struck through the medium of a keyboard (as described by Cecil Forsyth), or suspended and played with soft beaters in a manner not unlike tubular bells. Certainly either of these would be suitable, as the true harmonica would not, for the *Carnival of the Animals*, which includes *glissandi* and trills. It is perhaps some indication that Saint-Saëns actually describes the xylophone, in a footnote to the score of the *Danse Macabre*, as *un instrument . . . analogue à l'Harmonica*, which suggests that the glass bars of his instrument were laid flat. Sometimes the suspended type of instrument consists of bars made not of glass at all but of soft wood, which gives a similar gentle resonance.

Mozart wrote for the harmonica on two staves, both mostly in the treble clef with a range of (sounding an octave higher). Forsyth cites the ranges of the keyboard instrument as , which is much wider than Saint-Saëns uses, writing only on a single stave, and in fact performances of the *Carnival of the Animals* customarily employ a glockenspiel. In *Die Frau ohne Schatten*, Strauss writes on the two staves like Mozart, but limits himself to slow motifs within a range of

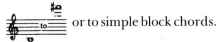 or to simple block chords.

Since many of these have eight notes, the part is played – as at the Royal Opera House, Covent Garden – on two vibraphones. In the event, it is barely audible except for a particularly magical moment, its first entry in fact, at the key point in the opera when the Kaiserin is suddenly granted her long coveted shadow.

Other glass contrivances prescribed by composers include the 'glass balls' of Ernst Toch's Third Symphony and the '4 Glasses (Cristals)' (*sic*) indicated in the *Symphonies de Timbres* by Haubenstock-Ramati. As these were no doubt created either for, or even by, the composers concerned, documentation is lacking here too as to exactly what they meant. Perhaps Honegger's **bouteillophone** – a row of tuned bottles scored for in his *Le Dit des Jeux du Monde* – strictly belongs in this category with a similar question mark attached, since one cannot be quite sure whether they were intended to be struck or blown across as during a Hoffnung concert.

GLISSANDO

This sliding effect (*glissez* in French) is necessarily of widely varying significance both in sound and technique, according to the potential of the many different instruments to which it is applied.

1 Strings

Where the strings are concerned an out-and-out *glissando* is a more extreme form of *portamento*, examples of which are sometimes extended to cover the entire length of the string or even to continue across the strings, though this requires ingenuity on the part of the players to disguise the inevitable cheating necessary to create the illusion of one gigantic sweep, as in Ravel's *La Valse*.

Glissandi present problems of notation, especially when they begin or end in the middle of a bar. In such cases there is no invariable custom and composers differ in their solutions, putting stemless notes in brackets, or bracketed rests, or even noteless stems as Xenakis does in his *Pithoprakta*. Although in the score it seems clear enough what is meant, the part can be quite perplexing to the player who loudly protests that there are not enough beats or notes in the bar.

It is rare to find the speed of the slide in a *glissando* mentioned or indicated in any way. In quick passages such as those extreme examples from Ravel's *La Valse* there is no difficulty, and this kind of quick slither in both directions was a favourite trick of Ravel's, and was taken over by many subsequent composers. But in slower tempi the speed of the slide may become very much a matter of style or judgement, as does the moment during a longer note when the *glissando* should begin. Unless the composer specifies to the contrary, as occasionally happens, it is usually assumed that the slide will start only towards the end – i.e, at the up beat to the end note – to avoid an ugly, grotesque or at worst comical effect.

Nevertheless, in many contemporary works it is precisely the very slow *glissando* that is wanted in the overriding desire to extend the orchestral palette. Avant-garde composers are strangely blind to the truth that the sound is comical and inevitably arouses levity in the audience. Any suggestion of this is apt to be rejected indignantly, yet the danger of hilarity certainly remains and should not be ignored.

Another *glissando* effect is one of PIZZICATO, but undoubtedly the most sheerly magical is the *glissando* of HARMONICS exploited by Stravinsky in *The Firebird*. Britten also extended this idea with particular success in the opening 'Parade' of his song-cycle *Les Illuminations*. The result is one of extreme delicacy, producing by gliding the finger gently over the surface of the string with just the least hesitation at the points where the lower harmonics occur. It can therefore be done only softy, although Ravel, in his *Rapsodie Espagnole*, marks it *mf* and describes it graphically in a footnote: *glissez en affleurant la corde . . .* adding *. . . du côté du chevalet*, i.e. near the bridge, a most interesting but difficult variant.

The *glissando* has less often been exploited in *staccato* since this naturally counteracts the characteristic slither. Nevertheless, Strauss uses a *spiccato glissando* to depict the flowing of gold dust in the ballet *Josephslegende*. His most famous example is, however, for the solo violin in *Till Eulenspiegel* – although this is a borderline case, for the notation is misleading and has more often than not led to a wrong interpretation. For whereas in a true

staccato glissando the player would be left free to play an indeterminate number of notes, in this particular passage Strauss prescribes exactly thirty – i.e, falling into five groups of sextuplets so as to correspond with the bottom of the run, which he notates as two written-out groups of the new $\frac{6}{8}$ bar. The same use of the term can be found in the little violin solo at the end of Rawsthorne's *Street Corner* Overture. In all such examples the passages should be actually fingered without true sliding even though the style and rapidity of execution is undoubtedly imitative of a genuine *glissando*.

2 Woodwind

In this respect the strings, with their ability to play infinite gradations of intonation, have here the advantage over the woodwind, all of whose instruments are constructed with a view to the twelve-note octave and can fake smaller gradations only by means of artificial adjustment of lip or breath. Of the wind it is above all the clarinet who, with a soft reed and dexterous manipulation of the keys, can accomplish a true rising *glissando* over its whole compass – as is proved in the memorable opening bars of Gershwin's *Rhapsody in Blue*. This fantastic show of virtuosity simply does not come into question with the other woodwind, the flute in particular – having no reed – being hardly able to simulate a true *glissando* at all, though some degree of pitch variation can be contrived with the lip. In the 'Songe d'une nuit du Sabbat' from Berlioz's *Symphonie Fantastique* one of the eeriest passages prescribes a *glissando* for piccolo, flute and oboe; in practice none of these instruments can properly be made to depress the note more than a tone at most before the sound drops to the lower octave. Yet such *glissandi* are not infrequently sought, as by Mahler in 'Um Mitternacht', one of the *Rückert Lieder*. Players sometimes try to solve the difficulty by sliding with the use of the keys, somewhat in the manner of the Gershwin, but the result usually comes closer to a quick scale, patently contrary to the desired intention. Yet just how near to the composers' requirements it is possible to come can vary from one player or even one instrument to another, and in the case of the bassoon the results can be surprisingly successful – as Schoenberg showed in the last movement of his *Fünf Orchesterstücke*, Op. 16, which has been known to make a splendid smear.

3 Horns

Horns can produce a tolerable *glissando* by pushing the sound with the lip across the harmonics; it works better upwards than downwards and is hardly viable at anything less than full speed. Typical examples occur, once again in the original score of Stravinsky's *Firebird*, marked 'gliss. dei suoni naturali sul 3 pist.', emulating an earlier instance in Gabriel Pierné's *Les Enfants à Bethléem*, published in 1907. Since Pierné conducted the first performance of Stravinsky's ballet three years later, perhaps it was he who suggested the idea to the younger composer.

Roussel's Third Symphony gives a later (1931) instance, in which his notation with many diatonic notes linking the harmonics show that he was reckoning on more than just open notes. Admittedly by skilful cheating – a combination of a free half-juggling with the valves and flexibility of the hand in the bell – horn *glissandi* can be simulated to a far greater extent than the strictly theoretical account of their technique suggests, though they tend to remain clumsy and inaccurate. Nevertheless by such means even slow and soft *glissandi* can be contrived to cover such requirements as that of the already mentioned instance in Berlioz's *Symphonie Fantastique* where the 3rd horn has to imitate the 'quasi-impossible' downward *glissando*. The fact is that the horn can get nearer to the idea of a continuous smear than the woodwind ever manage. But this is still not a technique normally appearing in the repertoire.

4 Brass

In respect of the heavy brass, whereas the *glissando* hardly exists on trumpets and tuba it is a built-in speciality of the trombone family, with their freely movable slides, and composers exploit it to the full. The most spectacular instance is probably the *glissez fantastico* in Elgar's Overture *Cockaigne*, but a special mention is due to the famous *glissandi* in Bartók's *Concerto for Orchestra* by means of which he derides in no uncertain manner a theme from Shostakovich's *Leningrad* Symphony. Nielson also provides splendid instances in the hardly less notorious 'contemptuous yawns' of the Sixth Symphony (as they are described in a footnote) and the Flute Concerto. The span of the *glissando* is, strictly speaking, limited to the length of the trombone's slide, i.e. the interval of a diminished fifth. Consequently the *Cockaigne* example actually has to be carried off by spectacular faking, as is suggested perhaps by the *fantastico*, since all the intervals are minor sixths.

The *glissando* of the trombone is, curiously enough, a two-edged weapon. So easy to exploit and to accomplish, it is on the other hand difficult to avoid when it is not wanted, as, for example, in very *legato* solos where the notes are adjacent, or in chromatic passages such as occur in the first ('Vorgefühle') of Schoenberg's *Fünf Orchesterstücke*, Op. 16. Where Schoenberg really did want the trombones to play *glissando* he made it absolutely clear, as in a passage in the *Gurrelieder* for alto and bass trombone where he even added a footnote detailing the method of execution, the two instruments sliding to and fro in octaves.

5 Timpani

Since the development of machine drums the timpani have joined the ranks of instruments capable of dramatic or even poetic *glissandi* by means of manoeuvring with the pedal. Nielsen was again among the first to exploit this dramatically in his Fourth Symphony, the *Inextinguishable*, composed in 1916, and Bartók gives countless instances of general *glissandi* on the drums in his *Music for Strings, Percussion and Celesta*, the Violin Concerto (1938) and other works. In these he writes both for *glissandi* executed during a roll as well as by a single ringing stroke that lasts long enough to allow for the slide of the sound without restriking. The pedals are, moreover, accurate enough to halt the *glissandi* exactly on a given note as required. Such *glissandi*

are equally successful upwards or downwards and can even go up and down on a single stroke, though this is rarely called for.

6 Percussion

The other instruments of percussion specializing in *glissandi* are the range of glockenspiels, xylophones, vibraphone and the like, where the hammers can so easily sweep up and down the bars or plates. Probably the most famous example of a glockenspiel *glissando* is in the 'Can-can' of the Rossini–Respighi *Boutique Fantasque*, and of a xylophone (with *glissandi* simultaneously in both directions) in Britten's *Young Person's Guide to the Orchestra*. Britten also contrived, with the aid of that doyen of percussionists, James Blades, a *glissando* on the tubular bells for the opera *The Turn of the Screw*.

7 Harp

The harp is naturally the *locus classicus* for *glissandi*. Indeed, sweeping the hands up and down the harp strings is so obviously dramatic that its over-use by many a composer has been the object of much criticism. Harpists often use both hands for greater sonority but the single line with which it is usually indicated rarely shows whether the composer would have wished for this. In fact harp *glissandi* are variously notated, whether with one of the octaves written out in full to show the tuning required; or with one octave but in two sections, giving half the notes at the top and half at the bottom; or even Holst's instructions, e.g. 'up in 3 beats' – 'down in 2 beats', printed between the single extreme notes of each hand, as in 'Neptune' from *The*

Planets. In such a case, of course, the tuning of the strings is necessarily added by listing all the notes individually by name, viz: A♮ B♯ C♮ D♯ E♭ F♮ G♮.

The direction of the *glissando* can be changed rapidly and this is sometimes featured in dramatic to-and-fro sweeps, such as in the famous *Scheherazade* solo, which, notated by a graphic arrow design, is often over-embroidered by virtuouso players in a style evoking that great master of the instrument, Harpo Marx.

The *Scheherazade glissando* also shows how one of the many pedal settings results, by dint of enharmonic duplication, in the chord of the diminished seventh and this is another very useful way of exploiting the *glissando*. Strauss takes it so much for granted that he does not always bother to indicate the tuning method by which it is accomplished but marks the notes with double strokes.

A miscalculation often made in the writing of *glissandi* is in the time required to travel from one end to the other. Mahler is one of the very few composers to recognize this problem – in the revised version of his Sixth Symphony, he altered the number of beats duration in several instances. For the most part the error is one of allowing too much, rather than too little time, so that the *glissando* becomes too slow to work effectively. Harpists in such circumstances often double over with the other hand, or make little changes of direction in the middle to spend the excess time and yet keep the brilliant speed of the *glissando*, or, simplest of all, add an extra octave to

the limits prescribed. This last may be artistically wrong inasmuch as the change can be audible and, furthermore, assuming that the composer has taken into account the resultant sacrifice in volume, a slow *glissando* may just possibly be what was meant. In such cases the actual appearance of the word *glissando* in the score and part is of primary importance, since otherwise such passages could perhaps be fingered out, i.e. with each note separately plucked.

8 Piano

While hardly less colourful than those on the harp, piano *glissandi* are more limited in their choice since there can be only the diatonic *glissando* on the white or the pentatonic on the black keys. The score will generally indicate which is required but often enough it is obvious. Falla uses both in quick alternation in *El Amor Brujo* and they can even be done simultaneously. In *Lulu*, Berg actually goes one better still and plays all the notes together in block clusters, to depict the athlete Rodrigo. Ives also uses both forearms for a colossal smudge in the last *fff* bars of his *Three Places in New England*, recalling a parallel place in 'Uranus' from Holst's *The Planets* in which an even more monumental cataclysm is prescribed for, of all instruments, the full organ. While actually written as a *glissando*, this is often played, like the Ives example, with the forearms to obtain the maximum sheer power.

Glöckchen (Ger.), *see* GLOCKENSPIEL, 2

Glocken, *see* BELLS; GLOCKENSPIEL, 6

GLOCKENSPIEL

1 Species

Two completely different species of glockenspiel are still in existence: the usual standard instrument consisting of two rows of steel plates mounted so as to correspond with the black and white notes of the piano and played with hammers; and the'keyboard glock' which is a contraption usually with rather limited range and doubtful action but which, having a keyboard just like an actual piano, is capable of a few effects not strictly practicable with hammers.

2 Names

The word glockenspiel, while clearly German in origin, is also used in other countries, though the French have their own **jeu de timbres**, which properly (though not invariably) applies specifically to the keyboard glock. The Italians have their own word, **campanelli**, which does cause occasional confusion with small bells, or **carillon** as Respighi writes in *The Fountains of Rome* – uniquely for him, in order to differentiate from his usual *campanelli* – indicating the keyboard glock, as he here writes figurations hardly possible on the hammered variety. Forsyth gives 'campanette' but I have never seen this in a printed score. Puccini, having previously used 'carillon' or 'campanelli' (**campanelli a tastiera** = keyboard glock in *Madam Butterfly*) reverted to 'glockenspiel' from *Fanciulla* onwards. Curiously Strauss, in *Don Quixote*, writes **Glöckchen** although elsewhere he writes normally for 'Glockenspiel'; possibly he meant to specify some

difference. Kurt Atterberg in his Sixth Symphony writes especially for the keyboard glock (as emphasized in a footnote) designating it, amid his otherwise Italian terminology, as 'timbre'. Debussy and Dukas also use 'glockenspiel', and in *La Mer* Debussy wavers between this instrument and the celesta. *Grove 5* baldly states that Debussy was writing for the keyboard glock (despite the choice of term), but this can only be surmised, possibly on the grounds of the alternative celesta, itself a keyboard instrument. The best and simplest identification of the keyboard glock is, however, where the score describes it as being *avec* – or *à* – *clavier* (Fr.), *mit* **Claviatur** (**Klaviatur**) (Ger.), etc.

3 Keyboard Glock

A number of instances can be found of composers stating that it is the kind of glockenspiel they require – Mahler for his Seventh Symphony, Ravel for *Ma Mère l'Oye*, Dukas for *L'Apprenti Sorcier*, etc. – but partly because keyboard glocks rarely have a compass of more than (sounding two octaves higher) and partly because so few are reliable, percussionists will usually try to persuade the conductor to accept the normal hammer glock even if it entails calling on two players to cover the situation. Sometimes, as in the Mahler, this works well enough, but *Ma Mère l'Oye* as well as various scores by Messiaen such as the *Turangalîla-Symphonie* set such problems that they are really impracticable except with the keyboard instrument. Fortunately some do exist, especially on the Continent, with the necessary three-octave range.

The archetype of the keyboard glock must surely be the one Mozart used in *Zauberflöte* and which we know he played himself. Details no longer survive of exactly what this was, but undoubtedly it would have been a softer-toned affair sounding more like a DULCITONE or CELESTA, which is substituted for it these days.

4 Hammer Glock

Normal hammer glockenspiels have a compass of two and a half octaves:

(again sounding two octaves higher) but composers such as Honegger in his Fourth Symphony (*Deliciae Basiliensis*), or Prokofiev in his First Piano Concerto, Op. 10, write for a three-octave glockenspiel, sounding *one* octave higher. But these instruments are rare, and many players will be found taking the top or bottom notes of a passage up or down the octave in order to bring the part within the range of the smaller set, however much the line may be distorted in the process.

5 Notation

In writing for the *jeu de timbres* Messiaen specifically states that the sound is two octaves higher. This is by no means invariable practice; Wagner certainly writes for the glock to sound one octave higher, and both Mahler and Strauss follow his example, as does Prokofiev. But since other composers very rarely indeed state the octave sound required it can for practical purposes become academic, and pas-

sages will generally be played simply wherever they lie most conveniently for the available instrument. For the conductor or score reader, however, the issue remains a complicated one – and arises not only with the glockenspiel, but equally with the xylophone and vibraphone.

6 Glocken

Dohnányi, who again does specify a transposition of two octaves, also asks in his *Variations on a Nursery Tune* for a second glockenspiel of 'exceptional purity and clarity of sound' which he writes at actual pitch: . He states that this is what he means by the term **Glocken** in order to differentiate from the normal 'Glockenspiel', which he uses in a later variation, but unfortunately it is not very clear exactly what instrument he had in mind, and many players are wrongly led to substitute the tubular bells. The best solution is undoubtedly a vibraphone played without the vibrators.

In the last movement of Sibelius's Fourth Symphony there is another conundrum over the use of the term 'Glocken'. Sibelius is reputed to have said that this was a misprint and certainly the passages are more usually played on a glockenspiel today. But it is more than possible that his intention was indeed for a ring of BELLS such as was signified by the old use of 'glockenspiel' and which should sound as written. It is also significant that when in the tone poem *The Oceanides*, written only three years later, he really did want our present-day orchestral glockenspiel he described this unconven-

117

tionally if accurately, as *Stahlstäbe*.

Like Dohnányi, Orff writes for a large glockenspiel under the designation of **metallofono** in *Catulli Carmina*, using both treble and bass clefs, with a range of .

The chief difference is that the bars are of bronze. Other similar instruments are the **litofono** (or STEINSPIEL) and TUBAPHONE.

7 Techniques

Theoretically, chords (with more than one beater in the hand or hands) and GLISSANDI (the beater swept up or down the bars) are practicable just as on xylophone or vibraphone, but are not written to anything like the same extent as for those instruments.

Trills are a commonplace, though the indication *tr* can be equivocal. With the keyboard glock it can mean across only two notes such as 𝄞 (b or

♮) but with the hammered glock it is ambiguous as it could equally well signify repetitions of the same note.

8 Use of Single Bars

The individual steel bars of the orchestral glockenspiel, being slung only loosely on the frame, can easily be detached and held up for striking. In this way they are sometimes used as a very tolerable substitute for antique cymbals in, for example, *l'Après-midi*, but Hindemith in his *Kammermusik No. 1* actually calls for *Der Stab aus einem Glockenspiel*, meaning that one

bar should be used on its own in this manner.

9 Lyra

In *Enter Spring*, Frank Bridge specifies a **Military glockenspiel** presumably intending the upright **lyre-glockenspiel** as used in bands on the march, but this is not actually used in performance. Strauss in *Panathenäenzug* also uses this instrument, simply describing it as *lyra*.

Gong Drum, *see* BASS DRUM

GONGS AND TAM-TAMS

Consideration of the gong family is confused by the fact that the generic titles are also used for the quite different subspecies. In English-speaking countries the word 'gong' comprises all the various gongs and tam-tams whereas on the Continent the all-embracing term is 'tam-tam' – 'gong' being used only occasionally as a term of differentiation. English dictionaries further confuse the issue by giving 'tam-tam, see tom-tom'; it is maddening that there is actually a grain of truth in this thoroughly confusing and inadequate definition because the African tom-tom is sometimes known ethnically as 'tam-tam'.

Essentially, the difference between gongs and tam-tams (both exist in all sizes) lies in their very shape, and this of course crucially affects the sound they make. True gongs are flat with a broad flange, like the domestic dinner gong in fact, although most orchestral gongs are considerably larger. They will usually give off a more or less definite pitch but in any case they have a well-focused boom. Since they come from the Far East they were, until recently, introduced into the orchestra only for local colour in such works as *Turandot* or Strauss's *Japanisches-Festmusik*, in both of which they are written at actual pitch. Vaughan Williams in his Eighth Symphony then deliberately borrowed the *Turandot* set of gongs and amused himself by scoring for them. But Berg, Webern and subsequent composers also called on the 'gong', *hoch* or *tief* (high or low) without specifying pitch, in order to add variety of colour by contrasting it with the more conventional tam-tam.

The tam-tam is of various shapes but in particular lacks the flange of the true gong. Tam-tams can have a widely varying depth of sound according to size, but are always of indefinite pitch (although if struck in the centre, some instruments will give a recognizable bell-like note – Delius, in his *Mass of Life* actually writes a deep Eb for the tam-tam to suggest the tolling of Nietzsche's 'midnight bell'). Tam-tams may be Chinese (and some of the more beautiful have dragons beaten out on their central portions), but also can be Turkish, though unlike cymbals the difference is academic and never mentioned in scores.

The real tam-tam sound is a great wash of shimmering tone which can even swell slightly after the initial impact of a single well-poised blow. In fact to achieve punctuality, especially with a mighty blow, players will often prepare the tam-tam, subtly setting the instrument in motion by rubbing it with the stick ahead of the moment when the roar is required. Too abrupt

a *fff* thwack will also produce a crude metallic quality foreign in most cases to the tam-tam's purpose. It is thus particularly significant that the terrific stroke with which Sindbad's ship sinks at the climax of Rimsky-Korsakov's *Scheherazade* is skilfully marked only a single *f*.

Orchestration books tend to ignore the duality of gongs and tam-tams; certainly many composers write indiscriminately for a tam-tam or gong as if the terms were wholly synonymous when what they actually mean is the deep tam-tam, such as Tchaikovsky in *Francesca da Rimini* or the Second and Sixth Symphonies. Hence the 'gong' in Delius's *Eventyr* is exactly the same instrument as the tam-tam of the same composer's earlier scores; Bax also uses the term 'gong' in his orchestral works, as does Britten, although when adding the dramatic stroke to the climax of the Passacaglia of *Peter Grimes* for the concert version he marked it 'tam-tam', as he did again in the Cello Symphony. The possibility exists, of course, that he really meant two different instruments but this is not borne out either by the musical contexts or by his practice in other works. Even Hindemith unexpectedly calls for a *grosse Gong* in his Violin Concerto in circumstances that make it unlikely that he really meant to differentiate.

Outside the standard orchestral world there are all sorts of different gongs such as Javanese (in Orff's *Antigonae*, where they are called **Buckelgongs**) with a pronounced nipple and accordingly having a particular tone of their own, though they remain more like gongs than tam-tams;

and with the contemporary passion for introducing specialized instruments from every corner of the globe the very similar Burmese gongs have now found their way into the orchestra in the works of Messiaen and his followers. Messiaen himself tends to write for tam-tams as the bass instruments of the gong ensemble, for example, in *Et exspecto*.

Gongs and tam-tams are normally struck with a heavy but soft-headed beater in order to minimize the metallic clang tone. But Strauss in *Macbeth*, and again later in *Elektra*, deliberately seeks just that crudity by instructing the tam-tam to be 'rubbed with a triangle stick', a terrifying effect.

The unchecked sonority of a high-quality tam-tam can persist for a very long time and it is always necessary to consider where it should, however gradually, be damped, especially when the score fails to specify. One inherent danger, not always sufficiently allowed for either by composers or performers, is that repeated strokes can cause the sound to grow to immense proportions, the roll becoming submerged in an all-enveloping mass of resonance. As a result, rhythmic patterns become difficult to discern unless the player resorts to very hard beaters.

Good tam-tams are hard to come by, and it has not been unknown for quite reputable orchestras to make do with what are little more than glorified tea-trays. Hardly less than the timpani, and perhaps to a greater extent than the cymbals, the quality of the tam-tam can be said to reflect the artistic standard of an orchestra.

GOURDS

Maracas and Other Rasps

Since it is from gourds that maracas are originally derived, some confusion is apt to arise when a score such as Copland's *El Salón México* specifies 'gourd'. But in fact the maracas are treated so differently from the gourd family that it is sensible to assume that they are to be used only when actually so specified. Basically the important distinction is that maracas are shaken so that the seeds inside the hollow heads rattle, whereas gourds are rasps scraped with a furrowed stick. Maracas are so essentially Latin American in character that they are mostly used in that context. However, while their rhythmic swishing is naturally indigenous to composers such as Carlos Chavez, Varèse's *Ionisation* introduces them largely because this pioneer adventurer set out to use virtually everything he could think of. Maracas have also been introduced in recent years by Pierre Boulez, who exploits various pitches as well as techniques in *Une Dentelle s'Abolit*.

Copland's gourd is actually first cousin to Stravinsky's *une* **rape guero** (literally 'a gourd rasp'), which makes its brief but notorious appearance in *Le Sacre du Printemps*, the strangeness of which, together with its odd notation, mystified so many of us before such exotics became a relative commonplace. Villa-Lobos's **reco-reco** is another scraper, though he notates it on a single line and without bothering about Stravinsky's up and down strokes, which look so confusingly like bowing marks. Other rasps, though no longer linked to gourds, are **choucalha** or **xucalhos** of either metal or wood, again used by Villa-Lobos (in his *Choros* Nos. 8 and 10) as well as Milhaud's **guicharo** used in *Saudades do Brazil* and *Le Boeuf sur le Toit*. Oddly, in a footnote on the first page of the latter score the composer allows the substitution of sandpaper on a plank, but it is in fact a Latin American metal 'torpedo' scraped with a comb such as is used to produce an Afro hair style. But perhaps the most hilarious is the **râpe à fromage** (literally the homely **cheese grater**) of Ravel's *L'Enfant et les Sortilèges*.

Gramophone, *see* NIGHTINGALE

Gran cassa, gran tamburo or **tamburo grande** (It.), *see* BASS DRUM

Grelots (Fr.), *see* JINGLES

Griff (Ger.), handle of drum stick; *see* TIMPANI, 12

Griffbrett (Ger.), fingerboard; *see* BOWING, 5

Grosse-caisse (Fr.), *see* BASS DRUM

Grosse Ratsche (Ger.), *see* RATTLE

Grosse Rührtrommel (Ger.), *see* DRUMS, 1

Grosse Trommel (Ger.), *see* BASS DRUM

Grosses Orchester (Ger.), *see* FULL ORCHESTRA

Guero, *see* GOURDS

Guicharo, *see* GOURDS

GUITAR

The guitar is a six-stringed wooden instrument not altogether unlike the violin family though simpler in construction, and always plucked directly with the fingers and fingernails, never bowed.

Apart from its special and soloistic operatic use, as in Rossini's *Barber of Seville*, the earliest appearance of the guitar in the symphony orchestra is in the second *Nachtmusik* from Mahler's Seventh Symphony. The fact is that much like the HARPSICHORD but to a far greater extent, the guitar is at a serious disadvantage when being used within, or pitted against, a symphony or chamber orchestra of whatever size. Indeed, although theoretically gradations of expressive dynamics count among the guitar's richest virtues, in practice anything less than the sound of fully spread chords over the six strings of the whole instrument is immediately rendered totally inaudible unless the orchestra is sternly subdued to below a *mezzo piano*.

Generally speaking, in spite of two or three popular concertos, the guitar occupies a world even more of its own than that of the organ, the freemasonry of solo players making careers of pronounced exclusivity solely through the unaccompanied recital. Hence the only very occasional importation of guitar players into the orchestra, initiated by Mahler and the Schoenberg school, has carried with it the hazard that there is a notable dearth of accomplished executants who are geared to the meticulous precision of ensemble playing, let alone experienced in the discipline of subordination to a conductor's beat. A few *routiné* players have now sprung up since a certain demand has been established, but even though the repertoire in which the guitar is required has grown, it still remains relatively tiny and a handful of key players tends to control the market.

When contrasted with the broader spectrum of orchestral sonorities the subtle intimacy of guitar colours, entirely controlled by the player's fingers, is easily lost and players are content to fill in their lines in a simple firm tone quality. At the same time it should be added that these variations of technique are never specified in printed copies but are left to the resourcefulness of the player's own artistry.

The conventional tuning of the guitar is:

and the normal range is between

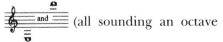

(all sounding an octave lower). The standard notation is on a single stave in the treble clef and sounds an octave lower than written, but Mahler takes it into the bass clef for a passage going down to the low C. Schoenberg, according to his custom from Opus 22 onwards, writes for the guitar in his Serenade, Op. 24, at concert pitch using treble and bass staves and this is also how the player's part is printed; it is accordingly useless and the work is performed from renotated manuscript copies. Schoenberg, un-like Mahler, clearly recognized the standard tuning, as notes lying below E (which he does occasionally include) are put in brackets. He also uses harmonics in his Serenade, Op. 24, which fortunately, being chamber music, makes allowance for the fact that these are, of course, softer still than the guitar's natural voice.

The guitar is normally placed as near to the audience as possible in orchestral layouts to give it the best chance of being heard, but when it comes to concerto work even this cannot overcome its congenital lack of volume in any but the smallest halls. As a result ELECTRICAL AMPLIFICATION has come to be regarded as indispensable, even though this carries with it a not altogether beneficial change of quality as well as the sacrifice of the guitar's essentially intimate character.

See also: ELECTRIC GUITAR

Guitara, quasi, *see* PIZZICATO, 3

HAMMER

This apparently simple term covers a multitude of possibilities. The idea originated from Mahler, who in his Sixth Symphony inserted three hammer blows of fate, the last and most important of which he later deleted out of superstition, as it was to have 'felled the hero' (i.e., himself) 'like a tree'. All he said of its execution was that it should sound like the blow of an axe.

This is, of course, all very well but unfortunately it is somewhat difficult to produce a thud that drowns an orchestra of a hundred and twenty complete with bass drum, timps, etc. It requires, moreover, much ingenuity with regard to what the hammer should strike in order to obtain a deep-toned 'whomp' rather than the high-pitched 'crack' that any hollow platform or box would produce (even if it did not split under the assault). As for the hammer itself, this is usually a large sledge-hammer, since although undoubtedly imposing in appearance, a wooden mallet of whatever size is simply not heavy enough.

Regardless of all these problems, Schoenberg and Berg at once took over the idea in *Die glückliche Hand* and *Drei Orchesterstücke*, Op. 6, respectively. Milhaud also uses a hammer in *Les Choéphores*, but clearly with a different, much lighter effect in mind as he stipulates a plank (*coups de marteau, sur une planche*) and writes a series of fairly rapid strokes in varying rhythms, adding the word *maillets* (literally, 'mallets').

HAND DRUMS

Broadly speaking, this is a generic term for a variety of drums, mostly oriental in origin, that are played with the bare hands and fingers, such as Bantock pressed into service in his *Omar Khayyám*. Other exotic hand drums are the DAIRA, an oriental-Russian variety used by Khachaturian in his *Gayaneh* ballet; the tarbuka, which are used by Berlioz in *Les Troyens* and by Ibert in his *Suite Symphonique* (where they are, however, termed DARBOUKKA), and the Indian **tabla**, which have come into their own with avant-garde composers such as Boulez, Berio, ApIvor and others.

Technically it could be argued that the BONGO/TOM-TOM family also qualify but they are more readily identified by their own names and in their own right. The term 'hand drums' is thus usually applied to the rarer ethnic instruments.

Harfe (Ger.), *see* HARP, 1

Harmonic Series, *see* HARMONICS

HARMONICA

This is a double-edged term, referring either to the GLASS HARMONICA (which is often simply called 'harmonica' or even **armonica**, the name many dictionaries insist is its true one) or confusingly to the mouth organ, whose proper description is no doubt considered too undignified by its virtuosi and devotees. But since the mouth organ has no place whatever within the orchestra (indeed its very appearance on the orchestral platform is limited to a handful of concertos), the ambiguity is not very important.

HARMONICS

1 Harmonic Series
The mainstay of the entire Western art of music has always been, and –*pace* the atonalists and contemporary sonic or electronic experimentalists – is likely to remain, the inescapable scientific truth of the harmonic series. On this is based not only our understanding of the relationships between notes and tonality but the very construction of our instruments. The fact that a note an octave higher or lower still sounds like the same note is not a mere subjec-

tive reaction but a fundamental reality based on the fact that the frequency of vibrations, of string or column of air, is exactly double or half respectively: i.e., in the proportion of 1:2. The perfect fifth, that next truest of intervals, which gives us our so immediately recognizable phenomenon of dominant–tonic relationship and on which the tuning of the orchestral string family is rooted, derives from the relative frequency of vibrations being in the proportion of 2:3, and so on.

The intervals get progressively smaller as the pitch rises, and the formula in simplified terms given, for argument's sake, as it applies to the lowest string of the violin, is shown in the music example below.

No. 1 (the open string in these terms of reference) is called the 'fundamental'; Nos 7, 11, 14 and 15 are marked 'x' because within our scale sytems they sound out of tune, and beyond No. 16 the intervals become smaller than a semitone and therefore lack identity to our ears, accustomed as they are to a twelve-note octave.

2 Strings

Where the string orchestra is concerned the scientific existence of harmonics has far more relevance than the mere tuning of the strings. It makes provision for a whole range of specially obtained notes produced by touching the string lightly at various clearly defined places along its length; the vibrations are split up and dif-

ferent notes, of a white purity, are obtained. The French and Germans call these sounds **flageolet** (abbreviated to *flag.*) since they are indeed flute- or, rather, recorder-like (flageolet being another name for the recorder); but the English term, following the Italian **armonico**, remains 'harmonic'.

Theoretically harmonics are obtained by touching the string half-way, two-thirds-way, three-quarters-way, etc., up its length, but in practice by Nos. 5 or 6 of the series the finger has approached so near to the bridge that these harmonics become rapidly less and less feasible. Nevertheless it so happens that by touching the string lightly in the same way at various other points between Nos. 1 and 2 some of these harmonics also result in an irregular order, viz:

(a) a minor third above the open string sounds two octaves and a fifth above (= No. 6)

(b) a major third above the open string sounds two octaves and a third above (= No. 5)

(c) a fourth above the open string sounds two octaves above (= No. 4)

(d) a fifth above the open string sounds one octave and a fifth above (= No. 3)

(e) a minor sixth above the open string *does not exist* (N.B.)!

(f) a major sixth above the open string sounds two octaves and a third above (= No. 5)

(g) an octave above the open string sounds one octave above (= No. 2)

1 2 3 4 5 6 7 8 9 10 11 12 13 14 15 16

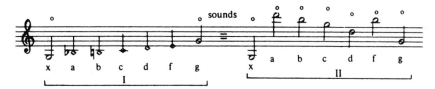

3 Notation

Set out in notation this will appear as shown above (again, by way of example, in relation to the G string).

Here the symbol 'x' represents the open string – i.e., No. 1 of the harmonic series – while g is in fact No. 2 of that same series. For this reason in both I and II they are notated with the usual round notes with an 'o' placed over the top, for it is general practice to write in this way both open strings and such natural harmonics as can be reached (amounting, as is explained above, only to the first few).

But all these notes of II (which sound as they are written) are notated thus not merely for simplicity's sake but because according to one school of thought it is the best way of writing any note required to be taken as a harmonic. The executants are then left to work out which way they may prefer to find the notes on their instruments. It is with this method in mind that Forsyth somewhat rashly wrote that 'the notation of harmonics is simplicity itself'. That it is the very opposite even a superficial exploration of the repertoire will disclose.

This is, however, clearly the least confusing method for the score reader, as it is for the inexperienced composer, although it carries with it the danger of writing impracticable or unrealistic harmonics without perceiving the implications. Certainly it is used in orchestral literature to an appreciable extent, though still mostly to designate what are perhaps misleadingly known as ARTIFICIAL HARMONICS, which consist of an almost infinite range of extra harmonics that can be produced on all the strings including the double-bass.

Altogether string harmonics and their notation represent a problem that virtually every composer has, in the absence of standardization, had to solve afresh – with resultant pitfalls for the score reader, conductor and, not infrequently, the players themselves.

4 Woodwind

It could be claimed that all the woodwind instruments, in theory, are able to obtain harmonics by 'overblowing'. In practice, however, only those of the flute are used orchestrally and even these are a specific series overblown at the twelfth: i.e., while they are written at pitch with an 'o' placed over them – just like string natural harmonics – they are actually fingered a twelfth below. Hence ♪, obtained by fingering ♪ is the lowest of these harmonics ever written in orchestral works. A particularly well-known instance occurs in Daphnis's dance in the first scene of Ravel's *Daphnis et Chloé*. The sound is hollower and can be very telling, though it is not always reliable, especially with regard to intonation. Nor is it in every instance immediately recognizable that one of these harmonics is being played. One clear characteristic is the absence of vibrato in the tone, but it is still sometimes argued that if any difference can be detected it is simply that the result is inferior to a note obtained normally, though to the flute fraternity this is no doubt heresy and unwarrantable cynicism. However, composers do call for these flute harmonics, and Stravinsky in *Pulcinella* goes so far as to give in the score itself an illustrative diagram of the keys and holes showing exactly the fingering he has in mind.

The reason why none of the other scientifically recognizable harmonics on the flute, or indeed any at all on the other woodwind instruments, are written for by composers, is shrouded in technicalities. Walter Piston's excellent book on orchestration goes some way towards discussing the details but even he fails to pursue the issue to the point of a comprehensive explanation relating to all the woodwind.

5 Horns and Brass

With the horns and brass, on the other hand, it is an entirely different story. The main difference between harmonics on horns and brass and those on other instruments lies in the fact that, instead of being a special effect, the pitching of different harmonics is the basic method of production. For, much as the way in which the strings are linked technically to the harmonics of their open strings, so the horns and other brass families are all rooted on the harmonic series of open notes available without the use of valves, or – in the case of the trombones – their slides. Which actual sounds result will, of course, depend on how the instruments are built or, in the case of the older horns and trumpets, how they were crooked. Moreover, there is an analogous practical aspect that has to be taken into account, which is that whereas on the one hand the fundamental tone (No. 1 in the chart above) is hardly available to horns and trumpets other than those in the highest CROOKS, so conversely those above No. 12 become more and more inaccessible to instruments other than those in the lower crooks.

6 Harp

With the harp, however, for which harmonics are also written, these are once again a specific extra colour and technique. They are obtained by stopping the string with the base of the hand while plucking with the thumb of the same hand. Harmonics are normally played with the left hand except for the higher notes which are more conveniently taken by the right. Above

♯ o harmonics become increasingly impracticable as the strings are too short, but Ravel writes up to G in the 'Feria' of his *Rapsodie Espagnole* and Schoenberg even to B♭ in his *Variations for Orchestra*, Op. 31. Equally the bottom covered strings of the harp are quite unsuitable and the lowest for which harmonics are written is in the region of

♭ o , e.g. in the 'Berceuse' from Stravinsky's *Firebird* or in Vaughan Williams's *Pastoral* Symphony, which goes a tone lower and is often regarded by harpists as unrealistic.

The two hands frequently play harmonics together to provide chords and although, owing to the angle, the right hand can play only one harmonic at a time, the left hand is capable of playing two, three or four harmonics within the span of up to a fifth so that four- and even five-note chords can be found entirely made up of harmonics – as again in Ravel's *Rapsodie Espagnole*.

The standard notation for harp harmonics is, once more like the strings and flutes, an 'o' over each note; but the difference is that these notes are written an octave lower than they sound. This is because, being the second harmonic of the series – and no other harmonics are possible on the harp – they always sound an octave higher than the string on which they are played. Nevertheless, needless to say, many exceptions to this notation can be found, which causes immense confusion. Stravinsky wrote the harmonics at pitch in the 'Ronde des princesses' from *The Firebird* but sounding an octave higher in the 'Berceuse' of the same work. Even in scores as late as Bartók's Violin Concerto (1938) the harp harmonics are notated at pitch and in many instances one can decide only by internal evidence at what pitch a passage should sound, as in Mahler's Third Symphony. In Debussy's 'Nuages' from the *Nocturnes* there is merely the indication '8ª bª . . . ' (*sic*) printed over the notes, but reference to the original Froment edition (in which the passage is played in the normal manner) reveals that this is no more than economy on the part of the publishers when preparing the revised score; hence what is meant –

though not stated – is that the passage should be *played* an octave lower, but should sound as written through being taken as harmonics. A recent reprint of the score misrepresents this issue still further.

7 Piano
As for the piano, a method of exploiting what are described as harmonics was invented by Schoenberg and introduced into many works by his pupils and followers. The idea is to put down certain keys so gently that the hammers are not brought into operation: this is indicated by **Tonlos niederdrücken**, or similar words, and these notes are shown with diamond noteheads: clusters of lower notes are then struck very strongly and abruptly damped, upon which the strings of the upper held notes can be heard gently vibrating in sympathy. In chamber music or solo passages the device can be magical, but in orchestral music it has to be conceded that these so-called harmonics are for all intents and purposes inaudible. The same is also true of the carrying power of guitar harmonics – which Schoenberg prescribes but fortunately only in a chamber work, the *Serenade*, Op. 24.

HARMONIE

This is a term used by both the French and the Germans to denote a wind ensemble containing either or both woodwind and brass, sometimes with percussion but usually without strings – or at the most only double-basses. Thus Stravinsky's Piano Concerto of 1923–4, which is scored for just such a combination, is described as being *pour piano suivi d'orchestre d'Harmonie*, and publishers in Germany like Breitkopf & Hartel describe the wind parts of even a full orchestral work as the *Harmoniestimmen*.

HARMONIUM

This is a keyboard instrument with reeds built in a manner not unlike a kind of small domestic organ, the bellows being worked by two large vertical pedals operated by the feet alternately. Therefore although there are a few stops like an organ's to vary the timbre a little, it has obviously no pedal keyboard as the feet are permanently fully occupied with the pumping operation. Moreover, this is in itself an arduous occupation, for if the player's feet stop for anything above an instant the contraption lapses rapidly into voicelessness.

Its name is the same in all languages, the word 'harmonium' even more than the organ conjuring up associations with evangelical functions. It is therefore surprising to discover that, for example, the extended part in the 'Purgatorio' movement of Liszt's *Dante* Symphony or the great solo at the end of Tchaikovsky's *Manfred* Symphony, the latter always in fact pealed out in the fullest registration available on the grand organ, are given in the printed score to none other than the humble harmonium with the organ only as an optional alternative.

Strauss frequently wrote for harmonium as a support for his orchestral wind, either as an off-stage instrument, as in *Salome*, or in the pit as an important and active member of the orchestra itself, as in *Ariadne auf Naxos*. This latter may indeed represent the pinnacle of the instrument's orchestral career, for Strauss took the trouble to set out in detail the stops and colouring he wanted used by the highly complex and developed species he had discovered and was writing for. These instructions, however, never reached the full score but reside hidden in the original edition of the player's copy. However, they have come to be of little more than historical interest, as that specific instrument is now scarcely ever available; nevertheless the interested player is given much guidance as to the kind of sounds intended. In fact Strauss seems to have had an unaccountable affection for the instrument, his celebration offering for the wedding of his son being none other than a *Hochzeitspräludium* for two harmoniums.

It is hard nowadays to find harmoniums of tolerable quality and in any condition of reliability; certainly the usual Moody and Sankey sounds that, with much wheezing and groaning, emerge from the normal run of instruments, hardly fit in with the ethic and atmosphere of a symphonic or operatic performance.

The equivalent of the organ's *grand jeu* is operated by the knee, but the difference is that its effect is dangerously instantaneous in summoning the instrument's maximum volume.

The overall range of the harmonium is usually the five octaves from C below the bass clef to the C an octave above the treble , but the Schiedmayer instrument specified by Strauss for *Ariadne* seems to have extended a great deal lower, for he wrote down to G♭.

Piston states that the harmonium has two manuals, but such instruments are rare, despite Strauss's example in *Ariadne* and Stravinsky's intended use of such a machine in an early abandoned version of *les Noces*; in Britain they are virtually unknown. The harmonium has one patent advantage over the organ, that it is relatively mobile, but it is usually placed as far to the rear of the orchestra as possible since its very bulk is apt to create hazards.

HARP

1 Descriptions

The harp is the foremost in the group of heterogeneous instruments – partly stringed, though not bowed, and partly keyboard – which in the orchestral score lie between the percussion and the main body of the strings.

Where the terms or species of the harp are concerned there are few complexities; all the names in different languages are closely allied and readily recognizable – **arpa**, **harpe**, **Harfe** (to cite the Italian, French and German forms) – and the few variants of the instrument itself, such as the little Irish harp, make no appearance in the orchestra. There is a smaller version of the true full-sized orchestral Gothic or Concert harp, called the Grecian harp, but in all practical details it is the same and is unsuitable for use with full orchestras only because of its relatively small sound.

Unlike the piano, the other most prominent instrument in this section of the orchestra, the harp has separate strings for only the notes of the diatonic major scale. Experiments were once made to create and popularize a fully chromatic harp but, although Debussy's *Danse Sacrée et Danse Profane* was actually written for this very purpose, the instrument proved too cumbersome to secure a foothold. The full chromatic range is therefore achieved by means of **pedals**, each of which controls simultaneously all the octave strings of any one note and in three positions: flat, natural and sharp. Academically speaking the harp is tuned in C♭, and this is certainly the instrument's dormant state with all the notes in flats; but a less confusing way of presenting the matter is to think of the harp as being in C major with all pedals in the central position in naturals.

2 Range

Since the harp has forty-seven strings with a range of six and a half octaves it thus has an overall range of

to

although the topmost F♯ (= G♭) may have to be tuned especially as required because harps lack the pedal mechanism for the highest and shortest string, the top F. Yet in *Das klagende Lied* Mahler actually writes not only the top G♭ as part of a series of rising arpeggios, but the B a third higher still, though this is not normally obtainable on any harp. A similar problem also attaches to the extreme bottom strings, C and D at the opposite end, which have to be manually retuned so that the player has to bring the tuning key into service in order to obtain the extremely low Bb and Db in the third act of Berg's *Wozzeck*.

3 Notation

The standard notation for the harp is similar to that of piano music, i.e., across two bracketed staves with treble and bass clefs, even though early instances can be found laid out on a single line, such as in Gluck's opera *Orfeo*. Exactly as with the piano, however, these clefs can be used freely on either stave as both hands can play in any register even though the lower compass is properly the province of the left hand and the upper that of the right. But harp technique does differ substantially from piano playing, and composers (who are more likely to play the latter than the former) rarely organize harp parts to the satisfaction of the players, who accordingly re-mark the music to suit their own needs.

The same applies to chromatic passage work, with the result that harp parts are generally thick with players' marks, lists of notes, enharmonic alterations or rewritings for the sake of practicality. Some composers, like Ravel, try themselves to work out how the strings need to be organized, usually by listing the seven diatonic notes with the sharps, flats or naturals added to show the pedal positions to be prepared for the opening as well as changes during the course of a work or movement. Yet harpists continue to tackle the problems in their own and personal way.

4 Tuning and Strings

The tuning of the harp is another extremely important part of the player's expertise, and the harpist is always to be seen at rehearsals or performances tuning the instrument long before the rest of the orchestra assembles. Every opportunity is taken during the session to adjust different strings, which are all too apt to go out of tune. Occasionally the upper harp strings can break during rehearsal or performance; yet, annoying as it may be, this is by no means the total disaster it is when a piano string snaps. At the first opportunity the player will whip out a new length of string and an experienced harpist can effect the repair surprisingly quickly. The lower covered strings are more troublesome to deal with but are by their nature far less prone to unforeseeable demise.

5 Use of One or Two Harps in an Orchestra

The introduction of the harp into orchestral literature was at first a very slow and gradual process. Gluck's use of the harp in the second act of *Orfeo* had obvious programmatic purpose where the hero subdues the monsters of the underworld, but this is an isolated early example. Even though the harp had no place in the orchestras of Bach or Handel, it is known that it did sometimes serve as a continuo instrument: hence its usage by conductors such as Beecham for *Messiah* or by Albert Coates for Bach's B minor Mass. This has come to be derided, but it does in fact have historical justification.

It was, moreover, by no means unknown as a concertante instrument. One of Handel's organ concertos (in Bb, Op. 4 No. 6) is commonly known as his Harp Concerto, suggesting that he was writing specifically for an instrument with whose technical requirements he was well acquainted, yet the score cites the harp as no more than one of many solo instruments on which it would be equally valid to perform the work.

Mozart too never scored for the harp except as a solo instrument together with the flute in the C major Concerto (K. 299), and in all Beethoven's orchestral music the harp can be found in only one brief number of the ballet music *Prometheus*. Beethoven's unique introduction of the harp into his orchestra for the ballet should be linked with that of Gluck for the opera, since in those early years of orchestral history harps were found only in the theatre.

That Paris was always in the lead where the harp was concerned accounts for a Frenchman, Berlioz, being the pioneer who scored for harp in his *Symphonie Fantastique* as early as 1830. In keeping, moreover with the resources he was accustomed to finding at the Paris Opéra, Berlioz calls for not one but two harps, writing for them later in other works for the concert hall such as the *Romeo and Juliet* Symphony, his instrumentation of Weber's *Invitation to the Dance* and so on, in all of which he exploits many different and novel harp techniques.

After such appearances the harp quickly took its place in the orchestral scene, though it was still for some time sternly excluded from purely abstract symphonic forms. For instance the harp has no part to play in the symphonic work of that implacable classicist Brahms, who, nevertheless, gave it a most poetic role in his *Deutsches Requiem* and who had in his early years composed the magical *Gesänge* for women's voices, two horns and harp.

Hence César Franck's inclusion of harps in his Symphony of 1888 was regarded as revolutionary, even though by that time the instrument had gained the widest acceptance in programmatic orchestral works. In general it continued to be the French school who remained in the foreground of orchestral harp writing, and it is remarkable how rarely French composers deprive themselves of the instrument, mostly indeed writing for two harps in works for larger orchestras.

In this, however, they were soon not alone. Liszt predictably features the harp in his symphonic poem *Orpheus*, though going one better than Gluck, as it were, by using two; Smetana scores for two harps in *Vyšehrad*, Balakirev in *Russia* and *Thamar*, Sibelius in *The Oceanides*, Strauss in *Ein Heldenleben* and so on. Nor is it only in large orchestras that they are found; Strauss's *Ariadne auf Naxos* numbers two harps among its 35-piece chamber orchestra.

Nevertheless the second harp can often have a curiously discouraging time. In *Otello*, Verdi reserves it for a single short passage in the second act. This is only one of several works where the second harp appears purely as a DOUBLING instrument – others include the finale of Franck's Symphony, the Brahms Requiem, and many works by Rachmaninoff and Shostakovich – or in which it appears primarily in that capacity, e.g. in Elgar's *In the South* and the two symphonies. Yet – especially in the case of Shostakovich – it would be entirely incorrect to regard the use of the second harp as optional.

6 Multiple Harps

The presence of more than two harps is a rare event. Stravinsky produced a curious and isolated example of three harps in the original ballet score of *The Firebird*; Schoenberg's *Gurrelieder* calls for four harps and the score of Mahler's Sixth Symphony specifies four harps though, strange to say, only in one place during the scherzo. D'Indy's *Forêt Enchantée* is ostensibly for eight harps but like the Mahler Symphony there are actually only two different parts and both works are generally played with no more than two. The outstanding example of multiple harps is, of course, Wagner's *Ring*, which is scored for six, each with a separate part, in which he was imitated by Mahler in the original version of *Das klagende Lied*. However, in the recently published material for the (ultimately rejected) first section, 'Waldmärchen', the six harp parts prove to have been redistributed by the publishers exactly like the orchestral material of the *Ring*, so that in practice all the important passages are fully covered when only two harps are used. The purpose of using more than one harp is patently for extra sonority, although, while hardly one of the most powerful of instruments, the harp is capable of considerable penetration in even the fullest orchestral tuttis when used skilfully. Yet beyond two it is curious how little additional harps add to the total weight of tone. I once had the privilege of conducting a work for twenty-eight harps in a concert given by the UK Harpists' Association and was astonished to discover that the benefit of so many of these beautiful instruments lay far more in the varieties of possible textures than in the power or sonority of their massed tone.

7 Length of Resonance

Like the harpsichord, the harp lacks the sustaining pedal that is so salient a feature of the piano. Nor, however, has the harp any device for damping the strings, and left to itself its resonance is very perceptible, even beyond that of the tutti orchestra unless specifically terminated. This is done by using the hands and arms as dampers, and, since in the majority of instances there is no appropriate injunction in scores or harp parts, this becomes an instinctive element in a harpist's style and technique. Moreover, the deliberate curtailing or extension of the harp's resonance is a positive feature of orchestral colouring and the terms **laisser vibrer** (**klingen lassen**, etc.), which are often applied to the cymbals and other percussion instruments, can also be found applied to the harp. The opposite, i.e, the injunction to damp the strings immediately, is **secco** (= dry) or the German *kurz* (= short); the French use **étouffez le son**, which needs to be differentiated ˙from the more extreme **sons étouffés**, requiring a particular technique of damping each string immediately after it is plucked, whereas the former injunction requires the player to use the forearm to stop the vibration of all the strings at once. Another Italian term for this needs to be mentioned: Bartók, following the confusing example in

Verdi's *Otello*, marks the end of some harp entries in the second of his *Two Portraits*, Op. 5, *con sord*, during a passage where several other instruments (including percussion) are similarly marked. It is clear that this does not signify that the harp should be played with a mute but that the sound should be damped immediately. For there is in fact no method of muting the harp in the sense conventionally applied to the string or wind families.

8 Other Effects

Occasionally harpists are instructed to interlace the strings with paper or other materials, as in Bax's *Spring Fire* or Arbós's orchestration of 'El Albaicin' from Albeniz's *Iberia*; but these are special *ad hoc* devices of the kind to which the harp, like every instrument, has become increasingly the prey.

To obtain the true ring of the harp, the player normally plucks the strings near the middle. But there are also other methods that can vary the quality, such as the less resonant sound that results from playing near to the soundboard, i.e, at the bottom of the strings. The French use the instruction **près de la table** for this effect and indeed so much is this a French-orientated technique that it is hard to find equivalents in other languages; however, Mahler's **Resonanz** deserves mention as it is not always recognized as such.

Another rarely understood Mahlerian harp term is **Mediator**, which occurs in the Sixth and Seventh Symphonies. This is actually a plectrum (as for a mandoline) but in practice players use their fingernails to get the required hard and twangy sound –

which Copland also uses in *Appalachian Spring*, though marking the passage explicitly *with the nail, like a guitar*.

The usual method of plucking is with the tips of the fingers and harpists develop hard corns in the course of training. So important a protection do these become against what could otherwise be quite a painful occupation that harpists are rarely able to take a holiday for any length of time away from their instruments.

Occasionally instructions appear requiring the use of other implements. In the first movement of Bartók's *Concerto for Orchestra* the 2nd harp is directed to use a metal stick for a short quasi-*tremolando* passage. Apparently straightforward enough in principle, in practice it is excessively difficult to change direction quickly enough unless the rod is extremely light; hence in the event many harpists use some ready-to-hand object like a pencil, which also works perfectly well.

Actually, the very fact that harpists have to pluck the strings, instead of merely pressing down keys as in keyboard instruments, makes rapid reiterations both clumsy and unreliable. This is reflected by the harp writing and notation of some composers, but is ignored by others who write *tremolos* and trills as if for the piano and leave it to the player to work out the best or nearest approximation.

Dvořák writes a series of quick repetitions of a single string in his symphonic poem *Die Waldtaube*, and although this is by no means impossible Dukas in *La Péri* contrived a better solution, showing more understanding of harp technique. This consists of rapid rearticulations of a single pitch but played enharmonically on two adjacent strings. This ingenious device was quickly emulated by Bartók, Honegger and others, Holst even using enharmonic juxtapositions of whole chords for the atmospheric passages of 'Neptune' in the closing pages of *The Planets*.

Such rapid alternation of the two hands is also the standard technique in *fortissimo*, as in Mahler's Second Symphony, Delius's *Appalachia* and so on, while *pianissimo tremolos* are often marked **bisbigliando**, signifying 'murmuring' or 'whispering', as in a familiar passage in Strauss's *Don Juan* where the hero is despairingly recalling past conquests. Most peculiarly Mahler adds the instruction *bispigliando* (*sic*) to his harps in his Seventh Symphony. This remains a mystery for, while there is no such Italian word, he cannot have meant 'bisbigliando' in its true meaning as the relevant passage occurs at a fully scored climax and is marked *ff*. The probability is that he intended a form of double *glissando* using the two hands.

See also: ARPEGGIANDO, GLISSANDO, HARMONICS, PLATFORM ARRANGEMENT, SCORE LAYOUT

Harpe (Fr.), *see* HARP

HARPSICHORD

The harpsichord is a keyboard instrument in some ways not unlike the piano though with an entirely different sound quality. This is because its strings are not struck by hammers but plucked with quills.

Harpsichords come in all sizes and even shapes, the smallest being called a SPINET. The largest instruments, however, have more than one manual and are equipped with stops and **pedals**, the latter – unlike the organ's – being merely foot-operated stops. The stops have the dual purpose of changing both the quality of the sound and the octave pitch. There are also coupling stops that link the manuals, thus enabling more than one octave to sound at a time when only single keys are actually being played. This is all patently very closely akin to organ terminology; even the pipe lengths are transferred, though they have no true application to string lengths – '8 foot' signifying stops sounding at actual pitch, with '4 foot' an octave higher and '16 foot' an octave lower. Equally, as in organ parlance the use and handling of these stops is described as 'registration'.

The range of harpsichords varies widely from period to period as well as from instrument to instrument. The smaller spinets usually have a keyboard of three and a half octaves while the larger varieties, by the use of the many stops and pedals, are able to extend the range to five octaves from , which Strauss typically extends still further to G at the top in his 'Couperin' Suites.

Registration indications are very rarely found in harpsichord parts, but an outstanding exception is Frank Martin's *Petite Symphonie Concertante*. This gives a variety of instructions, though without mentioning the 'harp-stop' often asked for in connection with very soft passages as it greatly reduces the notorious jangling quality described by Beecham as 'skeletons dancing on a tin roof'.

The harpsichord has virtually no range of expressive dynamics, not even an equivalent of the organ's swell box, and it cannot therefore follow the orchestra's fluctuations of volume as can the harp and piano. Nor has the very concept of a sustaining pedal any reality: *forte* and *fortissimo* are supplied by means of octave couplings (which thicken the texture and so give the impression of loudness), regardless of the notation in the score, and *pianissimo* by whatever variety of stops the instrument may boast. It is therefore still rarely used outside chamber-orchestral combinations despite its spectacular return to favour during the course of the present century.

For the principal orchestral role of the harpsichord once lay in the field of CONTINUO, in which capacity it had reigned supreme in the baroque era only to be considered subsequently as archaic and of limited validity. In this respect, however, its re-establishment has become total and it is now accepted that replacement by a piano is an anachronism and that the harpsichord is indeed the instrument to be used when a **cembalo** is prescribed.

This is, however, a situation needing a certain disentangling. The word 'cembalo' originated as a shortened form of **clavicembalo**, not to be confused with the **clavichord** – a quite separate instrument with a very very soft tone; perhaps for that reason the clavichord, for which Bach wrote the

'48', has never been used orchestrally. 'Clavicembalo', strictly speaking, means no more than 'keyboard instrument', and is in fact synonymous with the German **Klavier**. But 'Klavier' has come to denote specifically the piano and similarly where baroque or continuo playing is concerned 'cembalo' has turned into the international term for the harpsichord. Hence in Strauss's 'Couperin' Suite and the opera *Capriccio* 'cembalo' is used in preference to the dictionary word for the instrument, **Klavizymbel**; and in Stravinsky's *The Rake's Progress*, where the instrument list is given in English, 'cembalo' is used instead of 'harpsichord', even though the latter is well established colloquially. The Stravinsky example is of wider interest, however, since the listing also gives 'pianoforte' in brackets. This could imply that Stravinsky was using the word 'cembalo' in its broadest sense, the keyboard instrument actually to be used being the piano. His own recordings, however, negate this theory and it is clear that the reference to the piano was intended as no more than an emergency substitute. Certainly the piano would be a poor replacement for the eerie effect of the harpsichord in the penultimate scene where poor Tom plays a desperate game of cards with Nick, his soul standing as stake, and the harpsichord has since been frequently used to evoke the supernatural in film music.

On the other hand when the French school of composers of the present century started to write for the harpsichord as part of the orchestra or as a solo instrument, they would often use their own word for the instrument,

clavecin. Nevertheless, Falla, in *El Retablo de Maese Pedro*, held to 'clavicembalum', perhaps because, like Strauss and Stravinsky, he was using the harpsichord not merely as an orchestral colour but for its period associations.

On the platform the harpsichord is usually placed as centrally as possible, especially when used for the continuo; this is not only to give its tone the best chance to project (the lid is opened to its fullest extent or removed), but also to seat the player as near as possible to the principals, especially to the cello whose line he is elaborating. Players often possess and bring their own instruments and will probably tune them, for the maintaining of a harpsichord is as exacting a part of the job as playing it. ELECTRICAL AMPLIFICATION is sometimes resorted to in larger halls, though more often in solo rather than ensemble work.

Hautbois (Fr.), *see* OBOE

HECKELPHONE

Bass oboists are passionate in their assertions that the heckelphone is entirely different from their own beloved instrument, to which it is – however – obviously at least analogous.

Strauss was the first to introduce the heckelphone into the orchestra in his opera *Salome*. This was in 1905, the year after its invention (by Wilhelm Heckel, after whom it is called). It is coarser, if more powerful, than the BASS OBOE and has the particular advantage over that instrument of an extended range at the lower end of its compass. Anthony Baines cites it as

going down to its bottom A but in *Elektra* Strauss writes a semitone lower still, notating it – unlike some users of the bass oboe – in the treble clef sounding an octave lower. At the upper end it can theoretically reach the top A or even B♭ (sounding above the stave in the treble clef) but the need for such high notes does not normally arise as they are not the purpose of the instrument's existence; even Strauss writes no higher than F.

Heel, *see* BOWING, 2

Herdengeläute (Ger.), *see* COWBELLS

Herdenglocken (Ger.), *see* COWBELLS

Hoboe (Ger.), *see* OBOE

Holz, **Holzbläser** (Ger.), *see* WOODWIND, 1

Holzblock (Ger.), *see* WOOD BLOCK

Holzharmoniker (Ger.), *see* XYLOPHONE

Holzklapper (Ger.), *see* WHIP

Holzplattentrommel (Ger.), *see* LOG DRUMS

Holzschlägel (Ger.), wooden drum stick; *see* DRUMS, 3; TIMPANI, 12

Holzschlitztrommel (Ger.), slit drum; *see* LOG DRUMS

Holztrommeln (Ger.), *see* LOG DRUMS

Holz- und- Strohinstrument (Ger.), *see* XYLOPHONE

HORNS

1 Status

Although sometimes pedantically designated the alto member of the brass ensemble, the horn is in reality a species in its own right with links towards the woodwind just as much as towards the heavy brass. Horn players accordingly take pride in their special status lying apart from the main brass ensemble; indeed, if a conductor merely calls for the brass in rehearsal, the horns will most probably remain obstinately silent. There is something more than just snobbery here, although there is perhaps an element of this, as there is a consciously aristocratic side to an orchestra's horn section. Quite as important as the more robust facet of the horns' ambivalent character is the amount of time they spend playing alongside the woodwind and blending with them, and this requires refinement of a special order.

2 Names

Where the printed page is concerned the colloquial English term **French horn** really survives only in tutors and instrumentation books. This may be partly due to the superseding of the old narrow-bore French or French-type instrument, with its upright pistons, by the wider-bore German horn with the more convenient rotary-valve action. Certainly not all 'French horns' were made in France any more than all 'German horns' are made in Germany, but the fading of the term 'French horn' among players themselves roughly corresponds with the arrival during the 1920s and 1930s of the more reliable and consistent German instruments.

An earlier development in the history of the horn is revealed by romantic composers of the early nineteenth century such as Schumann, for instance, as well as the young Wagner, the opening of whose *Tannhäuser* presents an outstanding example. Both specify the simultaneous use of both *Waldhörner* and *Ventilhörner*, the former being the old hand-horns without any **valves** or pistons (= *ventile*) and thus limited to the open notes of the harmonic series. Among French composers, Berlioz also provides obvious instances, and strangely enough works as late as Chabrier's *España* of 1883 include both **cors** *ordinaires* and *cors chromatiques*, while Ravel's *Pavane pour une Infante défunte*, orchestrated in 1910, is still scored for *2 cors simples en sol*. But the Italians have always used only **corni**, the international term. The one really confusing name of the horn is the Spanish, which, oddly enough, is **trompa**. This appears in works such as Turina's *Danzas Fantasticas*, published in a relatively rare Madrid edition, where the *trompas en Fa* look deceptively like trumpets.

3 Tone and Style

The accepted tone quality of the horn varies enormously from country to country, possibly more so than that of any other orchestral instrument, ranging for example from the tremulous vibrato (not unlike a saxophone at times) of many French, Russian and East European players, to the thick mellifluous horns of the Vienna Philharmonic. It seems a far cry from the days when Brahms resolutely championed the hand horn, complaining that the introduction of valves muffled the fine ringing quality that characterized the true horn tone. For this ideal has receded more and more over the last decades with the universal adoption of wide-bore instruments until a true horn tone has even come to be discredited in some countries. Italian players, for example, so far from holding the bell aloft to aim at resonance and vitality, will often turn the instrument over so that the sound goes directly towards the thigh, and when asked to raise the bell in an attempt to lighten the thick 'tubby' sound will protest that to comply would be to jeopardize their position in the orchestra.

Even in Britain and America, where the tradition of a slender tone – more graceful yet entirely free from vibrato, firm but round and warm – long continued to fight a rearguard action, the tendency has been growing steadily towards a fatter sound in the pursuit of a more homogeneous blend both within the section and together with the other wind and brass groups. This has been achieved by the use not only of wide-bore instruments, but also of instruments with shorter lengths of tube and therefore pitched in higher harmonic series.

4 Cracked Notes

Both these factors are also believed to lessen the risk of cracked notes (that bane of horn playing) and, in the presentday pursuit of flawless reliability, are a prime reason for the sacrifice, much deplored by purists, of the characteristically vivid and hauntingly beautiful tone of the older instruments.

The constant bogey of cracked (or split) notes – an occupational hazard

more for the horn than for any other brass instrument, even the trumpet – is an age-long source of distress, no less within the orchestras themselves than to audiences curious to understand the cause. It is important to recognize that fluffing need not be the result of faulty technique, but may afflict even the greatest virtuosi through atmospheric or acoustic circumstances or the slightest untoward distraction. This is because virtually every note is produced in exactly the same way (horn playing is very much like singing in this respect); and it remains an inherent difficulty in many a horn solo merely to come in on the right note, let alone with a clean attack. Naturally the risk of mispitching becomes the more acute where the harmonics lie closest together – i.e., from the middle to the upper register – though even lower down the horn player should not be thought free from anxiety; the solo for the 8th horn sets in motion the vast span of Wagner's *Ring* is one of the cruellest tests of reliability and requires an iron nerve, simple as it looks on paper. Nor is it a matter of taking extra care (although the capacity for unswerving concentration is a first prerequisite for a reliable player). Indeed, an over-careful hornist is a liability to his section and his orchestra; the very psychology that aims to steer clear of trouble through caution will rob him of bravura, which has ever marked the greatest players, as well as landing him sooner or later into the very fallibility he so assiduously aims to avoid.

5 Range

The compass of the horn is basically

from its bottom written pedal F $\begin{smallmatrix}\end{smallmatrix}$ to its top C , although a few more notes at each end have been written – and can be obtained by good players. These notes as quoted are given in the conventional notation for the standard horn in F, the horn being a TRANSPOSING INSTRUMENT. In concert pitch this normal range of the horn would read:

6 Notation

Horn notation is by no means a straightforward matter. It is clear that both treble and bass clefs are used but bass-clef notation brings its own complexity amid never-ending controversy. By tradition the notes in the bass clef are transcribed an octave down, so that the transposition to concert pitch becomes a fourth upwards (corresponding to some extent to the old-style CELLO writing) in order to evoke an instinctive technical response, since the lowest notes are played with a different EMBOUCHURE and have a strong vibrant resonance. These are the PEDAL NOTES and so deep do they feel to the player that their low notation with plenty of ledger lines is a psychological and technical aid to performance.

Most orchestration manuals condemn this notation out of hand and the situation has to be faced that however popular 'old notation' may continue to be among players, 'new notation', whereby the anomaly is corrected, has gradually come to be favoured by composers, so that bass-clef notes are made to transpose in the same way as those in the treble clef. In the end the fact

remains that both notations exist side by side in scores, and it is not always obvious which octave is intended without pre-knowledge of the relevant composer's normal practice, or even (in some extreme examples) from internal evidence of the music.

Generally, however, 'old notation' reveals itself sooner or later in the course of a work since notes are usually encountered that would be too low to be practical if transposed down instead of up. Doubt arises in the player's or conductor's mind only when 'new notation' is used – another strong argument against it, especially from the player's point of view, where the least trace of uncertainty can lead to unreliability in performance.

7 Orchestral Section

The normal section of the symphony orchestra is of four horns. Broadly speaking, it is only by the mid- to late-nineteenth century that this four-horn group became standardized, when Brahms, Dvořák and Tchaikovsky – to cite only a few key romantic composers – all used four horns as a matter of course in their large-scale symphonic works. Nor is this by any means completely uniform throughout the repertoire, although by far the greatest number of works do call for horns in multiples of two.

The tradition of using horns in pairs can be traced back to baroque times, in Bach's Brandenburg Concerto No. 1 and the Christmas Oratorio, for example, while Handel (typically more prodigal) sometimes uses four horns, which are still, however, treated in pairs. Actually a single horn can occasionally be found in

Bach, as in the cantatas and above all in the 'Quoniam' of the B minor Mass. But these examples of solo horn writing are all concertante in character and are today regarded as virtuoso engagements commanding a soloist's fee, whereas the incorporation of a single horn as an integral member of the wind group emerged only during the present century. This is partly because one horn sounds strangely lonely and unsupported, but it is also to some extent bound up with the fact that the bassoon provides a poor foundation for the wind group, so that the more satisfactory low notes of the 2nd horn in, for example, Wagner's *Siegfried Idyll* fulfil a dual purpose, having links both with the 1st horn and with the woodwind ensemble.

Orchestral music is thus primarily orientated around a horn section built in pair units, a single pair sufficing for the standard eighteenth-century orchestra with the occasional addition of a second pair. It is sometimes not even very important, from the point of view of the scoring (as distinct from that of the players), which of the two pairs takes priority, a situation that extends into the romantic era. In Beethoven's Overture *Leonora No. 3*, for example, all the meat is given to the 3rd and 4th horns, while even in as late a work as Brahms's Second Piano Concerto the organization of the section is quite misleading. Indeed it is only by working out from movement to movement which players change crook that one discovers that in the second movement the D horns, who are enjoying all the solo work and are printed in the score on the upper of the two horn staves,

are in fact the 3rd and 4th players and are so printed in the orchestral parts.

8 Crooks

The use of horn pairs playing in different CROOKS had the purpose of adding melodic notes to the instrument in the days when only the 'open' notes of the hand horn were pure and round in tone. This principle was also sometimes exploited by Haydn and Mozart when using only two horns in all. Haydn's Symphony No. 44 in E minor (the *Trauer*) and Mozart's G minor Symphony (K. 550) provide examples of each of two horns being differently crooked, their available notes handled with splendid resourcefulness and skill. French composers took this a step further and passages can be found, for example, in Berlioz's 'Queen Mab' Scherzo from his *Romeo and Juliet* Symphony, in which each of the four horns is crooked differently, presenting a marvellous teaser to the score reader. As long as the crooks really were detachable objects in regular use, the purpose of the instructions 'in G', 'in Bb alto', etc., was specifically to tell the player which to attach to his instrument, whereas with today's standardization of the F horn they merely tell him (and the conductor or score reader) in which way the part will need to be transposed.

But a curious situation exists in some of Wagner's earlier scores. In *Lohengrin*, for instance, he retained the characteristic style of horn writing based on the open notes even though he was by now using valved instruments. This he achieved by a method of notation in which he prescribes a range of instantaneously changing crooks, even though, taken literally, such an activity would be completely, ludicrously, beyond the realms of possibility. It is thus self-evident that the instructions must mean something different; i.e., Wagner reckoned that the depressing of the relevant piston in effect transposed the instrument in the same way as a change of crook. This was not by any means improbable reasoning, except that his to-and-fro alternation of horns in G, E, D and Ab makes a riddle of which instrument he thought the players were actually using.

9 Other Effects

The horn is capable of all the playing styles associated with wind instruments – DOUBLE- AND TRIPLE-TONGUING, FLUTTER-TONGUING, GLISSANDI, LIP TRILLS, and so on. Moreover, one of the more amusing tricks – though not achievable by every player – is the execution of chords. Weber wrote a whole assortment in the middle section of his *Konzertstück* but by and large they are pure fantasy and it is a mystery how he was led to believe that they could ever be played. The most readily attainable are a series of chords with three notes in which either the top *or* the middle note is sung while the bottom one is played; the third note (the middle or top one, as the case may be) emerges as a kind of buzz – but still a recognizable note through the scientific effect known as 'differential' or 'summation' tones. Although occasionally brought out of the hat for a solo *tour de force* (one of the better examples is the cadenza of Ethel Smyth's Con-

certo for Violin and Horn) the use of chords has never been used within the orchestra.

10 Water Emptying

The sight of horn players emptying the water out of their instruments by turning them over, taking the slides out one by one and blowing through them, continues to intrigue onlookers. Horns are not equipped with spring escape valves like all other brass instruments because the water (largely condensation rather than pure spit, it may be disappointing to learn) collects in too many obscure bends of the endlessly curving tube. In many atmospheric conditions the accumulations of water in the bowels of the instrument can be a real hazard, distorting the tone and even contributing to the odd split note or bubble in a *legato* solo. Nor is the player always able to locate the trouble instantaneously, and if it lies in one of the least accessible places there may simply not be time to take the horn to pieces until, say, the end of a movement. The conductor will therefore often be seen to wait for his horn players to reassemble their plumbing before restarting.

See also: AEROPHON, BELLS UP, BOUCHÉ, BUMPER, CUIVRÉ, GLISSANDO, HARMONICS, PLATFORM ARRANGEMENT

Incudino (It.), *see* ANVIL

JAZZ BAND

Jazz bands can vary in their constitutions as widely as any chamber or symphony orchestra, from the simplest 8-piece New Orleans 'traditional' to the concert bands such as the famous Paul Whiteman group, which sparked the Ferde Grofé instrumentation of Gershwin's *Rhapsody in Blue*. Nevertheless they retain their identity as 'bands' rather than orchestras in that strings are used only as specially imported visitors, and even then usually as soloists rather than as a basic section of the ensemble.

In juxtaposing (with greater or lesser success) the jazz band with a symphony orchestra, as Liebermann and Seiber did in their Concerto (1952) and *Improvisations* (1961) respectively, both used an identical ensemble consisting of five SAXOPHONES, four each of TRUMPETS and TROMBONES, PIANO, DOUBLE-BASS and DRUMS (using what are known as traps). This can thus be taken as a fairly standard group, one outstanding characteristic of which is its extraordinary range of sheer decibels: for in the performance of both the Liebermann and Seiber works it transpired that the jazz band had only to strike up for the orchestra to fade into virtual inaudibility, and certainly to become totally incomprehensible.

Jeté, see BOWING, 11

Jeu de timbres (Fr.), *see* GLOCKENSPIEL, 2, 5

Jeu ordinaire (Fr.), *see* BOWING, 3

JINGLES

Already featured by Mozart in 'Die Schlittenfahrt', a movement from one of his most famous *Deutsche Tänze* (K. 605), these are sets of small spherical bells attached to a harness strap and shaken. What they really are, of course, is **sleigh bells** and in English and American scores this term is sometimes used instead of 'jingles'. Mozart's **Schellen** are actually written as pitched instruments, but by the time of their more familiar symphonic or operatic appearances, such as in Vaughan Williams's *London* Symphony, Mahler's Fourth Symphony, Strauss's *Arabella*, Massenet's *Manon* (**grelots**), Respighi's *Feste Romane* (**sonagliera**), etc., it is assumed that they are of indefinite pitch though written in the treble clef.

Sleigh bells are not, however, the only jingling instruments, among which must also be included such effects as **jingling johnnie**, **Turkish crescent**, BELL TREE, etc. There can be some mystery about composers' intentions when these terms arise, as in Rossini's *Barber of Seville* or Berlioz's *Symphonie Funèbre et Triomphale* for example, as such contraptions mostly derive either from antiquity or from the military bands in various foreign parts. They can be built in any number of shapes and sizes, but all bear clusters of little bells. Berlioz writes his **pavillon chinois** (translated into Italian for the Breitkopf score as **cappello cinese**) on a single line, as does Rossini his **sistro**.

Jingling johnnie, see BELL TREE, JINGLES

Ketten (Ger.), *see* CHAINS

Kettle-drums, *see* TIMPANI, 2

Keyboard, *see* PIANO, ORGAN, HARMONIUM, HARPSICHORD, CELESTA; for **Klavier**, **Clavichord**, **Cembalo**, **Clavicembalo**, *see* HARPSICHORD; for other keyboards **Claviatur (Klaviatur)** *see* GLOCKENSPIEL, ACCORDION

Keyed Bugles, *see* OPHICLEIDE

Klaviatur (Ger.), keyboard; *see* GLOCKENSPIEL, 2

Klavier (Ger.), *see* HARPSICHORD; PIANO, 1

Klavizymbel, *see* HARPSICHORD

Kleine Flöte (Ger.), *see* PICCOLO

Kleine Militärtrommel (Ger.), *see* DRUMS, 1

Kleine Pauke (Ger.), *see* TIMPANI, 4

Kleine Trommel (Ger.), *see* DRUMS, 1

Klingen lassen (Ger.) allow to vibrate; *see* CYMBALS, 2; HARP, 7

Knarre (Ger.), *see* RATTLE

Kontrabass (Ger.), *see* CONTRABASS

Konzert (Ger.), *see* CONCERTO

Korean Blocks, *see* WOOD BLOCKS

Laisser vibrer (Fr.) allow to vibrate; *see* CYMBALS, 2; HARP, 7

Lang gestrichen (Ger.) long bows; *see* BOWING, 9

LEADER

According to standard and immutable convention the primary figurehead of the players of an orchestra is the No. 1 1st violin. That is to say, he is the leader not just of the 1st violins or even of the string department, but of the whole orchestra. The Americans, for whom the word 'leader' may often signify the conductor, call this primary figure **concert master**, a direct translation of the German *Konzertmeister*. The French use either **chef d'attaque** (a splendidly graphic title) or more usually *premier violon*, corresponding with the Italian *primo violino*, although *la spalla* is also sometimes used, *spalla* meaning 'shoulder' – for the conductor to lean on (figuratively perhaps) since the leader, with his overall authority, is the liaison between conductor and orchestra. He may also act as spokesman for the orchestra *vis-à-vis* the management, except in matters that properly fall into the province of an appointed union steward. But in addition the leader may share his authority with the chairman of a representative committee formed by the members of the orchestra in such duties as addressing the assembled players on points of procedure or internal dispute.

In recognition of the leader's position and responsibility it is the custom in Britain for him to receive special mention, as it is also to make a solo entrance on to the platform, both at the beginning of the concert and after the interval. He also takes the initiative of choosing the strategic moment to lead his colleagues off at the end. These marks of distinction are nevertheless not universal, and on the Continent the leader will mostly take his place together with the rest of the orchestra, though he may stand up to obtain silence and either give or request the A for the orchestra to tune.

One worldwide tradition is that the conductor shakes hands with the leader at the end of the concert. This courtesy provides the conductor with the opportunity to show his appreciation of the whole orchestra, as well as of the leader's co-operation. Many conductors signify their enthusiasm by shaking hands also at the very beginning of the proceedings, a Continental custom that is gaining increasing currency also in Britain.

Despite the importance of the leader's broad role in the functions of orchestral life, however, it should never be overlooked that as a first priority he needs to be an exceptionally fine virtuoso performer on his instrument. Indeed many leaders are highly regarded soloists in their own right, playing concertos with their own orchestras or as a guest artist with others. The solos that fall automatically to the leader are also often of veritable concertante importance and difficulty such as those in Rimsky-Korsakov's *Scheherazade*, for example, or Strauss's *Heldenleben* and *Bourgeois Gentilhomme*. The leader's authority in dictating BOWINGS or matters of violinistic style and technique must depend on the unquestioning respect of colleagues throughout the string section based on their knowledge of the leader's own accomplishments, personality and experience.

See also: PRINCIPALS, VIOLIN

Legni, i (It.), *see* WOODWIND, 1

Legno (It.), wooden drum stick; *see* CASTANETS; DRUMS, 3; WOOD BLOCK

Legno, col (It.), *see* BOWING, 6

LIBRARIAN

The orchestral librarian is a central figure in the matter of concert giving with responsibilities not only to the orchestra but to the conductor as well.

The librarian's first priorities naturally lie in supplying the material for the players. This will involve either the hiring of the music for each programme, a duty itself requiring considerable expertise in an area of immense complexity, or the formation and tending of a library of such materials belonging to the orchestra and hence carrying the marks and bowings, etc., carried over from earlier performances. A good orchestral librarian will need to have a wide experience of the different publishing houses (both at home and abroad) as well as knowledge of the fluctuating problems of the laws of copyright as they may apply to the various composers.

Orchestral musicians often look to the librarian for the parts of some more demanding works in good time for them to be able to familiarize themselves with any especial problems in advance. This requires a good relationship with the publishers, many of whom do not readily send out music far ahead of performance dates or may make heavy charges for doing so.

The music once obtained, the regularization of REHEARSAL LETTERS or figures may need attention, numbering of bars, or the BOWING of string parts after the section leaders have marked the master copies. The removal and cleaning up of unsightly or illegible marks left in from earlier usages is another irritating and time-consuming occupation.

One area where the librarian's advice should be sought is when the management is booking extra players or special instruments. Catalogues cannot necessarily be relied upon to have the correct details, since publishers' lists are notoriously fallible and often omit mention of instruments making unexpected and perhaps brief appearances in later movements, or even towards the very end of a work. It is by no means unknown for a rehearsal to be held up when it is discovered that, for example, the need for a cor anglais has been overlooked in respect of the Berlioz Te Deum; the 3rd trumpet for Mendelssohn's Overture *Calm Sea and Prosperous Voyage* is another notorious pitfall, as is also the 3rd horn who appears without warning for a few bars only during the slow movement of Weber's Clarinet Concerto No. 1.

To the conductor, the orchestral librarian can be one of his closest allies, with once again very varied responsibilities. In the first place he may be asked to provide the scores for a programme, as the conductor will not always possess them or be in a position to procure them elsewhere. Yet it is often the conductor who is expected to initiate contact with the librarian for any scores he needs, failing which scores from the orchestra's library, or those automatically hired with the material, will generally be placed on the conductor's stand at the first rehearsal as a precaution.

Conductors, however, do sometimes have tasks for the orchestra's librarian that can be arduous and are often assigned at short notice. It is not unknown for star international conductors to send scores in advance of their own arrival with instructions that the orchestra parts are to be marked, revised, bowed or whatever, in accordance with the markings to be found within. On the other hand some conductors possess their own libraries of marked orchestral materials and thus need no more than an assurance from the librarian that only these will be placed before the players. During the early years of the Royal Philharmonic Orchestra that doyen of librarians George Brownfoot was ever at hand working loyally and under considerable stress to serve the moment-to-moment last-minute whims of the founder-director Sir Thomas Beecham, an ardent believer in the thorough marking of orchestral parts.

Librarians do not always attend their orchestra's public concerts, nor tour with them, but sometimes they may prefer personally to superintend platform arrangements and put out – and change between items – the different scores on the conductor's stand. At film or recording sessions too, the presence of an efficient and skilful librarian may be of untold value in view of the frequent abrupt changes of plan requiring new materials or the immediate and unexpected copying of parts or scores. A first-class librarian can thus all too often be worth his weight in gold.

145

LION'S ROAR

An entirely different contraption, similar though it sounds, from the BULL ROARER, this instrument is also – if less graphically – known as the **cuica** or **string drum**. Although it has no standard shape, being usually a rough and ready object looking as if it has been put together in someone's back garden, it is a not very large drum-like cylinder, round or maybe octagonal, closed at each end but with a hole in the top just large enough for a resined gut string to be passed through and fastened with a knot on the inside. Held taught with one hand, the string is then rubbed with the other, holding a piece of leather, upon which it makes the ferocious noise that gives it its name. Not often encountered orchestrally, it does nevertheless appear in the occasional score, for example Varèse's *Ionisation*, where it is described as **tambour à corde**. Varèse writes for it with a variety of effects including a long sustained *crescendo*, but in practice this is virtually impossible as its outburst of growling is necessarily brief, being dictated by the length of the player's arm as he is tugging at the string with all his might and main.

LIP TRILLS

These are the exclusive speciality of the horns. Horn TRILLS can actually be achieved conventionally with the valves but, where the two trilling notes consist of adjacent HARMONICS not more than a tone apart, they may be accomplished purely by lip flexibility. This is because many of the horn's upper harmonics lie close enough together in the instrument's most comfortable part of the compass. In classical music indeed, composed before valves were invented, the only horn trills written had to be those obtainable as lip trills, such as the Mozart Concertos. Yet today even these examples are not always taken in this way because valve trills, though much less smooth, are considerably easier and therefore often substituted, though at some sacrifice of style.

The most hilarious example of lip trills occurs in Mozart's *Musikalischer Spass*, where the upper trill for the 1st horn presents no problem as the next adjacent harmonic is very close, but the lower trill, entailing a to-and-fro of a fourth, is hardly possible and the player's efforts cannot fail to sound comical in the extreme, as Mozart well knew.

Litofono, *see* STEINSPIEL

LITUI

The lituus was essentially an Ancient Roman military brass instrument, its exact physiological details being somewhat conjectural. The intrusion of litui into the orchestral scene depends purely on their unexpected revival in a few baroque works and especially in Bach's Cantata No. 118, 'O Jesu Christ, mein's Lebens Licht'. It seems unlikely, however, that in such a context the antique band instrument will have been used, musicologists being unable even to decide whether the two litui in Bach's work approximated more nearly to high horns (they are pitched in B♭, sounding a tone lower than written) or trumpets. For our performance of the Cantata at an Aldeburgh Festival some years ago it must be admitted that we used cornets, which seemed to provide very much the quality the music suggested.

LOG DRUMS

These are essentially what their name implies – large hollowed-out logs, though with horizontal slots carved on their upper sides whose differing lengths vary the pitch when struck. The full score of Stockhausen's *Gruppen*, the most important work to date in which they have appeared, gives a very clear photograph of a pair of log drums – **Holztrommeln**, he calls them – on their home-made stand. James Holland describes and illustrates a formalized substitute that has come into circulation due to difficulties in obtaining the real things out of the African jungle; but, despite the advantage in obtaining the precise tunings some of the avant-garde have begun to prescribe, perfectly shaped rectangular objects obviously lack the romantic ethnical appeal of the originals. They are also known as **Holzschlitztrommeln** (**slit drums**) and are one of various species of native drums used by Orff and Stockhausen, such as also **Holzplattentrommeln** (**woodplate drums**).

Louré (Fr.), *see* BOWING, 9

Luce (It.), *see* COLOUR ORGAN

Luftpause (Ger.), *see* COMMA

Lyra (Ger.), **Lyre-glockenspiel**, *see* GLOCKENSPIEL, 9

Mailloche (Fr.), large round soft-headed stick; *see* BASS DRUM

MANDOLINE

Mandolines exist in various sizes – I myself possess a score of Cimarosa's overture *Il Matrimonio Segreto* arranged for mandoline orchestra scored for, among others, mandolini soprani, mandole tenori (*sic*), mandoloncelli and mandolone. But the only one used orchestrally is the standard mandoline with a range of three octaves from the G below the treble clef to the G high above it, the most common Neapolitan instrument having four double strings tuned in fifths like the violin. It is written on one stave in the treble clef at pitch and, unlike the guitar (with which it is often unfairly coupled) is played with a plectrum, having a strongly penetrating angular quality.

The first orchestral appearance of the mandoline is usually considered to be Mozart's brief use in Don Giovanni's serenade 'Deh vieni alla finestra' but this is again a special case, analogous with the guitar in *The Barber of Seville* or Beckmesser's lute in *Die Meistersinger*. A more genuine orchestral use of the instrument, though still introduced for the sake of local colour, is that of Respighi's *Feste Romane*, composed in 1929, which is always played with the characteristic *tremolando* though this is not indicated by the notation in the score.

The *tremolo* is indeed so indigenous to the instrument that it is commonly thought that all passages must automatically be played in this way, with ruinous consequences to the other school of orchestral mandoline writing – that inaugurated as early as 1908, together with the guitar, by Mahler in his Seventh Symphony and which he pursued in the Eighth and in *Das Lied von der Erde*. In the last two of these he abandoned the guitar whereas Schoenberg continued to write for both instruments as a pair in his Serenade, as did Webern in his *Fünf Orchesterstücke*, Op. 10. In the works of these composers the *tremolo* is clearly indicated wherever required, although in Mahler's Seventh Symphony some confusion has arisen through the Mengelberg practice, too often followed, of allowing *tremolo* to intrude everywhere, so that Erwin Ratz – the editor of the Mahler Society Revised Edition – was misled into adding *tremolo* strokes to almost all notes of longer value (such as minims), even though Mahler clearly showed whenever he positively wanted the effect. Ratz's preface is of interest in this respect, however, referring to different schools of mandoline playing not otherwise commonly known.

On the platform the mandoline is normally placed to the fore side by side with the guitar – even though when the two are used in conjunction the considerable difference in the strength of their tone puts the guitar at a notable disadvantage. It is, however, usual to feature the mandoline in this way also since, as in the case of the guitar if to an even greater extent, so few orchestral works include the instrument that players regard themselves – not without justification – as specialists in a colourful, even exotic, field.

Maracas, *see* GOURD

Marcato, *see* BOWING, 10

MARIMBA

The marimba corresponds to some extent to the bass XYLOPHONE, though it differs in character partly in the softer material of the wood used, partly in the curved shaping of the bars, and partly also in the use of resonators fixed beneath each bar. Furthermore, unlike the bass xylo, the marimba has the full range of four octaves, thus corresponding to the large virtuoso-model xylo, though sounding an octave lower (i.e., at the notated pitch) and much gentler in timbre.

Any confusion that has arisen over the past decades has been due to the adaptation of the modern xylo to include such marimba features as resonators, and even the extension of the range to a total of five octaves. The resultant hybrid has been christened a **xylorimba** since it can – and frequently does – serve as an all-purpose instrument capable of playing parts written for either of its parents. In the end it fulfils this function even though something of the more aggressive characteristics of the xylophone have inevitably been sacrificed in favour of the more ingratiating resonance of the marimba.

It is only in the most recent scores that the three instruments are differentiated and specified by name, and even so composers of the avant-garde have been known to go astray in trying to master their ranges and pitch differences, writing too low for the xylo, too high for the marimba, etc. But it does not matter: the players shrug their shoulders and play everything on their xylorimbas, and at the most convenient pitch.

Markiert (Ger.), *see* BOWING, 10

Marqué (Fr.), *see* BOWING, 10

Martelé (Fr.), *see* BOWING, 10

Martellato (It.), *see* BOWING, 10

Martelli sul incudini (It.), hammers on anvils; *see* ANVIL

Matráca, *see* RATTLE

Mazza (It.), mallet; *see* BASS DRUM

Mediator (Ger.), plectrum; *see* HARP, 7

Metà (It.), half; *see* DIVISI

Metal plates, *see* BELL PLATES

Metallofono (It.), **Metallophone** (Eng.); *see* GLOCKENSPIEL, 6

Metallrohr (Ger.), *see* BELLS

METRONOME

This device was originally invented by Maelzel in 1815 and imitated jocularly by Beethoven in the *Allegretto scherzando* of his Eighth Symphony. The intention was never that it should itself be a musical instrument, its regular loud

ticking being purely a measuring guide to establish and maintain musical speeds for tempo setting or documentation purposes. Nevertheless three metronomes representing **balanciers** are scored for by Ravel as part of the *accessoires* of the orchestra, at the beginning of his hilarious opera *L'Heure Espagnole*, being set in motion at different tempi to suggest some of the numerous clocks crowding the stage. They are marked to be set at respectively 40, 100, and 232 (the last presenting a problem as it is faster than the average metronome can play) while the basic tempo of the music is given as $\quarternote$ = 72, this being a typical 'metronome mark' signifying seventy-two crotchets per minute, the well-known military pace of a slow march (the quick gait of the 'march past' being widely memorized at $\quarternote$ = 120).

Whereas, however, Ravel's *balanciers* must proceed at mechanically exact tempi, it is not normally required that metronome marks should be rigidly adhered to. The figures added by Beethoven to his symphonies are notoriously unreliable and Schoenberg, whose metronome speeds are recklessly fast, stated specifically that they were not to be taken literally but were no more than an indication (*Andeutung*). In any case it is very rare for tempi in art music to remain inflexibly at a uniform pace for more than a few bars at a time, even when – as used by Stravinsky and his followers – metronome marks totally replace the usual verbal descriptions of pace and mood.

Metronomes are also commonly used for practice and training purposes, their familiar triangular form gracing many a piano in studio or rehearsal room, although metronomes shaped and activated like 'hunter' watches have to some extent come to replace the old format, and electronic digital gadgets have also recently come into existence.

Militärtrommel (Ger.), military drum; *see* DRUMS, 1

MILITARY BAND

This is the largest and most variegated body after the orchestra, which it follows in most of its instrumental details except that it has no strings other than basses, and even these are less indigenous than imported for special concert purposes. As its name suggests, the military band's prime function is for army parades and hence largely for outdoor ceremonial activities requiring mobility, such as marches, church parades, funerals, etc. Military bands do, however, give concerts in or out of barracks, again frequently in the open air occupying, for example, bandstands rather than concert halls.

This accounts to a large extent for the absence of strings, which project least well out of doors. Their place is taken partly by clarinets, who feature in great profusion, commonly divided into four or five main sections: solo – the solo clarinet being the corresponding figure to the leader of an orchestra; ripieno (often corrupted in printed scores and parts as 'repiano' – a meaningless term); 1st, 2nd and 3rd clarinets. Cornets also form a strongly representative tutti body with an important soloist at their head. The equivalent to

the cello line in the orchestra is often the euphonium, who is yet another primary soloist, and a group of saxophones may provide the filling supplied in orchestral terms by the violas and tutti cellos.

Admittedly works specially for the military band have gradually been written by composers such as Elgar, Holst, Vaughan Williams, Malcolm Arnold and others in Britain, or Hindemith and Schoenberg in America, but the widely differing constitutions of military bands in other countries, especially across Europe, has continued to prevent bands from acquiring a universal basic repertoire such as that enjoyed by the orchestra. Much of their work depends essentially on arrangements of orchestral music, frequently transposed (rather drearily) into flat keys to suit the overriding characteristics of so many of their constituent instruments – clarinets, cornets, trombones, saxophones and tubas all being built in flat keys and most, moreover, specifically in B♭.

Military band conductors are customarily officers of the various services, commissioned officers or NCOs (warrant officers or sergeants), whose rise to their more or less exalted rank may or may not relate to their musicianly knowledge or prowess. Some of the more accomplished will have trained at recognized military academies of music. Conductors of musicians in the armed services are generally known colloquially as 'bandmasters' but they themselves abhor this derogatory term and the correct official designation is 'Director of Music'. They conduct for the greater part from what are called 'piano–conductor' scores, which are condensations of the music arranged on to two or three staves with some indications of the more important instrumental colours. While no doubt intended by publishers to provide simpler guides for less skilled score readers, practice has proved repeatedly that these are handicaps to efficient rehearsal, analogous to finding one's way round country lanes equipped only with a map of the world.

The German and French word for a military band is generally **Harmonie**, but the French also use *musique* as in 'Musique de la Garde Republicaine'. The 'Concert' or Wind bands that have sprung up comparatively recently, mostly in the USA, are really an offshoot, civilian ensembles concentrating on works written for the medium. Yet a fairly varied repertoire is gradually evolving, from the pioneering examples of Grainger and others to those of contemporary composers who have taken an interest particularly in amateur and youth groups.

Military Drum, *see* DRUMS, 1

Military Glockenspiel, *see* GLOCKEN-SPIEL, 9

Military Tambour, *see* DRUMS, 1

Mit dem Bogen geschlagen (Ger.), *see* BOWING, 6

Mit Verschiebung (Ger.), *see* MUTES, 8

Modo ordinario, in (It.), *see* BOWING, 3

MOTOR HORNS

These are not so much *bona fide* orchestral instruments as members of the special effects department of the percussion group. They are introduced both by Poulenc and by Gershwin in his *American in Paris*, where they appear in four different – but unspecified – pitches to represent the vociferous Parisian taxis, and must therefore be of the rubber-bulbed variety common enough in the 1930s but long since relegated to the world of car museums. The actual pitches used for taxis (a), (b), (c) and (d) are usually – but by no means necessarily correctly – chosen to correspond with the pitches maintaining in the rest of the orchestra, namely G, A♭, A♮ and B♭, although in the score they are all notated on a single line.

Musical Glasses, *see* GLASS HARMONICA

Muta in (It.), change to (another instrument, or crook) *but see also* TIMPANI, 9

MUTES

1 Terminology
These apply to most, if not quite all, orchestral instruments. Muting is not merely a device for softening the tone but a colour in its own right. The terminology in other languages is **sordini** abbr. *sord.* (It.), **sourdines** (Fr.), and **Dämpfer** (Ger.) to which must be added a few of the multilingual instructions for putting them on and taking them off, since these are by no means standardized and many of them far from straightforward. The commonest indication

151

in Italian is, of course, *con/senza sordini* but one will also meet *levare i sordini* – or the more graphic *via sordini*, i.e., 'away with mutes'; Tchaikovsky, in his *Pathétique* Symphony gives the rare *alzate sordini* (literally, 'lift' or 'raise the mutes'). Again, the French equivalents *avec/sans sourdines* are clear enough as also surely *préparez/enlevez les sourdines*, but while the German *mit/ohne Dämpfer* rarely causes hesitation (although the frequently met abbreviations *m.D.* and *o.D.* are less readily grasped), many is the time when *Dämpfer auf* and *Dämpfer ab* (on and off respectively) are misinterpreted to denote the opposite of their true meaning. *Dämpfer weg* also appears from time to time, being the German corresponding to *via sordini*, as does *Dämpfer vorbereiten* (*préparez les sourdines*).

2 Strings

Mutes for the string ensemble are of every conceivable shape and species, wood, metal or plastic. At one time the majority were like elaborately designed letter Ms, which led to the symbols often put by players into their copies (⌐⌐ and ⌐⌐) for mutes on and off, though these are never found in print. With the exception of the basses, however, mutes are no longer necessarily independent objects fixed over the bridge, but may be a sliding contraption remaining permanently on the instrument. This has the clear advantage of speed in application or removal as well as in the matter of storage when not in use. But while the change of tone from one type or substance to another in different mutes is very slight, so that convenience would

seem to be the overriding factor, players do consider that they themselves are aware of a noticeable loss of quality in modern substitutes.

Composers sometimes neglect to indicate where the mutes should come off and *ad hoc* decisions have constantly to be made (see, for example, the last movement of Rachmaninoff's Third Piano Concerto, or the 'Scène d'amour' from Berlioz's *Romeo and Juliet*). One result is that there are places in the repertoire where the unmuting directions seem to have been omitted whereas the composer may well have intended the veiled tone to persist even in loud passages. One of the best-known instances of this dilemma is the central climactic passage of the Largo of Dvořák's *New World* Symphony, which is often played unmuted although there is no such indication, whereas in fact the sound of muted strings against a strong surge of orchestral sound makes a remarkable and beautiful effect.

The sheer contrast of colour between muted and unmuted strings, whether soft or loud, has been variously exploited. Reger was particularly fond of dividing his string group for this purpose into two antiphonal groups, each with their own identity, a technique he employed in several works and in subtly varied ways.

Although naturally all the strings can be equally muted, bass mutings are less often scrupulously observed since the difference in sound is minimal and most bass players reckon that conductors hardly ever notice whether mutes are used or not. Nevertheless bass mutes certainly do exist and in the hands of first-class players can make good sense of composers' practice of writing for them. An outstanding instance when bass mutes are essential is in the opening bars of Holst's *Egdon Heath* where a phrase for muted basses is alternated with a similar one for other divided basses unmuted. It is also perhaps revealing that Mahler elected to write for a muted bass in the 'Frère Jacques' solo at the beginning of the slow movement of his First Symphony.

Many instances occur where string mutes are prescribed for excessively short periods – even for a single note or chord – and players often simply cheat with a very soft **sul tasto** rather than take risks. One particular instance in which compromise is desirable is where a movement ends with muted strings but leads *segue* (i.e., without a break) into a new movement to be played unmuted. Rather than lose the dramatic hush and immobility at the all-important moment of transition it is often preferable to allow the players either to remove the mutes early and finish as softly as possible, or conversely to unmute only after the new movement has been launched.

All the various devices of string techniques are used and written for in conjunction with mutes – **ponticello, col legno**, harmonics, etc. – but in practice the mute merely reduces (if not actually negates) the character of the effect. String players therefore often try to ignore the muting indication rather than fight against what seems to them unreasonable odds in the pursuit of unrealistic aims.

3 Woodwind

Mutes, in the form of actual objects such as the strings and brass use, do not really exist for the woodwind. Nevertheless the need to improvise some sort of muting does occasionally arise for these instruments. Liadov marks both the oboes and bassoons *con sord.* in his *Enchanted Lake*, as does Stravinsky in the choral piece *Zvezdoliki* (*Le Roi des Étoiles*), although it is far from obvious what he expected to happen; similarly Elgar writes for a muted clarinet in *Dream Children* and Britten for a saxophone *con sord.* in *The Prince of the Pagodas*. When Strauss, in his 'souffleur' (prompter) scene of *Capriccio* instructs all the woodwind to mute, he adds a footnote leaving the manner of execution to the players' ingenuity. Berlioz, in his *Treatise of Instrumentation* writes of leather bags, but these have never become standard equipment although the comparable use of a handkerchief held between the knees is a method often deployed not only for these specified occasions but also for such passages as the last fading oboe phrase of the 'Berceuse' from Stravinsky's *Firebird*. Clearly, however, these devices offer no remedy to either flute or bassoon families and it is a moment of high entertainment to orchestra and spectators alike when in Ligeti's *Lontano* the 3rd bassoon is instructed to reach over to his neighbour, the contra, and insert a horn mute into the inverted bell of the player's instrument.

4 Horn

Horn muting can be effected in a number of different ways. The simplest of these is patently by means of a muting agent, of which a large variety exists made both of metal and of papier-mâché, though these differences are not specified by composers as they are in trumpet muting. A muffled tone can be obtained without difficulty over the whole compass of the horn by means of a mute, which is one advantage it has over a second but no less important method, which is that of hand-stopping or BOUCHÉ. At the same time, although varieties of mutes can supply degrees of edginess in the tone, few can quite achieve the savage bite of the best *bouché* notes. Unlike these, incidentally, the insertion of a mute in the bell does not affect the pitch at all and no transposition is necessary.

Muting by means of actual mutes is prescribed by *sourdines, Dämpfer, sordini,* etc., exactly as in string writing, and not by the symbols '+' and 'o' which are specifically reserved for hand-stopping. But composers are not always precise in their instructions and Walton, for instance, will often write *chiuso* and *aperto* without regard to the method of obtaining the sound. Moreover, time is needed to insert or remove mutes, and many instances exist when the composer has marked *con sordini* or *senza sordini* without even allowing so much as a semiquaver rest to enable the player to carry out the instruction. Where the part lies high enough he will then simply handstop, and indeed the different forms of muting are frequently interchanged according to convenience. It is, however, a mistake to regard instantaneous manipulation of a mute as impossible. A player may have to carry on even if

the hand in the bell is inconveniently holding a mute in readiness, or conversely has not had time to dispose of it, as in Beethoven's *Rondino.*

Some indications often taken to be associated with muting need not actually refer to it at all. The term *echo* for example, as given by Delius in his piece for small orchestra *Summer Night on the River* could imply a muted effect (and is sometimes wrongly played so) whereas on the contrary a true echo is far better produced open, a good player being able to achieve miracles of *pianissimo* without muting.

5 Brass

Where the heavy brass is concerned mutes are of comparatively recent origin, with the exception of those for trumpets, which are prescribed in scores as early as Haydn's Symphony No. 102 in B♭. The *Andante* of this work provides a quite extraordinary example giving an odd effect, since the horns are not muted to match. There is nothing to tell what kind of trumpet mutes Haydn would have expected. Yet unlike horn mutes, the numerous varieties of trumpet and trombone mutes are quite often specified in twentieth-century scores. This to a large extent results from the influence of jazz or other forms of popular or dance music, but the lack of standardized terminology either among players or even in makers' catalogues causes a highly complex situation, especially since many of the mutes stipulated by Bartók, Stravinsky, Milhaud, Gershwin, etc., and which were everyday objects at the time they were writing, have either changed out of all recognition or no longer exist at all.

Different types of trumpet mute encountered in printed scores include:

Cardboard mute
    (Bartók, Violin Concerto, 1938)
Metal mute
        (Villa-Lobos, *Choros* No. 8)
Straight mute (= fibre mute)
    (Bartók/Serly, Viola Concerto)
Double mute
    (Bartók, Violin Concerto, 1938)
Harmon (which is similar to, but
not identical with:)
Wa-wa mute   (Walton, *Façade*)
Hat (this really is made to look
like a small bowler hat)
    (Gershwin, Piano Concerto)
Felt crown
    (Gershwin, Piano Concerto)
Cup mute ⎫ (Copland, as in Piano
Hush mute⎬ Concerto and other jazz-
Jazz mute ⎭   orientated works).

A decision often has to be taken with regard to the quality of sound best suited – in the opinion of player and conductor – to different styles and periods, especially as with changing fashions players tend to favour different mutes, made of totally varying materials. This arises equally in the interpretation of classical or romantic works where no more than the simple *con sordino* is indicated. Metal or fibre mutes were once the most frequent alternatives (the latter having a sharper, thinner quality), and it is therefore particularly disconcerting that in recent years they have strangely fallen into disuse.

Trumpet and trombone mutes can be put on or off in a trice, though many players are loath to acknowledge the fact. Ravel tends to exploit this potential while in Stravinsky's Violin Concerto the 1st trombone is given virtually no time to get the mute in between phrases.

The whole question of trombone mutes is similar to that of trumpets, though the variety and complexities are less because, on the whole, composers have been less demanding or imaginative with muted trombones.

Tuba mutes are a different proposition altogether. All tubas, bass and tenor alike, do have mutes but once more composers do not at any time specify different types, and all kinds are to be seen. The reason is not that there is any intentionally marked difference in their sound but that there has never been any standard tuba mute. The various different mutes in use include some very picturesque pagoda-like contraptions and many of these are actually constructed by the players themselves, since commercial mutes are often clumsy affairs and may well be out of tune.

The tuba is usually marked *con sordino* with the rest of the brass simply as a matter of course, but occasionally muted tubas really are used in pursuit of a new and individual tone colour, as in Strauss's *Don Quixote* or Britten's *War Requiem*. Even the Wagner tubas are supplied with mutes, though neither Wagner nor Bruckner ever prescribed them. Strauss, however, introduced them into *Elektra* and Schoenberg wrote a splendid veiled solo passage for muted Wagner tubas at the beginning of Part 3 of *Gurrelieder*. Nevertheless, undeniably effective and even magical though this passage is, the use of mutes for Wagner tubas remains a side issue. It was perhaps inevitable that mutes would be supplied for them as for all other brass instruments, yet their use to some extent negates Wagner's very purpose in inventing them in the first place.

6 Percussion

Of the percussion department it is most likely the drums that may be required to mute; the standard method of reducing the resonance of drums is to place pads on the heads. This is certainly one form of muting, but alternatively the timpani may be wholly covered with cloth, as for example in a military funeral procession. It is this that is clearly expected when composers (whether as early as Mozart's *Idomeneo* or as recently as Walton's Violin Concerto) use the term **coperti**. Other indications are *muffled* or words used for muting other instruments (*gedämpft*, **voilé**, *con sord.* etc.). But whichever term may appear in the score and part, players today more usually revert to the pad because of its conveniently simple application and removal – although the effect is not the same; Berlioz, in particular, comments on the notably lugubrious sound of the covering cloth.

In the case of snare drums muting is really synonymous with *muffled*, which in its turn is also widely regarded as an instruction for *snares off* (*senza corde*, etc.) since this gives a much less strident quality, especially with the side drum. But the intention may well be that these instruments too should be draped with cloth, even though, as with the timpani, players may not always have either the time or the inclination for so

elaborate a process, and more often than not content themselves with placing a handkerchief or pad on the skin. There are times, however, where no such substitute will quite serve the purpose, as in the closing bars of Elgar's *Falstaff*, where it is specifically the lugubrious sound of a muffled drum that marks poor Falstaff's death. Yet this is not to say that a muffled drum need be soft: in *Till Eulenspiegel* the terrifying *fortissimo* roll with which Till is arraigned before the judges is marked *dumpf*; in such a case it is not probable that a pad or cloth was intended, and the passage is played simply with snares off.

It is very rare to find muting applied to other percussion instruments, but Bartók does give the instruction in the second of his *Two Portraits*, Op. 5, not only for the side drum but for the cymbals and triangle all to play *con sord.* As these are instruments capable of the most refined *pianissimo* without having recourse to special muting devices, it is not obvious what this instruction signifies. However, the solution lies in some footnotes in the parts, though they do not appear in the score. It is indeed further varieties of colour that Bartók is exploring here: in the case of the cymbals these are to be struck 'with the hand', the side drum is to be played 'with a hand placed on the skin while striking', and the triangle too is 'to be clutched whilst being stirred (*gerührt*) by a larger or smaller stick'. These are therefore not conventional muting devices such as apply to the other sections of the orchestra.

7 Harp

In the same piece Bartók also marks *con sord.* for the harp, another instrument for which there is no way of muting in the conventional sense. It is therefore clear that Bartók cannot have intended that the harp should be played here with any sort of mute but rather that the sound should be damped immediately.

8 Piano

The piano, on the other hand, can indeed be muted, the soft (left) pedal being the instrument's equivalent even though neither the word 'mute' nor any of its translations is used in relationship to the piano, other than Debussy's exceptional use of *con sord.* in 'Claire de lune'. This can be confusing for the odd reason that *senza sordini* was occasionally used in classical times, as by Beethoven, to indicate the use of the *sustaining* **pedal** – i.e., without dampers. The most general term for piano muting is **una corda**, even though the action of the soft pedal on the modern piano no longer causes the hammer to strike only a single string but – over most of the compass – two of the three strings. The contradiction is correspondingly **tre corde**, even though this again does not accurately apply to the piano's lower octaves, which have only one or two strings. Similarly, other damping and muting devices are incorporated into cheap or upright pianos but the terminology is not affected.

The French term for the soft pedal (**petite pédale**) does not appear in scores, but the German **mit Verschiebung** (literally 'with shift' indicating

the resultant movement of the entire keyboard of the grand piano) can occasionally be seen, especially in Schumann, as in the opening of the *Konzertstück*, Op. 92.

Since orchestrally the piano is more usually exploited for its resonance or its percussive quality, the soft pedal is less often prescribed. Prokofiev, however, uses it in *Ala et Lolly*, and Casella in the Pastorale of his *Scarlattiana*; Falla askes for *les 2 ped.* at several places in *El Amor Brujo* as does Stravinsky in the 1945 version of the *Firebird* Suite.

Nacchere (It.), *see* CASTANETS

NATIONAL ANTHEM

There was a time, not at all long ago, when most concerts in Britain were automatically introduced by the National Anthem. The exceptions were for the greater part concerts in a series, or operatic and other such performances in a season, when the anthem would be played only at the first and last nights.

Today this custom has largely lapsed except for very special occasions, or when royalty is present, and it is less usual to hear the instruction flying round the orchestra 'Queen in G' (or 'in Bb' if a choir is involved) as the musicians take their places on the platform at the beginning of a concert.

There is both gain and loss here. The necessity before every musical occasion, however unimportant, of going through the formalities of the introductory drum roll, the audience dragging itself reluctantly to its feet, followed by an often routine run-through of the anthem before the proper business of the performance could begin, all too easily degenerated into a travesty of its purpose, acting rather as an orchestral warmer-up or ice-breaker with no more than a perfunctory show of loyalty to the sovereign.

Yet the fact is that the British are blessed with an unusually impressive and musically rewarding piece of music for their national anthem. Quite apart from its royalist significance – and there continue to be many in every concert audience to whom this is a positive reality – 'God Save the Queen' can, at the hands of an imaginative conductor, create a most stirring effect. Sir Thomas Beecham was in the habit of making it into a highly dramatic, if personal, pronouncement, with exaggerated rubatos at the climaxes and a long held fermata at the close, and many visiting orchestras created furores with their individual interpretations; that of the Mexican National Orchestra, in particular, was quite unforgettable and was greeted with waves of enthusiastic applause. It is in fact still known, especially at festivals, for foreign orchestras to pay their hosts the compliment of beginning with a rendering of the British anthem, and in the same way British orchestras need to be prepared to reciprocate when touring abroad. This may even occur within Britain's multinational society since on several occasions, such as Eisteddfods, it is required to give a spirited rendition of, say, the Welsh anthem 'Land of our Fathers', during which the audience can be relied upon to join in; and woe betide the conductor who neglects to repeat the refrain.

Whilst every professional orchestra is expected without warning or advance preparation to be able to render the 'Queen' in its standard version and harmonization, for major functions there have been special arrangements produced by a number of foremost British composers, such as Elgar and Britten. The Elgar version in particular is a huge canvas in which all three verses are set in various vocal combinations including solo soprano and a solo quartet of voices. This is often used for occasions such as the Last Night of the Henry Wood Promenade Concerts, to bring the proceedings to a close.

The anthem's origin in earlier centuries enables it to be introduced without incongruity into chamber orchestral concerts, a version by the eighteenth-century composer Thomas Arne being an especial favourite in such circumstances.

The national anthems of other countries are far more rarely summoned into service in the British orchestral scene, although military bands attending state functions may have to be more regularly prepared for the necessity. For diplomatic reasons, however, or the visit of a foreign dignitary, it does occasionally happen that some unfamiliar anthem has to be performed, the orchestra reading from a hastily summoned set of parts and trying not to look too gauche as they squint down at their desks from a standing position (except for the cellos, harps and timpani whom convention releases – for obvious reasons – from the necessity of rising).

One additional national anthem that is a particularly fine piece of music is the 'Marseillaise', of which Berlioz's superb realization, for soloists, chorus and large orchestra, is hardly less than a masterpiece in its own right. Other familiar anthems are the Austrian and German to a great and well-known melody by Haydn; the Israeli, which is virtually identical with the famous theme in Smetana's *Vltava*; and the American 'Star-Spangled Banner', memorably quoted by Puccini in *Madam Butterfly*. But none of these has been cast in versions of outstanding musical interest, either by their authors or by composers of the first rank.

Naturale, nat. (It.), *see* BOWING, 3; CYMBALS, 2

NIGHTINGALE

There are a number of orchestral nightingales, usually imitated by the flute, as in Beethoven's *Pastoral* Symphony or Stravinsky's *The Song of the Nightingale*, but also by a comical little contraption for the *Toy* Symphony (once believed to be by Haydn though now attributed to Leopold Mozart).

The solitary real nightingale in the orchestral repertoire, however, is the one imported into the concert hall by Respighi for his *Pines of Rome*, which he effects by means of a **gramophone**. The actual 78 rpm disc is listed in the score, catalogue number and all, but sadly the old-style gramophone is now replaced far less romantically by an off-stage TAPE recorder.

Nut, *see* BOWING, 2

OBOE

Conical, double-reed instruments, the oboes are the second from the top of the woodwind section, while the smallest representative of the family in the orchestra is the oboe itself. Below it, in turn, come the OBOE D'AMORE, the COR ANGLAIS and the BASS OBOE.

The French name for the instrument, **hautbois** – literally 'high wood' – was once in use in England and spelt 'hautboy'; in both English and German, however, the Italian 'oboe' has become standard, although the Germans sometimes restore the 'h' to make **Hoboe**, which appears, for example, in many (but by no means all) of the works of Richard Strauss. Like the flute, the oboe is written at concert pitch and only in the treble clef.

Its range is normally taken to be from [musical notation] to [musical notation] although

Stravinsky actually writes a top A in *Pulcinella*; fortunately this is well covered by doublings in the woodwind ensemble, whereas Peter Maxwell Davies makes no bones about top Gs and As in his *Second Fantasia on John Taverner's In Nomine*, sustaining them unmercifully across long bars. In the event top Fs and Gs are not uncommon in the repertoire but Gs such as the solo example in Stravinsky's *Jeu de cartes* remain notorious hurdles.

At the bottom end, it is so taken for granted that Bb is the oboe's lowest note as given in orchestration books that it may be surprising to discover that instruments exist, especially on the Continent, that go no lower than

159

Bᵇ. While admittedly the Bb is not vastly common in orchestral parts, it is certainly frequent enough to be regarded as essential; there being an instance already in the 'Intermezzo' from Mendelssohn's *Midsummer Night's Dream* music (in the same passage that provides a well-known example of an extension to the flute's range).

The oboe possesses the highest degree of sheer cutting power of the whole woodwind department. This, owing to a particularly strong fundamental in its harmonic structure and its vibrant expressiveness, is certainly among the characteristics that have led to the oboe being adopted as the standard arbiter of pitch for the orchestra as a body, 'giving the A' (*see* A) being one of the principal oboist's more important responsibilities. Although it might be going too far to call the 1st oboe the leader of the woodwind, he nevertheless remains the key figure. His pre-eminence in the matter of pitch, together with his instrument's inherent virtues and limitations, its maximum expressive power on the one hand and its relative lack of flexibility on the other, causes the other members of the section normally to pay him the courtesy of working to him in matters of ensemble as well as intonation – i.e., in chord placing, or unison passage work, etc.

For with its small double reed the oboe is harder to control than either flute or clarinet and is also relatively clumsy in rapid passage work as well as in ultra-quick tonguing. The familiar hurdle of Rossini's Overture *La Scala di Seta* would have presented no difficulty to either of these other instruments.

Kodály's *Dances of Galanta* contains a notorious challenge for the tongue of any but the most virtuoso of oboists. The passage, which occurs several times in different keys, is also given to flute and clarinets without presenting anything like the same difficulty. Britten also wrote diabolical tonguing passages in the 'Tarantella' of his *Sinfonietta*.

The oboe's very quality of penetrating expressiveness can also be a mixed blessing, as for instance in the low register, which is very hard to control in soft dynamics. This causes hazards when trying to match the soft ensemble of the other woodwind, the Czech school (especially Dvořák) being notably demanding on the 2nd oboe in this respect. In such cases a conductor of experience and understanding may suggest that the other wind gauge sympathetically what degree of *piano* is practical in order not to present the 2nd oboe with unnerving or unrealistic demands on technique. A particularly feared low 2nd oboe entry occurs between the peasant's dance and the moonlight scene in Smetana's *Vltava*, and that doyen of Czech conductors, Vačlav Talich, used to obviate the risk of a gawky disturbance at this magical moment by replacing the unfortunate oboe with a clarinet. This expedient can still be encountered in Czechoslovakia but is surely going too far, the character of the passage being unduly sacrificed in the interests of safety.

Much depends on the nature and therefore the choice of REEDS, with the result that the very making – as well as the adjustment – of the oboe's complicated double reed usually lies in the province of the player, who is for ever scraping, testing, binding, etc., in the pursuit of the perfect reed for a given solo. This is very much a skill in its own right and one that has to be mastered by every aspiring artist alongside his studies in the playing of the instrument.

The oboe also has greater problems than the flute and clarinet where breathing is concerned, not indeed because more breath is needed, but, on the contrary, because so very little is released at a time through the tiny aperture between the reeds, thus requiring tremendous stamina and control. Long solos, as at the beginning of Ravel's *Tombeau de Couperin*, are as much tests of endurance as they are technical challenges. Some of the greatest virtuosi, such as Leon Goossens and Heinz Holliger, solve this by acquiring a curious skill whereby the cheek is used as a kind of bagpipe sack that can continue to supply air during an extended solo while the player relieves the pressure on his lungs. This is, however, one of a number of highly specialized accomplishments – an important one of which is known as circular breathing – which are nevertheless by no means standard practice.

See also: BELLS UP, EMBOUCHURE, MUTING

Oboe da caccia (It.), *see* COR ANGLAIS

OBOE D'AMORE

This is the second member in descending order of the OBOE family, its name being the same in all languages except only that of the French, who translate it straightforwardly into *hautbois d'amour*. Theoretically it is the alto of the family, although its role as such as has been largely supplanted by the deeper and thus slightly thicker and heavier COR ANGLAIS, since the oboe d'amore almost became extinct after the baroque era. It has nevertheless continued to remain an occasional visitor to the orchestra.

The oboe d'amore lies midway between the oboe and the cor, sounding a minor third lower than notated. Therefore, while Bach wrote for it at concert pitch in works such as the *St Matthew Passion*, such romantic scores as have revived the instrument notate it as a transposing instrument in A, e.g. Mahler's pioneering Rückert Lied 'Um Mitternacht' followed by Strauss's *Symphonia Domestica* and Debussy's *Gigues*. (Holst's *Somerset Rhapsody*, where the oboe d'amore solo is admittedly given at concert pitch, hardly counts since the passage is designated for oboe, with the oboe d'amore shown in brackets as a highly desirable alternative.)

The range of the oboe d'amore is similar to that of the oboe although with certain reservations. Nowhere is it taken quite as high, top E being about the limit, and at the lower end it is generally stated in orchestration manuals that it does not have the bottom B♭. In *Gigues*, however, Debussy (or Caplet who carried out the completion of the score) did take the instrument down to B♭.

OCTOBASS

It is doubtful whether a case could still

be made for Berlioz's octobass, wistfully dreamed up in his ideal orchestra and once actually built, standing no less than ten feet high. It was to have been pitched an octave below the DOUBLE BASS, but in the event it was never scored for, not even by Berlioz himself, as sadly practice proved theory at fault and the mighty instrument had to be abandoned. Moreover, could it ever have been played – and this is in itself highly improbable – its sound, by analogy with the tone of the basses themselves, might well have proved a woeful disappointment.

OFF-STAGE EFFECTS

One of the most exciting adjuncts to concert-giving is off-stage effects. Yet they are not without their problems and a major allowance of rehearsal time has always to be made for their organization. This is partly because no two halls are alike in their provision for such exercises, some of the more recently built in particular being woefully inadequate in their back-stage facilities. Many therefore are the *ad hoc* decisions that need to be made – for example, the presence of an assistant conductor who, in the absence of closed-circuit television, may be necessary to cue the players or singers waiting in the wings to perform a fanfare or some more extended passage, and without whom they may not know whether the right effect has been produced, either with regard to ensemble with the orchestra, or even whether their pitch matches, as distance can play formidable tricks on intonation.

The most usual terminology in other languages is *sulla scena* (It.), *sur la scène* (Fr.), or *auf dem Theater* (Ger.), even for music to be played in a concert hall. One of the earlier examples, as well as the best known, originally derived from the opera house, is the trumpet fanfare in Beethoven's *Leonora No. 3*. (The No. 2 Overture has a similar fanfare far less well known and even more technically difficult.) The popular anecdote of the player being marched off by a policeman (''Ere, you can't do that, sir. Don't you know there's a concert going on inside?'), although an old chestnut, is still a possibility that has to be taken into account. One of our most eminent players quite recently managed heroically to achieve the famous solo while in the process of being dragged away by an irate attendant. Moreover, such distant calls, as well as the three trumpets in the battle scene in Strauss's *Ein Heldenleben*, often have the slightly ridiculous side effect of the players' more or less discreet reappearance on the platform after their off-stage work is over, since they also form part of the main orchestra. Even in this more enlightened age members of the public have been overheard complaining of the orchestra's poor discipline ('Fancy the trumpeters arriving late' or 'Do you know, they actually went off for a quick smoke during the performance'). Conductors have, perhaps for these reasons, been known to instruct the players to remain in the orchestra in this as well as for the opening of Mahler's First Symphony, perhaps even playing the passages muted, thus totally sacrificing the dramatic intention even though some mutes are reputed to give an off-stage effect.

Any member or members of the orchestra can be liable for off-stage service. Hindemith in his *Sinfonia Serena* places a solo violin in the wings on one side, and a solo viola on the opposite side, in order to play in alternation with their respective leaders in the manner of the 'Deposuit' from the Magnificat of Monteverdi's *Vespers* of 1610. Berlioz places a string trio behind the scene towards the end of his Symphony *Harold in Italy*, forming with the solo violist on stage a curiously far-flung string quartet. This produces all kinds of managerial problems since it would be both disturbing and destructive for three of the best players from the front desks to leave their places during the performance. Yet back-desk players are not always sufficiently authoritative and it may be necessary to subpoena extra players of the requisite calibre.

Berlioz was ever a lover of theatrical devices and gives two examples of off-stage playing in his *Symphonie Fantastique*, one for oboe and another for a tubular bell; here again more than one appropriate back-stage location needs to be sought and tried out; the same applies to the side drums and flügelhorn in Mahler's Third Symphony. But a far more exacting effect is required in Massenet's *Scènes Alsaciennes* where the *Retraite* is to be heard behind the platform approaching and disappearing into the far distance. Not every hall (nor every group of musicians who have to play on the march) is equipped to bring this off successfully.

Holst's double women's chorus in 'Neptune' from *The Planets* is another perennial nightmare unless the hall is suitably endowed with galleries, stairs or passages, as the sound of the chorus (ultimately unaccompanied) has to vanish imperceptibly – a door being closed behind the singers – the performance coming to an end only when they have become totally inaudible.

Some of these more complicated operations never lose their perilous aspects – such as the *Grosse Appel* in the last movement of Mahler's Second Symphony, requiring impeccable synchronization by a large and varied back-stage group including trumpets on opposite sides. On the other hand individuals or small groups of players often actually prefer to manage by themselves when circumstances allow.

Curiously enough, off-stage theatrical devices mounted within the main body of the auditorium can sometimes produce just as impracticable situations as those placed out of sight. The brass bands of Berlioz's *Grande Messe des Morts*, one at each corner of the auditorium, or those of Walton's *Belshazzar's Feast* and Mahler's Eighth Symphony, in which they are instructed to be placed entirely separately from the main corpus of performers (*Isoliert Postiert* as Mahler stipulates), can be incredibly awkward – and occasionally even impossible to mount in a hall otherwise much admired for its enlightened platform and auditorium planning, but where the architect lacked either the briefing or the requisite knowledge of orchestral life to allow for such unusual, but no less important extravaganzas.

ONDES MARTENOT

Of all the exotic musical instruments that have been contrived during the past half-century since the development of electronic sound, the only instrument to survive so far remains the *Ondes* (= 'waves') invented by M. Martenot in the late 1930s. The reason for its supremacy, whilst no doubt owing much to its intriguing possibilities of varied sonority, must be primarily attributed to the works by important composers that include a part for it.

Honegger's *Jeanne d'Arc au Bûcher* and Messiaen's *Turangalîla-Symphonie* as well as his *Trois Petites Liturgies* are outstanding examples, but there are many others, mostly French, such as Koechlin who wrote for the Ondes in his *Seven Stars Symphony* to describe the film actress Marlene Dietrich.

In character it is like a wild, penetrating, inhuman wailing musical saw; yet it is eerily fascinating and by no means necessarily disagreeable. It is exclusively a melodic instrument and as such is notated on a single stave.

The Ondes Martenot actually consists of a fairly elaborate set-up. A keyboard is situated behind three speakers, which are described as *principal*; *métallique* – equipped with an orchestral tam-tam; and *palme*, a lyre-like object fitted with twenty-four tuned strings. Visually the most picturesque feature, it is all the sadder that apparently the *palme*'s days are numbered in favour of much more staid-looking electronic substitutes.

The instrument is played in two primary ways, described in its notation as *au clavier* and *ruban*. The former uses a six-octave keyboard from C to C, although a seventh octave is rendered available through the agency of a button, giving the Ondes a range similar to that of the piano but without the three bottom notes. It has, however, the additional capability of a very wide vibrato and of microtones, both obtained through the flexibility of the keys, which are in this respect unlike those of the piano. *Ruban* gives the other style of playing, the ribbon being threaded through a metal ring that the player controls with his right forefinger. With this the keyboard is again unpianistic, serving as no more than a guide to pitch, every kind of *portamento* and – above all – *glissando* being its chief stock-in-trade. It has, moreover, an incredible range of dynamics from a whisper to a positively ear-splitting shriek.

Honegger, like most composers, leaves the many complex details of possible execution to the performer (much like organ registration), at most contenting himself with the primary instructions *au clavier* and *ruban*. Messiaen, however, is not only well acquainted with Ginette Martenot (the original executant of her husband's creation), but his sister-in-law Jeanne Loriod is also a skilled performer on the Ondes. He has thus been able to fill his score with every kind of technical instruction including the variations of tone production (by means of curved arrows), degrees and species of resonance (indicated by numbers and letters corresponding to the controls manipulated with the left hand) and the choice of the three available speakers. Messiaen uses numerous other words and instructions as well, including suggestions for the orchestral tone colour that should be simulated, as one of the characteristics of the Ondes is the ability to imitate orchestral timbres.

OPHICLEIDE

The word 'ophicleide' is in actual fact the Greek word for 'keyed serpent' although unlike the SERPENT itself it is a tall brass instrument. Until a few years ago the picture of an ophicleide, long and ungainly, survived on the weekly front cover of *Punch*, played by an angel in full flight, but now even that historical design has been relegated to limbo. However, in these days of passionate authenticity, a few specialist players are attempting to resurrect the monstrosity with its undeniably humorous qualities.

The best-known orchestral appearance of the instrument is in Mendelssohn's Overture to *A Midsummer Night's Dream*. While only one of numerous appearances of the ophicleide in orchestral scores, this is unusual in that the tuba is not automatically substituted in modern printings of the score as it is in most other relevant works. For the two instruments are not at all similar in character, even though Berlioz, an ardent writer for the ophicleide, already anticipated the usurping power of the much fatter-voiced tuba, then a newcomer, by giving it as an alternative in his *Symphonie Fantastique*.

Where the masterly Mendelssohn overture is concerned, such a substitute – now invariable practice – has never been more than *faute de mieux*, as the boy composer was caricaturing the comic figure of Bottom with his ass's head, and the smooth round tone of the tuba is far less suitable for this purpose than the raucous and somewhat crude ophicleide.

Only bass ophicleides have ever been summoned into orchestral service, although others did also exist. Berlioz wrote in detail about alto ophicleides in E♭ and F, though he never used them. The smaller members of the family are generally described as **keyed bugles** these being, however, primarily military or band instruments.

Two bass ophicleides were once in use, pitched in B♭ and C, although that in C was by far the more common. Berlioz wrote for both, the one in B♭ being notated as a transposing instrument. They were always written in the bass clef, especially as they were not taken very high. Berlioz himself hardly writes above E♭, though he lists the range in his *Treatise of Instrumentation* to be from B below the bass clef to the A above middle C, regretting that 'perhaps sufficient advantage has not yet been taken of the very high notes'.

The ophicleide survived long enough to be used as the bass to the trombone ensemble in the seat now occupied regularly by the tuba. Examples of this exist both in Wagner (*Rienzi*) and in Verdi who, as late as 1874, specified 'officleide' in his Requiem.

ORCHESTRA

This, the very subject of the present book, is an instrumental body which

165

includes a STRING section. Orchestras can, of course, be of different sizes, from the FULL ORCHESTRA used for symphony concerts down to the CHAMBER ORCHESTRA. Instrumental groups lacking strings come mostly into the category of BANDS: MILITARY BANDS, BRASS BANDS, dance bands, and so on.

It is a standard prerequisite that the strings of an orchestra are made up of players most of whom play the same line as others of their subsection – violins, violas, cellos or basses – as is normal in orchestral works such as the Beethoven symphonies. If this is not so the group would otherwise generally be called an ENSEMBLE. But here too there are isolated exceptions, such as those works by the contemporary Greek composer Xenakis in which every single player in the substantial orchestral string section of, for example, *Metastasis* or *Pithoprakta* has a separate line.

The usual formation of an orchestra includes corresponding groups of WOODWIND, BRASS, PERCUSSION and other miscellaneous instruments, e.g. harp, celesta, organ, piano, etc. But unlike the strings none of these is integral to the identification of the group as an orchestra, nor is indispensable to its function in that capacity.

ORCHESTRA LISTS

These are of various species and different purposes. In the first place there is the list showing the actual instruments required for each work to be played. This is necessary for programme planning and of prime importance to the orchestra manager for the engaging of the necessary players. Publishers' catalogues and orchestral files carry comprehensive lists of this kind laid out according to formulae, usually based on groupings such as, for example: 3.2.2.3: 4.2.3.0: Timp. 3 Perc. Str. This, which gives the essential instrumental forces required for Beethoven's Choral Symphony, shows the woodwind, brass, percussion and strings in their conventional order, with the woodwind subdivided to show the numerical strength of in turn flutes, oboes, clarinets and bassoons, and the brass subdivided to show the strength of horns, trumpets, trombones and tuba, the latter still shown even if with a zero, indicating that none is required. This use of zeros keeps the formula clear even in the case of very small forces – an early Haydn symphony might, for instance, be represented by: 0.2.0.1: 2.0.0.0: Str. At the other end of the scale, extra instruments not part of this scheme may be added separately by name, such as saxophones, harps, celesta, etc.; also some lists identify doubling instruments specifically, such as piccolos, cors anglais, cornets and so on.

Strings are rarely listed numerically even when composers state their preferred strength. This is perhaps because however desirable the fullest body of strings might seem, it is hardly ever categorically essential, and economic as well as sheer platform considerations often cause unavoidable reductions in the numbers actually employed. Where string strengths are cited, moreover, there is a twofold custom of referring either to desks, as for example 8.7.6.5.4 in a full orchestra, or the less conventional formula of 16.14.12.10.8 showing the number of players, and confusion has sometimes been known to arise in borderline cases. Where string enumeration is specified in the scores, however, it is always listed by players, not desks.

The orchestra manager will always carry personnel lists giving the names of every player; the conductor too may wish to have a copy of this in order to identify players, recall the names of familiar faces, or have the ability to address players by name rather than with the impersonal '2nd clarinet' or 'Mr 1st horn'. There are, however, traps here as Mr X frequently turns out to have been replaced at short notice by Mr Y. Even more hazardous is the growing custom of using first names, since the formal names of many musicians correctly given on any list are often not those by which they are actually known.

Permanent orchestras will sometimes be listed in full in the programmes of their concerts. This is a splendid custom, much appreciated by audiences, but the lists can be misleading when the personnel, laid out in such detail, turns out to be the official contractual register instead of the names of those players who are in fact on the platform.

Another confusion of such listings occurs when the seating is not fixed, the names of the players of any one instrument being given alphabetically, so that it is impossible to guess which of the many names apply to which players. The purpose in publishing the list, as in the case of the contract list, is thereby to a large extent negated.

ORCHESTRAL MATERIAL

An orchestra works from individual parts like all instrumental groups but unlike vocal ensembles. Thus a set of parts of an orchestral work will consist of several of each string line (violin 1, violin 2, viola, cello and bass) and a set of wind, etc., one for each instrument. String parts for the numerous desks are identical to the master copies, divided lines – if these should occur – all being included so that the individual players need to mark for themselves which strand concerns them. In many classical works the cellos and basses play together for long periods or sometimes even throughout, in which case only a single cello/bass part is supplied. Conversely, if the music is sufficiently complicated, the string lines dividing constantly, separate front- and back-desk parts are printed, as in some of the Strauss tone poems, where the parts are marked (a) and (b), or notably as in Smetana's cello parts, the 2nd cello joining with the basses for much of the time, leaving the front desks to enjoy an independent existence.

Where the wind and brass are concerned, some publishers – especially in England and France – used to provide only one copy for the 1st and 2nd of each instrument printed together, their parts being shown the one above the other on two bracketed staves. Although obviously to some extent inconvenient, the stand having to be placed between the players who both have to squint sideways at it, there was also some gain in the way they thought and played together as a single unit.

167

For long this was accepted as a fact of life, and a virtue made of necessity, but over the years most wind players have rebelled and now categorically insist on duplicates being provided, even if some photocopies have to be made at the eleventh hour. Double-bass players in some orchestras also insist on having each a stand and part to himself.

Percussion parts produce quite special problems and as a result there is no standard procedure for dividing them between players. Often the publishers will concoct some kind of division with, say, bass drum and cymbals on one part, triangle, tambourine and tam-tam on another, xylophone on a third and so on; but errors of judgement are frequent, causing much inconvenience and confusion. It is all too easily forgotten, for instance, that the bells as well as all the glockenspiel – vibraphone –xylophone group of instruments must have plenty of time and room for manoeuvre. Many composers try to avoid complaints by providing a multiple part containing all the percussion, with a copy supplied for each player, who can then select his own line as it best works out. But theoretically ingenious, even foolproof, as this may seem, the result in a work with a great deal of complicated percussion can not only look horrifically intricate, but may take up so much space on each page that the players find themselves endlessly struggling with impossible and frequent page turns.

The system of individual parts for each player is to some degree a specifically instrumental practice, choruses or vocal ensembles being accustomed to working from 'vocal scores' (in which the voice parts are given complete over a piano arrangement of the remainder), except where the CHORUS is used quasi-instrumentally as an extra colour in the orchestral spectrum.

It is the LIBRARIAN's responsibility to provide the orchestral material either by purchase (increasingly rare these days), or hire from the publishers, or from the orchestra's own library. The latter is obviously the most efficient but tends mostly to be limited to works from classical or earlier romantic periods where the composer has long been dead and is thus out of copyright. In contemporary works orchestral parts are rarely engraved or even printed, and are often supplied in more or less legible manuscript. All too frequently publishers' hire libraries have very few sets of parts of even quite important works, and the materials can be in atrocious condition with endless contradictory marks or BOWINGS scrawled over them from earlier performances, which the publishers' librarians seldom if ever clean up before reissue, despite labels on the covers to the effect that if marks are put into the parts an extra charge will be made for removing them. It is, however, inescapable that marks will have had to be put into copies, often in direst haste during rehearsal, and as a result no notice is taken of such warnings. The copies thus soon deteriorate to the point at which complaints are an everyday occurrence, especially in view of the ever increasing hire charges coupled with the non-availability of the music for purchase. It has occasionally been suggested that performances should be cancelled if the parts are considered to be demonstrably substandard but, logical as such a step seems, it has only very infrequently been carried out. In music, as in other works of public presentation, 'the show must go on' continues to be an honoured maxim.

See also: COPYISTS, EDITIONS, REHEARSAL LETTERS

ORGAN

1 Description
The organ is the largest of all the keyboard instruments, being normally equipped with several manuals and a full **pedal** keyboard in addition.

The most usual manuals are (from top to bottom): the Swell, specializing in the reeds; the Great, the manual of the diapasons and the loud brassy stops; and the Choir, the softest toned. Above the Swell some larger organs have a fourth manual called the Solo and the largest of all yet a fifth, the Echo manual.

The conventional playing (as opposed to sounding) range of the manuals in a modern organ is the five

octaves from   to   . In general the basic manual stops are the 8-foot and 4-foot, so called after the length of the largest pipe of the set; the 8-foot play at pitch and the 4-foot sound an octave higher than written. Then there are 2-foot stops sounding an octave higher again and two intermediary stops called the Quint and the

Twelfth, which automatically add consecutive fifths to everything that is played, with polytonal effect.

The playing range of the pedals is two and a half octaves from C below the bass clef to G above middle C, the stops being 16-foot, sounding an octave lower than written, while in the largest organs there will be the enormous 32-foot sounding two octaves lower which makes everything vibrate including, it may well be, the very building itself. (The 32-foot stops in the magnificent organ of Lincoln Cathedral were for long actually debarred from use lest the cathedral should shake to the point of actual collapse; nevertheless 64-foot pipes have been installed in the recently completed Anglican Cathedral in Liverpool; the notes cannot really be said to be audible at all, but only felt.) These low stops, however, are particularly desirable for such opening rumbles as in Strauss's *Zarathustra* and Verdi's *Otello*.

2 Use in Combination with the Orchestra
The appearance of the organ in orchestral work is always an occasion. Its size, visual impact, potential strength and associations all mark it as a distinguished visitor and it is mostly with this in mind that composers have introduced it orchestrally rather than as a continuo instrument.

3 Continuo Playing
Where continuo playing is concerned the organ is as much in evidence as the harpsichord, but is even more closely associated with religious functions, so that in the church music of classical composers up to the time of Beethoven

the organ has no individual existence outside its role as part of the basso continuo. Hence it is written only as a figured bass, which is how it still appears in Beethoven's Mass in C, Op. 86. But by the Missa Solemnis a change can already be seen with the organ now given its own staves even though many passages are oddly shown fully worked out and then countermanded with the words *senza org.*, i.e, *tacet*. No doubt the purpose of this was to show the player the framework of the music even when he is not occupied.

The place in the score for the organ is generally above the strings, but in Berlioz's sacred choral works, such as the Te Deum, where the organ has a considerable solo part to play, the lines are again put at the foot of the score. Even in an example as late as the Brahms Requiem the organ's contribution is not absolutely fixed, although later full scores such as the reprinted Peters or the Breitkopf do contain a specific part, still at the foot of each page, not given in earlier editions or in the miniature score.

In fact, whenever the organ is functioning as continuo, the realization of its notation will largely be a matter of choice for the player. Moreover, the very degree of his participation may be a matter for individual judgement; hence performances are given of, for example, Bach's Passions or Handel's oratorios in which the organ may supply the continuo for choral movements while a harpsichord will take over for solo numbers according to the conductor's feeling for, or knowledge of, period style.

Again as with the harpsichord realizations (by no doubt worthy scholars) of the organ's figured-bass line exist in the published materials of many well-known works; but an experienced artist will more likely prefer to work on his own directly from the full score.

Sometimes, as for example in the recitative section of Mozart's *Exsultate Jubilate*, the orchestral string parts are printed with a full realization of the organ continuo laid out in self-contained harmonies, even though no sign of this exists in the score. Such practice emphasizes the problem, never absent where the organ is concerned, over the quality or even the very availability of an instrument in the building where the performance is to take place.

4 Problems of Availability I: Character

In this respect the organ magnifies immeasurably the pianist's occupational hazard – the different instruments he may have to contend with from one location to another. The multiplicity of stops, the number of manuals, the subsidiary extras such as swell box, composition buttons (couplers), mixtures, etc., will all vary or may be lacking in different organs. If the hall has no built-in organ at all the question may arise of whether or not an electric organ should be hired, its 'tubby' synthetic tone being all too often a dismal substitute for a genuine pipe organ, especially at full volume and with regard to the deeper notes. Some replacement is more easily tolerated, of course, when the organ is needed as no more than a continuo instrument, though even then an inadequate substitute may seriously mar the success of a major choral work. It is true that very large electric organs do now exist and give a surprising illusion of the right quality, but even these are rare and can be alarmingly fallible. Small portative organs as well as the similar but not identical Royals, or Positives, also exist, but are not used as replacements for the grand organ; more usually they are brought in either for old music, such as the Monteverdi *Vespers*, which needs a portative as well as a grand organ, or for very new music, such as many works by Peter Maxwell Davies, whose *Five Motets*, as well as his opera *Taverner*, specifically require the delicate, subtle sounds of these beautiful instruments.

II: Pitch

Even if the concert venue boasts a grand organ the question of its pitch may be a hazard as organs are all too often tuned to a different pitch from that used by orchestras. If the variation is not too great the orchestra can, though with some difficulty, partially adjust to the point where the performance is at least able to take place. For an organ can never simply be retuned on the spot; if a piano takes hours to tune, a large organ would take days. Hence, before rehearsing or performing any work using an organ, the orchestra takes a new A from that instrument, and even then needs to take care to listen, for an organ tends to sound flat when set in abrupt apposition to the combined living tones of massed orchestral players.

It transpires therefore, that in certain circumstances plans to include a work containing an organ may either have to be abandoned or, on the contrary, specifically included because of the presence of a fine instrument.

5 Examples of Repertoire in Orchestral Scores

Bearing all these considerations in mind, it is understandable that composers do not write lightly or casually for the organ. The Third Symphony of Saint-Saëns, a notable work in this respect (following Liszt's initiative in the Symphonic Poem *Hunnenschlacht* and the choral epilogue of the *Faust* Symphony), is widely known as the 'Organ Symphony' although the organ is used very sparingly and only in two of the four movements. Similarly, the organ entries in Strauss's *Also sprach Zarathustra*, Janáček's *Taras Bulba*, and Vaughan Williams's *Job* are surprisingly few, and are thus the more dramatically arresting. Elgar even uses this impressiveness to increase the stature of works like the *Enigma Variations* and the overture *Cockaigne* by adding the organ to the closing pages, although he cautiously marks it optional (*ad lib.*).

Larger opera houses are usually equipped with organs, for the instrument occupies a substantial niche in the world of opera, especially in such obvious contexts as the church scenes of Gounod's *Faust*, Massenet's *Manon*, Puccini's *Tosca*, Britten's *Peter Grimes*, etc.

The organ also plays a vital part in large-scale choral works such as Mahler's Eighth Symphony; Janáček's *Glagolitic Mass* has spectacular solo passages for the instrument, and sacred works from all schools up to the late romantics tend as a matter of course to feature the organ. The Requiems of Fauré and Duruflé are outstanding in this area, the latter (as befits a work by a prominent organist) being full of detailed registration and written out on three staves.

6 Notation

Strictly speaking, it is on three staves that the organ should be notated, the manuals sharing the upper two and the pedals always having the lowest to themselves. But although solo organ music is usually so written, it is by no means the rule in orchestral organ parts. These, on the contrary, are frequently shown simply on two staves like piano music, the mode of execution and distribution of the lines between manuals and pedals being left to the player, apart from a few scattered indications showing some notes intended for the pedal keyboard.

Liszt in his *Faust* Symphony, Elgar, Strauss, Respighi, Bruckner, Mahler, Vaughan Williams and Britten are all punctilious enough to write their organ parts in full on the three staves, showing that it is not a matter of period or of country but of the individual composer. Nor does the custom give any indication of the extent or importance of the organ part in a given work. Saint-Saëns notates it on only the two staves, as does Holst in *The Planets*, and the same is true of most operatic parts, as for example in *La Forza del Destino*, *Cavalleria Rusticana*, *Faust*, *Tosca*, or Massenet's *Manon*, this last having an extended solo representing a Voluntary at the seminary of Saint Sulpice.

These all use the organ to represent genuine organ music played in churches, but in every case the composer has given only a two-dimensional figuration of what is essentially three-dimensional music. Yet this restriction cannot be said to imply ignorance on the part of the composers or inadequacy in the presentation of their music, but rather that they were content to use what amounts to a short score (not perhaps unlike that used for stage bands) in the firm knowledge that their intentions would be fully realized by any competent organist on the basis of the notation supplied.

7 Registration

In fact very little technical detail is indicated in the organ parts of most orchestral scores. This is perhaps primarily because any registration specified by a composer based on an instrument known to him would in any case have to be reorganized by the player in the light of available resources on each separate occasion. Nevertheless, bearing in mind that a change of registration amounts to no less than the equivalent of a total re-scoring of the orchestral wind parts, and that solo organ music is on the contrary normally published with copious suggestions for registration, it may be thought remarkable that, apart from works by notable organists (Fauré and Duruflé have already been mentioned in this connection) not even the choice of manual is indicated in most orchestral music, Brahms's *man. oben* (i.e. 'upper manual' – presumably the Swell) in the *Deutsches Requiem* being exceptional.

The term 'full organ' (German, *volles Werk*; French, *grand jeu*; Italian, *organo pieno*) is used when maximum tone is required with a ringing diapason supporting reeds and brass-type pipes. In this, the doubling of octaves twice and three times above and below the written notes is presupposed.

8 Dynamics

A curious impediment of the organ is its difficulty in making subtle gradations of dynamics. One can add or reduce the stops but this gives a stepwise *crescendo* or *diminuendo*; hence the only means of gradual rise or fall is the swell box controlled with the feet, and the opening and shutting of a box hardly corresponds to the infinite tonal gradations at the disposal of every orchestral musician.

9 Communication

The platform position of the organ has, of course, generally to be accepted precisely as it stands because in most buildings the console cannot be moved. This often means that communication between organist and conductor can be achieved only through a system of mirrors; indeed in some cathedrals the organ console is totally hidden from the conductor and vision is possible only on a one-way basis by means of closed-circuit television. But whether the communication is by mirrors, television or any other such artifical contrivance, it creates a highly inconvenient situation that is accepted only because of the understood fact that the organist is an exceptionally accomplished specialist in his own field and is almost by courtesy, as it were, entering into the conventions of orchestral practices.

Ottavino (It.), **see** PICCOLO

Ottoni (It.), *see* BRASS, 1

Pandero sia sonajas (Sp.), *see* TAMBOURINE

PARTICELL

This is a shortened version of the FULL SCORE, not – it should be emphasized – designed to be readily playable on a piano, although it can sometimes be so used, but created by a composer as a preliminary working model from which the orchestration can be carried out. A particell is, indeed, generally laid out on several staves so as to accommodate possibilities for numerous instrumental colours as well as polyphonic strands, harmonies, etc. Debussy's particell of the *Prélude à l'Après-midi d'un Faune*, laid out on sometimes four, sometimes five staves, and using different coloured inks, is so beautiful that it has received a limited circulation thanks to the benefaction of the Robert Owen Lehman Foundation in Washington.

A particell might or might not include every detail of a composition as it will appear when finished. At one period of his output Schoenberg actually published the particells of his orchestral works in preference to making full scores; but this turned out not to be a success, partly because it resulted in the cramming of innumerable and indecipherable details on to the few allotted staves, and partly because the composer himself was no longer able to visualize – and hence create – the same degree of subtle colourings that a full score renders possible, and thus Schoenberg's own works of this period are cruder in their orchestration than those of his earlier fully worked-out scores.

Conversely, however, such a particell can sometimes be used for rehearsal purposes and – if more rarely – for performances. The complicated vocal scores of operas and ballets such as Berg's *Wozzeck* or Delius's *A Village Romeo and Juliet* benefited greatly by their publication in the form less of piano reductions than of particells.

Pauken (Ger.), *see* TIMPANI, 2

Pavillon chinois (Fr.), *see* BELL TREE, JINGLES

Pavillons en l'air (Fr.), *see* BELLS UP

Pedal Clarinet, *see* CONTRABASS CLARINET

PEDAL NOTES

Contrary perhaps to expectation, these have nothing whatever to do with the pedals on the piano, harp, organ or even timpani, but fall within the province exclusively of the HORNS and brass. Pedal notes on the horns, trumpet and trombones are those created by the lowest harmonics and accordingly with a relaxed and often 'inset' EMBOUCHURE. They have an unmistakably characteristic rumbling quality used quite often by composers as a special effect, such as Beethoven's and Brahms's horn pedals supporting vehement passages for the soloist in their Eb ('Emperor') and D minor Piano Concertos respectively.

So deep does their strong vibrant resonance actually feel to the player that in the case of the horns and trumpets they gave rise, in classical times, to a method of notation that, lying below the stave in the bass clef and an octave lower than the corresponding notation in the treble clef, is of positive psychological and technical aid to performance, although this practice has come to be condemned by theorists and composers as illogical.

Berlioz was especially fond of the effect of the trombone pedal notes, using them for many a grotesque moment – as in the macabre 'Marche au Supplice' from the *Symphonie Fantastique*, though the editors of the Breitkopf Gesamtausgabe so little understood his intentions that they reorchestrated the relevant passages, switching the trombone and tuba lines. Consequently it became necessary to re-engrave several pages when, in a more enlightened decade, the true originality of the music was at last recognized. Undoubtedly however, the extreme example of idiosyncratic exploitation of pedal notes is in the same composer's *Grande Messe des Morts* where six trombones play them in unison, descending as low as a growl on the deepest G♯, alternating with only the high bare sound of three flutes. Berlioz was so proud of these extraordinary sonorities that he described them in detail, quoting the whole passage, in his *Treatise of Instrumentation*.

It is, nevertheless, obviously more usual to find these trombone pedal notes cloaked in some kind of orchestral texture. Examples of the kind were introduced frequently by Janáček, in, for instance, the *Sinfonietta* or the *Glagolitic Mass*, as well as by Alban Berg who makes splendid use of them in his *Drei Orchesterstücke*, Op. 6. Lambert features a solo trombone pedal note in *Summer's Last Will and Testament*, facetiously marking it *come lampone* (Italian for 'raspberry').

Pedal Timpani, *see* TIMPANI

Pedals, *see* HARP, HARPSICHORD; MUTES, 8; ORGAN, 1; PIANO, 4

PERCUSSION

1 Names and Members
This is the widest and most diverse department of the orchestra, comprising every instrument played by striking or shaking with the exception only of the TIMPANI (which are a law unto themselves) and the keyboard group. Some composers or editions do in fact couple these with the percussion, as well as the CELESTA, but this is contrary to the normal conventions of orchestral practice.

The collective term in other languages is **batterie** (Fr.); **Schlagzeug**, or sometimes **Schlagwerk** (Ger.); while the Italian word corresponds to the French – **batteria** – although both, if more rarely, do also use the term analogous to our own (*percussion* and *percussione*).

It will never be possible to make any ultimate and exhaustive list of all the multifarious instruments, devices and effects in which every percussionist has to be expert, from the relatively simple (triangle, cymbals, bass drum) to the extremely skilled (snare drums, tambourines, xylophone, etc.). The following catalogue, however, contains most of those found in orchestral scores up to the present day:*

Definite Pitch

ANTIQUE CYMBALS, (ANVIL), BELLS, BOUTEILLOPHONE, COWBELLS (*cencerros*), CROTALES, FLEXATONE, GLASS HARMONICA, etc., GLOCKENSPIEL, GONGS, MARIMBA, [MOTOR HORNS], Roto-toms, (Tenor Drum), VIBRAPHONE, XYLOPHONE, Xylorimba

Indefinite Pitch

ANVIL, BASS DRUM, BELL PLATES, BONGOS, [BULL ROARER], CASTANETS, CHAINS, Chinese BELL TREE, CLAVES, COCONUTS, CONGAS, (COWBELLS), (CROTALES), CYMBALS, GEOPHONE, GONG (tam-tam), GOURDS, HAMMER (and mallets on plank), HAND DRUMS, JINGLES (sleigh bells), [LION'S ROAR (string drum)], LOG DRUM, Maracas, [METRONOME], Military Drum, Pavillon chinois, Rasps and Gourds, RATTLES (various), Rute (VERGHE), SANDBOX, Side Drum, [SIREN], Sistro, Tabor (*tambourin*), TAMBOURINE, Temple Blocks (Korean), Tenor Drum, [THUNDER MACHINE], TIMBALES, TOM-TOMS, TRIANGLE, Turkish Crescent, WHIP, [WHISTLE], WIND CHIMES, [WIND MACHINE], WOOD BLOCK (Chinese)

As indicated in all this massive heterogeneous collection, there is one chief dividing line separating two main groups: those instruments with and

---

* As throughout this book SMALL CAPITALS denote a separate entry.

those without definite pitch – although, in the case of a small number (those in round brackets), different composers have used them in either a tuned or untuned capacity. But there are also a few devices (in square brackets) that it has to be acknowledged are not proper percussion since they are neither struck nor shaken, yet are still handled by this department.

2 Number of Players

There is a dichotomy unique to the percussion group between the number of different instruments used in a work and how many players may be required to operate them. In nineteenth- and early twentieth-century scores it is rare to find in orchestration lists any indication of how many percussion players the composer had in mind. Ravel's *Daphnis et Chloé*, for instance, lists twelve instruments (in additional to timpani) that actually require no more than eight players. Moreover, where more than one timpanist is essential to play a further set of drums, he will generally be co-opted from the percussion group of players. Conversely, Moeran's *Serenade in G* is laid out with no fewer than six percussion lines for seven instruments on the first page of score, but scrutiny will reveal that, surprisingly enough, two players (still always in addition to timpani) can cope with all they have to contribute.

More recently, however, composers reckon to have worked out the problem and usually list the number of players at the head of the score, but it is a mistake for the orchestral manager to order the forces accordingly; it lies in the province of the principal percussionist to report on the minimum number of players he regards as necessary for a given programme. This may depend on a number of factors, including the location or importance of the performance. For it is astonishing how much of an apparently extravagant percussion ensemble can if necessary be managed by a smaller group of willing and resourceful musicians, though the practice is understandably resisted on ethical grounds by the highly organized percussion freemasonry of the larger symphony orchestras.

Nor can one turn to even the most efficient composer for reliable guidance: the full score of Strauss's *Rosenkavalier* stipulates *3 Spieler* against the ten percussion instruments listed, but a glance at the heavier moments of the opera shows that five or even six players are necessary, while Stravinsky's *The Rite of Spring* contains a careful roster of the vast orchestra but nevertheless forgets the cymbals.

3 Notation

In the score the standard position for the percussion is immediately below the timpani, although it may occasionally stray either above, to confusing effect, or – as in Smetana's *Má Vlast* – underneath the strings at the very foot of the page. But where the different members of a multiple percussion group are concerned, there is virtually no uniformity of order. It might be thought that on the whole the higher, lighter instruments – triangle, side drum, tambourine, etc. – would be at or near the top, with bass drum and tam-tam at the bottom, but although this is a principle often followed it is no more than that.

Because of their close association bass drum and cymbals are often written on a single stave, in which case the very universality of the phrase 'bass drum and cymbals' rather than 'cymbals and bass drum' may all too easily suggest that the bass drum is always notated on the upper line and the cymbals on the lower, whereas the opposite is normally intended. The different instruments are usually specified by name (and hence on each page of the score) and are notated on conventional staves headed by clefs; yet none of this can be taken as standard practice. Where the listing is concerned it is not at all uncommon to find a set of six or more lines of percussion without a single indication of what is playing and it is necessary to check back to the first page of, for example, Balakirev's *Thamar* or Shostakovich's First Symphony. Indeed, in the latter work the lack of indication in the original score has led to a common misreading, since in the slow movement a later printing makes a guess at 'piatti' where 'tam-tam' is surely more likely to have been the composer's intention in this particular context.

Another unfortunate custom, especially in more modern scores, is when composers indicate the percussionist by number instead of by the instrument. In the heat of the rehearsal, the sign 'Perc. 3' is little help to a conductor who may address the right player but without knowing instinctively what to expect of him.

The use of staves with conventional clefs for percussion of indefinite as well as definite pitch is quite common, although non-pitched instruments are sometimes placed on single lines, either headed by some neutral symbol such as ◀—— or even without anything at all. But where a range of different-sized drums, gongs or tam-tams (even maybe combined with cymbals, etc.) is used to suggest higher or lower sonic relationships, several such symbols are often placed together on staves, as in the melodrama from the second act of Britten's *The Rape of Lucretia*, or the notes are indicated with crosses instead of heads like Walton's *Scapino* and *Façade*; or even token staves are used, with no more lines than the number of instruments portrayed. Notation with tails up and down may be used to identify two different instruments on the same stave, but is of course also used to signify a single drum played with two sticks.

If clefs are used to symbolize instruments of indefinite pitch it is normal to find only treble or bass, the former to suggest high-sounding effects such as triangle, tambourine, side drum, etc., the latter for deep sounds – bass drum, tam-tam. So much is obvious, as also that borderline cases can be found, the composer making his own *ad hoc* decisions. Of these, the outstanding example is that of the cymbals, which are surprisingly often notated in the bass clef (the opposite of Tchaikovsky's curious way of writing for both deep tam-tam and bass drum in the treble clef) even when given a separate stave from the bass drum to which they surely supply the contrasting high sounds. Exceptions to this can, however, be found in Delius's *Eventyr* (but not *Paris*), Strauss's *Heldenleben* (but not *Til Eulenspiegel*), and especially the Adagio of Bruckner's Eighth Symphony in which the composer actually ascribes to the percussion different notes, G, Bb and Eb, as if he imagined both the cymbal clashes and triangle strokes harmonizing with the climaxes they decorate. Moreover, though they are all in a dynamic of *fff*, one may well feel that the higher notes are intended to be the stronger, and Mahler must have thought the idea strongly evocative as he followed Bruckner's example repeatedly in his Seventh Symphony.

4 Orchestral Use

Whereas percussion other than timpani was initially introduced into the orchestra through the increasing popularization of colourful Turkish band effects (as in Haydn's *Military* Symphony, Mozart's *Entführung aus dem Serail*, Beethoven's Choral Symphony, etc.), during the romantic era it soon came to be used for extra sonority or brilliance in climaxes, on the one hand, and to enlarge the orchestral spectrum on the other. It is however interesting to observe composers' economy as well as their extravagance in the use of percussion: the total abstinence on Tchaikovsky's part in his Fifth Symphony as well as his careful self-control in the *Pathétique*; the surprisingly few percussion instruments and players required for the enormous orchestra of Wagner's *Ring* (it is an instructive occupation to count the tam-tam strokes of the entire epic). These are perhaps more positive hallmarks of the composers' resourcefulness than the self-indulgent batteries of so many twentieth-century scores.

At the same time it has to be recognized that in the latter part of this century the percussion section, with its myriad techniques and evocation of ethnic cultures from all over the globe, has blossomed into by far the most extensive of the entire orchestra. The variety has become virtually infinite, and so too has the potential range of dynamics, from the cataclysmic to the most delicate and imaginative sonic effects, which its manifold resources have aroused in the creative minds of so many composers.

See also: PLATFORM ARRANGEMENT, SCORE LAYOUT

Perfect Pitch, *see* ABSOLUTE PITCH

Petite flûte (Fr.), *see* PICCOLO

Petite pédale (Fr.), soft pedal on the piano; *see* MUTES, 8

Petite timbale (Fr.), *see* TIMPANI, 4

Pianino (It.), *see* PIANO, 1, 5

PIANO

1 Names and Types

The piano is known by its full name, 'pianoforte', primarily in scores using Italian terminology; otherwise it usually appears in the familiar colloquial abbreviation. Strangely enough the Russians still use 'fortepiano' as the full name of the instrument, a form elsewhere reserved for the eighteenth- and early nineteenth-century predecessor of our modern piano. Of other languages, only German preserves in current use an entirely independent word, **Klavier**, which though in common usage has come to mean the piano, strictly denotes not merely that instrument but any instrument with a keyboard, as in Bach's *Klavier Konzerte*, once widely accepted as piano concertos but today played mostly on the HARPSICHORD. Indeed the French also use 'clavier' specifically to denote just the keyboard itself.

Moreover, a grand piano, as opposed to an upright or even a baby grand, is known in German as **Flügel**, Strauss, for example, specifying a *Konzertflügel* in the orchestra list for *Ariadne auf Naxos*.

As a rule a grand piano is taken for granted unless otherwise stipulated, e.g. in Glazunov's *The Seasons*, or Berg's *Wozzeck*, where an upright piano is described as **pianino** in the latter instance precisely because of its home-spun sound, representing a pub piano on the stage. Peter Maxwell Davies similarly uses what he describes as an 'out-of-tune "honkytonk" piano' in his *St Thomas Wake*. Upright pianos are, however, not normally used orchestrally since, apart from their greatly inferior tone quality, the player is virtually unable to see the conductor or other players for accurate ensemble playing.

2 Range

The standard range of the piano is the seven octaves from  to

and this applies to the different kinds of instrument, whether upright or grand, with the exception only of a few mini-pianos, which are sometimes used in small orchestra pits for continuo or recitative work.

In addition, however, many high-grade pianos have extra top notes extending the range to C and these are used not only in piano music by composers such as Debussy but also in orchestral works, for example, Prokofiev's Fifth Symphony – making them indispensable for practical purposes. Still further extensions, this time at the bottom end, were introduced by Bösendorfer for their largest concert grands, taking the range down to F and even to the very bottom C for the largest of all, the 9½ foot model. But these additional low notes have never been used by composers and only add to the tone by sympathetic sonority. Moreover, the change in appearance of the extended lower end of the keyboard upsets the player's orientation and the manufacturers found it necessary to provide a felt or wooden cover for the bottom notes 'when not in use' or, in the case of the latest models, to paint the extra keys black.

3 Notation

Although extra staves are sometimes added for extremely complex passage work, the piano is normally notated like the harp – above which it is usually placed in the score – on two bracketed staves, the upper in treble clef for the right hand, the lower in bass for the left. However, these can naturally vary as required even while the relationship of hand to stave is retained wherever possible. Where the right hand is required to take notes on the lower stave or vice versa, some indication (such as *R.H.* or the French *m.d.*) is often added.

4 Pedals

Where the simple indication *Ped.* appears, it is always the sustaining (right) pedal that is meant. This is not to say, however, that in the absence of any such pedal marks none is to be used. On the contrary, it is taken for granted that the player will add pedalling according to his musical taste and judgement much as string players use **vibrato** and **portamenti** or the harp ARPEGGIANDO; a score such as Strauss's *Ariadne auf Naxos*, for example, gives extremely few indications and the pedal marks that are given occur mostly at places where the player might otherwise be misled, as for instance by rests. Sometimes, however, composers do positively want either a great deal of sustaining or none at all, and then specific instructions (*mit viel pedal, senza ped.*, etc.) are put into the piano parts.

The soft (left) pedal is the piano's equivalent to its MUTE. Some larger pianos, but only those of certain makers, are further supplied with a third pedal; this enables the player to catch and hold notes individually while those played subsequently are not sustained. Although useful and standard equipment on all modern Steinways, and

hence available to composers and players throughout the world, this device is very rarely specifically prescribed, nor has it indeed any terminology other than 'third pedal'.

5 Orchestral Use

Not every symphony orchestra carries a pianist on its regular strength; but if he is a member, the player will also be responsible for other keyboard work, such as the celesta and, though more rarely, the keyboard glockenspiel. He may also be asked to take on continuo playing, but on the other hand he may or may not be an organist or harpsichordist with this expertise and as a result a specialist may need to be engaged for the purpose.

Although to the layman the most familiar of all instruments, the piano occupies a slightly curious position in the orchestra. Its role is unusually composite, being sometimes featured in a semi-concertante manner, joining the orchestra in closely integrated ensemble work as well as emerging from time to time as a soloist (e.g. d'Indy's *Symphonie sur un Thème Montagnard* or Stravinsky's *Petrouchka*); alternatively it may be scored for as a kind of replacement for the harp (e.g. Shostakovich's Symphony No. 1, Martinů's symphonies or Falla's *El Amor Brujo* – Falla even marks it *quasi arpa* in one place); or it may serve as an extra colour in addition to the harps and celesta (e.g. Prokofiev's Fifth Symphony or Bartók's *Dance Suite* and *Music for Strings, Percussion and Celesta*). In Stravinsky's *Symphony in Three Movements*, the first movement is scored with piano, the second with harp, while the third has both.

Such incorporation of the piano into the body of the orchestra is a comparatively recent development, emerging gradually out of its more conventional role as continuo (as in Mozart, who is known to have used a small **pianino** in place of harpsichord for the Da Ponte operas, and later in Rossini and Donizetti, whose *L'Elisir d'Amore* specifies a piano for the recitatives). Berlioz gives the piano as an *ossia* for the bells in the *Symphonie Fantastique* (although this is never done); Glinka writes for a piano together with the harp to imitate the Russian minstrel's *guzli* in *Russlan and Ludmila*, and Rachmaninoff (unbelievably) prescribed a small upright piano as a possible DOUBLING instrument for the harp in his Third Symphony.

But in general the piano tends to be denigrated in orchestral manuals, and certainly it is surprising how unfavourably it often compares with the harp in orchestral works that use both, or when used in apposition with harp and harpsichord in a score such as Frank Martin's *Petite Symphonie Concertante*, whose object is specifically to flatter each of the three instruments equally. It is interesting that the piano in the original ballet version of Stravinsky's *The Firebird* which appears together with the three harps and celesta has very little to do, but the elaborate part it has to play in *Petrouchka* derives from the fact that the material for the second tableau, in which it is featured, was at first planned as a *Konzertstück* for piano and orchestra. On the other hand, in *The Firebird* Stravinsky greatly augmented its role

when rescoring the music in 1919, turning it into a strident kind of celesta (which however he retained as an *ossia* in the 'Berceuse') in keeping with his own increasingly astringent taste in colour.

It is indeed particularly composers with a brittle style, or who are prone to spiky textures, who tend to add the percussiveness of the piano to their scores – Copland, Britten, the later Russians (Scriabin's *Prometheus* is sometimes cited but here the Chopinesque piano arabesques are treated in a concertante manner) and many contemporary composers. In his *Concerto for Orchestra* Tippett partners the piano with the xylophone in a manner richly indicative of this aspect of its character.

6 Small Ensembles

One further function of the piano is as a key member of small salon or pit orchestras and it is with this in mind that, for example, Ibert and Strauss include the piano in their *Divertissement* and *Bourgeois Gentilhomme* respectively. In *Ariadne auf Naxos* Strauss further emphasized its light-music connotations by specifically associating the piano with the theatrical *buffo* figures, while reserving the harp for the classical world of the *opera seria*.

7 Duets

Excellent examples of purely orchestral piano writing date from as far back as Saint-Saëns's pioneering Third Symphony, more famous for its introduction of the organ, but equally remarkable for its use not merely of the piano in the Scherzo but of a piano duet – i.e., one piano, four hands –

for a short but beautifully colourful passage in the Finale. Perhaps this was the inspiration for the unconventional scoring of Debussy's early *Printemps* whose texture embodies the *piano à 4 mains* in Henri Busser's orchestration published during the composer's lifetime. Respighi and Bartók also use a four-handed piano in various works, but piano-duet playing (even in the present retrogressive days of hi-fi and television) continues to recall music-making in the home, and it can look a little cosy as the two players sit side by side intimately at work.

Stravinsky scores for two pianos in the orchestration of the *Symphony of Psalms*, as does Villa-Lobos in his *Choros No. 8*, while there are no fewer than four pianos in the totally unconventional instrumental forces Stravinsky finally decided on for *Les Noces*. These are exceptional, however, partly perhaps because of the inescapable attendant problems of placing such large instruments satisfactorily on the platform (*see* PLATFORM ARRANGEMENT, 8) and also on account of the sheer matter of ensemble; few things are harder than for two pianists to strike a chord absolutely together without having developed that sixth sense by constantly working as a virtuoso two-piano team.

8 Tuning

In company with the organ, whose tuning is an operation of the most enormous magnitude, there is nothing whatever the player can do about the piano if it is out of tune. In such an event a tuner has to be summoned, and indeed a tuner's presence is always necessary at concerts, both before re-

hearsal and again (for touching up) between rehearsal and performance, especially, of course, in concerto work; during recording sessions a tuner may even be kept permanently on hand, since if only a single important string goes out of tune it is still outside the player's scope to put it right. The art of the piano tuner is an independent *métier* and a highly skilled accomplishment.

9 Unusual Effects

Various types of 'prepared pianos' have been introduced experimentally over the past half-century, the first of which is surely Ravel's *piano (luthéal)* in his *L'Enfant de les Sortilèges*. This seems to have corresponded more or less to a type of piano, usually upright, found occasionally in Britain, equipped with an extra pedal converting the sound into a jangling quality not unlike that of the harpsichord. Ravel says that in default of the *luthéal* an ordinary piano can be fitted, where indicated, with a sheet of paper over the strings *pour imiter la sonorité de clavecin*. In the event these indications consist only of the encircled numerals 1 and 4, alternating with 2 and 3 and with appropriate cancellations, that invite speculation on the exact nature of Ravel's instrument, which has long since vanished without a trace.

John Cage was the prime mover in popularizing prepared pianos among avant-garde composers such as Denis ApIvor. The preparation starts from the Ravel-like stretching of tissues over the strings, but goes much further with the alarming use of drawing pins, screws, metal bolts, rubber wedges *et alia*. The use of sticks with which to strike the strings is also not uncommon, as in Peter Maxwell Davies's *St Thomas Wake*. Reginald Smith Brindle gives a full and entertaining account of all this activity in his book *Contemporary Percussion* (the piano being here included primarily in that capacity), in which he also discusses 'pizzicato' (putting the hand inside the instrument and plucking the strings), muting with strips of cloth and various other forms of artificial activities, both delicate and brutal. He than adds the following paragraph:

> There are also several other percussive roles for the pianist, of a rather more banal character. For instance, in Maderna's Oboe Concerto the 2nd piano player is instructed to play 'on the surface of the piano' with light sticks; in pieces by John Cage the player has to slam down the piano lid; while in Křenek's Flute Sonata there is a passage where the pianist plays on the cover with a metal coin. None of these effects is particularly ingenious or musical, and care must be taken to reserve such and similar usages for moments when they are apt. Otherwise, from an aesthetic point of view, the result can be catastrophic.

Piano Accordion, *see* ACCORDION

Piatti (It.), *see* CYMBALS

PICCOLO

The smallest and highest of the flutes, as indeed of the whole orchestra, the piccolo is the commonest sub-member of the family. Its name is an abbreviation of the Italian **flauto piccolo**, but whereas this is the international term, the Italians themselves always use **ottavino**, as do Carl Orff, Ernest Bloch and other such Italian-orientated composers. The French and Germans both use direct translations of *flauto piccolo*; **petite flûte** and **kleine Flöte**.

The piccolo is now always written in C an octave lower than the actual sound. Transposing piccolos were once widely used, though principally in wind bands; Mozart wrote for piccolo in G in *Die Entführung aus dem Serail* but the part survives in this form only in an appendix to the full score.

In the printed page of score the piccolo usually occupies the topmost line of all although, logical as this would seem it is not always the case as it can conflict with other considerations (*see* SCORE LAYOUT).

The actual range of the piccolo is from the low D only, , to the uppermost C, , thus extending slightly less far than the flute in each direction. Similarly, however, to the flute's low B, the Continental repertoire abounds with instances of the bottom C, whether in Verdi's Requiem, in Mahler's *Leider eines fahrenden Gesellen* or numerous Strauss works (*Rosenkavalier, Bourgeois Gentilhomme*, etc.). On the other hand the subterfuge of arranging for the missing note to be covered is relatively simple since any unoccupied flute can do this imperceptibly.

At the extreme top the piccolo becomes very hard to control at anything less than an earsplitting *fortissimo*;

composers have nevertheless been merciless at times, as is shown by the cruel passage from Schoenberg's *Gurrelieder* at the beginning of the section entitled 'Des Sommerwindes wilde Jagd'. Here four piccolos alternate in sustaining the upper Bs in octaves *pp* over a period of no less than twenty-four bars. So excruciating was this when I was rehearsing the passage with the LSO that one of the players ingeniously contrived to substitute a small whistle that produced exactly the right sound and pitch in, moreover, a true effortless *pianissimo*.

Although it is normally the 2nd or 3rd flute players who are expected to double on piccolo, the principal flautist is quite often called on to do so. Indeed composers such as Dvořák (in, for example, the *New World* Symphony) actually give the piccolo solos to the first player – although this is rarely carried out today. Moreover, all the members of the section can be required to play piccolos – whether two (Sibelius's First Symphony and *The Return of Lemminkäinen*, etc., or Britten's *Peter Grimes*), three (Kodály's *Háry János*), or four (Mahler's Third and Ninth Symphonies). Occasionally a principal flute will, however, insist on an extra player being engaged for the purpose in order to avoid unsettling his embouchure.

Unlike the flute, the low notes of the piccolo are very faint and while the instrument is delicate if handled in transparent ensemble work, it lacks penetration in any but its highest compass, a fact that composers sometimes fail to take into account. This is possibly because the sound is an octave higher than written, suggesting a greater shrillness than is actually produced. Players accordingly often play trills and flourishes up an octave – as at the end of Borodin's Second Symphony or the passage describing the St John's Rapids in Smetana's *Vltava*, which as written are scarcely audible, but in which the piccolo's whole purpose is to add brilliance to a fully scored woodwind ensemble.

On the other hand the piccolo can have a truly sparkling glitter that has been widely exploited in the depiction of flames (Wagner's 'Fire Music' from *Die Walküre* or Strauss's *Feuersnot*) as well as lightning flashes – which are always the essential province of the piccolo (Berlioz, 'Royal Hunt and Storm'; Verdi, *Rigoletto* Act 3, etc.).

The piccolo can present particular problems of intonation in a woodwind section, certain groupings causing especial discomfort – such as the placing of the piccolo in, for example, the final chords of both Strauss's *Don Quixote* and *Ein Heldenleben*. In piccolo solos too, where a composer may be using the instrument only intermittently, intonation is something the piccolo player has to be unusually aware of as the particular quality of the instrument can make it sound suspect unless he is constantly sensitive to the prevailing pitch.

PICCOLI TIMPANI ORIENTALI

Ippolitov-Ivanov introduces these into his *Caucasian Sketches*, writing for them in the treble clef on F and high C. It is, however, only by a stretch of the imagination that they can be rated as timpani, for all Ippolitov-Ivanov's use of the word. As Tom Wotton wrote entertainingly in the *Musical Times* of July–September 1930:

> These drums, of which the Russian name is apparently **timplipito,** may be described as a couple of ginger jars of different sizes, bound together by a strip of rawhide, which also serves to secure the two membranes. The pair are played with a couple of little drumsticks, and cannot be tuned, remaining at the pitch decreed by Providence and the vagaries of the drying hide. The choice of jars of appropriate size may ensure the notes being approximately a fifth apart.

Piccolo timpano (It.), *see* TIMPANI, 4

Pitch, *see* A, ABSOLUTE PITCH, SCORDATURA, WOODWIND, 8

PIZZICATO

1 Definition

After the normal methods of playing with the bow, *pizzicato* is the style of execution most often used by the string section. It indicates that the strings are to be plucked directly with the fingers and is always designated by this Italian term (abbreviated to *pizz.*) since strangely enough no equivalents in other languages have ever been introduced.

If no specific instruction is added, the string is normally plucked at the nearest convenient place on the edge of the fingerboard by one or sometimes more fingers of the hand holding the bow. The use of extra fingers is relatively rare but is necessitated in passages of exorbitant speed.

2 Technique

It was once thought integral to *pizzicato* that the thumb should be anchored to the corner of the fingerboard and the index finger used. Nowadays this is no longer regular practice and the resultant freedom of the hand allows the middle or other fingers to be used and at different points along the fingerboard. Although there is a certain loss of firmness and power there are also the compensatory qualities of greater flexibility and variation of colour. Certainly the anchoring thumb has to be dispensed with when two or more strings are plucked with flamboyant effect, as in the last *fortissimo* chord of Elgar's *Introduction and Allegro*.

Sibelius in the 'Pastorale' from his *Pelleas and Melisande* writes for the violas a repeated succession of Abs directed to be played *mit dem Daumen, Instrument frei*, an unusual instruction for a similar manner of execution.

When *pizzicato* is used in rapid alternation with *arco* – and especially for a single note – the string can be plucked near the scroll by the left hand. When the composer positively wants this the correct notation is a cross sign (+) over each note, but players will often adopt this method as a convenience in quick to-and-fro *pizzicato* even when not so instructed. This is not always as desirable as it is practical, since a different sound emerges, thinner and more twangy.

3 Other Methods

Properly the + sign always indicates a left-hand *pizz.*, but in the 'Funeral March' from *Grania and Diarmid* Elgar exceptionally uses it in a cello passage of chords that cannot possibly be played so; perhaps he meant the players to pluck vertically, away from – instead of across – the instrument. This *upward* way of playing chords using a finger for each string is also sometimes employed by personal choice, as, for example, in the *Scherzo* from Dag Wiren's *Serenade for Strings*, since scores normally give no guidance where this manner of execution may be in question.

In their pursuit of special effects, contemporary composers may instruct that the strings should be plucked with the fingernail or very near to the bridge, the latter sounding very dry (not at all squeaky like *arco ponticello*) and having little carrying power. Players, however, generally resist such effects, which they regard as unrealistic and frustrating as well as having a disagreeable tendency to deposit resin on the finger.

Chords can also be plucked in rhythmic succession in a to-and-fro motion, often appropriately designated **alla chittarra** or **quasi guitara**. This is variously notated, whether by the use of up- and down-bow symbols, as in Rimsky-Korsakov's *Capriccio Espagnol*, or with up and down arrows, a style used by Bartók in his *Music for Strings, Percussion and Celesta*. An arrow is also the normal symbol for indicating that a chord is to be plucked in the opposite to normal direction, i.e., if it is to sound downwards from the top towards the bottom note. If no instruction appears it is assumed that the direction will be from bottom to top, but this is not necessarily correct. In the popular

Marcia, again from Dag Wiren's *Serenade*, the cellos' open-string three-note chords could well be thought to be more striking when spread downwards towards the resonant bottom C.

In Roussel's *Suite en Fa*, gliss surprisingly denotes the throwing of the plucking fingers right across the instrument; similarly Respighi in *The Birds* writes *Pizz. strisciando il dito* for the same effect, while Debussy in *La Mer* wrote strong dramatic *pizzicato* notes for the violins with the injunction *à vide* (i.e., open string).

If executed over-enthusiastically such vehemence can cause the string to rebound off the fingerboard giving a snapping crack. Mahler was the first actually to prescribe this exaggerated over-plucking in the Scherzo of his Seventh Symphony, while Bartók exploited it to such an extent that he invented a special symbol ♩, which he uses even in quite soft dynamics though the string cannot actually be made to snap at less than *forte*.

An additional aspect of *pizzicato* is that the sound can be encouraged (by the manner of plucking, by *vibrato*, etc.) to ring on for long enough to allow the pitch to be altered so as to produce a *glissando* (upwards or downwards). This is never very loud, especially compared with the initial plucking from which it derives, but it has enough reality to have entered the range of string effects in orchestral literature. One example of the problems associated with this device is that the notation often fails to make it clear whether the sound of a slurred pair of notes is replucked or not. It is thus sometimes disputed whether, for example, Bartók really meant a *glissando* effect when, as in the *Elegy* of the *Concerto for Orchestra*, he wrote such pairs, the second notes then serving merely to indicate the extent of the plucked sounds' rise or fall.

Composers have sometimes written extremely rapid *pizzicato* passages that are often bowdlerized to *arco* on the assumption that they are impracticable – as in the Scherzo of Liszt's E♭ Piano Concerto. But in a large string section the impression may be adequately and effectively conveyed even though each individual is achieving something less than total accuracy, so that the abandoning of a composer's intention is unnecessary and highly regrettable.

Free massed plucking has, however, been used deliberately for the 'thrumming' *pizzicato tremolo* of the *Cadenza accompagnata* in the last movement of Elgar's Violin Concerto, which is directed to be executed *with the soft part of three or four fingers across the strings*.

Pizzicato is sometimes specially marked muted, but players rarely obey this as they regard the effect as indistinguishable, except for its inferior quality, from an unmuted *pizzicato* played truly *pianissimo*.

4 Bows Down

When a *pizzicato* continues over an extended period and there are sufficient rests before and after the adjacent *arco* passages, the players often lay down their bows. This is naturally the custom in movements played *pizzicato* throughout, such as the 'Divertissement' from Delibes's *Sylvia* or the Scherzo from Tchaikovsky's Fourth Symphony; it is also obligatory for such devices as occur in the Fête scene from Debussy's *Ibéria*, where the violins are instructed to be held under the arm.

5 Slapped

However much a conventional *pizzicato* may be the most usual method, it is certainly not the only one. For example, the strings may be slapped with the whole hand, as in dance-band double-bass technique. (Indeed in the context of popular music the bass is rarely played with the bow.) Some contemporary composers, especially Americans, have experimented with this for the whole string group, though with only moderate success.

See also: ARCO, BOWING

PLATFORM ARRANGEMENT

1 Usual Form

The normal disposition of a symphony orchestra on the CONCERT PLATFORM is with the percussion along the back, in front only of the organ and chorus (if any); then in turn the horns and brass, and woodwind generally in two tiers placed as centrally as possible, and the strings across the front – spreading to the sides but in principle nearest to the audience.

There are, of course, innumerable exceptions to this arrangement according to the variations of space in each hall, seating preferences of the orchestral members and the wishes of the conductor. There are also a number of different layout possibilities within each department of the orchestra.

2 Strings

Firstly, the five sections of the string ensemble are grouped nearest to the conductor with the smallest instruments, the violins, towards the front and the basses, being so vastly larger than their nearest relation, the cello, placed in majestic rows to the rear. Conductors with a keen eye for histrionic effect such as Leopold Stokowski have, especially in America, experimented by placing the basses in a single impressive line across the back of the entire orchestra; but this has not ultimately proved itself a preferable arrangement as it is far from ideal for the players to be so remote from the remainder of the strings.

The disposition of the string sections is based on recognized formulae of which the oldest established puts the 1st and 2nd violins on opposite sides to the left and right of the conductor respectively. This is the classical grouping favoured by most of the past generation of traditionally minded conductors; but over the years this feature of having all the violins nearest to the audience along the entire width of the platform has come to be supplanted by a formation whereby the violins are all grouped together to the conductor's left, the cellos now being placed to his right, with behind them the double-basses. Advocates of this arrangement hold it advantageous that all the higher sound is on one side and all the lower on the other, while others oppose it for the very same reason.

Placing the 2nd violins on the opposite side to the 1sts has the virtue of featuring them as a separate entity with a character of their own, and also preserves the to and fro of antiphonal writing that is found not only in classical times but also in the world of the romantics. Many a passage where the composer treats the 1st and 2nd violins in this way, such as Rimsky-Korsakov's *Capriccio Espagnol*, is reduced to nonsense if the violins are all huddled together on one side of the platform. Tchaikovsky's extraordinary interplay between the sections in the *Adagio lamentoso* of his *Pathétique* Symphony must also have presupposed the antiphonal seating arrangement. There is also the important issue of the psychological impact on the 2nd violins. Much playing that is the merest drudgery when representing no more than a subsidiary section of a great mass of fiddles can become of liveliest interest when the 2nd violins are in apposition to their colleagues of the 1sts as well as being themselves in full view of the audience.

Yet there are equally numerous counter-arguments; one is that the quality of the 2nd violins when they are placed on the right is substantially weakened owing to the tilt of their instruments away from the audience, a consideration that should then apply with no less force when the violas are so placed, as they too are now coming increasingly to be. Yet in fact this theoretical loss of tone is largely illusory; what comes across instead is a (surely desirable) variation of quality, and certainly in the case of the violas this disputed place to the conductor's right has the advantage of spotlighting a group that, of all the strings, possesses the least penetrating power.

Another serious objection to the wide separation of the 1st and 2nd violins is that it causes unnecessary difficulties of ensemble in the numerous passages they play together. With training, and where lavish rehearsal time is available, this can certainly be overcome; but in our less than ideal professional world frustrations and loss of time may prove overriding factors.

The placing of all the violins together on the left has, moreover, also acquired strong musical points in its favour, and in view of its current prevalence a number of works have entered the standard repertory that take it so much for granted that it can often become indispensable on practical grounds. An extreme instance occurs in Shostakovich's Fifth Symphony where the violins are re-divided for just the slow movement into an exactly equal number of 1sts, 2nds and 3rds, the three lines being printed in full in both the 1st and 2nd violin parts to enable the distribution to be made.

Further complications arise when the music is scored for double string groups. Cellos in particular occupy a quite disproportionate amount of space, so that a work such as Stravinsky's *Apollon Musagète*, which uses throughout a double cello section, has to have its own replanned seating formation. Reger habitually divides all his strings into two groups, half muted and half unmuted, needing at least the upper strings to be seated in double files, and the same is true of Elgar's part-writing in his *Introduction and Allegro*. But certain scores are fully laid out for double string orchestra, and this raises

quite specific problems; Bantock's *Omar Khayyám*, a work for full orchestra and chorus, is scored throughout in this way while a host of string pieces – such as Tippett's *Concerto for Double String Orchestra* and *Fantasia on a Theme of Corelli* – treats the double strings both individually and antiphonally, necessitating completely mirror-wise seating for two self-contained string groups with the cellos and basses arranged to the rear.

Conversely many works treat all or varying quantities of violins as a single group, whether the total body of violins is used, as in Hindemith's *Konzertmusik* for strings and brass, or only a few, such as the six in Strauss's *Bourgeois Gentilhomme*, Stravinsky's *Dumbarton Oaks* and Ibert's *Divertissement*.

Yet another seating situation arises where there are no violins at all. Brahms's Serenade in A, Op. 16, is written for an ensemble led by the violas, who may then occupy the place to the left of the conductor otherwise always occupied by the 1st violins. Stravinsky's *Symphony of Psalms* has no strings other than cellos and basses and requires an entirely individual formation centred around the two pianos, which play a primary role in the unusual orchestration.

3 Woodwind

Directly facing the conductor, and as near to him as the disposition of the strings will allow, come the woodwind, who occupy the first rises on the platform. They will generally be placed in two lines with the principals bunched together in the centre, the remainder fanning outwards in either direction.

The flutes, with the clarinets behind them, will then be on the left with the oboes and bassoons correspondingly on the right.

There are very few exceptions to this but when, however, the cellos and basses are disposed to the left of the orchestra, as in the classical and continental practice insisted on by conductors such as Toscanini, Klemperer, Boult, etc., the positions of the clarinets and bassoons are sometimes reversed, the former sitting behind the oboes and the latter behind the flutes. The clear purpose of such an arrangement is that the bassoons are brought across towards this alternative position of the cellos and basses with whom their lines have often much in common.

The woodwind are never ranged in more than two tiers and never, if they can help it, in a single long line. If the group is large this can safely be considered out of the question, but in relatively smaller ensembles the necessity can arise in small halls or for reasons of balance, with all the attendant problems of ensemble and intonation caused by the lines of communication being so spread out.

4 Horns

In Britain and America the traditional place for the horns on the concert platform is on the left (as viewed by conductor and audience); this sets them apart from the heavy brass ensemble, which is usually placed on the right. Recently, however, and especially on the Continent, the custom has arisen of moving the horns across to the right, together with the trumpets and trombones. But apart from the

unfortunate musical and psychological effect of their being positively identified as brass instruments, there is the additional practical disadvantage of the tone being dulled, since their bells are directed into the bodies and clothes of their colleagues seated centrally in the orchestra, instead of allowing the sound to project freely into the hall.

Of the two main seating possibilities:

$$(a) \quad 1. \quad 2. \quad 3. \quad 4.$$
$$or \quad (b) \quad 4. \quad 3. \quad 2. \quad 1.$$

once a matter of sharply differentiated schools of thought, (b) has for many years now utterly routed (a), which was the seating firmly championed by Aubrey Brain and continued into the 1950s by his son Dennis. The virtue of (a) lay in the 1st horn's bell being free and exposed, allowing maximum resonance and expression in solo passages; there was also the added advantage that the other members of the section were able to balance their tone with the true reflected sound of their leader, instead of receiving his tone in crude form direct from the bell. The difference is far greater than anyone would believe who has not had the personal experience of sitting in a section.

The advantage of (b), which has proved so decisive, is that the 1st horn is nearer the focal centre of the orchestra and in particular the principals of the woodwind. The value of this in delicate ensemble work is self-evident, but nowadays horn players have become so completely accustomed to (b) that they continue to adopt it even when moved to the opposite side of the orchestra, though here its *raison d'être* is entirely lost.

Of course platforms vary to an infinite degree and it is sometimes difficult to line up the horns satisfactorily either to left or right of the woodwind. In this case one variant that has come to be adopted is of placing the horns centrally *behind* the woodwind. But this too has its disadvantages, for with their bells pointing backwards any increasingly remote position is detrimental to both tone and precision, while this formation once again results in pushing the 1st horn over to the right and into the territory of the brass.

On some platforms a square formation is a better proposition:

4. 3.
2. 1.

and horn players often favour this block seating for ease of ensemble; but the magnificent effect of a row of horns is too great to be sacrificed lightly, being not merely a splendid sight but also producing a livelier and more ringing quality.

Horns must always be placed in such a way as to give plenty of lateral space between them, to allow their tone to 'get away'. For they are unique in respect of the true beauty of their tone being heard by reflection, the bells pointing half sideways, half backwards, in consequence of which they are also particularly sensitive to the acoustical properties of the back or side walls of a hall or theatre, a characteristic that should never be overlooked, or even underestimated, when the orchestral seating is being planned. At the same time it must be conceded that in some broadcasting studios or in recordings for films the sound engineers deliberately place the long-suffering horns against a resonating back wall or baffle to create a special effect.

Another consideration is that horn players will go to any lengths to avoid being placed immediately alongside or in front of the timps and heavy percussion. They are, of course, not unique in this, but have a special case to plead since the effect of sudden and violent reverberation travelling up the bell and on to their lips can have a seriously detrimental effect on reliability.

5 Brass

The heavy brass is usually placed to the rear right of the orchestra, where they may either be in block formation:

Trombone 1. 2. 3. Tuba
Trumpet 1. 2. 3.

or, if there is plenty of space on the platform, in a line, in which case the trumpets will reverse their positions so that the 1st trumpet is next to the 1st trombone:

Trumpet   Trombone
3. 2. 1.   1. 2. 3. Tuba

One advantage of this layout is that the trumpets do not suffer from the formidable blast of the trombones coming straight at them from behind.

Where there are two tubas, the second player sits on the far right – unless he is a tenor tuba, when he will more usually sit between the bass trombone and the bass tuba. But in Strauss's *Don Quixote* the tenor tuba often elects to sit away from the brass department and near to the bass clarinet, with whom he has many difficult ensemble passages. Understandable as this may be, it also

191

has disadvantages and is only reluctantly condoned by conductors. A more satisfactory solution is to adopt the reversed seating of the clarinets and bassoons, thus automatically bringing the bass clarinet into proximity with the tenor tuba's correct position in the brass ensemble.

Another variation of seating occurs when the Wagner tubas are in operation, for the bass tuba is then to a large extent scored for in conjunction with these rather than with the trombones. It may therefore be better in this case to seat all the tubas together, which means putting the bass tuba on the other side of the platform (with the trombones and trumpets reversed) in order that he should be close to the second horn quartet who are doubling the Wagner tubas.

6 Percussion

The placing of the often massive and bulky percussion department on the platform requires such forethought and ingenuity that it is rarely organized without the percussionists themselves being present. The timpanist is ideally situated centrally at the back but is nowadays often moved to the side with the remainder of the section ranged to his left or right. If the music needs a great variety of percussion this is often laid out in two tiers: the heavy, noisier drums, gongs, cymbals and so on behind, and the pitched agile glockenspiel, xylophone, vibraphone, etc., in front. This complicated arrangement of the individual instruments is always the responsibility of the players, bearing in mind their movements to and fro between, perhaps, xylophone, cymbals

and tubular bells, all of which may very well have to be addressed in turn by a single player. Nevertheless composers do sometimes make their own plans for a particular percussion layout with details of how they envisage the instruments distributed among the players – Henze's *Antifone*, for example, actually gives a graphic design on the front page of the score.

7 Harps

Instruments such as harps, pianos, celesta, or special visitors such as MANDOLINE and GUITAR, create their own individual problems. Ideally harps ought to be as near to the audience as possible to compensate for their relative lack of projection; more generally, however, they are set to the side and rear of the orchestra, since the height of the instruments themselves can all too easily mask any players behind unless they can take advantage of a stepped part of the platform.

A single harp may be placed on either side according to space or the way the music is written: in Mahler's First Symphony, for example, the harp often plays in unison with the lower strings and may be therefore better situated to the right; in Tippett's *Ritual Dances*, on the other hand, it has a great deal of intricate ensemble work with the upper woodwind and is therefore best placed towards the left centre, and so on. Harpists themselves ask not to be placed too far back, and on the whole express a preference for the left rather than the right because the harp being supported on the right shoulder, it is easier to see the conductor's beat, and moreover it is then the left ear which is furthest from the harp itself and which is orientated to the orchestral voices with whom ensemble has to be achieved.

8 Piano, etc.

Whereas the piano is also generally placed to the side, attempts are sometimes made to move the instrument to the centre of the platform, especially for works where the orchestral player has an important obbligato, as in Stravinsky's *Petrouchka*. The sheer size of the instrument always remains a deterrent, however, splitting the string group into two dissociated halves. Concert grands vary between 7½ and 9 feet long and this constitutes a considerable bite out of the available space for the orchestra. The long stick that raises the piano lid for solo work is rarely used when the piano is only orchestral, since the player may find it hard to see the beat; as an alternative, concert grands are supplied with a very short stick, or the lid may even be taken off altogether, though this has a biting and not always agreeable effect on the resonance.

Another consideration may be that the player is frequently required to double on celesta. If the two instruments have to be played in rapid alternation a suitable place must be chosen where the celesta can be placed adjacent, preferably at right-angles to the piano keyboard so that even while taking care not to mask the celesta from audience or conductor, the pianist is still able to swivel from one instrument to the other in circumstances such as occur in the 'Cortège' from Ibert's *Divertissement* or the last of Ives's *Three Places in New England*.

It is in any case always hard to place the celesta to best advantage on the platform; in addition to the piano, it should be as near as possible to the harps with whom it too is often closely associated in ensemble work. Yet so long as it is not too far away or submerged in a heavily crowded part of the platform, it is surprising how much of its tiny voice will tell across the orchestral texture.

9 Chorus

The commonest layout of the chorus is with the women (generally by far the more numerous) on the outside – sopranos to the left, altos to the right – with the men between them; the basses will then usually be at the back and the tenors, the smallest group in any chorus, in front of them.

Some works, however, definitely favour the more modern seating of S.A.T.B. in straightforward blocks from left to right. But where the switch to and from a double chorus is integral to the composer's writing, as in Walton's *Belshazzar's Feast*, it can be desirable to approximate to a layer formation of S.A.T.B. reading from front to back, thus allowing for more flexibility of division. Acute seating problems also arise when composers write for double chorus in isolated sections, as in Bach's B minor Mass and – to cite a modern example – Orff's *Carmina Burana*, only in a single movement. In such places the two choruses are treated separately and in apposition to such an extent that although it is for so small a proportion of the work the antiphonal nature of the music would be jeopardized unless the singers were disposed in two differentiated groups.

10 Soloists

Soloists are conventionally placed to the conductor's immediate left, taking care that contact between conductor and leader is not put too much at risk. Solo cellists have a rostrum to themselves, partly for reasons of sonority, partly to make absolutely sure that the cello spike will be securely fixed, and partly also for visual effect, seated as they are. In Strauss's *Don Quixote* it can be ingenious to make an exception and place the cello soloist on the conductor's right since the part is combined to an unusual degree with the orchestral cellos.

With respect to the concerto position for the piano there was for long a divergence between the practices in various different countries. In Britain the piano used to be placed between the conductor and the orchestra, a formation that, even after it had otherwise lapsed, lingered for a time in borderline concertante works such as Dohnányi's *Nursery Tune Variations* or Falla's *Nights in the Gardens of Spain*, the solo part needing to be particularly closely integrated into the orchestral texture. The established continental tradition, however, has always been to place the piano nearest to the audience with the conductor behind. The disadvantage of the piano being placed between the conductor and orchestra is primarily that, the lid being always fully up for concerto playing, the string players immediately in front (generally violas) are totally masked from the conductor, who, moreover, receives such an amplified sound of the piano that he can hear little of the orchestra while the soloist is playing.

On the other hand, the now universally adopted position of the conductor behind the piano is also not without its disadvantages. If the conductor stands in the conventional central position the raised lid now acts against him and he both receives a muffled sound and is out of touch with his soloist. For these reasons the conductor usually stands somewhat to the left of centre and diagonally, so that he has admirable contact with the soloist even though difficulties may be created for the right-hand group of string players who see hardly anything but his back for much of the time.

Where there are several solo singers the women are often placed to the conductor's left and the men to his right, but there are obvious variations to this, such as in Elgar's *Dream of Gerontius* where the tenor and mezzo-soprano representing the Soul and its Guardian Angel will certainly be together on the left, with the baritone on the right. In some works the solo voices may be placed to greater advantage not beside the conductor at all but immediately in front of the chorus. Beethoven's Ninth Symphony benefits particularly from such an arrangement, which also avoids the irrelevant presence of the four soloists sitting idle in front of the orchestra for the better part of three-quarters of an hour, or – worse still – making a disturbing entrance between whichever of two preceding movements.

Pointe (Fr.), upper end of bow; *see* BOWING, 2

Ponticello (It.), bridge; *see* BOWING, 4

Portamento (It.), *see* STRINGS, 10; TROMBONES, 5

Portato (It.), *see* BOWING, 9

Posaune (Ger.), *see* TROMBONES, 1

POSTHORN

This rare visitor to the orchestra makes two appearances in Mozart: in the Serenade No. 9 (K. 320), which is indeed known as the 'Posthorn Serenade', and in the last of the *Deutsche Tänze* (K. 605), subtitled *Die Schlittenfahrt* ('The Sleighride'). For these Mozart writes in various pitches, the Serenade being for a **corno di posta** in A, while in the *Schlittenfahrt* he uses two instruments, in Bb and F.

The range is from middle C to G above the treble clef (written) although the two posthorns in the *Schlittenfahrt* play only the two Gs. All these posthorns are notated as TRANSPOSING INSTRUMENTS.

The posthorns are fitted with trumpet mouthpieces and, like the Flügelhorn, therefore, they are always played by trumpeters, though using various substitutes for the old instruments that were played by the post, i.e., mail coaches, of earlier centuries. In England these were long and straight natural instruments but on the Continent they were small and coiled, looking indeed not unlike a tiny horn, as shown by the emblem on many European postage stamps, and which replaced the original posthorns proper during the nineteenth century, especially in Germany and Austria.

The extended off-stage solo in the third movement of Mahler's Third Symphony is another orchestral appearance of the posthorn, and, being in Bb, is perfectly suited to the Flügelhorn – to which instrument it was ascribed in the first edition of the score and on which it is still always played. Mahler's intention in changing the part to *Posthorn* is unknown but could perhaps have been with some pictorial programmatic idea in mind.

Poussez (Fr.), up bow; *see* BOWING, 7

Près de la table (Fr.), *see* HARP, 8

Près du chevalet (Fr.), *see* BOWING, 4; CIMBALOM

PRINCIPALS

Professional orchestral musicians are employed on three scales of seniority: principals, sub-principals and rank-and-file. Of these, the last applies only to the strings and does not exist in any other department, whereas the terms principal and sub-principal apply throughout the orchestra. In the strings they refer to the two players at the first desks of 2nd violins, violas, cellos and basses; the 1st violins are, however, a special case and here it is the No. 2 and No. 3 players who are respectively the principal and sub-principal of the section, since No. 1 1st violin is the LEADER of the whole orchestra with a unique position and special responsibilities.

In the wind it is again the No. 1 player of each species who is the principal and No. 2 the sub-principal, but in terms of fees and salaries all

195

players are graded as principal or sub-principal, and where the latter (i.e., seconds) are regularly required to double on piccolo, cor anglais, bass clarinet and contra, their contracts make provision for this dual role. Third players, however, are usually principals, since their chief occupation is probably the accessory instrument itself. The same applies equally to the brass since the third trumpet carries the principalship of the accessory smaller trumpet or of the cornets, while the 3rd trombone is again a principal on bass trombone. The horns are similar but to a more extended degree and for a different reason. For although the horn does not possess a subspecies or accessory instruments (other than the Wagner tubas, which are a completely special case), its historical role in the orchestra has led to its section being built up mostly in two-horn units regardless of the size of the group. Hence each 1st player (i.e., 1. 3. 5. 7.) is a principal in the structure of the orchestra and each 2nd (2. 4. 6. 8.) a sub-principal. This continues to apply even when there is, exceptionally, an odd number in the three-horn sections of, for example, the *Eroica* Symphony or the Dvořák Cello Concerto; the 3rd horn is still a principal.

With regard to the percussion, there is a 1st player apart from the timpanist who is of course also a principal in his own right. Moreover, if in a larger ensemble a player of the more skilled instruments (drums, xylophones, etc.) has a part of especial virtuoso or solo-istic character he too may expect to be rated as a principal.

Finally, where there is only one member of a family, such as the celesta, organ, guitar and so on, the player will automatically qualify for principal status or perhaps even for specially negotiated terms according to prestige and responsibility.

See also: DOUBLING, RANK AND FILE

PROGRAMME BOOKS AND NOTES

There was a time when concert programmes were enormously informative. There were always, of course, the pages listing the works to be played, the identities of the performers, biographical details of soloists and conductor, complete ORCHESTRAL LISTS and often even the chorus names; but in addition one could almost always count on extensive descriptive notes on the items, liberally interspersed with music examples, these being not only marvellous aids to concentration in absolute music but virtually essential for any degree of perception of what the piece was about in programme music. The lights in the halls were habitually at full strength throughout the performances so that it was possible to – and many an earnest listener commonly did – follow the music both aurally and visually by relating the sounds to the section-by-section descriptions. Some of these essays even outlived their original function – such as those by Donald Tovey written for his own concerts at Edinburgh University and subsequently selected and published in book form.

With ever rising costs, as well as with changes of fashion (there are, after all, as many different ways of listening to music as there are of writing about it), this valuable aid to musical appreciation has come to be replaced, where notes are supplied at all, by more general information about the composer and his music. Yet, when and how the audience is expected to imbibe such scholarship is far from clear, especially with the increasingly widespread custom of lowering the house lights. Instead there is a growing tendency for concert-goers to be expected to sit back and simply enjoy the sound of the music.

Another kind of programme book is the one generally expensively produced for special occasions or charity concerts in larger and glossy format. Although these are always sold at vastly inflated prices, they consist largely of advertising material and the amount of helpful information they contain is usually in inverse proportion to the splendour of their appearance.

However, one advantage of such splendid printing is where the programme book contains the notes and information for all the concerts of a whole subscription series or festival. This, though expensive for a single visit, usually makes provision for further interesting articles, whether on the composers or perhaps on peripheral activities. These are certainly a help in co-ordinating the disparate festival events into a homogeneous whole.

See also: AUDIENCE

PROGRAMME PLANNING
1 Number of Rehearsals
There are innumerable and widely differing considerations that have to be taken into account when approaching this highly complex operation. For example, the amount of REHEARSAL time allotted to a concert may be the first consideration. The inclusion of a new and complicated score will require extra rehearsals, whereas a concert budgeted for preparation within the minimum rehearsal time of three hours on the day of the performance will need to be built around music within the players' repertoire. This is often the case in popular, box-office-orientated concerts known to the orchestras as 'one-offs'.

2 Soloist
The engagement of a soloist, and accordingly the choice of his solo item, may exert an important influence on the rest of the programme. The selection of the soloist himself, even his very nature, whether instrumentalist (and what kind) or vocalist, is often a matter of careful deliberation, based on a number of factors: would a piano be desirable on account of popularity or unsuitable either because of platform limitations or over-exploitation in the recent past; should he be young (a recent competition winner, perhaps) or well known; home grown or foreign, and so on.

3 Duration
Concert duration has always to be taken into account, and in working out the arithmetic it is necessary to be aware of certain facts: for example, in Britain a concert is expected to last in the region of two hours, in which case the total playing time of the music should be no more than some 85 minutes. This can be slightly increased

if the number of items is fewer than four, but proportionately decreased if there are five or more. On the Continent, however, it is more usual for concerts to be rather shorter, 70–75 minutes of actual music, or even less, being not uncommon.

4 Forces Available

Much may depend on the constitution of the forces available. Naturally if neither money nor space on the platform are of any account Schoenberg's *Gurrelieder* with its absolutely mammoth forces may be programmed with impunity, as it is from time to time for a special occasion. Or if complete cycles of a composer's works are in prospect, such as the complete Beethoven or Mahler symphonies, provision will have to be made to accommodate the more extravagant of these, such as Beethoven's Choral or Mahler's Eighth, the so-called 'Symphony of a Thousand'. More often, however, there is a given specification or budget around which the programme is expected to be planned. The basic size of the orchestra; the positive desire to, or not to, include a chorus; the presence of a good organ in the hall or, on the contrary, the known lack of such an amenity – these are only a few elements governing the choice of works to be performed. If extras are to be engaged for a particular piece there is often scope for ingenuity in using them again in other works.

5 Suitability for Venue

In selecting a programme it is generally necessary to be aware of the music to be played in the particular venue during the season. There is a considerable art in slotting in music that may be of a nationality or category otherwise neglected either through oversight or because of local unfamiliarity. There can even be an enjoyable pioneering element in combining popular favourites with lesser-known works by the great masters. There is, moreover, an important responsibility, wherever financial considerations will allow, to represent the contemporary schools and the young composer struggling for a hearing; the avant-garde of the past thirty years has so alienated the large majority of concert-goers, to whom the very words 'modern music' are now virtually anathema, that the inclusion of a newly written piece can often guarantee an empty hall. As a result new music may be lumped together in all-contemporary programmes for specialist audiences, the regular series of symphony concerts becoming a museum-like activity concentrating mostly on a repertoire of favourite pieces written within a time span of barely two hundred years. It requires an enlightened conductor and management, through clever planning collaboration, gradually to break down this unfortunate syndrome and to woo audiences towards greater interest and confidence in maintaining music as a living and progressive art form.

But the conductor is by no means always allowed a free hand in the programme, either in part or whole. In many instances he is invited to take on an assignment with an already built-in list of works; or it may be the solo item that has been fixed and around which the conductor will have to find suitable bedfellows. This need not be a drawback; where one is given absolute *carte blanche* it can be quite a problem to find exactly the right kind of music for any given occasion. The choice can in fact be too wide and some constraint can be a help rather than an encumbrance.

6 Shape

The shaping of a programme can all too easily become stereotyped into the conventional overture–concerto–interval–symphony format; but it can also, with imagination, be capable of infinite and interesting variations. On the whole, promoters tend to like a concert to begin with an overture or some other short piece to allow for late-comers, who are generally forbidden entry until the first break in the music. Yet longer works that open stunningly but end softly, such as Strauss's *Don Juan* or Brahms's Third Symphony, make better opening than closing music. Conductors often make too much of a fetish of avoiding soft endings to a concert but there is no escaping the fact that symphonies with *fortissimo* endings such as Beethoven's Seventh or Tchaikovsky's Fourth have virtually built-in ovations.

Concertos are generally placed before the interval, but this too is by no means an invariable rule. Some of the longer examples – Beethoven's Violin Concerto or both the Brahms Piano Concertos – make an excellent effect placed by themselves in the second half (assuming that the conductor is not too vain to share the applause at the end of the concert).

If, on the contrary, the solo work is short the soloist may wish to play again after the interval. There are also concerts in which distinguished virtuosi perform three or more concertos, occupying the whole programme, or perhaps allowing the conductor the courtesy of a short opening item to establish his presence.

New or unfamiliar music is more wisely placed in the first half, thus being played to fresher ears as well as avoiding the danger of tempting the audience to make their escape during the interval. It used, however, to be Henry Wood's avowed policy, in planning his famous Promenade Concerts, to place all the adventurous works in the second halves, the music played before the interval being the much-loved single-composer features of Wagner on Mondays, Bach/Handel on Wednesdays, Beethoven on Fridays and so on – concerts were much longer fifty years ago than they are today.

7 Contrast of Keys

There are other guidelines in programme building. If the two halves are disproportionate in length or substance it is usually better not to arrange for the longer or heavier to come after the interval (although this maxim is conventionally disregarded when a short work is used as a curtain raiser to a major item such as Beethoven's Choral Symphony). It would generally be regarded as poor planning if the *Magic Flute* overture and the *Eroica* Symphony were chosen to surround Beethoven's *Emperor* Concerto, all three works being in the same key of E flat, even though not all listeners will be sufficiently key-conscious to be aware

199

of the uniformity. It also makes bad billing if the word 'symphony' or 'concerto' occurs too many times; hence a concert such as:

Bach: Brandenburg Concerto No. 3
Mozart: Piano Concerto in F (K. 459)
Bartók: Concerto for Orchestra while making excellent musical sense, would look odd in the advance publicity unless drafted for a special purpose.

8 Lollipops

Some conductors enjoy building programmes made up of a collection of shorter compositions. Sir Thomas Beecham made a speciality of this, many of his *trouvailles* coming to be known as 'lollipops'. Where the pieces are 15–20 minutes long, such as Delius's *Eventyr* and Sibelius's tone poem *Tapiola*, the result can be singularly successful; but the danger always lurks that the total result can become too fragmented and lacking in real substance. Finally the element of taste must always be a guiding factor, the amount and proximity of loud and soft music, profound and theatrical, sensuous and haunting with brash and virtuoso. Programme planning at its best is an art in itself and needs to be the product of much thought and heart searching.

See also: AUGMENTATION, CONCERTO, ENCORES

Pultweise geteilt (Ger.), *see* DIVISI

Punta (It.), point of bow; *see* BOWING, 2

Q, abbreviation for *Quartette* or *Quintette*, which are themselves ab-

breviations for *Streichquartette* or *-quintette, see* STRINGS, 1

Raganella (It.), *see* RATTLE

RANK-AND-FILE

This status applies collectively to the tutti members of the string group below the ranks of PRINCIPAL and sub-principal. They are accordingly the lowest paid, bearing as they do the least individual responsibility. However, although rank-and-file players are all administratively equal in status, they may compete avidly for desk positions, outside and inside, nearer the front or back, first or second violins, etc., and this often causes strife and discontent within a badly disciplined orchestra.

Experiments have been made in some organizations with a rotation system of rank-and-file players. This is, however, not without its drawbacks, since, despite an obvious overall increased responsibility, the apparent gain in interest through being rescued from the oblivion of the back desks is offset by the loss of incentive for promotion. Moreover the conductor's closer personal contact with the players he otherwise sees and controls only from a distance is counteracted by the unsettling effect on the players of having to readjust to new partners and environment. Apart from training orchestras, therefore, such schemes remain the exception rather than the standard practice.

See also: BACK DESKS, ORCHESTRA LISTS

Râpe à fromage (Fr.), *see* GOURDS

Rape guero (Sp.), *see* GOURDS

Rasps, *see* GOURDS

Ratsche (Ger.), *see* RATTLE

RATTLE, RATCHET

While conceding the (strictly correct) dictionary differentiation between the two words 'rattle' and 'ratchet' (confusingly reinstated in the *New Grove*), in orchestral parlance rattles are objects that can be swung round like those at football matches. They are used in the orchestra for special effect in works such as Beethoven's *Battle Symphony* (where there are two – one for the French, one for the English side), and also for moments of hilarity or violence as in Strauss's *Till Eulenspiegel*, Walton's *Façade*, Milhaud's **crécelle** in *La Mort d'un Tyran* or Respighi's **raganella**, in his riotous *Feste Romane*. For such purposes their noise is usually indicated as a trill, mostly of reasonable duration as shorter trills give the player little chance to get the thing going so as to give the maximum furore over the heads of the whole orchestra.

The rattle also turns up in unlikely scores, such as Nielsen's *Pan og Syrinx*, where it is curiously indicated by the two words *Crotales* and *Schnarre*, the one vertically above the other. Strangely CROTALES is indeed a dictionary word for rattle, though in percussion terminology it means something entirely different. The German

Ratsche and **Schnarre**, or even **Knarre**, are certainly occasional alternatives although none of these is the everyday word, which is more often *Gerassel*; this, however, is never used in scores.

Sadly percussion departments are often disappointingly prone to fall back on a small ratchet, which is not quite the same as a proper orchestral rattle. Ratchets are really most suitable for individual clicks not unlike those produced by castanets or claves, but sharper as well as deader – less resonant. To obtain the clicks accurately in a prescribed rhythm, a handle is often fitted to a little ratchet which is just like the '**carraca** (piccolo raganello)' *(sic)* used by Falla in his *El Retablo de Maese Pedro*. In fact Strauss's **grosse Ratsche** in *Rosenkavalier* is often so executed on account of the precise rhythmic pattern prescribed, even though this later changes to a *ff* roll, and Ravel in *L'Enfant et les Sortilèges* goes as far as to specify a **crécelle à manivelle**, i.e., with a crank. There are also various South American rattle-like instruments such as **matráca** and **caraxá** scored for by Villa-Lobos and Milhaud.

RECORDERS

These are the simplest of all wind instruments, being essentially sophisticated versions of the penny whistle. There is a considerable range of different members in what is strictly called a 'chest of recorders'; the family members most commonly used orchestrally are the treble recorder – generally believed to be the instrument used by Bach and Handel – which sounds as written; the descant, which sounds an octave higher; and the very tiny sopranino, which also sounds an octave above the written note.

Other names for the instrument are **Blockflöte** (Ger.), **flauto dolce** (It.) or **flûte-à-bec** (Fr.), while in this country it has come to respectability as the recorder, a more favourable term than the once official name 'fipple-flute'. The simple word 'flute' has for nearly two centuries automatically meant the transverse FLUTE and it has therefore ceased to be necessary to specify, as it was for Bach, exactly which kind of flute is intended.

Indeed, for a time any species other than the transverse flute had come to be considered archaic and of solely historical interest. In the last decades, however, as part of the widespread revival of authentic interpretations of baroque and pre-baroque music, the recorder has made a strong comeback. Thus Bach's Brandenburg Concertos Nos. 2 and 4, for which he designated flûtes-à-bec (unlike No. 5), are now frequently played on those instruments, though players and scholars are by no means agreed over which size should be chosen or even at which octave the lines should be played.

If the recorder then remains predominantly a solo – even a concertante – instrument, it can have an orchestral function in authentic performances where it is used in such ensemble writing as in, for example, the Monteverdi *Vespers*. This work calls for a group of three or four players who must have a thorough understanding of the possible doublings and alternations with strings and cornetti, few of which are definitely prescribed as in a modern score.

The recorder's relationship with the orchestral world remains, therefore, essentially a profession apart; when one is required, an expert is engaged who may arrive with a Gladstone bag full of bits and pieces which he will assemble as he sees fit without anyone – least of all the majority of conductors – knowing what he is about, let alone being able to challenge him on his view of the requirements presented by the music. In contemporary works, however, composers are usually more precise. It is, for example, the treble and descant recorders that Britten uses in *Noye's Fludde*, though in the score he notates the descant recorders at actual pitch.

It has to be admitted that the recorder cannot compete with the rich characterful quality of tone which enabled the transverse flute to oust it in the first place, and in particular the sounds produced by the attractive-looking deeper instruments (resembling some exotic and ancient bassoon) remain sadly disappointing. However, it is important to stress that the recorder group does not need to have that desperate watery, thin quality with which it is often all too justifiably associated.

The recorder has furthermore a distinct educational virtue in providing a readily available introduction to the joys of co-operative musical activities with a minimum requirement of skill or preparation. But, as Britten has cleverly shown in *Noye's Fludde*, this aspect of the instrument can be exploited while at the same time revealing the degree to which the recorder may have a pronounced character of its own if expertly handled by composer and performer.

Reco-reco (Sp.), *see* GOURDS

REEDS

The reed is to the woodwind (excluding only the flutes) what the string is to the violin family, that is to say, the medium by which the air is set in motion and the sound produced. The CLARINETS and the SAXOPHONES have unsophisticated single reeds carefully curved, shaped and widely tapered to fit over the mouthpiece where they are held in position by metal clasps. OBOES and BASSOONS, on the other hand, are double-reed instruments, and the production of the composite piece of equipment whereby the twin, narrow reeds are bound with twine and inserted together into the top of the oboe or the crook of the bassoon is a complicated and exceedingly skilled operation.

Single reeds are commonly purchased in moderately priced boxes, a fair quantity at a time, out of which, however, only a small proportion will be serviceable. Double reeds, on the other hand, and those for bassoons and contras in particular, can be so expensive – and still no less fallible – that most players learn to make their own as an integral part of their training.

Since reeds are mostly quite literally derived from the natural product (although needless to say plastic clarinet reeds have now made a questionable appearance) they can vary to an enormous extent not merely in quality but in character, and players can be seen at rehearsals endlessly sucking, scraping and moulding in pursuit of the ideal reed for specific passages. A hard reed may give a louder but also more raucous tone and become unreliable in subtle phrasing; a soft reed can be a precious and carefully nursed object (being very easily damaged) for soft melting solos such as abound in Delius. Particular effects also need special reeds which are accordingly kept on one side for the purpose, such as the pliable clarinet reed essential for the *glissando* opening of Gershwin's *Rhapsody in Blue*, or the harder oboe and bassoon reeds – but which must still have refinement – for imitating the duck and the grandfather respectively in Prokofiev's *Peter and the Wolf*.

Nor are reeds remarkable for longevity, and the passing of a favourite reed just before an important assignment can be an occasion for mourning and anxiety.

Some organ stops control pipes fitted with 'reeds', usually (if not invariably) as part of the Swell manual, which may be specified when a composer introduces into the score instructions for a preferred registration, such as Vaughan Williams in his *Sea* Symphony. However, these 'reeds' are now only terminology for they are in fact made of brass.

REHEARSAL LETTERS OR FIGURES

The way that orchestral scores and parts were at one time printed made no provision whatever for stopping and restarting in the middle of a movement or work. Rehearsing music published

203

in this way can naturally be an intensely hazardous occupation, since valuable time is lost and tempers frayed in the effort to find a recognizable place in the music without risk of miscounting.

In the course of time it became customary to insert letters, at first at widely spaced intervals but later with greater frequency. In longer works figures might be substituted as the limitations of the alphabet can necessitate reverting to the beginning again with the variation of lower case letters, or double – or even triple – lettering (AA, or Aa, AAA, etc.), which is relatively clumsy. Above all, whether letters or figures, they were for long always placed at musically identifiable places, a consideration of primary importance. As an additional aid, some publishers give also the bar count at the beginning of each line of music. Unfortunately the apparently irrefutable logic of this system has gradually led even composers to use the bar count as the very choice of place and designation of the rehearsal figures, often spaced out regularly every five or ten bars regardless of the sense of the music. It is strange how unaware the many devotees of this method are of the confusing effect it has on those players who have long periods of rest. For miscounting will always occur, resulting in false entries, when the strong musical moment – to which conductors will usually refer in rehearsal – is at some unmarked point between numbered bars, while the numbers themselves fall at arbitrary points unrelated to the musical structure.

Some COPYISTS go even further and give only the bar counts at the beginning of lines, with the result that instruments with relatively less to play will constantly have to work out complicated and unreliable arithmetical formulae in their attempt to find where the conductor has decided to start from. In some works the publishers have saved themselves yet more time and trouble at the expense of the musicians through the total omission of longer resting passages, with words like tacet until 74, even when there is the added complication of changing time signatures. The player can then have no idea, even when a cue is supplied a few bars before the next entry, of how long it might be before figure 74 will flash past.

Schoenberg went to the other extreme in his later works, numbering every single bar so that there are no rests, the part showing each bar full of either cues or notes to play. This too is so bewildering as to invite accident. Bartók conceived the ingenious method of putting the figures in musically sensible places but making the figures themselves the correct bar count. The fact that this too went awry for a number of foolish reasons was hardly the fault of so practical a performing composer.

Today, despite a few enlightened composers experienced in orchestral practice, the situation is becoming increasingly standardized by copyists, composers and publishers alike into the simplest use of the bar count. As a result the cost in delays and frustration at rehearsal continues unabated for the lack of frequent placing of figures or letters at carefully chosen places consistent with the logic of the musical structure, as can be seen in most of the scores by truly practical performer–composers, such as Mahler, Strauss, Stravinsky or Britten.

See also: EDITIONS, ORCHESTRAL MATERIAL

REHEARSALS

In Britain the simplest repertoire orchestral concert takes place after a single 3-hour rehearsal, which, by union ruling, has to be held on the same day, though not necessarily in the same venue, as the performance. If, however, works are included in the programme that are unfamiliar or difficult – and especially first performances of contemporary music – extra rehearsals become indispensable. This causes the cost of the concert to rise steeply, as each rehearsal over and above the first 3-hour unit involves pro rata extra fees for the players, apart from other incidental expenses such as the hiring of a suitable hall for the purpose. Nevertheless important and prestigious concerts of even repertoire programmes can command as many as four or five extra rehearsals in order to achieve the necessary standard of execution or to satisfy the demands of a star international conductor.

Freelance orchestras in Britain normally work in 3-hour periods with a statutory interval of 15–20 minutes. Contract orchestras, on the other hand, have in theory a greater flexibility of schedule planning, the players being engaged on a scale of hours per week rather than per concert. Even so, 4- or

even 5-hour rehearsals common on the Continent are rare in Britain.

Continental orchestras on the contrary usually concentrate their rehearsals into such extended periods (with numerous intervals) in order to finish work early in the day, two 3-hour rehearsals such as are customary in Britain being relatively unknown. Nevertheless a move is afoot – also in Britain and particularly in radio orchestras – to make more use of 2½- or even 2-hour rehearsals on the grounds that the last half-hour or so of a 3-hour session loses efficiency because of reduced concentration from tired players with their eyes on the clock. At the same time it can be argued that the last half-hour of *any* rehearsal may very well suffer in the same way regardless of duration.

With the exception of studio orchestras, few can regularly hold their preliminary rehearsals in the venue where the performance is to take place. An orchestra such as the Royal Liverpool Philharmonic, which can boast its own hall, is exceptionally fortunate; but often it is only the final rehearsal on the morning or afternoon of the 'show' that can take place in the hall, and accordingly matters of balance or platform organization have to be deferred until that time.

One of the most frustrating practices among orchestral players can occur where a concert carries several rehearsals or even repeat performances, not all of which are convenient to every musician. Rather than have empty chairs with missing solo cues, which are obviously detrimental to co-ordination, players are sometimes allowed to send a

205

deputy. The abuse of this privilege was at one time extremely widespread and there was a well-known story of a conductor who became so outraged at the continual change of personnel from one rehearsal to another that he ran up to the one musician who had been unfailingly constant in his attendance at every rehearsal and embraced him publicly – only to be met with the answer, 'Thank you, but the pity is I cannot be present at the concert.' Fortunately standards have risen so markedly during the last decades that the practice has largely declined except in amateur or student orchestral work, where for a number of practical reasons it still has often to be tolerated, however reluctantly.

A particularly valuable form of preparation can be sectional rehearsals. Liszt actually advocates this system at the foot of the scores as the ideal method of work for his symphonic poems. Today these are no longer considered so exacting that they require such detailed rehearsal, but there is no doubt that many programmes as well as many orchestras benefit greatly from spending time and patience over BOWING styles in a string rehearsal, or ENSEMBLE and intonation in the wind, unembarrassed by the members of other sections waiting restlessly.

The CONDUCTOR is frequently asked to supply a rehearsal order some days ahead and has to plan and organize his time even in the face of unforeseeable complications. He must know fairly accurately the duration of the different items in the programme as well as the probable degree of relative difficulty they are likely to present to the players.

If the instrumentations of the pieces differ greatly he will be expected to discuss with the management the merits of beginning and ending with the largest or the smallest forces, at what point in the rehearsal he would prefer to work with the soloist, and so on.

Rehearsal technique is in fact one of the most vital skills of a conductor. It is not generally realized outside the profession what an immense degree of concentration and expertise is exercised by conductor and orchestra alike in order to spend every precious second of available time to the greatest possible advantage. The enemy is the clock; waste of time the one unforgivable sin. The conductor who cannot get what he wants without endless harangues is the least efficient, and it is the players who are eternally on the alert to get on with the job of putting the music right, of playing better and more together. On the other hand, therefore, the conductor who, conscious that time is slipping away, fails to correct or rehearse errors, or who seeks to court popularity by letting pass inadequate playing in order to let the orchestra off early, can expose himself as an inferior artist.

There are no golden rules in rehearsal, only principles, and it is the exercise of judgement that must ultimately be the only guidance: how much to play; how often – indeed *when first* – to stop. How much to put right at any one time; the need to allow the orchestra to *play*; the ability to detach oneself and compare what one is actually hearing with what ideally one would wish to hear; how at rehearsal to be primarily working and not already giving the performance; how to rehearse the orchestra for *its* benefit and not for the conductor's own.

Important as the conductor's psychological involvement with his players may be however, his first preoccupation at rehearsal must always be that of working to the highest standard of which he and they are capable within a given time schedule; and in this respect an element of firmness, if necessary even of ruthlessness especially in the maintenance of discipline, may well be essential.

See also: PROGRAMME PLANNING

Resonanz (Ger.) *près de la table*), *see* HARP, 8

Ricochet (Fr.), *see* BOWING, 11

Rim-shot, *see* DRUMS, 2

Roto-toms, *see* TIMPANI, 4

Röhrenglocken (Ger.), *see* BELLS

Rührtrommel (Ger.), *see* DRUMS, 1

Ruthe, Rute (Ger.), birch; *see* BASS DRUM, VERGHE

Saiten (Ger.), string, snare; *see* DRUMS, 1

Saiteninstrumente (Ger.), all instruments of whatever family that have strings; i.e., piano, harp, violins; *see* STRINGS, 2

Saltato (It.), *see* BOWING, 11

Samuels Aerophon, *see* AEROPHON

SANDBOX, SANDPAPER BLOCKS

Hindemith writes for a metal canister filled with sand (*Sandbüchse*) in his *Kammermusik* No. 1; Orff in *Die Kluge* asks for several under the name of *Sandrasseln*. Sandpaper blocks rustled together are called for by Copland and others, such as Britten who uses them to imitate the shuffling feet of the Prodigal Son in his church parable. These all come into the category of the effects department and are of course operated by PERCUSSIONISTS.

SARRUSOPHONES

The French have a predilection for a CONTRABASSOON made not of wood but of brass. This is in fact the double-bass sarrusophone, the lowest and only surviving member of its family (the name, like the SAXOPHONE's, being derived from its inventor). Described merely as 'sarrusophone' in the different scores where it appears, it is actually intended to be (and to all intents and purposes is) a simple and direct *alter ego* of the contra, like which it is notated in C, an octave higher than it sounds. In recent years, however, it has become increasingly rare, despite the claims once made on its behalf of both power and tone quality, no doubt the original purpose of its invention in 1856 by M. Sarrus, a French bandmaster.

Parts for the sarrusophone where the contra is the normal substitute occur in Debussy's *Jeux*, Ravel's *Rapsodie Espagnole* and on one page only of *Daphnis et Chloé* (where it looks as if Ravel had either momentarily forgotten which he was using or regarded it as literally synonymous with contra), and Delius's *Eventyr*.

But the sarrusophone has become a lost cause. The oddest revival (still of only the double-bass member) has been in Stravinsky's *Threni* of 1958, but here too it is hard to find anything in the tiny part for the instrument for which the contra would not serve at least as well.

Sautillé (Fr.), *see* BOWING, 11

SAXHORNS

Saxhorns are such very rare visitors to the orchestral BRASS section that when they do appear in scores the problem is not so much just exactly what they are, but rather which other more familiar instrument they most nearly resemble, and are accordingly replaced by, in countries such as Britain where they are not indigenous.

In appearance they are either horizontal, such as the FLÜGELHORN, or upright, like the TUBA family, according to size and key. Of the seven varieties the two uppermost are used by d'Indy in *Fervaal* under the name of *petit bugle en Mi♭* and the *bugle en Si♭*. This identifies these smaller saxhorns as corresponding to the Flügelhorn. In the march that concludes his Te Deum Berlioz wrote for a *petit saxhorn en Si♭ alto*, adding a footnote to the effect that it sounds a seventh higher than written. This seems to establish it as an even smaller and higher instrument. In *La Prise de Troie* he also uses two small members of the family, although he describes these as soprano and contralto saxhorns (again in E♭ and B♭). They transpose respectively a minor third higher and a tone lower than written. It is these B♭ instruments that correspond with Respighi's FLICORNI *soprani in Si♭* in his *Pines of Rome*.

The next saxhorn in descending order is the alto in E♭, also used in both Berlioz's and d'Indy's ensembles, although unlike d'Indy (who does call it 'saxhorn alto') Berlioz actually names it a *saxhorn* **tenor** *en Mi♭*. This is otherwise unknown in orchestral literature, but corresponds closely with the ALTHORN, an instrument known in military- and brass-band circles – where it often replaces the French horn – as an 'upright grand'; it transposes a major sixth down.

Then comes a tenor in B♭, which is much like the so-called BARITONE of British bands, an instrument similar to the EUPHONIUM and with the same range but lighter in character and tone quality. It is the tenor saxhorn which, described on the Continent either as Barytone or **Tenorhorn**, is used by Mahler in the first movement of his Seventh Symphony; perhaps the strangest feature of this isolated appearance is that at no time does the tenorhorn take part in the brass ensemble, but appears purely as a solo voice with its own particular theme. In this country it is generally taken by a tuba player but wrongly on a euphonium or a tenor tuba (both of which are too heavy and clumsy for Mahler's intention) instead of our more suitable 'baritone'. Mahler writes for the tenorhorn conventionally in the treble clef a ninth higher than it sounds, as does Respighi, to whose *flicorni tenori in Si♭* in his *Pines of Rome* this instrument corresponds; but the British 'baritone' is normally written like the euphonium at concert pitch in the bass clef.

The most bewildering of the sax-horns is the fifth in the list, for it is also in B♭, with a similar range to the tenor but differing in character, weight and constitution. This really does correspond to our euphonium, and is given the bass supporting role by d'Indy in his quartet of saxhorns in *Fervaal* (though maddeningly under the name of *saxhorn baryton en Si♭*) and by Respighi as the deepest of his **buccini** again in his *Pines of Rome*, where he describes his analogous instruments as *flicorni bassi*. Moreover, the two composers differ in their notation, for d'Indy writes a ninth higher in the treble clef as for the tenorhorn (indeed one cannot be absolutely sure that he was not confusing the two instruments), whereas Respighi writes a tone higher in the bass clef.

The sixth of the saxhorns is a **bass saxhorn** in E♭, first used by Meyerbeer in *Le Prophète* and also incorporated by Berlioz into his saxhorn group in *La Prise de Troie*. Here it is notated in the bass clef but, perhaps unexpectedly, a minor third lower than it sounds, and under the description of *saxhorn contrebasse en Mi♭*. This was not an accurate name, however, as a true *saxhorn contrebasse* does exist and is the seventh of the family, a very low B♭ instrument and corresponding to our BOMBARDON or Wagner's *Kontrabass Tuba*. This appears in Massenet's *La Terre Promise*, where it is notated in the treble clef two octaves and a tone higher than it sounds. It has also been written for in recent years by Messiaen

in *Et exspecto resurrectionem mortuorum* (notating it in the bass clef at concert pitch in a score written entirely *en sons réels*). He describes it as *saxhorn basse en si bemol* and cites its range in his *Nomenclatures des Instruments* as:

In the event, however, he uses it primarily in its lower register, taking it lower than he does the tuba.

Practically speaking, this is all so complicated that players end up by suiting their own convenience, playing the various parts on whatever brass instrument of the TRUMPET, tuba or saxhorn family corresponds best with the range and style of the work in question.

SAXOPHONES

The invention of the saxophone was always a logical development of the wind section. If the double-reed conical instruments are the oboe family and single-reed cylindrical ones are the clarinets, someone was bound to build a single-reed conical family of instruments if only to see what happened. And this is precisely what Adolph Sax did in 1816, although he actually went one stage further and built them exclusively of metal. (It still remains for some enterprising instrument builder to complete the cycle and invent a family of double-reed cylindrical instruments.)

The saxophone family is quite varied and covers a wide range of no fewer than six members from the SOPRANINO AND SOPRANO, via the ALTO and TENOR, to the BARITONE and BASS. Nevertheless few developments in the history of instrumentation are stranger than the fate of the saxophones, for they somehow failed to establish themselves as anything but special-purpose instruments until they came to be adopted as one of the mainstays of dance bands and jazz, both as solo instruments and in group work. This in turn gave them such strong prejudicial associations that they could never again compete orchestrally with the other WOODWIND on an equal basis. Even Strauss's experimental use of a saxophone quartet in *Symphonia Domestica* is marked *ad lib*, which is just as well, as he unfortunately chose for his purpose Sax's original subsidiary set, which, pitched in C and F alternately, quickly became obsolete; for those that became the standard instruments of today are (again alternately) in Eb and Bb. The opinion has been aired that Strauss muddled them with SAXHORNS but, apart from the imputation of ignorance against one of the most knowledgeable masters of the orchestra, this suggestion is wholly belied by the woodwind-style flexibility of the parts given to the ill-fated foursome. It should be added that Strauss himself never insisted on them in his own performances. Josef Holbrooke frequently incorporated virtually the whole of the family into his woodwind, especially for the larger-scale works, but perhaps because of the heavy glutinous effect his precedent has remained unfollowed.

Thus the saxophones remain only occasional visitors to the orchestra and it is very rare for more than one of them to be introduced into the woodwind group; Ravel's *Bolero* is an exception with its sopranino (an unusual member in F) and soprano as well as tenor, while Gershwin uses a family of three (alto, tenor and baritone) in *An American in Paris*, although their status as visitors is emphasized not only by his treatment of them exclusively as an inseparable group at isolated moments during the course of the work, but also by his placing of them on the printed page much like soloists between the percussion and the strings. There is in fact no uniformity at all in this matter, Strauss putting his saxophones between the clarinets and bassoons, and Ravel most oddly below the brass but above the percussion. Prokofiev, like Strauss, places the saxophone stave between the clarinets and bassoons; Britten between the bassoons and horns, while different editions of Bizet's *L'Arlésienne* give it in each of the above positions. Berg, however, placed his saxophone between the oboes and clarinets, while Milhaud in *La Création du Monde* conceived the highly original and unconventional idea of using the saxophone as a substitute for the viola in his string group, even placing it there in his score layout.

The general rule is for an extra player to be engaged whenever a saxophone is required, but it can be taken as a DOUBLING instrument in the clarinet department on account of the similarity of its single-reed mouthpiece and of its fingering technique. Oddly enough Ravel organized his orchestral version of Mussorgsky's *Pictures from an Exhibition* so that the saxophone should be doubled by the 2nd oboe, but this is never done in practice.

Schalltrichter in der Höhe (Ger.), *see* BELLS UP

Schellen (Ger.), *see* JINGLES

Schellentrommel (Ger.), *see* TAMBOURINE

Schlagzeug, Schlagwerk (Ger.), *see* PERCUSSION, 1

Schmetternd (Ger.), literally 'blazing'; *see* CUIVRÉ

Schnarre (Ger.), *see* RATTLE

Schwammschlägel (Ger.) soft-headed drum stick; *see* TIMPANI, 12

SCORDATURA

Composers sometimes instruct the strings to adopt unconventional tunings. This is always an unpopular requirement and is strenuously resisted by players who say – with some justice – that it throws out all the fingerings and that changes in string tension can upset the instrument. Such re-tunings, known as *scordatura*, have a long and venerable history and may be applied to all four strings of an instrument, though in this case it usually concerns only a single player, i.e., a soloist or the leader. A well-known solo instance is in Mozart's *Sinfonia Concertante* (K. 364) where, to brighten the tone, the viola is tuned up a semitone and written as a transposing instrument in D. A notorious example for the leader of the orchestra is Mahler's Fourth Symphony; in this case the player has to bring on to the platform a second retuned instrument, which he keeps by his side for quick changeover during the Scherzo.

There are instances of all sorts of retunings for special purposes or effects such as the fiddling skeleton in Saint-Saëns's *Danse Macabre*, whose E string tuned down to E♭ forms so amusingly grisly a feature of the score.

In fact by far the commonest *scordatura* is for a single string to be retuned and this is the usual requirement when applied to whole sections. Such a change may be required in order to obtain an otherwise non-existent natural HARMONIC, as in Stravinsky's *The Firebird*. But it is most often a matter of lowering the bottom string to extend the range. Mozart already wrote a low F♯ for the 2nd violins in the finale of the E♭ Symphony (K. 543), marking it *N.B.* although he makes no suggestion as to how the note should be played. Hindemith instructs the 2nd violins to tune their G strings to F♯ in the slow movement of his *Symphonic Dances*. Here he uses a very unconventional notation: as the only note to be played after retuning is the open string he writes it as a G and adds a footnote to explain that it is to sound F♯. But the more usual and simpler expedient is to keep to conventional notation and simply use the extended range, as does Bax in his First Symphony, where his 2nd violins actually tune down to F♮ and his violas to C♭. Similarly the cellos and basses have to tune right down to bottom B♭ in Strauss's *Panathenäenzug*.

Strauss in particular was so prone to use instruments below their normal range that he came less and less to bother about writing into the score where and when it needs to be done. In *Don Quixote* he does in fact specify where the viola should tune to low B for the famous Sancho Panza solo, but in *Salome* the violins find themselves confronted with passages containing the low E entirely without warning. The story goes that during a rehearsal the players expostulated, only to receive from Strauss the curt retort, 'Well, what did you expect me to write, a G?'

In fact Strauss did not always expect the players to tune down for such instances, which abound in his works right up to the end of his long life, as for example in *Metamorphosen*. For there was always, in this most professional of composers, considerable method in his apparent madness. In his more patient moments he would explain that if the player *thought* the unobtainable note strongly enough and tried hard to look as if he *was* playing it, the audience would never know it was missing.

Where a composer positively intends that the players should tune down he normally allows time with rests for this to be done. But one grotesque yet valid effect must be allowed for, in which the players change the tuning while actually playing the string concerned. Haydn characteristically used this joke effect in his Symphony No. 60, 'Il Distratto'.

SCORE LAYOUT

1 Standard Form

While the layout of the FULL SCORE is broadly standardized, with the WOOD-WIND at the head, the BRASS in the middle and the STRINGS at the foot of the page, there are exceptions, deriving mostly from earlier practices. Until the early nineteenth century all kinds of arrangement were in current use and the manuscripts of Mozart, Beethoven and even Schubert will often show the upper strings at the top of the score, the bass line at the bottom, and the wind and brass in the middle. The scores of Suppé's overtures present a splendid conundrum to the modern score reader in this respect, it being an excellent trial of scholarship to ask a conductor to identify the bassoon part out of all the mixed-up lines in the original Siegel edition. Modern scores have tried to introduce uniformity as a matter of policy, but curious survivors of older methods still exist, such as in the Prelude to *Tristan und Isolde*. Here one system – but only one – is given in archaic manner on the second page, showing the extent to which, despite Wagner's advanced thinking and apparent modernity in stylistic experimentation, he was at heart a traditionalist. Indeed his operatic scores present yet another throwback to earlier custom – that of placing the vocal line within the string block directly above the cello/bass line.

2 Solo Line

This derives from the basso continuo, in which, for the sake of the keyboard performer who would be playing from score, the solo line used to be placed immediately above the figured bass. This custom was also carried over at times into instrumental concertante works with the result that well-established editions of the classical concerto repertoire exist with the solo part (including piano) in that position.

Although early keyboard *(Klavier)* concertante parts are still often retained below all the strings, at the very bottom of the score, in modern scores the normal placing of the solo line, instrumental or vocal, is above the whole string group.

3 Woodwind

In the case of the woodwind, which normally occupies the head of the page, the standard procedure is for the flute department to be at the top followed in descending order by the oboe, clarinet and bassoon families, each as a rule together in blocks.

There are, however, all kinds of exceptions, as the result of composers' different idiosyncrasies. Tchaikovsky, for example, sometimes puts the cor anglais not among the oboes but below the clarinets; many of his most familiar works are laid out in this way, such as *Romeo and Juliet*, the Overture *1812*, etc. His reason for this change from the usual pattern must have been in order to maintain the regularly descending pitch range down the score rather than meticulously segregating the instruments by family. In the same way the bass clarinet is sometimes placed below the bassoons, as by Wagner in *Tristan und Isolde*, or even, oddly enough, above the other clarinets, as in the original Bote & Bock edition of Dvořák's *Scherzo Capriccioso*.

4 Order within Families

Within each of the woodwind families themselves the instruments are usually ranged in the score in descending order of pitch with the highest at the top. On this basis the piccolo would naturally find its proper place at the head of the page. Yet even this is not always the case, as the logical layout by pitch conflicts with another consideration: that of the top line being given to the principal player of the group, here the 1st flute. Hence there are two quite distinct practices: when the piccolo is used throughout a work, that is to say without changing to 3rd (or 2nd) flute, the line will indeed appear at the top of the score. But when the 2nd flute doubles on piccolo, his role of subsidiary flute takes priority and the piccolo line comes beneath that of the 1st flute.

As a result of complicated doublings with the piccolo, and sometimes more than one, not to mention perhaps also an alto flute, the lines in some scores get mixed up; perhaps the 2nd piccolo (played by the 1st flute) may be put above the 1st piccolo with the alto flute somewhere in between. It is not even unknown for the composer himself to become confused over how the distribution should work out, and accordingly the players' staves can change their relative positions from page to page.

Similar problems may arise in the clarinet department, where the E♭ is normally placed above the 1st and 2nd B♭ and A, unless doubling occurs. But the situation with oboes and bassoons is trouble-free as the subsidiary instruments are all pitched lower than the parent instrument.

Although in some scores each player's line is laid out individually, it is more usual for the 1st and 2nd of each instrument to be combined on a single stave. When they sometimes play in unison, they may then be shown with only single stems to the notes and marked *a* 2, this indication having exactly the opposite meaning to its use in the string department where it generally signifies a form of DIVISI playing.

5 Horns

The usual place for horns on the page is at the head of the brass, i.e., below the bassoons and above the trumpets, but bracketed with the latter. There are, however, two other alternative layouts. The first, initiated by Berlioz, is based on the principle that since the horns work in closest conjunction with the woodwind they should therefore appear, in order of pitch, between the clarinets and bassoons. The other is a diametrically opposite school of thought. Wagner himself in the *Siegfried Idyll* and in only one or two isolated pages of the *Ring* abandons his normal method of grouping the horns with the woodwind and places the trumpets above the horns, some composers following this procedure as their invariable practice. Prokofiev, for example, wrote for the horns, again in seemingly logical order of pitch between the trumpets and trombones, but thereby identifying them too closely with the heavy brass. This layout has at various times been toyed with by other composers, such as Reger, Lalo and Shostakovich, though the two latter curiously tried it only in certain works, as if they became conscious that it was unsatisfactory.

Horns are rarely written out in open score with a stave to a part, unless either they are all pitched in different crooks or where the interplay of the lines would otherwise present too confusing an appearance. By far the most usual is for two horns to share a stave – even, as occasionally, when they have different clefs, presenting the rare sight of treble and bass clefs one above the other at the head of a single stave.

6 Brass

The brass traditionally appear below the horns and above the percussion. They are also reasonably placed in descending order of pitch though keeping the family members together, i.e., trumpets, including bass trumpet; trombones, including bass and contra-bass trombone; and tuba(s), headed by the tenor tuba if there is one.

There are, however, as always, exceptions, beginning with the arrangement discussed above whereby the trumpets are placed above the horns. The consequent unification of the horns and brass by this practice has a certain logic in maintaining the entire brass section together in strictly descending order of family pitch level, the horns now representing the alto voices of the brass choir, however much this disregards their more sensitive affiliations with the woodwind.

A further and greatly perplexing variation of brass format appears in many early scores, especially vocal or operatic scores. Here the trombones may be isolated below the timpani as in Mozart's *Zauberflöte* or Beethoven's *Fidelio*, this being perhaps indicative of their being included in the orchestra as a special importation. Yet Beethoven, and Mendelssohn after him, transferred this odd arrangement across to their symphonic works; and Mendelssohn's *Reformation* Symphony actually places the trombones above the trumpets, an extraordinary scheme in which he was followed by Berwald in his Overture *Estrella di Soria*.

There is little uniformity in scores over whether the brass are given independent staves or are laid out in groups. Instruments most frequently placed together on a single stave are the 1st and 2nd, as well as the 3rd and 4th, of both trumpets and trombones. If there are only three the 3rd trumpet will normally have a stave to itself (unless of course all are playing in unison) whereas the 3rd trombone usually shares a stave with the tuba. The mixing of these instruments on a single stave makes it important to add some specific identification (*3rd* or *col tuba*), and when a composer fails to do this it can be none too clear whether he really intends the combined sound of the tuba playing in unison with the bass trombone.

The situation of the tuba or tubas, although mostly with or below the trombones, is also apt to be thrown into some confusion when the work includes WAGNER TUBAS. The troubles arise partly because these are hybrid animals and really belong together with the horns, by whose players they are handled mostly as DOUBLING instruments. Where this occurs the Wagner tubas are generally placed in the score with the horns and above the trumpets. This at least preserves their identity, though it appears strange for the deepest genus of the brass family to be placed so high on the page and so widely separated from the true bass tuba (in these circumstances generally called the contrabass tuba), which con-

tinues to be placed conventionally below the trombones. In view of the oddity of splitting up the tuba group in this way, the Wagner tubas are moved in some scores down to their logical position between the trombones and the (contra-)bass tuba.

7 Timpani, etc.

The traditional score presentation of the timpani line is under the brass and above the other percussion: the harp(s), celesta, etc., then come below these. Needless to say, however, there are again variations. Schoenberg puts the harps, etc., above the percussion group, and in a few works the timpani line is placed below that of the other percussion. Berg usually keeps to the standard layout, but in the *Drei Orchesterstücke*, Op. 6, which has an immense number of percussion parts, the timpani appear variably in the score, beginning below the mass of other percussion staves but shifting their relative placings as the work progresses – sometimes to the middle, sometimes even to their conventional place at the top. Reorientating of the timpani occurs to a considerable degree in contemporary works, especially where there is an elaborate percussion department, such as in Zimmermann's *Canto di Speranza*, and this can be quite misleading.

8 Double-staved Instruments

Where a score has a wide assortment of harps, piano, celesta, organ and so on, each of which has at least two staves, they can occupy an inordinate amount of space in the middle of a page and can be in any order. The original ballet score of Stravinsky's *Firebird* gives a good example, with its three harps together with both piano and celesta; but Wagner's six harps in *Das Rheingold* in fact produce the unique situation where the publishers decided against making the score big enough to include the complete instrumentation, and the six harp parts are relegated most inconveniently to an appendix – so that no complete conductor's score exists for the pages devoted to the 'Entrance of the Gods into Valhalla' at the conclusion of the opera.

See also: COPYISTS, FULL SCORE, PARTICELL, REHEARSAL LETTERS

Secco (It.), dry; *see* HARP, 7

SERPENT

This is a very rare bass to the brass group, used for example by Mendelssohn in his Overture *Calm Sea and Prosperous Voyage* as well as in operatic scores by Spontini and Bellini, where it is called *Serpentone*. Although this is virtually the same name as the Greek word OPHICLEIDE (i.e., 'keyed serpent') the serpent itself, also keyed, is an entirely different instrument with a much stronger claim to the name since, unlike the ophicleide, it does at least look like a large snake. It is, however, not a brass instrument at all but, like the ZINKE, of which it is the bass, is wooden and covered with leather yet blown with a mouthpiece, so that it is to a great extent hybrid, with links both to woodwind and brass.

The serpent has occasionally made isolated appearances, being specially imported for its grotesque, uncouth quality (for which Berlioz berates it).

The sound is not unlike a kind of draconian contrabassoon, though of course without the real buzz of that unmistakable woodwind instrument. The serpent has the same range as the ophicleide and is notated at concert pitch in the bass clef.

SHOFAR

This is a ram's horn adapted for use in Jewish ritual as a focal point of the traditional service. It can be of various sizes and pitch and has in reality no place in the orchestra except that Elgar imitates its effect in *The Apostles*, where he gives it two notes, an E♭ rising to C, saying in a preface that its effect should be imitated by an extra trumpeter playing preferably a straight trumpet. Strangely the one work in which it might have been expected to appear, Ernest Bloch's *Sacred Service* (a full setting of the Jewish Service), the shofar has no place whatever.

Side Drum, *see* DRUMS, 1

Signalhorn (Ger.), military bugle; *see* BUGLE

SIREN

This is one of the several effects for which the percussion department makes itself responsible, hardly qualifying as a musical instrument but making an occasional *coup de théâtre* in some of the more exotic twentieth-century scores.

There are various kinds of siren, most of which can be found somewhere in orchestral works, and of these the greater number are characterized by the fluctuations in pitch all too familiar in their extra-musical associations, such as ambulance or air-raid sirens. Nevertheless Varèse used precisely these electrically operated sirens with their melancholy wailing for purely musical purposes in works such as *Ionisation*. Hindemith used a siren, probably expecting one of the smaller and simpler hand-operated variety, in a strongly satirical vein in his *Kammermusik* No. 1 as one of the many typically 1920-ish send-ups.

An entirely different kind is a ship's siren, also called a ship's hooter, which in contrast maintains a single constant pitch. Satie uses this in *Parade*, as does Bliss in his ballet *Miracle in the Gorbals*, the latter to suggest the sinister proximity of the Clyde shipbuilding yards at the climax of the ferocious drama.

Sistro, sistrum (Lat.), *see* BELL TREE, JINGLES

Slapstick, *see* WHIP

Sleigh Bells, *see* JINGLES

Slit Drum, *see* LOG DRUMS

SLUNG MUGS

This home-made device is neither more nor less than its name implies, a row of a dozen or so mugs threaded on string. It was suggested to Benjamin Britten by Imogen Holst, who first called it into service as part of her work in the field of local amateur music-making. Britten used slung mugs with

great ingenuity to suggest raindrops in *Noye's Fludde*, where they are struck with wooden spoons as part of the unskilled department of the children's orchestral groups. They have a random quality not unlike Mahler's use of cowbells, but naturally enough with far less resonance as the mugs are supposed to be of china rather than metal.

Slur, *see* BOWING, 12

Snare Drums, *see* DRUMS, 1

Snares, *see* DRUMS, 1

SOLO

This is primarily an indication to tell the player that the passage in question is of individual importance and should be projected over and above the printed dynamic. On this basis the word is used (both in the score and the players' material) especially for solos in the wind, brass, percussion, etc. On the other hand, where the strings are concerned it has the additional significance of requiring the line to be performed by a single player, usually the leader of the relevant group.

Even in the strings, however, the word *solo* is not infrequently added in the parts and/or score to indicate that the line is of solo importance, and not that it is necessarily to be rendered by a single player. This may need a decision from the conductor – aided perhaps by whether or not the word *tutti* appears by way of contradiction later, as in Chausson's *Poème*, Op. 25.

Further confusion may arise in

concertos where the words *solo* and *tutti* are repeatedly added to the orchestral parts, not, however, with reference to these at all but purely to identify sections in which the concerto soloist is or is not playing, and hence as a guide to where the tone should be moderated in the interests of accompaniment.

Sonagliera (It.), *see* JINGLES

Sons étouffez (Fr.) damp each sound immediately; *see* HARP, 7

SOPRANINO AND SOPRANO SAXOPHONES

These two highest-sounding SAXO-PHONES are more properly jazz than orchestral instruments. Their outstanding appearance in the orchestra is in Ravel's *Bolero*, but even here a single instrument (the soprano) and one player serves for both. Normally they are pitched in Eb and Bb respectively, but curiously Ravel chose a sopranino instrument in F, now long extinct.

SOPRANO

The women's upper singing part in solo and choral singing alike. It does not, however, apply to boys whose top line is called 'treble'. Nevertheless in the full and vocal scores of works where boys' voices may be preferred, such as Fauré's Requiem or Stravinsky's *Symphony of Psalms*, the word 'soprano' will still conventionally be retained in most instances.

In choral writing, female sopranos can be used over a range extending from middle C to the C two octaves

above, but with boys' voices the compass will be considerably reduced at either end.

The soprano clef (C on the bottom line) is still used in many old or scholarly editions, especially in sacred music or throughout Mendelssohn's works, but otherwise the treble clef is the norm.

Sordini, sordino (It.), *see* MUTES, 1

Sourdines (Fr.), *see* MUTES, 1

Spiccato (It.), *see* BOWING, 11

SPINET

The smallest HARPSICHORD. This contains only one manual and no stops or pedals. It is not used orchestrally except by way of continuo with a small ensemble.

Spitze (Ger.), upper end of the bow; *see* BOWING, 2

Springbogen (Ger.), *see* BOWING, 11

Stab (Ger.), *see* STAHLSTÄBE

Staccato (It.), *see* BOWING, 11

STAHLSTÄBE

(Ger. literally 'steel bars'). Mahler writes this in a footnote during the finale of his Seventh Symphony to describe his concept of deep untuned BELL PLATES; Sibelius, on the other hand, unconventionally uses the word to denote the GLOCKENSPIEL, as in *The Oceanides*, while Hindemith scores for a single *Stab*, i.e., one bar of the same instrument held up and struck, in his *Kammermusik* No. 1. In itself, however, a *Stab* can be simply a metal rod, such as is used for a triangle beater.

Steg, am (Ger.) *(sul ponticello), see* BOWING, 4

STEINSPIEL

(Ger.); **litofono** (It.). This fringe percussion instrument, invented by Orff and used in *Die Kluge*, consists of a row of suspended stone slabs struck with wooden beaters. Some stones are more prone than others to give off quite a recognizable note.

Stierhörner (Ger.), *see* COWHORN

Streichorchester (Ger.), string orchestra

Streichinstrumente, abbr. *Streiche* (Ger.), bowed instruments, as distinct from *Saiteninstrumente*, which also includes harp, pianos etc., *see* STRINGS, 2

Strich für Strich (Ger.), separate bowing; *see* BOWING, 8

String Bass, English term for double-bass used sometimes in bands, where strings are in the minority

String Drum, *see* LION'S ROAR

STRINGS

1 Members
The standard orchestral string section consists of groups of four related instruments, all members of a single family subdivided according to size and hence register: VIOLINS, VIOLAS, CELLOS and DOUBLE-BASSES. These are, however, most usually divided into five groups by the conventional subdivision of the violin strength into 1sts and 2nds, each of which is as much a complete and self-contained unit as any of the others. The Germans refer to the strings equally as the *Streichquartett* or *Streichquintett* according to whether or not the 1st and 2nd violins are considered collectively as a single instrument genus. In this context these terms, normally associated with the solo string quartet or quintet of chamber music, are used occasionally in the instrumental lists at the beginning of orchestral scores, or in analyses. The abbreviation **'Q'** may thus also occur in piano arrangements or vocal scores in German editions where these give indications of the instrumentation.

However true it may be that the repertoire ranging from early to contemporary music shows similar divisions into 1st and 2nd violas, cellos and basses, or different divisions (into three, etc.) or no divisions at all, for violins or for any of the others, these variations are far less frequent and do not affect the constitution or administration of the orchestra.

2 Names
The English 'strings' is paralleled by the French **les cordes**, but the Germans, with typical punctiliousness, specify **Streichinstrumente**, i.e. 'stroked instruments' as distinct from **Saiteninstrumente**, a blanket term including equally all stringed instruments,

whether bowed, plucked, hammered or whatever, such as harp, piano, harpsichord, mandoline, guitar, etc. Hence Bartók's *Musik für Saiteninstrumente, Schlagzeug und Celesta* is a title hard to translate since the straightforward English equivalent (*Music for Strings, Percussion and Celesta*) fails to indicate that the score includes harp and piano. In the German title only the celesta has to be singled out since its keyboard operates hammers that strike not on strings but metal bars.

The Italian term for the string group is again different. Although the word for string is *corda* (similar to the French) the section as a whole is called not *le corde* but **gli archi**, i.e., not the strings but the bows.

3 Position

The string body occupies a primary status in the orchestra. This is not merely so in a visual sense – at the front of the concert platform – but because the very presence of multiple strings can be taken to determine whether a group of instruments should be described as an orchestra at all. Even the presence of single strings (that is, one player of each department) is barely sufficient to qualify an ensemble as an orchestra, though borderline cases exist such as Jean Françaix's *Serenade*, which, scored for twelve instruments including five solo strings, is actually – if perhaps incorrectly – described as being *pour petit orchestre*.

4 Quantity

There is no absolute number of strings constituting a symphony orchestra, but the full strength aimed at for prestige concerts in the capital cities of

the world may be said to be 16 1st violins, 14 2nd violins, 12 violas, 10 cellos and 8 basses. At other times one desk less all round is very common, although every conceivable variation is employed and, indeed, written for.

Composers, when they specify at all, vary widely in their preferences. Berlioz habitually stated *at least 15. 15. 10. 11. 9*, a curious strength since it presupposes a single player at most of the back desks, a situation generally found unsatisfactory. Also it will be noticed that Berlioz enumerated more cellos than violas – an unusual though not unique practice. Debussy in *La Mer* asks at one point for no fewer than 16 cellos, although nowhere else in the score is there any indication that he is thinking in terms of an abnormal string strength. Wagner in *The Ring* lists a string body of 16. 16. 12. 12. 8 against a wind body that might have been thought to require even more extravagant forces. The largest body actually prescribed, on the assumption that it must and will be made available, is for Schoenberg's *Gurrelieder*. The numbers scored for are: 20. 20. 16. 16, plus an unspecified number of basses, the whole – he says – to be further reinforced. Even London's Royal Festival Hall platform had to be measured carefully to see if it could accommodate such a vast gathering of players, let alone any 'further reinforcements'.

Although it is by no means regular practice to give exact figures of string strength, there are a surprising number of scores where they are in fact noted, especially when the composer is anxious that the force should not be too large for good balance in accompaniment. Thus most of Strauss's operas and orchestral *Lieder* have carefully adjusted string strength with this in mind. Again Stravinsky stipulated no more than 8.8.6.4.4 *players* (not desks) for his Violin Concerto, while a similarly small group is insisted on by Poulenc as the background to a solo harpsichord in his *Concert Champêtre*.

It is where the composer leaves no instructions that the conductor's responsibility and artistry begins. For example, Honegger gives no indication in his *Pastorale d'Éte*, but no sensitive conductor would play this delicate fragment with a body of strings worthy of Strauss's *Ein Heldenleben*. Programmes can easily come to mind that could benefit from variations of string strength for every item.

5 Classical Numbers

Fashion can also play a part: classical works – by Haydn, Mozart, Schubert, etc. – that would once have been played by the full orchestra under every international conductor from Bülow to Toscanini will generally be played today with greatly reduced strings in the pursuit of stylistic purity. Yet Mozart once wrote to his father in delighted excitement after hearing one of his symphonies played by 40 violins with the rest of the orchestra augmented in proportion. Performances of the Beethoven symphonies have recently been given, on grounds of authenticity, with an orchestra of reduced strings such as Beethoven himself would have found at his disposal. But it is improbable, to say the least, that this was what he really would have liked, in particular for the odd-numbered, large-scale symphonies. In any case opinions will always differ over the right artistic demands of every work while also bearing in mind the acoustics of each individual hall.

6 Smaller Ensembles

One has also to remember that the fewer the players the higher the standards of execution must be. Far less than a full symphony orchestra can a chamber orchestra afford to have passengers in the rank-and-file strings, since any imperfection is the more immediately perceived. Moreover, personal responsibility is likely to be greater, since as soon as the lines divide each may be taken by two players or even only one solo.

The fewer the players on any one line, moreover, the harder it is to match the tone quality. Two players – i.e., a single desk – is certainly the hardest of all. Yet composers have been known to choose precisely this effect, such as Liszt and Brahms in their E♭ and D minor Piano Concertos respectively, a device Tchaikovsky echoes with his two cellos in the slow movement of the ever popular B♭ minor Piano Concerto. If they can force the conductor's hand, players tend to shirk this all too revealing exposure, leaving such passages to the leader of the section. Certainly there is no need to court disaster by trying, for instance, to play the *Siegfried Idyll* with two players to each string part, as was once advocated in all seriousness by an eminent critic.

The use of individuals from the ranks, including the BACK DESKS, forms part of an increase of responsibility that is a growing feature of present-day orchestral life. There is, however, both gain and loss here: gain where renewed interest leads to a rise in standards, loss where soloistic responsibility may lead to special fees being established in connection with some works, thus causing orchestral managements to relegate them to the background of fringe repertoire.

Nevertheless there is no evading the existence of a sizeable repertoire of orchestral or chamber-orchestral music using smaller string forces, whether in the pursuit of finesse in classical works or for specific twentieth-century compositions such as the Ibert *Divertissement* or Stravinsky's *Dumbarton Oaks*, both of which require as few as three violins (written as a single line), three violas and two each of cellos and basses, and down to Schoenberg's *Kammersymphonie*, Op. 9, scored for single strings—that is none other than a solo string quintet.

7 Solo Playing

The timbre of a single string player is so different from the mass quality that its use in apposition to the main body is often comparable with the contrasting use of a solo wind instrument. Members of each of the sections can be found spotlighted in this way, including the double-bass. One of the most striking instances of solo work for the leaders of their respective groups occurs in Tchaikovsky's Piano Concerto No. 2 in G, Op. 44. For much of the slow movement the solo piano is joined by the leader and first cellist in a piano trio, both players enjoying short cadenzas. Although violin cadenzas

are quite a feature of Tchaikovsky's orchestral music (as, for example, in the *Theme and Variations* from the Suite No. 3, the *Mozartiana Suite* and numerous places in the ballets), this is such an exceptional instance that the leader often stands to perform it, as he has also been known to do in the beautiful extended cantilena in the 'Benedictus' of Beethoven's *Missa Solemnis*.

It could be argued that such behaviour is inappropriate, being too soloistic for the contexts, but there is a legitimately histrionic element in symphonic music that should not be underestimated, least of all derided, although taste and changing fashion will always need to be taken into account. For it is by no means unknown for the whole string group to play standing (excluding the cellos, who do not even attempt to stand for National Anthems). Sir Henry Wood used to play the Third Brandenburg Concerto with the massed strings standing, and just at the time when this practice was coming to be regarded as out of keeping with the classicism of baroque music, along came the Adolf Busch Chamber players, the Lucerne Festival Strings and other such groups offering a style of presentation thought in other respects to show a return to purism but in which all the players regularly perform standing.

8 Strings

Controversy continues to rage over the actual strings themselves. Once made of sheep- or cat-gut, the highest violin string—the E (also designated in scores by the Roman numeral I)—was the first to be replaced by steel wire. The G string – the lowest, and designated IV – came, on the other hand, to be covered spirally with metal, to be followed by the D and A. Today steel strings are often used for all four, although the resultant sacrifice in tonal warmth and beauty is deplored even by string players while admitting their greater reliability.

It is in fact widely recognized that there are other factors of convenience that cannot be ignored: for instance, it is only with steel strings that it is possible to fit an adjuster whereby fine retuning can be carried out quickly and easily even in the course of the music. This can also be of particular advantage in cases where the composer prescribes changes of tuning (SCORDA-TURA) during a work.

One of the chief hazards to which the string players can be subject concerns the innate unreliability of even steel strings, which, unless in perfect condition, may be untrue especially in higher positions. Furthermore new strings tend to stretch so that they drop in pitch until they settle, thus needing constantly repeated checking and retuning, while old ones deteriorate in quality and are liable to snap. In the event of a soloist or even a leader suffering a broken string during a concert, a quick substitution of instruments may take place so that a back-desk player can scuttle off the platform to replace the broken string, while the players with most responsibility carry on as little disturbed as possible by the emergency. But often enough the unfortunate musician will have to carry on as best he may by playing as much of the part as he can on other strings in unfamiliar and ungainly positions.

Strings are also greatly affected by atmospheric conditions of temperature or humidity. It is generally believed that as hall and instruments warm up the wind will rise in pitch while the strings will drop. In actual practice, however, the strings rise as well, though for a variety of reasons including the psychological fact that players tend to keep adjusting their intonation in an upward direction.

9 Tremolo

The to-and-fro bow strokes may be treated not purely as means of expression, but as a dramatic method of extending the sound. In these instances various forms of accompaniment figurations result, such as the so-called *ostinati*, which as they become more rapid approach the **tremolo**. This latter should, however, really come into question only when the number of to-and-fro bow strokes is indeterminate.

However, the signs for this: ♪ , ♪ , ♪ ,

or even sometimes only ⌒ , are indis-criminately used to the point where it is all too often debatable whether the composer really intends a tremolo or an actual measured figure, especially when the tempo is slow enough for the exact number of notes to be played in rhythmic repetition, as at the beginning of Mahler's Seventh Symphony. On the whole, three strokes ♪ is standard tremolo notation, but Haydn for one was in the habit of writing ♪ , and many such passages in his symphonies are often interpreted as exact slow-moving semiquavers. Conversely, Tchaikovsky actually meant demisemiquavers when he used three strokes and added a fourth when he wanted tremolo.

Sometimes the clue to what might seem an unlikely interpretation is given by printing out in full a first specimen group, as in the slow movement of Dvořák's D minor Symphony, Op. 70, or 'Siegfried's Funeral March' from Wagner's *Götterdämmerung*. Occasionally composers do add *trem.*, but it is very rare to see the opposite indication *non trem.* (i.e., measured) although one such does occur in Strauss's *Don Quixote*. Yet there are countless borderline cases where either of the two essentially different effects is equally possible and it must be admitted that in the absence of any obvious choice players tend to take it for granted that they should play *tremolo*.

Duparc, in his orchestration of the song *L'Invitation au Voyage*, calls for **trémolo ondulé**. This device was certainly known in the seventeenth and eighteenth centuries and was exploited orchestrally by, for example, Gluck in his opera *Alceste*. Forsyth, in a section of his book on orchestration called 'The Obsolete Undulating Tremolo' describes the action as 'a series of pressures exerted by the fingers of the right hand on the bow during the course of a long *legato* bow stroke. The fingers exert and relax the pressure as the bow proceeds on its course.' Today few players have so much as heard of the technique and opinions in orchestras tend to be divided over what they might be expected to do as well as how it is supposed to sound.

10 Style

In these days of chromium-plated purity of style, impeccable cleanliness in changes of position, however wide, is considered to be an essential yardstick of orchestral standard. Yet audible, even quasi-*portamento*, shifts, as well as actual slides between the notes, were once a recognized means of expression. Composers took this method of execution for granted, as is shown by the performances Elgar conducted of his own works. It would therefore not normally be specifically indicated, though pronounced slithers or extravagant GLISSANDI for special purposes would be notated by a line drawn between notes. This would generally be a straight line but in some avant-garde scores wavy lines are substituted to suggest more elaborate smears.

Such **portamento** effects might be realized through the deliberate exaggeration of shifts of position, extra ones being taken over and above those actually needed by the normal fingering of the passage in question. But even greater suggestion of parodied sentiment is achieved by the use of a single finger sliding up or down the string; Mahler asks specifically for this in, for example, the Fifth Symphony, and even goes so far as to prescribe a smeared shift between two identical notes taken on different strings.

11 Vibrato

Just as the *portamento* was until recently an accepted method of playing to indicate a sensitive expression of musicianship, so too was the **vibrato**, since its appearance with the passing of the viols. This shaking to and fro of the left wrist and hand has now long been the standard method of tone production for all stopped notes and is cultivated by every player in his own way in the pursuit of style and a beautiful quality from his instrument. All forms of *legato* and sustained playing are subject to *vibrato* – with the exception of harmonics, for the lightly touching finger cannot produce a true *vibrato*. Indeed *vibrato* – with the exception of HARMONICS, for the lightly touching finger of pure harmonics, since its purpose lies in the production of warmth and a colourful tone.

Broadly speaking it is the use and degree of *vibrato* to which composers are indirectly referring when using such terms as *dolce* (Ger., *zart*; Fr. – though more rarely – *doucement*) or *espressivo* (Ger., *ausdrucksvoll*; Fr. *expressif*). Hence, when a composer stipulates that a passage be played *senza espress.* (*ohne Ausdruck*, etc.), it is often taken to mean 'without vibrato' although this is not necessarily the right interpretation. For when strings really do play without any *vibrato* whatsoever a bare unbeautiful sound ensues, a special effect that may or may not represent the composer's intention.

In some contemporary scores, therefore, the specific term *senza vibrato* has come to be used, together with *con* (or *senza*) *vibrato poco a poco*, where the warmth of colour is to be added (or withdrawn) gradually (Fricker, Violin Concerto; Goehr, *Little Music for Strings*, etc.). Moreover, so automatic is the normal use of *vibrato* that the appearance of the actual word itself generally signifies that more – or perhaps a slower, wider – *vibrato* is required than the players would naturally produce. This could be to create a special degree of intensity, or perhaps even for parody or the grotesque, as in Bartók's Second Suite, Op. 4.

12 Characteristics

It is to a large extent the combination of many individual *vibrati* that is the predominant characteristic of the string mass, and which gives it its unique colour, the very colour that identifies the symphony orchestra itself. It is also the one colour of which for some indefinable reason the ear never tires, unlike that of any other group of instruments.

The string orchestra can thus be a fully self-contained entity which has indeed a large and splendid repertoire of its own ranging through every period of musical history from the Baroque school to the present day. As a result countless string ensembles have come into being and have acquired international reputations without the need for more than the occasional co-opted wind or timpani player in order to add a particular work for some special concert or programme.

At the same time, although the strings have this clear advantage over the wind, the latter can boast a compensating quality in the carrying power of even quite small formations. This accounts for the specifically outdoor nature of wind ensembles, from the divertimenti and serenades of the Haydn–Mozart era to the entire gamut of military music and brass bands. In the open air string quality disperses hopelessly, and any orchestra depends on some kind of artificial amplification, as the organizers of park concerts or the creators of open-air auditoriums such as the Hollywood Bowl well know.

Another outstanding and curious feature of the string timbre is that it cannot be imitated in any way. This is a fact electric organ builders and other devisers of electronic equipment are reluctant to face, since it is contrary to all the theories they most vehemently hold and assert.

Finally the string body is outstandingly flexible and intuitive. Miracles of instinctive and instantaneous response can be achieved by a highly trained string orchestra in which, it should be remembered, most of the members lack that element of individual contribution enjoyed by every wind player. And, oddly enough, when groups of wind players take over the string rank-and-file roles, as in the military band, they never quite achieve a comparable finesse. Whether in nuances, in interplay with each other of tone and dynamics, in response to a conductor's freedom of expression or *rubato*, in variations of style or technique, or even in the matter of endless give-and-take in accompaniment within the orchestra itself as well as in concerto and operatic work, it is the strings who have the edge on every other section. And where traditional rhythmic freedom is concerned, such as in the waltzes of Johann Strauss or the opening of the Scherzo of Dvořák's D minor Symphony, Op. 70, an alert string section can accomplish as one player, and even without rehearsal, subtleties of phrasing that could never be written down or explained, and that would require hours of preparation and rehearsal with

the other soloist-orientated groups.

Although, therefore, life as a RANK-AND-FILE string player is often bemoaned as soul-destroying in the long run, the corporate string section – made up to some extent though it may be of individuals each aspiring to greater opportunities for self-expression – remains the essential foundation on which the symphony orchestra firmly rests.

See also: PLATFORM ARRANGEMENTS, SCORE LAYOUT

Su (It.), up bow; *see* BOWING, 7

Sul ponticello (It.), *see* BOWING, 4

Sul tasto (It.), *see* BOWING. 5

Tabla, *see* HAND DRUMS

Tabor, *see* DRUMS, 5

Taille, *see* COR ANGLAIS

Talon (Fr.), **Talone** (It.), heel of bow; *see* BOWING, 2

Tambour, *see* DRUMS, 1

Tambour à corde (Fr.), *see* LION'S ROAR

Tambour de basque (Fr.), *see* TAMBOURINE

Tambour militaire (Fr.), *see* DRUMS, 1

Tambourin (Fr.), Provençal long drum, *see* DRUMS, 5

Tambourin (Ger.), *see* TAMBOURINE

TAMBOURINE

Tambourines exist in all sizes – in Sicily I once saw a real monster, more than twice the usual diameter, giving a reminder both in appearance and use of its origin in the drum (tambour) family – but orchestrally this has little reality. The same is true of the hoop tambourine without parchment – nothing but the frame with jingles – or its opposite – hoop with parchment but no jingles – both of which exist but are no more than occasional visitors to the orchestral scene; Falla uses the latter in *El Retablo de Maese Pedro*, calling it a **Pandero sia sonajas**.

One awkward feature of the tambourine is the similarity of its name to the **tambourin**, i.e. the Provençal long drum. The French get out of the difficulty by calling the tambourine the **tambour de basque**, as do the Germans with one of their words for it, **Schellentrommel**; this is, however, rarely used and the standard German name is in fact none other than **Tambourin**, completing the confusion and leading to the famous howler of using a tambourine for Bizet's *L'Arlésienne*. The Italians use both **tamburino** and **tamburo basco** but the Breitkopf Berlioz edition uses *tamburi piccoli* in, for example, *Le Carnaval Romain*, which is as unusual as it is dangerously ambiguous.

It is rare to find technical methods prescribed for the tambourine as it is mostly either struck (usually with the fingers as in the 'Brigand's Orgy' of Berlioz's symphony *Harold in Italy*) or shaken; it is never played with a stick. Nevertheless a number of important variants make up the player's technique, of which the most usual in the printed score is *Mit den Daumen* or *avec la pouce* (with the thumb), referring to the method of producing a trill or rapid figure by licking the thumb to increase the friction and juddering it over the surface of the skin. Poulenc's *Concert Champêtre* and the 'Danse Arabe' from Tchaikovsky's *Nutcracker* both call for this method, though the latter, being slow and measured, is an instance where it is particularly difficult and players rarely obey the instruction. This thumb technique is in fact standard practice for a soft and shortish unmeasured roll, but for anything longer and louder it is more usual to shake the whole thing, especially if the roll ends in a dramatic tap, for which the tambourine can even be raised above the head with great panache. In complicated sections players will also use the knee, either to rest it on, or to strike it against, or both. One of the hardest technical problems is to play the tambourine really softly. The jingles will ring out at the slightest vibration and the catastrophe of a dropped tambourine is not infrequent and in every way as disastrous as a dropped cymbal. However, Stravinsky actually asks for a tambourine to be held above the floor and then dropped in the last scene of *Petrouchka* at the moment when the puppet's neck is broken by the Moor.

Single taps or rhythmic passages can be placed either on the skin of the instrument or, turning it over, on the frame. The quality is, of course, different and it is odd that composers do not show awareness by specifying one or the other. In *Falstaff* Elgar wrote a passage that is often taken to mean a short roll and is therefore played with the thumb or even by shaking the tambourine briefly, whereas there is an authentic tradition that Elgar himself asked for it to be played 'struck lightly on the parchment'. This is typical of the doubt that pervades tambourine notation. More precise is Khachaturian who in *Gayaneh* specifies a composite technique with *on the rim* alternating with *on the centre.*

The use of more than one tambourine is rare, but Berlioz writes for two (in unison throughout) in the overture *Le Carnaval Romain* as well as in *Harold in Italy*, a splendidly imaginative stroke.

Tamburino (It.), *see* TAMBOURINE

Tamburo (It.), *see* DRUMS

Tamburo basco (It.), *see* TAMBOURINE

Tamburo di legno (It.), *see* WOOD BLOCK

Tamburo grande (It.), *see* BASS DRUM

Tamburo militare (It.), *see* DRUMS, 1

Tamburo piccolo (It.), *see* DRUMS, 1

Tamburo rullante (It.), *see* DRUMS, 1

Tam-tam, *see* GONGS AND TAM-TAMS

TAPES

The combination of pre-recorded electromagnetic tape together with live orchestral forces has been introduced by various contemporary composers and in numerous different ways. Owing to the sharp acceleration of evolution in the field of electronic recording since the Second World War, the ethical principle has become established that a tape recorder may be set up in an auditorium and its sounds projected, on its own or simultaneously with those of performing musicians.

Tape recordings for such purposes have been created by composers either out of natural sounds – instrumental or vocal, and untreated or distorted in various ways (the latter sometimes called *musique concrète*) – or of artificial effects created through the agency of different kinds of oscillators. Karl-Birger Blomdahl introduced a tape of splendid noises into his opera *Aniara*, which has a science-fiction scenario, to simulate the 'voice' of the space ship that carries the survivors of mankind to their doom. Similarly Roberto Gerhard, who had a particular interest in the possibilities of tape, created a number of pre-recorded 'bands' to be played in conjunction with the orchestra in his 'Collages' (Symphony No. 3). In such cases, of course, no notation could be concocted to indicate the sounds of the tapes, and instructions or thick lines simply designate where they are to be operated.

As far as natural sounds are concerned it is possible for the composer to be more explicit. John Tavener's *In Alium* combines a wide range of effects with the live performers, including the voices of children playing or saying their prayers in different languages, all sorts of tongue-clicks and kisses, noisy breathing and a pre-recording of a soprano singing exaggeratedly high chords achieved through superimposition and by means of running the tapes at double speed. Music has also been composed for solo instruments with tape in such a way that the player appears to play a duet with himself over a kind of loop in time, as in the Viola Sonata by Thea Musgrave.

Nevertheless, despite the limitless ingenuity of such effects it is significant that whereas tapes have been widely exploited, and indeed seemed to constitute hardly less than a major new dimension, they have become less of a standard medium than might have been expected. In the event it would seem that the artificiality of electronic sound has, up to the present, prevented the use of tapes from taking the place of the essential art of musical expression through the direct agency of live and physically present interpreters.

Tarbuka, Arabian hand drums; *see* DARBOUKKA

Tárogató (Hung.), *see* COR ANGLAIS

Tarole, tarolle (Fr.), *see* DRUMS, 5

Tastiera, Tasto, sul, (It.), *see* BOWING, 5

Tasto solo (It.), *see* CONTINUO

Tavolette (It.), *see* WOOD BLOCK

Teller(n) (Ger.), clashed cymbals; *see* CYMBALS, 2

Temple Blocks, *see* WOOD BLOCK

TENOR

The male upper voice for both solo and choral work. In choruses tenors are frequently the smallest group, good high voices being relatively scarce, so they are often placed centrally to the front.

Whereas the tenor line may, especially in older scores, be notated in the tenor clef, it is the treble clef that is mostly used with the parts written an octave above actual pitch. To indicate this some composite sign is occasionally substituted such as 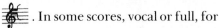, or

. In some scores, vocal or full, for reasons of space the vocal lines may be given not in open score but condensed on to two staves. This entails notating the tenors with the basses in the bass clef at pitch and as a result the tenor line in the score may then turn out to be at variance with the part, which is more likely to be notated conventionally.

The range of the tenors can be extraordinarily wide, (see CHORUS), and when used chorally to the full can exert an undue strain on the voices. Experienced CHORUS MASTERS sometimes resort to doublings (with 1st basses or 2nd altos as may be appropriate) in the interests both of strengthening and of alleviating the tenors' lot. If organized so well that it is undetectable this is obviously ingenious and effective.

Tenor Drum, *see* DRUMS, 1

Tenor Saxhorn, *see* SAXHORNS

TENOR SAXOPHONE

This is the second most common saxophone to be used in the orchestra. Its outstanding solos are in Prokofiev's scores (*Romeo and Juliet*, *Lieutenant Kijé*, etc.) but it also features as one of the trio of saxophones in Ravel's *Bolero* as well as those in Gershwin's *An American in Paris*. It is pitched in Bb, midway between the alto and baritone instruments.

TENOR TUBA

This important subspecies of the TUBA family, while not a regular member of the orchestra, is often brought in for special occasions such as Janáček's *Sinfonietta*, Strauss's *Don Quixote* and *Ein Heldenleben* or Holst's *The Planets*.

Unlike other tubas, the tenor is a TRANSPOSING INSTRUMENT but curiously its notation is not standardized, although it is universally built in the same key (Bb) with its set of harmonics an octave above the big CONTRABASS TUBA or BOMBARDON. German composers write for the tenor tuba in both treble and bass clefs sounding a tone lower, whereas Holst writes in the treble clef throughout and a ninth higher than actual pitch. This is strangely in contrast not only with the Continental practice, but also with English notation of the analogous EUPHONIUM, which is normally written in the bass clef at concert pitch.

The range of the tenor tuba stretches

from 𝄢 , its fundamental, over

some three octaves. Strauss writes a top

C♯ (sounding B) in *Don Quixote* and Holst in 'Uranus' goes a semitone higher still.

The tenor tuba shares with the other members of its kind the galumphing character for which Strauss chose it to depict the more ungainly elements of Sancho Panza's behaviour, but equally it emphasizes such degrees of both agility and lyricism of which tubas as a family may be capable. In this it contrasts with the tenor variety of the WAGNER TUBAS whose entire purpose lies in the providing of extra weight to the horns and brass.

Tenorhorn (Ger.), tenor saxhorn in Bb; *see* SAXHORNS

THUNDER MACHINE

This, another member of the percussionists' effects department, comes into its own primarily in the world of opera. Wagner uses it splendidly, for example, in the opening scene of the third act of *Siegfried* where the Wanderer (Wotan) enters amidst a violent storm. But Strauss ingeniously calls on its services on the concert platform for the huge thunderstorm that forms the climax of his *Alpine Symphony*.

Nowadays the thunder machine (**Donnermaschine**) is usually a great hanging sheet of metal (it is also sometimes called a thundersheet), which the player shakes with appropriately devastating realism, though other devices and contraptions were once used in theatres and opera houses. Strauss's machine is, however, said to have been operated like a WIND

MACHINE (i.e., revolved with a handle), although instead of the wooden drum being swished round against canvas, heavy balls tumbled about inside it.

It is amusing to recall that during the commercial recording of Carl Orff's opera *Der Mond* the point was just being reached at which St Peter hurls a thunderbolt at the earth when it was noticed that a violent thunderstorm was raging in the outside world. With exemplary speed a microphone was hoisted on to the roof of the studio and the actual thunder recorded; it was then incorporated successfully into the performance and can easily be recognized on the disc, thereby proving that however life-like the imitation there is no substitute for the real thing.

Timbales (Fr.), *see below and* TIMPANI, 2

TIMBALES

These are all too easily confused with the identical French word meaning timpani, which is – like the TAMBOURINE/**tambourin** muddle – a serious hazard to the investigation of proper timbales. Most reference books either omit them *in toto* or manage to entangle them with KETTLE-DRUMS, with which they are then combined in the index.

The timbales are South American instruments, not altogether unlike African TOM-TOMS but shallower and a little larger in circumference. They are single-headed, played usually with wooden sticks and written for in pairs. Their sound is hard and penetrating and has even been called metallic, although this depends on exactly where they are struck, as the different places

on the heads, let alone the rims and shells, all produce a wide variety of sounds.

A prominent feature of South American bands and popular music, the timbales were for long a rare visitor to the orchestral scene. Roberto Gerhard however introduced them into *The Plague* and they are becoming ever more prevalent in the manifold percussion sections of contemporary scores.

Timbales chromatiques, *see* TIMPANI, 5

TIMPANI

1 Status

While it stands to reason that the timpani are, technically speaking, part of the PERCUSSION, nevertheless this is not the whole story within the hierarchy of the orchestra. The timpanist is very much king in his own province, and in larger orchestras it is only in exceptional circumstances that he is called on to play any other percussion instrument whatever.

Normally he will not even participate when (as does sometimes occur) an odd triangle or perhaps cymbal stroke is printed in his part; nor will he touch isolated works, such as Sibelius's tone poem *En Saga*, which is scored wholly without timpani although it uses no fewer than three other percussion players. It is in the main only in smaller orchestras with limited percussion sections that a timpanist is sometimes engaged with the agreement that he will 'double' other instruments if required. The same may apply in chamber orchestras playing works containing a single percussion line of which the timpani form only a small part, such as Prokofiev's unconventionally scored Overture, Op. 42.

Visually, the timpanist appears enthroned, presiding as it were over the orchestra. Nor is this empty pomp or illusion; a good timpanist really does set the standard of the whole orchestra, electrifying the other players as well as the audience, for his role is far more an integrated musical part of the whole than any of the other percussion, however important or elaborate may be the special effects they provide.

2 Names

Timpani is, of course, the Italian name, though it is widely used internationally. The spelling sometimes varies, Dvořák and a few other composers or editions giving **tympani**. The singular form, less often seen since these drums are so rarely used singly, is *un timpano*. However, the French do use **timbales** – not to be confused with Latin American TIMBALES – and the Germans also have their own word, **Pauken**. Our own homely **kettle-drums** should also not be forgotten, though the name now sounds either old-fashioned or military and is no longer used orchestrally despite the championship of some English composers who have aimed at using English terms throughout their scores, such as Delius in *Eventyr*.

3 Number and Arrangement of Drums

The timpani require a great deal of space and consideration when the PLATFORM ARRANGEMENT is being planned. In the purely classical repertoire no more than two drums are necessary, but the majority of symphonic programmes calls for at least three and possibly four or five. Six drums or more require extra players and are laid out in appropriate clusters around the executants.

It has become the general custom in Britain for the timpanist to arrange the drums with the biggest (and lowest) on his left; but this is not entirely universal, Germany in particular being a stronghold of the opposite layout. In *Salome*, however, Strauss requires a timpani layout than is unconventional by either school, adding in a footnote exactly how a certain virtuoso passage is to be played.

4 Range

The timpani are the only orchestral drums that are always tuned to definite pitches. They come in various sizes and between them command an overall compass of some two octaves from $\bm{\unicode{x1D162}}$ to $\bm{\unicode{x1D162}}$. This is covered by the overlapping ranges of timpani measuring from 30 inches to 22 inches, with the addition of an even smaller one of 19 inches (and touchingly little it looks) for the upper notes, described as a **piccolo timpano** (Ger., **kleine Pauke**; Fr., **petite timbale**), as required in Strauss's *Salome* or Stravinsky's *The Rite of Spring*. Janáček tends to feature high timpani, there is a top D♮ in Ravel's *L'Enfant et les Sortilèges*, and Milhaud even scores for 2 *petites Timbales*, the upper in F♯, in *La Création du Monde*. Notes still higher are sometimes written by the most recent avant-garde, and are simulated by means of various exotic drums, such as the so-called **roto-toms**, but it could well be argued that the realm of timpani proper has long been left behind.

5 Development of Pedal Timps

At one time taps or handles for adjusting the tension of the skin were the sole method of tuning, these being placed at intervals around the circumference of the drums and used both at the beginning of a piece or movement and for minor adjustment of intonation. Their operation was both cumbersome and time-consuming, and composers had to make a point either of leaving suitable periods of rest, however short, or of contenting themselves with tunings that were often unsuitable for the prevailing harmony, as for instance in symphonies by both Schubert and Schumann. When Mahler wanted an instantaneous pitch change for a special effect in the finale of his First Symphony he actually wrote a footnote to the effect that the second timpanist should retune the first player's F to F♭ while he continued to play on that very drum.

Mechanically tuned drums, however, were already beginning to transform the orchestral scene around the turn of the century. Experiments were made with various methods of rapid chromatic tuning until finally **pedal timpani** swept the field and are now universally taken for granted. Not only has this enormously increased the speed and flexibility of tuning, but all kinds of new effects have become possible, including, for example, GLISSANDI.

Pedal timpani or other forms of 'machine drums' (as they are collectively known by the percussion fraternity) are seldom mentioned specifically in scores, although in the early days of their development they were indicated, in particular by the French, as **timbales chromatiques** at the beginning of certain scores or in the list of instruments, as in Florent Schmitt's *La Tragédie de Salomé*.

6 Limitation and Freedom of Notes

Since pedal or 'chromatic' timpani make practically any note available at a moment's notice, there no longer devolves on the composer the responsibility, hitherto largely accepted, of organizing how the drums should be tuned and retuned. Hence in Bartók's *Concerto for Orchestra* we find him writing whichever note suits him without working out how and on which drum each is to be obtained.

The pedals also give players the opportunity to amend earlier composer's timpani parts where these may seem inadequate or even downright incorrect, a freedom the virtuoso timpanists of today are often tempted to abuse. For, as in the examples already cited, it is actually surprising how often both classical and romantic composers would write notes quite foreign to the harmony rather than forfeit the colour of a drum stroke, confident that the pitch clash would pass unnoticed by all except the player himself. Strauss in his *Burleske* for piano and orchestra of 1886 anticipates the practice of such casual emendation by specifying notes that should be played only when chromatic timps are available, and in this he was followed by other composers, including, for example, Vaughan Williams, who gives alternative notes in his *Five Tudor Portraits*. Yet in Sibelius's Second Symphony a timpani roll is actually omitted altogether in a parallel return passage solely because the drums happen to be inappropriately tuned, a matter now easily enough restored by the use of the pedal if this is thought to be artistically justified. But textual revision is not always the simple ethical matter it may seem: Toscanini, often cited as a stern upholder of the sanctity of the printed text, used to add a timpani part of his own invention to the climax of the finale of Brahms's First Symphony, a most doubtful procedure and one rarely condoned or followed today.

7 Tuning

Despite modern technical aids, tuning the timps is still a highly skilled accomplishment. Players show a remarkable expertise in the sheer manner and speed with which they tune their drums. It can be done unbelievably silently during quiet passages and this is of particular importance, of course, when the timps have to be retuned while the orchestra is playing. Strange to say, a timpanist is still able to hear what he is doing when the orchestra is at full tilt: a flick of the fingernail may tell all that needs to be known; for more careful and accurate adjustment the player will lean over the drum with his ear to the skin as he taps it in different places to make sure that the tuning is true. Sometimes he can even be seen pressing the skin all over to stretch it into the required

condition; or he may hum softly into it, his mouth close to the head, to obtain a sympathetic vibration back in return. Skins may give off all kinds of harmonics in addition to – and more prominent than – the actual tuned note; drums can even be in tune when played *forte* and out of tune when *piano*, a real hazard in works where the same figure may be repeated at both extremes of the dynamic range, such as in the solo in the Finale of Shostakovich's First Symphony.

8 Notation

Strangely, it was not always thought necessary to indicate the timpanist's part in the score at all. In Mozart's *Haffner* Serenade (K. 250), there are no timpani although the scoring for trumpets presupposes their use, a fact not always realized and taken into account today. Actually a timpani part supposedly in Mozart's hand does exist, and is printed in the Eulenburg miniature score, though in an appendix. In the case of the Symphony No. 32 in G (K. 318), however, the situation is more complicated. The Breitkopf score includes a line for timpani – and a very curious one it is with high Gs Mozart himself never wrote – but with a footnote to the effect that the autograph contained no timpani. This is a half-truth: the autograph showed neither trumpets nor timpani, but trumpet parts in Mozart's own handwriting have survived, whereas the surviving timpani part is in another hand. In keeping with custom the timpanist would have been expected to invent a part for himself, which might to some extent explain the origin of the part subsequently included in Breitkopf.

Timpani are normally notated in the bass clef at concert pitch, but although this might seem self-evident it was by no means always so. In classical times when a single pair of timps was the standard complement, and traditionally tuned to the tonic and dominant of the prevailing tonality, the timpani were often notated as transposing instruments, the tuning of the drums being in this case stated at the beginning of the piece or movement and the notes written as C and G. This can be seen in many scores of the period, but curiously it was not a universal custom. Bach wrote his timpani in this way but Handel did not; Mozart did, but not Haydn; Beethoven did not – indeed by his day the practice was dying out and so he was able to tune his drums so daringly in octaves in his last two symphonies; yet Schubert kept to the old tradition in just his Second Symphony. These anomalies can be seen reflected in printed scores including many nineteenth- and twentieth-century editions, in which moreover still further anomalies can be found: the Breitkopf Gesamtausgabe of Mozart's works gives transposed timpani in some symphonies (e.g. the *Haffner* and the *Paris*) and not others (the *Prague* and the Eb (K. 543)), in which it is duly followed by the corresponding Eulenburg miniature scores.

In his *Treatise of Instrumentation*, Berlioz complained indignantly of so illogical a custom that could, as a result of limited availability of timpani pitches at that time, represent the sounds 𝄢 ♩ ♩ by the notation:

in A.E. 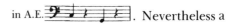. Nevertheless a most bizarre survival of the custom can be seen in Berwald's overture *Estrella di Soria* and in some sections (only) of his *Sinfonie Singulière*, where he wrote his tonic and dominant timpani notes oddly enough on C and G in their treble-clef positions though preceded by the bass clef.

9 Tuning

The traditional notation for the timpani line is with the pitch of the drums indicated by the names of the notes at the beginning of a work or movement; it will then be mentioned again only at each change of tuning, this being given with the words **muta in** ('change to' – sometimes **cambia in**, especially with Italian composers) or the equivalent in the different languages: Ger., **umstimmen nach** . . . ; Fr., **changez en** . . .

In view of the timpanist's limited range the name of the note would often suffice, since there is little likelihood of mistake in the octave. Timps in C and G would, for example, be unlikely to be tuned 𝄢 or 𝄢 unless especially marked: *timp in C tief, in G hoch*, etc., as can sometimes be seen in Mahler. This has nevertheless led to the nice style, adopted by some composers, of giving the pitch for the drums' initial tuning in actual notation on the first page of the score, as in Elgar's Second Symphony. Many of the late romantics, however, no longer bother to indicate timpani tuning at all. Strauss abandoned it after *Tod und Verklärung*; Debussy and Ravel in most of their mature and later works; Mahler altogether, and so on. Much depends on the nature of the writing: Sibelius, for instance, continued to indicate tuning until his last orchestral work, *Tapiola*, but omitted it where the use of different timpani pitches was very free, as in the Seventh Symphony written in the previous year, 1924.

10 Multiple Drums

The use of a third timp as standard equipment appeared only gradually on the symphonic scene. Brahms introduced it as no more than a special augmentation for one movement only (the Scherzo) of his Fourth Symphony, and Dvořák added it for just the very last of his symphonies, the *New World*. Moreover, the addition of a third timp did not by any means necessarily entail the abandoning of tonic–dominant tuning for the other two.

With a fourth timp a second player may well become necessary (although the five drums of Strauss's *Till Eulenspiegel* are handled by a single player) – especially if the four drums are written as two pairs; or for special effects the use of multiple timps could require a different player for each drum. Berlioz, whose passion for the timpani (which he played himself) led him to make every kind of experiment, used both procedures in the *Symphonie Fantastique*, the two pairs being employed in the last two movements; but in his thunder imitation at the end of

the 'Scène aux Champs' he requires four players. In the overture *Benvenuto Cellini* Berlioz also rides his hobby-horse of using his timpani to build up harmonies, stipulating one player per drum, even though there are only three drums; moreover, two players are expected to play on a single drum, a demand seemingly so unlikely that the Breitkopf material evades the issue by bowdlerizing the text.

The use of two timpanists in works using basically standard orchestral forces is more common than might be expected. Nielsen in his Fourth Symphony, *The Inextinguishable*, writes for more than one drum tuned to the same notes by two different players with remarkably dramatic effect. Moreover, for programmatic reasons, as well as clarity and contrast, he demands in addition that the two timpanists be placed on the extreme opposite sides of the orchestra. Walton's First Symphony, too, scored with remarkable economy in other respects, makes great and spectacular play of two drummers handling six timpani for the riveting climax of the Finale. Mahler of course, with his inflated forces, regularly takes such a double timpani section for granted, although in most instances the second timpanist will – unlike the PRINCIPAL – be co-opted from the percussion section.

For sheer multiplicity of timps, however, one still has to return to Berlioz, from whose *Grande Messe des Morts* the 'Tuba Mirum' still ranks supreme with its eight pairs of timpani specifically directed to be handled by ten players.

11 Tremolos and Trills

The roll is the drums' equivalent of the strings' **tremolo** and shares many of the notation troubles of that device. It is designed equally by 𝄢 (which unlike strings or wind notation does not mean a trill on two notes); or by any of the following, often used indiscriminately: 𝄢 .

Strangely the word *tremolo* (or its abbreviated *trem.*) is not often found in timpani parts, though Glazunov provides a few examples. As for the number of strokes added to the notes, this can be immensely variable. Haydn normally writes ♪ , and until recently timpanists have been strongly in favour of playing measured semiquavers, especially in slower tempi. Modern scholarship, however, holds that Haydn always intended the roll (even where he wrote *ten* ♩) and certainly the drum-rolls that give their name to the E♭ Symphony No. 103 are notated ♪ in the autograph, the third stroke in many modern scores being mere editorial addition. Mozart normally used *tr.*, in which he was followed by Beethoven, so that when Beethoven wrote ♪ , even in an allegro such as the first movement of the Ninth Symphony, he certainly intended demi-semi-quavers.

Another confusion of timpani notation lies in composers' different indications for extended rolls, in many of which it is uncertain whether the roll should be restarted in each new bar or not. Dvořák will often write

when he intends a continuous roll, and he is by no means unique. On the other hand in the Choral Symphony we find Beethoven writing

in circumstances where a continuous roll is not necessarily the intention.

12 Sticks and Style

Among Berlioz's other innovations for the timpani, was the indication in his scores of different types of stick, of which the outstanding alternatives were sponge-headed, leather-covered, and wooden; but of these he deplored the currently excessive use of leather as rough and crude, and hence actually prescribes only the first and last, in which he was followed by other composers such as Strauss. His French terms—**baguettes d'éponge**, **baguettes de bois** – are realized in German as **Schwammschlägel** and **Holzschlägel** and in Italian (though these terms are curiously rare) **bacchette di spugna** and **bacchette di legno**. Needless to say, over the years customs have changed and the instructions to use specifically sponge-headed sticks are ignored, sponge being regarded as unsuitable because it damps the quality. Instead, players use felt-covered sticks of various degrees of softness which they select as they consider the style of the part. It is quite normal to see a

237

player using different pairs of sticks during the course of a work although there is no indication in the score or the part. The conductor too may often express a preference for 'hard' or 'soft' sticks in respect of a particular passage, hard sticks giving greater clarity for a rhythmic figure but soft ones producing a more beautiful resonance.

The heads of the sticks also vary enormously in size and shape, from those with straight sides and flat circular ends to woolly-looking spherical heads not unlike young tennis balls, and timpanists make their choice from a surprisingly wide range.

The one variation that remains linked unquestionably to the composer's special instructions is wood. When this is prescribed players commonly change to light sticks with wooden knobs on the end, and to facilitate very quick changing felt-headed sticks are often fitted with wooden heads at the other end. Elgar actually stipulates the handle in *The Dream of Gerontius*, marking it *with the stick; mit dem* **Griff**.

The sound of wooden sticks is highly characteristic, and a very high proportion of the repertoire absolutely requires their use. Nevertheless timpanists sometimes try to avoid using them on the grounds of damage to the heads. There is some truth in this as a result of the introduction of plastic heads, which unlike the old skins can show alarming indentations after strong use with wooden sticks; however, sticks made of the softer balsa wood do produce the correct sound without inflicting damage.

It is generally on account of their extra stridency that wooden sticks are indicated, but they are also sometimes used *pp*. In this case a further variant is the indication of side-drum sticks (which are also wooden though with slenderer heads) for the shallow rattling they produce. Elgar in Variation XIII of the *Enigma Variations* wrote this requirement in the score, but it is well known that what he really wanted for so atmospheric a passage was two pennies (that is, the British old large penny coins) and it is coins of the realm of one sort or another that are to this day used by all who know the tradition.

In later scores the contradiction to *Holzschlägel* may be **gewöhnliche Schlägel**, literally, 'ordinary sticks', which is accordingly interpreted by players as they see fit and appropriate. But composers often forget to make it clear whether wooden sticks are indicated only for a specific passage or whether their use should continue for longer periods. Liszt's *Faust Symphony* gives one such example, for if the printed instructions are followed to the letter, one finds that the greater part of the long first movement is played on wooden sticks, not at all impossible but at times more than a little improbable.

Various composite uses of these colours are also to be found from time to time. Holst in *The Perfect Fool* instructs the player to hold a wooden stick in one hand and a felt stick in the other. Contemporary composers have also written for timpani to be played with some foreign body – a cymbal, a tambourine, etc. – placed on the drum head.

13 Conclusion

Although in theory there is virtually no

limit to the possible experimental devices to which timpani could be put, further adventures hardly come within their province to the same extent as the other percussion, whose *métier* is – on the contrary – primarily concerned with colouristic effects of every kind. In practice the timpanist continues for the most part to be held in especial respect by composers as an aristocrat in his own field; this role can, however, be double-edged, since a composer such as Messiaen regards it as so restrictive that, within the wide spectrum of colouristic effects that is the essence of the particularly lavish percussion section found in the majority of his works, he can find no place for the pure classicism of the timpani, which are thus conspicuously absent. This move away from the timpani, which has been pursued by a number of avant-garde composers from Honegger to the contemporary schools, can be traced back (apart from isolated instances such as Sibelius's *En Saga*) to Schoenberg's *Fünf Orchesterstücke*, Op. 16, composed in 1909, where the timpani have only a few notes in the first movement, and are thereafter totally ignored in favour of the other members of a large and varied percussion group. Yet the timpanist's days are very far from numbered, and his position as king figure remains firmly secure in symphony orchestras all over the world.

Timplipito, *see* PICCOLI TIMPANI ORIENTALI

Tirez (Fr.), down bow; *see* BOWING, 7

TOM-TOMS

In recent years these native drums have entered regularly into the symphonic repertoire. They are larger than BONGOS and are used either as a pair or occasionally three together. Like bongos they are played with the flat of the hand, but tom-toms can also be played with sticks, though composers rarely specify this. There is, however, a considerable problem over what type of tom-toms is required, their identity having been confused through the development – largely in connection with dance-band work – of another kind of tom-tom, which is hardly more than a very deep snareless side drum. A pair of these will most often form part of a drummer's 'traps' or kit – i.e., a whole grouping together of equipment that will enable the player to sit in its midst confident that he has all he needs for an evening's gig.

As a result players almost always produce a pair of dance-band tom-toms unless 'African tom-toms' are specifically ordered, even though such a definition is hardly ever written into scores. In fact the whole question is more complicated than many composers seem to recognize; and indeed CHINESE TOM-TOMS produce additional confusion, not to mention TIMBALES or even CONGAS. None of these instruments is of definite pitch although their sound can vary from deep to quite high; in certain circumstances, however, tom-toms may be tuned and this accounts for the *ossia* for high timpani given in Stravinsky's *Agon*.

Tom-toms may also be a possible interpretation for the little drums in

Hindemith's *Kammermusik* No. 4 (Violin Concerto) although he calls them **Trommeln**. Writing in 1925 when bongos, tom-toms and timbales were hardly known and in any case still essentially jazz instruments, he describes them in a lengthy footnote which also details his bass-clef notation for the four contrasted drums.

Tonlos niederdrücken (Ger.), *see* HARMONICS, 7

Touche, sur la (Fr.), on the fingerboard; *see* BOWING, 5

TRANSPOSING INSTRUMENTS

Transposing instruments are those built in a variety of lengths, and therefore keys, and whose parts are accordingly written so as to indicate the way the player reads and produces the notes instead of the way they sound.

There are two main reasons why this sometimes confusing state of affairs came about. In the case of woodwind instruments there was obvious benefit in a single method of fingering for any one family of oboes or clarinets (in particular) regardless of the numerous subspecies; for a player may be required to play any of them. Each will therefore, according to size and key, give out higher or lower ranges of notes as a result of the same fingerings read for the same set of notations.

This purpose has still largely survived although the gradual disappearance of some family members has led to the need for players to develop an expertise in transposition where a different instrument has to be used. The CLARINET in D, for example, or the bass clarinet in A, hardly exist today, and although some of the best-known and more exacting parts may have to be rewritten for the present-day substitute, the player cannot necessarily depend on such spoon-feeding in all circumstances. The C clarinet especially, widely used at one time, is generally considered an unsatisfactory instrument for general purposes and is now something of a rarity. But both the B♭ and A clarinets persist at least in Europe on account of the numerous simplifications of fingering they provide for passage work with complicated key signatures, the B♭ clarinet removing two flats, the A three sharps, at a stroke.

The player's increasing ability to transpose at sight complicated parts for inconvenient or unavailable instruments had, however, the unfortunate side effect of encouraging Schoenberg to expect players of his ferociously difficult works from Opus 22 onwards to read from material laid out according to his theories of 'logical' notation exclusively in concert pitch, 'using any instrument they may prefer'. This, however, carried the assumption of expertise far beyond the level of practicability, with the result that the works are usually played from bad and faulty manuscript copies transposed for B♭ clarinet, the beautifully printed and spotlessly clean copy (in C) lying neglected and abandoned.

The second main group of instruments which brought about the necessity for transposition consists of those, like HORNS and TRUMPETS, rooted on their HARMONICS (all of which represent the open notes produced without handstopping or, later, the use of valves) and built originally with detachable CROOKS.

Crooks of different sizes automatically change the length of tubing of the instruments and hence their basic harmonic series. The player had only to choose the crook corresponding to the key of the piece, or to the one nearest available, and thus simplify immeasurably both the thought and the technique necessary for performance.

All that remained was that the notation for these instruments should be uniformly notated in C both in the score and the players' parts with the addition of the instruction *in F*, *in D*, etc., to indicate which crook should be fitted; the resulting notes would then lie in the prevailing tonality while the player works primarily on or around the open notes – i.e., harmonics of the appropriately elongated or shortened instrument.

In the course of time, however, a degree of standardization has entered into both horns and trumpets, which, being now fully chromatic, no longer use detachable crooks, even though numerous alternative instruments built in different keys are summoned into service for a variety of technical reasons. Horn notation has accordingly tended to stabilize around the F instrument; trumpets around those in B♭ or C. Like their colleagues in the WOODWIND, therefore, the players, while working from a basic technique built on these standardizations, have learned to regard automatic transposition into other keys upwards or downwards as an essential accomplishment; indeed so instinctive is the process that the growing custom of converting classical horn and trumpet parts, conceived by composers in terms of different crooks, into a uniform F horn or B♭ trumpet notation, as has been done by some publishers, is highly unwelcome, particularly to horn players, and is oddly disconcerting.

On this same basis it might justifiably be thought illogical and strange that the TROMBONE family as well as the deeper TUBAS have never been transposing instruments (except in BRASS BANDS). One can only suppose that since these were never involved in the crook-changing system on the one hand, or a complex technique of fingering multiple keys and holes like the woodwind on the other, the necessity for a transposing method of notation in respect of these instruments never arose.

One further species of transposing instruments needs to be considered. In the case of the PICCOLO as well as the CONTRABASSOON and the DOUBLE-BASS it has proved an obvious convenience in the avoidance of multiple ledger lines to notate these respectively an octave below and an octave above their true pitches. Indeed, although Schoenberg and his followers unwisely ironed out these octave adjustments many composers continue to retain them even these days, when, in full scores if not in the players' actual material, all other transpositions have largely fallen into disfavour – an issue of mixed virtues and heated controversy.

Tre corde (It.), literally 'three strings';

used for the piano as contradiction to **una corda** after a passage with soft pedal; *see* MUTES, 8

Tremolo, *see* STRINGS, 9

Trémolo dental (Fr.), *see* FLUTTER-TONGUING

Trémolo ondulé (Fr.), *see* STRINGS, 9

TRIANGLE

The triangle is a treble instrument of indefinite pitch (at least it should be, although triangles that really are of indefinite pitch can be difficult to find). It is, with the bass drum and cymbals, the third indispensable member of the Turkish group in classical scores, such as Mozart's *Entführung* or Beethoven's *Ruins of Athens*.

Triangles come in different sizes, but this has little relation to the height or depth of the sound, and composers writing for a number of triangles with this purpose in mind create more problems than they cater for. For example, Boieldieu in *The Caliph of Bagdad* scored for alto and bass triangles; Bruckner in his Eighth Symphony mysteriously wrote two different notes (E♭ and B♭) for his single triangle at the cymbal-crested climaxes of the Adagio but he cannot really have intended these pitches to be reproduced in such circumstances. Nor would it seem that the pitch was intended to relate to dynamics as the lower note oddly occurs at the greater climax.

The range of dynamic power in a triangle is necessarily severely limited, but if held up high above the stand it is surprising how well the sound will carry against an orchestral *forte* tutti, especially in a roll. It is worth emphasizing this necessity for raising the triangle, as it is generally slung from a stand and in many halls its sound is lost amidst the mass of music and bodies. Yet it may be quite inconvenient to hold it aloft for each entry, especially in a work with complicated to-ing and fro-ing for the percussionists.

If no other stipulation appears in the score it is taken for granted that the triangle should be played with a thin metal beater (in German **Stab**). In fact other implements, such as wooden sticks for a more jangling sound, are only rarely used. Walton, however, in *Façade* instructs that the triangle itself should be struck against a cymbal.

Although seemingly a mild and delicate instrument, the triangle can add an excellent splash of colour, and it is not at all uncommon to find it the only PERCUSSION instrument other than the timpani in a symphony such as Schumann's First and Brahms's Fourth. Dvořák frequently used it in this way, as in the last movement of his early E♭ Symphony, Op. 10, and for the Scherzos of both his Symphony in F, Op. 76, and the *New World*. But for sheer genius in economy one of the most famous triangle solos in the repertoire is Richard Strauss's favourite: the single stroke in the whole second act of *Siegfried*, occurring very near the end.

Triple-tonguing, *see* DOUBLE- AND TRIPLE-TONGUING

Trogxylophone, *see* XYLOPHONE

Tromba (It.), *see* TRUMPET, 1

Tromba contralto in F (It.), *see* CONTRALTO TRUMPET

Tromba da Tirarsi (It.), soprano trombone; *see* TROMBONE, 2

TROMBONE

1 Names
The trombone family is part of the BRASS choir, coming next in descending order below the trumpets. Its name is the same in English and in all Latin countries, but the Germans use **Posaune**, which is of inestimable value for ready identification in scores, especially in respect of abbreviations, *Pos.* being unmistakable among all the other Ts. On the other hand **basun** is, curiously, the Scandinavian for trombone (a corruption of *Posaune*), a linguistic oddity that can lead to magnificent incidents at rehearsals in those countries; but fortunately *basun* does not normally appear in printed scores.

2 Species
There are no fewer than five members of the trombone family: the alto, tenor, tenor/bass, bass and contrabass. There may even have been a sixth, a soprano trombone, which oddity appears, for example, in the Breitkopf editions of Mozart's C minor Mass (although it is not substantiated in later more scholarly editions of the work). It might perhaps have corresponded with Bach's **Tromba da Tirarsi**, but it is somewhat doubtful whether Mozart would have known it. Nevertheless a soprano trombone is certainly cited as one of the instruments in Gluck's *Orfeo*

(though curiously enough as an *ossia* for the *cornetto*) and it does seem to have existed at one time. In the *New Grove* it is identified in some detail as having been pitched in B♭, an octave higher than the tenor trombone. The inclusion of a soprano trombone together with the alto, tenor and bass instruments in choral music probably followed the classical tradition of doubling all voice parts with trombones throughout, especially in sacred works. This custom is further reflected, for instance, in Schubert's masses, where trombones play with the vocal parts for pages on end. In practice this is not only unthinkable on grounds of sheer endurance but musically intolerable, and it is hardly credible that the trombonists of Schubert's day actually played all the notes as they appear in the score.

The ALTO TROMBONE, once thought obsolete, now enjoys an honoured status as a rare visitor, as does, at the other end of the range, the CONTRABASS TROMBONE. In between, the two standard trombones are the tenor and the bass, the conventional threefold trombone section on the strength of all symphony orchestras consisting of two tenors and a bass.

The tenor trombone is in B♭ but the bass trombone, which has always been built in F on the Continent, used to be in G in Britain, causing problems when composers wrote passages for the one lying badly or even impossibly for the other, as for example the *glissando* sneers in Bartók's *Concerto for Orchestra*. Schoenberg wrote a *glissando* in *Gurrelieder*, producing problems for everybody as he chose to call on yet another bass trombone, a still deeper one pitched in E♭. The disappearance of this purely German nineteenth-century military instrument has made it impossible to obey Schoenberg's implicit instructions to the letter.

One further member, the tenor/bass trombone, is a relatively newer composite animal of enormous practical value, which has caused it to become increasingly prevalent in orchestral work; Wagner wrote for it throughout *The Ring*, while Stravinsky's *L'Histoire du Soldat* and Berg's *Kammerkonzert* are other outstanding examples. It is in fact a double instrument built in B♭ and F and therefore ideal for the wide-ranged parts found in so many late-romantic and contemporary works, especially when only a single trombone is used.

3 Notation

Where notation is concerned all the different keys in which trombones are built are of no consequence, as the family is not one of TRANSPOSING INSTRUMENTS, all members being written alike at pitch. They are notated in different clefs, nevertheless, principally tenor and bass but also alto. The latter, apart from its obvious use for the alto instrument, often appears when composers such as Schumann, and after him the Russian group of Les Cinq, wrote for the 1st and 2nd trombones together on one stave in that clef regardless of which instrument, or combination of instruments, is actually reading the lines in question. The tenor trombone, in addition, habitually finds its part written in both tenor and bass clefs – the latter being, of course,

the only usual clef for the bass trombone except for the rare occasions where he may be in the upper register in unison with the others, as at Petrouchka's fury in the second scene of Stravinsky's ballet.

4 Range

Taken corporately the trombone family can command a comprehensive chromatic range from 𝄢 to 𝄡 .

The obvious instance of the full splendour of this lower range can be heard in Wagner's *Ring*, for which purpose indeed the deepest instrument, the contrabass trombone, was introduced by Wagner into the orchestra. The low notes from B♭ downwards are the PEDAL NOTES, with a characteristically rumbling quality like those of the horns, and which were especially beloved by Berlioz.

Where the upper range is concerned there has come to be surprisingly little difference between the extreme possibilities of the tenor trombone and the alto, this being clearly a strong factor in the latter's disuse for so many years. Strauss, for instance, writing for the normal trombone section consisting of tenor and bass instruments only, thought nothing of taking the first player up to the top D in *Also sprach Zarathustra*. The bass trombone, on the other hand, does not usually go much above G, this being already a very high region for what is essentially a heavy, even cumbersome instrument. Where the 3rd trombone is taken to exalted altitudes, it is generally because the composer is thinking in more general terms of the trombones as a group rather than of the 3rd player necessarily playing a bass instrument. Equally it is perhaps hardly profitable to consider in detail the upper possibilities of the contrabass trombone, whose chief virtue lies in its magnificent bottom notes.

5 Characteristics

Like those for the TRUMPET, extended trombone solos tend to evoke undesirable associations, especially on account of the instrument's outstanding characteristic, the slide. Indeed, because of this it is very hard to avoid a tastelessly obtrusive **portamento** throughout smooth passages. No doubt this is the reason for the valve trombone's brief appearance, although it never established itself and is now orchestrally obsolete. *Cantabile* solos are thus a rarity in symphonic literature and have become a major feature where they do occur, as in the slow movement of Berlioz's *Symphonie Funèbre et Triomphale*. Generally in trombone solos players try to avoid the inherently tiresome style of the slide-executed *legato* by using an enunciatory phrasing, as Mahler so cleverly advocated in the long solo in his Third Symphony, even though it is specifically marked *sentimental*.

The trombone solo that characterizes the 'Tuba Mirum' of Mozart's Requiem thus remains a curiosity, not merely for its own time but for any period at all; and it is understandable that in days less purist than our own it was always, after the first declamatory phrase, split up between various other instruments (horn, cello, etc.) in the belief that Mozart would surely not have written it as it stands today had he lived to complete the score. Yet it can be executed with considerable beauty, as the unprecedented refinement of present-day trombonists has proved.

See also: BELLS UP, BOUCHÉ, CUIVRÉ, GLISSANDO, MUTES

Trommeln (Ger.), *see* TOM-TOMS

Trompa (Sp.), *see* HORN, 2

TRUMPET

1 Names

The trumpet is the topmost member, the soprano so to speak, of the BRASS choir. There are few problems with names, all translations being virtually the same, only the Italian **tromba** occasionally leading to confusion either with the trombone, where abbreviations are used, or with the Spanish *trompa* which is, oddly, the word for 'horn' (the Spanish for trumpet being simply *trompeta*). On the other hand in eighteenth- and early nineteenth-century scores the archaic term CLARINO was often used, although this can also have a specialized meaning of its own.

2 Species

There exists, and has always existed, a large trumpet family with different sizes. Apart from the BASS TRUMPET and the CONTRALTO TRUMPET, which are separate subspecies, the largest member used to be the old standard trumpet for which composers from Haydn and Mozart to Mahler and Strauss most commonly wrote. This, like the handhorn, was originally fitted with CROOKS, and was therefore a

TRANSPOSING INSTRUMENT, which, except when the instrument in C is used, trumpets are to this day.

This noble ancestor has, however, sadly given way to the trumpet most used at present, which, being considerably smaller and shorter, works on an entirely different set of harmonics, an octave higher, pitched usually in Bb or C. The Bb trumpet used for a time to be fitted with a switch converting it into A, and the preeminence of this double instrument in the decades between 1920 and 1950 caused a very large number of works to be published in which these two crooks were taken for granted in a way exactly parallel with the Bb and A CLARINETS. Furthermore, many popular editions, including the American reprint of many Breitkopf & Härtel materials, give transposed parts for trumpets in Bb or A alongside the original notations, just as they do with the standardized horns in F.

The slightly smaller C trumpet (an entirely separate instrument, there no longer being any question of crooks), is today a regular alternative to the Bb in the orchestral world, although the latter still holds sway in military, brass or dance bands. Then, higher than the C, there are a number of still smaller trumpets in various different pitches; of these the trumpet in D is perhaps the most widely carried. Dukas had already used this smaller trumpet in his Symphony *en Ut* and D'Indy scored for a *petite trompette en Mib aigu* in his Second Symphony in Bb, Op. 57. It was Rimsky-Korsakov, however, who claimed the credit for the whole idea of a little trumpet. This is not without its problems, especially in respect of intonation, though it has come sufficiently into its own in respect of parts lying high for much of the time. Britten tended habitually to pitch his 3rd trumpet in D, placing it therefore above his 1st and 2nd C trumpets in chordal passages and even giving it much of the solo work (see *Peter Grimes, The Prince of the Pagodas*, etc.).

Next comes the little F instrument, often known as the BACH TRUMPET, not because it resembles the instrument of Bach's own day but because it is more reliable for the extremely high and exacting parts encountered in, for example, the Second Brandenburg Concerto, the Third and Fourth Suites and the B minor Mass. Nor is this the end of the story because in recent years an even tinier instrument in high Bb has come into favour for use in CLARINO parts. This touching little object (known among trumpeters as the pea-shooter) also has the virtue of a detachable shank with replacements, which can put it into other keys like the old horn crooks, the A shank, for instance, being suitable for very high parts written in D.

Generally, however, players make their choice out of all these instruments less in accordance with the corresponding transpositions given by the composers than for their technical convenience; in fact they may quite often arrive for a concert carrying several instruments as opposed to the horn player who rarely has more than one.

3 Notation

Trumpets are written almost entirely

in the treble clef; the very few exceptions occur either where the PEDAL NOTES of the old larger trumpet are given (as by Mozart in the Minuet of the *Jupiter* Symphony or the Overture to *Don Giovanni*) or where the lower notes are being used in a way that was more conveniently given without too many ledger lines for score layout. In the latter instances (Strauss's *Till Eulenspiegel* provides an example) the orchestral parts usually retain the treble clef.

On the other hand the pedal notes are a different matter, these exhibiting the same peculiarity as in the case of classical bass-clef notation for the HORNS, i.e., they jump to the octave lower. (The equivalent to 'new notation' on the horn – the bass clef as a direct continuation downwards from the treble – is very rare in trumpet writing, although an instance can be seen in Strauss's early Violin Concerto.)

4 Range

The range of the trumpet family as a whole is theoretically as wide as from

$$\text{♭} \quad (= \text{♭}) \quad \text{written by}$$

Stanford in his *Irish* Symphony as the pedal note of the classical trumpet crooked in B♭, though it is doubtful whether it was ever actually obtainable)

to , which excessively high

G appears in the first movement of Bach's Second Brandenburg Concerto. Bach's writing in this extreme register was customary, as instances of clarino playing which was common practice in

his day; but when the boy Schubert, composing his Overture to *Des Teufels Lustschloss* in 1811, wrote the top C for his F trumpet (sounding only a tone lower than Bach's G) this would have been for a very different instrument from Bach's, and it seems likely that he had not yet learned that such notes were far beyond the register of the current trumpets, which had changed materially from the Baroque instruments.

It stands to reason that none of the many trumpets can obtain the complete overall range of the family as a whole, and the textbook range of written notes, therefore, generally cited as

$$\text{♭} \quad \text{to} \quad \text{♯} \quad , \text{ is admittedly}$$

sound, if conservative, though the pitch will naturally vary considerably according to size and length of tubing of each instrument used.

The upper end of the trumpet's register is so immensely striking that it imposes as a direct consequence the severest strain on human nerves and psychology of any instrument in the entire orchestra; indeed the casualty rate over the years among trumpet players gives a certain cause for concern. The bright shining tone of the upper notes soars out with so dominating an effect that even moderately high passages, such as the moving solo from Walton's First Symphony, need a strong and confident personality with nerves in prime condition, while Strauss's famous fanfare in *Also sprach Zarathustra* actually remains a *tour de force*, though by presentday standards it too by no means takes the player to the extreme end of his compass. The same applies to Stravinsky's duet for two trumpets, one in D, the other in Bb, descriptive of the mocking spectre of Petrouchka.

5 Character

Where extended individual solo work is concerned, both the trumpet and TROMBONE carry inbuilt associations with other walks of musical life that need to be taken into account in respect of style. Long *cantabile* solos inevitably evoke military and brass bands, the Salvation Army, etc., unless executed in impeccable taste. The solo at the beginning of the second act of Donizetti's *Don Pasquale* (written indeed for trumpet and not, as the idiom leads one to expect, for cornet) or the out-and-out trumpet tune in Stravinsky's *Scènes de Ballet* can fall into vulgarity far more readily than corresponding solos on the horn or on any string or wood-wind instrument. Britten even carica-tures the effect in Thisbe's solo in the third act of *A Midsummer Night's Dream*. Here the question of *vibrato*, specifically marked in the score, is a salient factor since this is a manner of tone production very rarely demanded symphonically, even in those countries where horn players habitually indulge in it, but belonging rather to the world of military-, brass- and dance-band soloists.

See also: BELLS UP, BOUCHÉ, BUMPER, CUIVRÉ, GLISSANDO, MUTES

TUBA

The tubas (the name is universal in all languages) are for the most part the lowest, fundamental tones of the BRASS section. The family is actually quite large from the point of view of the possibilities open to the composer and his orchestral player, comprising, among others, the TENOR TUBA, BASS TUBA – of which there are a variety in regular use – and CONTRABASS TUBA. Of these, it is the bass tuba that is meant when the simple term 'tuba' appears in orchestral scores in conjunction with, and as the bass to, the trombone group, although which of the available bass tubas (F, Eb, C or Bb) is immaterial where the score is concerned. For, despite this plethora of keys, the bass tuba is not a TRANSPOSING INSTRUMENT but is written exclusively in the bass clef and at pitch (except in the rarest instances, such as, oddly enough, Bax's *Overture to a Picaresque Comedy*, where it is written in Bb, sounding a tone lower).

Taken as a whole, the tubas cover a remarkable range, going down to the very low C: . This note is taken not from an example in Wagner, who writes for his *Kontrabass Tuba* no lower than Eb, but from Berg's Violin Concerto, while Glazunov goes nearly as low in his Fifth Symphony, the Russians tending to take a very large tuba for granted. At the upper extreme Ravel writes a high G♯, , in 'Bydlo' from his orchestration of Mussorgsky's *Pictures from an Exhibition*. This can be regarded as an extreme instance for the ordinary tuba, but the tenor can of course go appreciably higher, Holst writing the high D in *The Planets*.

The tuba, despite its ponderous nature, which is after all its chief purpose in life, is capable of surprising agility. It is, however, rather indistinct in quick solo passage work and as a result composers tend to double it with instruments better able to supply edge to the tone, while the tuba concentrates on supplying weight. Moreover, an element of comedy is inescapable in acrobatic solos such as the Scherzo of Vaughan Williams's F minor Symphony, which really is intended to sound grotesque. It is no doubt the intrusive element of comedy that prejudices composers against extensive use of *cantabile* tuba solos in symphonic work; as a soloist the tuba must always remain a 'character', if in the best sense of the word.

TUBAPHONE

This instrument is near to the glockenspiel family, consisting of a row of metal tubes arranged horizontally and struck much like a small vibraphone. It appears, suitably translated into Italian as *tubafono*, in several movements of Khachaturian's *Gayaneh*

where it is given a range of ,

sounding an octave higher.

Tubular Bells, *see* BELLS

Tumbas (Sp.), *see* CONGAS

Tuning, *see* A

Turkish Crescent, *see* BELL TREE, JINGLES

Tutti (It.), all; used as contradiction after divided playing; *see* DIVISI

Tympani, *see* TIMPANI, 2

TYPEWRITERS

These, no doubt complete with secretaries, are scored for in Satie's *Parade*.

Typophone, *see* DULCITONE

UKELELE

This is a Hawaiian strumming instrument like a cross between a small guitar and a banjo but made of wood with four strings. It hardly qualifies as an orchestral instrument but has made the occasional appearance in works evoking folk music or scenes of popular life and a few scores by contemporary composers such as Hans Werner Henze.

Una corda (It.), the soft pedal on the piano; *see* MUTES, 8

Unisoni (It.), together; *see* DIVISI

Umstimmen nach (Ger.), tune to; *see* TIMPANI, 9

Valves, *see* HORN, 2

Ventilhorn, original name for French horn when it first developed valves; *see* HORN, 2

Vents, les (Fr.), *see* WOODWIND, 1

Verges (Fr.), *see* VERGHE

VERGHE

Strictly speaking *verghe* signifies a switch or birch. In *Intégrales* Varèse relates it to the French **verges** = **Rute** (Ger.), and similarly Rachmaninoff adds a part for verghe in his *Trois Chansons Russes*, but gives no indication which instrument the birch should be applied to, whether perhaps bass drum or cymbal. This intensifies the problem since, unlike the bass-drum switch of birch twigs, when a cymbal beater comes into question percussionists hold that the verghe should not be wooden and hence turn to the wire brush, which does not seem to be the best solution for Prokofiev's verghe on cymbal to describe the huntsmen in *Peter and the Wolf*.

Verschiebung (Ger.), *see* MUTES, 8

VIBRAPHONE

A relative newcomer to the symphonic scene, the vibraphone is normally extremely soft toned; its quality of pulsating resonance is of a characteristically evocative shimmer, whether in the use of isolated notes or chords, which latter are an especial feature and can be of up to as many as six notes (three beaters being held in each hand). Berg features the vibraphone in *Lulu* as part of his evocation of the 1930s jazz idiom, while Walton's Cello Concerto and Messiaen's *Turangalîla-Symphonie* may be cited as more recent works making prominent and pervasive use of the vibraphone. In the latter, indeed, the instrument is hardly less than a soloist in its own field.

In range and appearance similar to the MARIMBA (apart from its silvery metal bars), it is generally written at pitch although Messiaen sometimes requires it to sound an octave higher.

Although the vibrating fans are such an integral *raison d'être* of the whole instrument they are in fact a separate mechanism that has to be independently set in motion. It is, however, less usual for scores to specify when they are required than when they are not, as in the Adagio of Britten's *Cello Symphony*. Another important part of the vibraphone's equipment is a sustaining pedal, again hardly ever prescribed but used by Britten in *Death in Venice*, another score which specializes in the use of the vibraphone.

Despite the blurred effect of rapid vibraphone passage work, instances of this are appearing more and more in contemporary scores, after the pioneering example of Boulez's *Le Marteau sans Maître*.

The matter of different beaters also comes into question. One inherent difficulty with the vibraphone is that a generally undesirable 'clang' tone very soon becomes evident both in loud passages and especially when hard sticks are used. These are, however, sometimes deliberately called for, as in Roberto Gerhard's *The Plague* – as well as by Harrison Birtwistle, who features two vibraphones in his *Triumph of Time*, insisting on plexiglass or extremely hard plastic sticks to obtain the correct overtone intensity. He further instructs that they both use ELECTRONIC AMPLIFICATION.

Vibrato (It.), *see* STRINGS, 11

Viel Bogenweschsel (Ger.), *see* BOWING, 9

VIOLA

The third and central member of the violin family that makes up the STRING department of an orchestra. Unlike the violin its name is different in most other languages, only the Italian being similar to the English; the French use **alto** and the Germans **Bratsche**. The French term is certainly logical, though unexpected since all other French names are in line with the Italian, while *Bratsche*, commonly used in German editions, has in fact an Italian origin – i.e., [*viola da*] *braccio* (= arm) as opposed to [*viola da*] *gamba* (= leg).

The viola is only a little larger than the violin and is similarly tuned in fifths but without the upper E string and instead, a C string at the lower end:

It is thus exactly an octave higher than the cellos' tuning and commands a range of

roughly

. The uppermost Ab can be seen to correspond to a top Eb on the violins, being just under two octaves above the highest open string. This may seem a little limited when compared with the range of the violins, since theoretically the violas might be assumed to possess an identical register a fifth lower. But in practice composers mostly avoid using the extreme upper notes even when the violins are playing at the very top;

this is because the extra size of the viola puts these notes out of reach for most players and in any case this is not their purpose in life. As has been shown, they use both the alto and treble clefs.

The violas usually sit centrally in the string section though this may be to the left or right of centre according to the conductor's wishes or the orchestra's customary PLATFORM ARRANGEMENT. In recent years the Continental practice of placing them on the outside to the conductor's right has also been finding favour in Britain, ousting the cellos (or 2nd violins) in public prominence.

When the violas are positioned to the right centre *vis-à-vis* the conductor it can be difficult to know which of the two players at the front desk is the leader of the group as there is no hard and fast rule; it thus remains a matter of preference for the individual leader whether he wishes to correspond to the leader of the 1st violins on the one side of him or of the cellos (or perhaps the 2nds) on the other. This is an instance where the unwary conductor may make an unwitting *faux pas*, even occasionally giving considerable offence.

Despite their very similar appearance to the violins, the violas have in fact a very pronounced character of their own, much prized by composers who have over the years written some exceptionally beautiful passage work for them; warmth and mellowness is broadly their outstanding quality rather than brilliance, although they can make a splendid show of virtuosity if required. Mozart in particular greatly loved the violas and never failed to give them interesting and rewarding lines.

251

See also: ARCO, ARTIFICAL HARMONICS, BACK DESKS, BOWING, DIVISI, DOUBLE STOPPING, EARLY STRINGED INSTRUMENTS, GLISSANDO, HARMONICS, MUTES, PIZZICATO, RANK AND FILE, SCORDATURA, STRINGS

Viola da gamba, *see* EARLY STRINGED INSTRUMENTS

Viola d'amore, *see* EARLY STRINGED INSTRUMENTS

Viole (It.), plural form; *see* VIOLA

Violetta, *see* EARLY STRINGED INSTRUMENTS

VIOLIN

The highest and smallest member of the family constituting the orchestral STRINGS. The name of the instrument is generally the same in all languages, but the Germans sometimes use **Geige**, a word derived from the old Italian *giga*, since in its early days the instrument was closely associated with the jig. The English FIDDLE, corresponding to the German *Fiedel*, is also sometimes used, though primarily as a colloquial term.

The strings of the violin are tuned, like those of all the family except the basses, in fifths:

giving a potential range of something

over four octaves from

or even higher. The treble clef is used exclusively.

Where PLATFORM ARRANGEMENT is concerned the 1st violins always sit to the left of the conductor and at the front of the platform nearest to the audience. The 2nds on the other hand may either be with the 1sts, though towards the left centre of the platform, or – as may be required by conductors of the older school – on the opposite side, to the extreme outside right.

The first player of the 1st violins is always the LEADER of the whole orchestra, or concert master as the Americans call him (a direct translation of the German term *Konzertmeister*), and therefore occupies a strategic position of importance in the orchestral hierarchy, in respect of both discipline and the relationship of the players with conductor and management. He also enjoys the widest opportunities for soloistic display, ranging from the briefest of melodic strands to concertante sections such as those in Strauss's *Ein Heldenleben*, which exploits double stoppings in two-part counterpoint as well as complicated chordal passages *à la* Paganini. Similar and other spectacular techniques are introduced by Rimsky-Korsakov in his *Capriccio Espagnol* and *Scheherazade*, in addition to which works such as Strauss's *Bourgeois Gentilhomme*, Stravinsky's *Apollon Musagète* or *Agon*, and others too numerous to list but no less exacting, are famous for their solos and provide virtuoso shop windows for which no leader or prospective leader can afford to be unprepared.

Sometimes passages may be written with more than one independent obbligato violin part. In cases of a second solo this may fall either to the No. 2 1st violin, as in Mahler's Ninth Symphony, or to the leader of the 2nd violins. Handel's 12 Concerti Grossi, Op. 6, present a curious situation, since the solo 2nd violin plays sometimes in unison with the *tutti* firsts and sometimes with the *tutti* seconds, in addition to his duo-concertante work with the solo 1st player.

In the event such obbligati are normally played by the leader of the 2nd violins, who also automatically takes on the 2nd violin solo in such works as Elgar's *Introduction and Allegro* or Stravinsky's *Pulcinella*. On the other hand the No. 2 1st violin does also come into his own whenever the composer asks simply for a pair of solo players, as in Strauss's *Ariadne auf Naxos*, or the solo sextet that opens the same composer's *Capriccio*.

Sometimes, however, the composer fails to make it clear whom he is writing for, and the conductor and players are dependent on a decision made by the publishers when preparing the orchestral material. In the ethereal Prelude to *Lohengrin*, for instance, Wagner merely specified *4 einzele Violinen* in the opening bars, which he probably intended to come all from the 1sts. But in the part the lines are actually given to the first desks each of 1sts and 2nds and so perforce it is always played.

It is not unknown for the entire 1st violin section of the orchestra to be treated in a virtuoso manner. Rachmaninoff conceived the solo part in his instrumental version of the *Vocalise* for all the 1st violins to play together, standing in front of the accompanying orchestra, while Toscanini made a justly famous gramophone record in which all the 1st violins stood up to play Paganini's notorious *Perpetuum Mobile* in unison, and at breakneck speed.

The pre-eminence of the leader of the 1st violins, not only as figurehead of the string section but of the whole orchestra, further reflects the exalted position occupied by the violin itself. As a solo instrument it is, after the piano, justifiably the most popular of all and enjoys the widest and most distinguished repertoire. Its soaring qualities as melodist and breath-taking possibilities for brilliant and acrobatic display set it indisputably above its colleagues in the string section even though the cello has – especially in recent decades – hotly pursued it with evocative and virtuoso capabilities of its own. Nevertheless it is the violin that remains the leading instrument of the entire orchestral spectrum.

See also: ARCO, ARTIFICIAL HARMONICS, BACK DESKS, BOWING, DIVISI, DOUBLE STOPPING, EARLY STRINGED INSTRUMENTS, FIDDLE, FREE BOWING, GLISSANDO, HARMONICS, LEADER, MUTES, PIZZICATO, SCORDATURA, STRINGS, RANK-AND-FILE

Violino piccolo (It.), *see* EARLY STRINGED INSTRUMENTS

Violino spallo (It.), *see* LEADER

Violon (Fr.), *see* VIOLIN

Violoncello, *see* CELLO

VIOLONE

This is a precursor of our modern

double bass, although it is strictly a double-bass viol. The term is sometimes used by Bach and others, including, for example, Richard Strauss, when especially low notes are required.

Voices, *see* A CAPPELLA, ALTO, BARI-TONE, BASS, CONTRALTO, SOPRANO, TENOR, CHORUS, CHORUS MASTER

Voilé (Fr.), *see* MUTES, 6

WAGNER TUBAS

These are hybrid instruments, half tuba, half horn, invented by Wagner, who caused them to be especially constructed for use in *The Ring*. Their purpose, as he saw it, was to add to the horn section the potential of greater weight and breadth of tone, and thereby provide them with a bridge to the nobler aspects of the heavy brass and to their fundamental as personified by the deep brass tuba. The Wagner tubas are in appearance not unlike saxhorns although more oval in general shape. There are two varieties, tenor and bass, and, despite their name, they fall wholly within the province of the HORN department; indeed even the same mouthpiece is used. They are played by the 5th–8th horn players either exclusively, as in Bruckner's Seventh Symphony, or more usually as alternate DOUBLING instruments to the horn itself. Wagner tubas are usually treated as a quartet and consist of a pair of tenor and a pair of bass tubas. So much are they a matched quartet that players do not even possess their own instruments, which are acquired as a set of four by orchestras, opera houses, broadcasting stations, or occasionally conservatoires.

The tenor Wagner tubas are pitched in Bb, while the bass ones are in F. They correspond in length of tubing and manner of execution with Bb alto and F horns respectively, though they go a fourth lower, the Bb tubas down to F and the F tubas down to C.

The danger of confusion with the tuba family proper is considerable. In the first place, although universally known as 'Wagner tubas' and constructed entirely as a genus in their own right, they are nowhere so designated in scores, where they are indeed listed simply as 'tubas'. The question will inevitably arise at once: how are the uninitiated to know when it is Wagner tubas that the composer has written for? Undoubtedly the best guide would be a list of relevant works – and it is surprising in view of the importance of the Wagner tubas in the orchestral scene how few there are in addition to Wagner's *Ring* – Bruckner's Symphonies Nos. 7–9, Strauss's *Elektra*, *Die Frau ohne Schatten* and *Alpine Symphony*, Schoenberg's *Gurrelieder* – and the list is already practically complete. Other works often wrongly thought to include Wagner tubas are the Janáček *Sinfonietta*, *Don Quixote*, *The Planets*, etc., all of which are scored for the real tenor tuba in Bb. In *Elektra* Strauss describes all four Wagner tubas, tenor and bass alike, simply as *4 tuben* but in the later works be calls all four *Tenortuben*. Stravinsky's *Sacre* and Bartók's *Miraculous Mandarin* are both unusually scored for only two tenor tubas (used in each case briefly in alternation to horns). Stravinsky, as he already has two bass tubas in his brass section, reasonably reckons that he has no need for the lower pair of Wagner tubas, the two tenors joining the ordinary bass tubas to form an *ad hoc* quartet. In 1960 Elisabeth Lutyens took the rare step of reviving the quartet of Wagner tubas in her *Quincunx*, although at no time do the players double on horns.

It might be expected that the Wagner tubas would be notated like horns in the transpositions in which they are crooked, that is to say B♭ and F. Unfortunately Wagner himself complicated the issue early on during the composition of *The Ring*: in *Rheingold* all goes smoothly (although he retained the same octave when writing in the bass clef for the bass tubas, whereas he was still writing conventionally an octave lower when using the bass clef for horns). But the scores of the other three music dramas contain a footnote reading:

> In this, as well as the following/preceding scores, the tenor tubas are written in E♭, the bass tubas in B♭, because the composer believed this way easier to read; when copying out the parts, however, the keys of B♭ and F should be retained according to the nature of these instruments, and the notes must therefore be transposed.

This is complete confusion, especially as it is not entirely true; for in the *Vorspiel* to *Götterdämmerung* he experimented further, reverting to the B♭/F notation as in *Rheingold*, but in the treble clef an octave higher. However, he clearly came to the conclusion that this was a mistake because by Act I

he had changed back yet again to his so-called 'easier-to-read' double transposition of E♭ and B♭, in which they remain to the end.

Unfortunately Wagner's instructions were never observed and the orchestral parts are printed exactly like the scores; however, some opera houses have had special sets transcribed, which, in deference to the wishes of the players, retain the standard F horn transposition throughout.

Strangely, Wagner's E♭/B♭ double transposition was adopted by Schoenberg when he used the tubas in *Gurrelieder*; Bruckner, on the other hand, retained the B♭ and F notation, in which he was followed by Strauss. Sadly Bruckner got caught up in Wagner's muddle so that inconsistencies of all kinds bristle in the course of his last three symphonies.

One consequence of all this is that it is hardly ever obvious at which octave the Wagner tubas should play. In *Le Sacre du Printemps* either octave is feasible for the B♭ tenor tubas and it is primarily from internal evidence that the right decision is reached. Elisabeth Lutyens ultimately wrote for all four Wagner tubas in F on the practical advice of players and librarians, though this gives her score a unique appearance since in no other scores at all are the *tenor* tubas actually described as being F instruments.

The position of the Wagner tubas in the score is another case where no uniformity exists. Wagner himself placed them together with the biggest tuba, i.e., below the trumpets and trombones, not unreasonably since he was writing for a five-tuba ensemble.

This is also their position in Bruckner's Seventh Symphony but in the Eighth and Ninth he changed his mind since he was now thinking of them as part of the horn group, and they are placed above the trumpets, even bracketed with the horns. Strauss also had second thoughts on this matter, for in *Elektra* the tubas are grouped below the trombones but thereafter they are repositioned above the trumpets.

In range the Wagner tubas correspond broadly to the horns despite their extra weight, though the bass tubas are naturally less flexible than the tenors. But the upper notes are rarely found in the repertoire and Strauss's high writing in *Elektra* can be considered exceptional.

See also: MUTES, PLATFORM ARRANGEMENT, 5; TRANSPOSING INSTRUMENTS

Waldhorn (Ger.), original name for French horn in its natural state; i.e., without valves; cf. Ventilhorn; *see* HORN, 2

WHIP

The whip is another special-purpose instrument. Like the English, the French and Italian terms refer to what the instrument emulates: **fouet** and **frusta**, but the Germans and Americans, being realists, call it **Holzklapper** and **slapstick** respectively, which is what it actually is – two pieces of thin wood hinged together. Because of this, fast repeated strokes are possible in a way that could not be achieved with a real whip, and extended passages are written, like the relentless whip strokes in the *Scherzo* of Mahler's Fifth Symphony.

Nevertheless the whip is usually associated with single electrifying slaps such as at the climax of the first movement of Milhaud's *Protée* or the notorious first crack of Ravel's G major Piano Concerto, surely the most striking of all.

Whip strokes are generally loud; just as the real whip would not crack at all unless vigorously lashed, so the imitation model flapped gingerly creates little effect, though Britten does ask for a succession of *p* and *pp* strokes in the Cello Symphony.

WHISTLE

The feature of the whistle – unlike, for example, a similar 'effects' instrument, the SIREN – is its single constant pitch. It is, however, equally full of extra-musical associations such as the police whistle of Ibert's *Divertissement*, which, described as a *sifflet à roulette*, derives from the work's origin as incidental music to the play *The Italian Straw Hat*, where it represents the frenzied whistle of an outraged French policeman faced with an uncontrollable mass débâcle. The part is marked *fff* – which is just as well, as this kind of whistle hardly works any other way.

See also: PICCOLO

WIND CHIMES

These delicate objects were for long hardly more than adjuncts to the effects department of the percussion group, but have gradually entered the sphere of serious compositions, as for example, in John McCabe's *Chagall Windows*.

They originate from the Orient where they are not part of the musical scene at all but are either purely ornamental or serve as elaborately flexible door curtains rustling attractively in the wind. They can be made of various substances, such as glass, bamboo, shell or very light metal tubes, all of which, being lightly strung together, ring freely when disturbed by the hand or shaken. Composers rarely specify the material as it is the shimmer that is required and the exact effect is generally a matter of trial and error.

WIND MACHINE

This unwieldy contraption, although not percussion in the strict sense of the word, comes into the same orbit as the wind chimes as part of the effects department. It is a large wooden barrel-shaped structure that is rotated at varying speeds swishing against a canvas cover. It is cranked, by a percussionist, with surprisingly realistic effect; in fact, there is a school of thought that regards its imitative function as cheating, much like Respighi's NIGHTINGALE in the *Pines of Rome*, which is a real one played on a gramophone.

Strauss uses the wind machine in the storm of his *Alpine Symphony* as well as in *Don Quixote* to add realism to his graphic depiction of the Don's mock flight through the air in Variation 7. Vaughan Williams uses it much more nakedly for the spine-chilling gales in his music for the film *Scott of the Antarctic*, sections of which he afterwards reassembled for the so-called *Sinfonia Antartica*. Here, where it essentially replaces composed music with pure imitation, the accusations of cheating

have perhaps more foundation; a symphonic design should arguably be structurally integrated even to the point of stylization (such as the sheep in Strauss's *Don Quixote*), whereas in a film score the straightforward naturalistic effect is obviously valid.

Ravel uses the wind machine under the name of **éoliphone** for the manifestation of the god Pan in his ballet *Daphnis et Chloé*, but unlike the Vaughan Williams example, it serves merely as an extra colour in an already composed piece of music.

Since the only contribution the wind machine can ever make is the rise and fall of its rushing sounds, it is naturally enough notated by a trill (usually on a single line or note) with hairpins of *crescendo* and *diminuendo*. Tippett, when using a wind machine in his Fourth Symphony, tried to avoid this rise and fall of pitch by replacing it at first with an electronic amplification of the actual sound of human breathing, and subsequently with a synthesizer to create the same effect; but both venture even further into the department of realism and are in the event somewhat discomforting.

Wine glasses, *see* GLASS HARMONICA

WOOD BLOCK

Sometimes called the **Chinese block,** the wood block is precisely what its name implies: an oblong block of wood, but so fashioned that it gives a very resonant sound when struck. The primary difference from a single bar taken from a xylophone lies in its having no definite note, although wood blocks can be of all sizes with

257

consequent variations of pitch that are then sometimes used together – high, middle and low. The standard orchestral use, however, is of a single small block with high and acute tone, that may be termed (perhaps rather perfunctorily) simply **legno** as by Prokofiev in his Sixth Symphony; Blomdahl charmingly uses *pezzo di legno* ('piece of wood'); the Germans say **Holzblock**, as do the French, **bloc de bois**. In *La Création du Monde* Milhaud calls for a *bloc de bois* as well as a *bloc de métal*. This latter is essentially an ANVIL. There is some doubt over what, in his Sixth Symphony, Kurt Atterberg intended by writing *wooden box, Trälåda, Holzkasten, boite de bois* – and then, in the list of the orchestra, **tamburo di legno** (like Prokofiev in his Fifth Symphony), which is not necessarily the same thing. Puccini used the same terminology in *Turandot*, but what he probably intended was a drum similar to the one designated by the Germans as a *Holzplattentrommel* ('woodplate drum'), a native instrument not unlike a LOG DRUM. Another area of doubt surrounds the 2 **tavolette** in Respighi's *Feste Romane*; he writes a rhythmic pattern for them on a single line and they are played, at any rate in Britain, on two wood blocks; but they may well correspond with the Indian tabla or with some oriental HAND DRUMS, such as Bantock uses in his *Omar Khayyám* and which Respighi may have believed to have been in use among the Arab community in Ancient Rome.

Although it is unusual to find methods of execution, type of stick required, etc., detailed in scores, there are ample instances of the wood block used for rhythmic or colouristic effects with full range and gradations of tone; if the block is struck really viciously the resultant 'crack' can match the 'rimshot' on a side drum, though lacking the exciting dramatic impact of that effect. Xenakis uses the wood block stridently in works such as *Pithoprakta*, and the irregular, spaced-out blows once produced such unnerving shocks to the members of the Philharmonia Orchestra that they were unable to restrain themselves from recoiling at each savage *fortissimo* stroke; nevertheless the composer expressed disappointment that a particular Japanese variety of wood block with even greater brilliance could not be obtained.

Roberto Gerhard was particularly interested in wood blocks and his works are full of their exploitation in various sizes and pitches, going on from there to **temple blocks** and beyond these to **Korean blocks** (similar but larger and deeper), all in splendidly exotic rows of graded size and depth.

Temple blocks, also confusingly called Chinese blocks in some scores, look rather like skulls decorated with red and gold, and give a softer 'plopping' noise. They are usually rigged up three or more at a time, of different pitches, and are particularly often written for in groups of three, as in Walton's overture *Scapino*.

Woodplate drum, *see* LOG DRUMS

WOODWIND

1 Terminology
This section comprises all the wind instruments of the orchestra with the

exceptions of the horns and heavy brass. For although today not all the instruments are actually made of wood, they were when the term 'woodwind' first came into general use. However, the name continues to serve even though strictly speaking it has ceased to be accurate, either because wood has to a large extent been superseded by metal – as with flutes – or because newer instruments like saxophones, allied to the section, have been invented which have never been made of wood.

The German equivalent of 'woodwind' corresponds to the English, i.e. **Holzbläser** or just *Holz*, while the French and Italians always omit the '- wind', simply saying **les bois** and **i legni** respectively. In English the word 'wind' is used colloquially to mean only the woodwind, but the corresponding words **Bläser**, **les vents** and **i fiati** on the contrary imply the inclusion of all the brass as well.

It is rare for a work to be written for a symphony orchestra that omits woodwind altogether. Constant Lambert's *Rio Grande* is perhaps the outstanding example, while Hindemith's *Konzertmusik für Streichorchester und Blechbläser* is another well-known instance although, as its title shows, it has no percussion either. In general any ensemble qualifying as an orchestra is assumed to carry some woodwind, however diminutive the section may be.

2 Families

The woodwind consists of a variety of instruments normally falling into four main species: FLUTES, OBOES, CLARINETS and BASSOONS. All of these are reed instruments with the notable exception of the flutes, whose sound is produced by the direct application of the mouth blowing across a hole in the head-joint.

3 Subsidiary Instruments

Each woodwind family has subsidiary members, instruments on which the players may be required to alternate. This demands a degree of agility and adaptability of technique as well as the provision of appropriate aids in the form of furniture designed to make quick changes possible. Flutes, for instance, sometimes can be seen to have a box-like fitment attached to their stands to hold the instrument(s) not in use (for some reason these attachments are rarer than they used to be, and in any case the tiny piccolo can be conveniently kept snugly in the pocket), whereas clarinets and bassoons need more elaborate structures to support the tall and heavy bass members of their species.

Composers are not always realistic in allowing sufficient time for the change, which can be quite a cumbersome operation in the case of, for instance, the contrabassoon. In Mahler's Fifth Symphony the third clarinettist is instructed to handle no fewer than five different instruments, often with only three or four bars' rest to make the switch. But the ultimate is reached by Janáček, who allows no time whatever at certain points in his *Taras Bulba* – so causing the 3rd bassoon, who is directed to double contra, to make *ad hoc* decisions on how to adapt his part by playing some bars on the wrong instrument. The same happens with the oboe and cor anglais in Dvořák's Te Deum. In some instances players may make the switch earlier than marked, a recourse having the additional benefit of warming up the alternate instrument in time for an important solo, a consideration rarely taken into account by composers.

Moreover it is inconsiderate to require the player to change from the smallest to the largest member of a family (or vice versa), as, for example, the piccolo and the alto flute, or the little Eb and the hefty bass clarinet. Such different techniques are involved that players sometimes even refuse to take on such a part alone, insisting that an extra player be engaged.

4 Formations I: Double Wind

Unlike the strings, the flexibility of whose constitution is essentially a numerical matter, the constitution of the woodwind is wholly a question of the composer's requirements. Nevertheless the most basic group may perhaps best be regarded as 'double wind', i.e., two each of flutes, oboes, clarinets and bassoons. This is the body commonly engaged as the nucleus of orchestras that are of modest but not necessarily chamber proportions. Such a section can cover the broad classical and early romantic repertoire without either leaving players idle for too many items in a programme or needing too many extra players for this work or that.

Yet even so fundamental a formation as this cannot be thought of in terms of standardization where most programmes are concerned. Early nineteenth-century composers to whom the double-wind group may have represented the basic norm thought nothing of varying it from work to work as the character of each seemed to dictate. Thus Beethoven, whose symphonies are all essentially conceived on the standard double-woodwind pattern, used only a single flute in No. 4, but added a third player, in the person of the piccolo, in Nos. 5, 6 and 9 as well as a contra in Nos. 5 and 9. Brahms, who also thought in terms of the double wind, added a contra to the First, Third and Fourth of his Symphonies, but not No. 2; moreover, he used a piccolo but no contra in the *Tragic* Overture and both piccolo and contra in the *Academic Festival*, and so on.

In practice it is the 3rd flute who has seemed to be the commonest extra across the broad repertoire, and some double-wind orchestras find it worthwhile to engage just this one additional member on a permanent basis. At the same time, conversely, the flutes are also the family most often reduced to a single player against two each of all the other woodwind instruments, as in Beethoven's Fourth Symphony (already mentioned) as well as in some of his concertos, in Schubert's Fifth Symphony, and in a host of Mozart and Haydn works. The latter composers also show that where complete families are concerned it is the clarinets who are the most often altogether absent, though this is on historical grounds, as in the eighteenth and early nineteenth centuries the clarinet was a newcomer to the orchestral scene.

Variations of the double-wind pattern are, then, infinite. Even Berlioz, for all his gargantuan orchestral con-cepts, thought in terms of double wind except only in taking four bassoons for granted like most French composers, since their opera houses normally carried these players on the strength. Balakirev was prone to add a 3rd clarinet, though he used only a single oboe in conjunction with the cor ang-lais; Dvořák on the contrary tended to use a three-oboe section, and so on. Subtractions can naturally also be found other than the 2nd flute and/or the clarinets, but are associated mostly with the chamber-orchestral single-wind ensembles.

5 Formations II: Triple and Larger Wind Groups

In full-scale symphony orchestras the standard section is essentially triple woodwind. This is adequate for the bulk of the repertoire with only small variations involving a minimum of personnel left idle or no more than the occasional extra players.

Of the rarer subsidiary instruments, alto (bass) flute and Eb clarinet are carried on the orchestral strength of only the very largest international or-chestras with fourfold woodwind, where they will naturally come within the orbit of the 4th players, though the 2nd and 3rd players will need to be prepared to co-operate where com-posers such as Mahler and Strauss lay their scores out with complicated woodwind doublings, or need more than one piccolo, cor anglais, Eb or bass clarinet, basset horn or even contra. Such cases, though admittedly the exceptions, are by no means rare: Busoni uses a section of one oboe

combined with two cors anglais in the 'Sarabande' from *Doktor Faust*; there are two Eb clarinets in Mahler's Second Symphony and two basset horns in Strauss's *Elektra*; Webern scored for two bass clarinets in the splendid original version of his *6 Orchesterstücke*, Op. 6; and Stravinsky provides a spectacular example of two contras in the 'Death of Kastchei' from the ballet score of *The Firebird*.

The rarest instruments of all the woodwind, such as the oboe d'amore, bass oboe and pedal clarinet, are used too infrequently to be specifically engaged on a permanent basis, though if it transpires that a prospective member actually possesses a good bass oboe, for example, it naturally enhances his market value.

6 Formations III: Smaller Groups

At the other extreme end of the numerical scale there remains the woodwind ensemble consisting of only a single representative of each member of the four families. This CHAMBER ORCHESTRA formation is of compara-tively recent origin, appearing in such works as Stravinsky's *Danses Concer-tantes*, Britten's *Sinfonietta*, Honegger's *Pastorale d'Été*, etc. Earlier examples generally include a pair of at least one or other of the families, such as Wagner's *Siegfried Idyll*, which has one each of flute, oboe and bassoon, but a pair of clarinets.

A large number of classical works (and also several twentieth-century pieces written with an eye to inclusion by orchestras specializing in a classical repertoire) reduce the wind group by using just two pairs, or sometimes even only one, of woodwind instruments. A pair of oboes is probably the most frequently used of these, though bassoons may also be added on account of their role as part of the CONTINUO. More rarely, Mozart's Symphony No. 27 in G uses only flutes, and in his G major Concertos for violin (K. 216) and flute (K. 313) they actually alternate with oboes for the slow movement. (In Mozart's day both flutes and oboes would have been played by the same artists but this is wholly unknown now.) Another curiosity is Mozart's use of only clarinets and bassoons in his Horn Concerto No. 3 (K. 447). In such works, however, the diminutive woodwind group was more often than not combined with a pair of horns, which are treated as co-woodwind rather than as isolated members of the brass family, for this inclusion of horns in the woodwind group is a primary accessory quality of these instruments' character.

7 Individualistic Nature of the Section and General Remarks

Soloistic to a fundamental extent that can never be the case with the strings, less exclusive than the horns, more aristocratic than the brass, the woodwind department consists of a group of highly individual but interdependent artists whose work in the orchestra alternates between solo and ensemble playing. Hence arises the status, and accordingly payment, of the wind who are mostly PRINCIPALS with only a few sub-principals.

Wind players need considerable resources of patience and adaptability. Their solos may occur in the midst of gruelling stretches of *tutti* playing or after long periods of inactivity. In the one case there is the eternal spectre of the tired lip or worn reed, in the other the necessity to play a difficult and exposed passage on a cold instrument and when they themselves have, as it were, 'gone off the boil'.

Nor are these hazards confined to the specific responsibilities of playing solo passages for the woodwind group. The manifold characters, let alone the imperfections, of so many different instruments and variations of instruments, give rise to tortuous problems of intonation as well as precision of ensemble attack. The combining of woodwind into blocks of sound is not at all the exact science that Rimsky-Korsakov formulated in his beautifully logical *Principles of Orchestration*. All his carefully contrived dovetailing of timbres gives a sound as personal and as acoustically fallible as that of other composers whose individuality is revealed as much by their distribution of woodwind chording or ensemble work as by their very style of composition. Berlioz once said in bitter irony, but with perhaps unintended truth, that he had only to write down a chord of D major for the critics to shout, 'Impossible!" For his orchestration is often so idiosyncratic as to be unmistakable even in a simple woodwind chord.

The varied styles of different composers may present quite unexpected problems. Many a chord that looks harmless enough on paper presents unforeseeable clashes of overtones requiring the utmost skill as the players jockey for pitch position. Even highly accomplished artists may be unsure at times who is at fault or even whether they should personally adjust up or down, sharp or flat, in circumstances where the word 'truth' has no unequivocal meaning. The problem may also arise through the acoustical flaw in our use of the tempered scale. There is a notorious 6:4 chord near the beginning of Strauss's *Till Eulenspiegel*, which gives perennial trouble to the four instruments concerned, two flutes and two clarinets, where it is – strange to say – the tonic F, played by the 1st flute, that may have to be flattened with regard to the prevailing pitch before the chord will be tolerable and free of 'beats'. Sometimes the use of a certain degree of *vibrato* in, for example, the flutes may help; for the innate purity of the flute sound in itself can make it appear to be actually below pitch when combined with other members of the wind ensemble. The same can be true of the lowest register of the oboe, though for different acoustic reasons. These are matters that experienced and well-matched players will aim to correct as a matter of course. Such a wind section will often prefer to organize their differences and make any necessary adjustments among themselves, especially in the case of the well-known *bêtes noires* (Mendelssohn's overture *A Midsummer Night's Dream*, Rimsky-Korsakov's *Scheherazade*, the last chords of Wagner's *Faust* overture, Balakirev's *Thamar* and Strauss's *Don Quixote*, etc.). It must also be conceded that chords and passages do occur that hardly ever sound really satisfactory. There are even ghost notes, played by nobody and even inaudible to the wind group though perfectly clear to the conductor and the delighted strings. The conductor, therefore, if he is to arbitrate successfully, needs a specific understanding of wind problems, but it would be naive to believe that his skill in perfecting wind intonation will be due to an impeccable ear. Such an asset, enviable as it is, has been known to lead to a tiresome misuse of valuable rehearsal time and the consequent irritation of the players, who have long learned how to adjust momentarily to each other as occasion may warrant, while the wretched conductor embroils himself ever deeper in a fluctuating tonal quicksand.

8 Ensemble

Woodwind ensemble of attack is again an art and not a science. Orchestral leaders, sitting fretfully at their violin desks, have been known to express scorn and impatience at what they regard as the patent incompetence of wind players who appear to be unable to tongue precisely on the conductor's beat. Yet this view merely reveals a lack of sympathy with the inherent difficulties and techniques in wind playing, which are not only as specialized in every way as the numerous problems of precision with which the strings are constantly involved, but are also concerned to a far greater extent with the interplay of personal styles and the close collaboration of a few interdependent soloists. However much it may be desirable for the leaders of the string group to like and admire each other as people, as well as for their artistry, in the wind ensemble it is of paramount importance.

See also: ENSEMBLE, HARMONIE, PLATFORM ARRANGEMENT, SCORE LAYOUT

Xucalhos, *see* GOURDS

XYLOPHONE

The xylophone is first cousin to the GLOCKENSPIEL in that it has a similar arrangement of bars, with the chief difference that they are made of wood instead of metal. A further important deviation lies, however, in the way the instrument has developed from the **Holz- und Strohinstrument** of Strauss's *Salome* (this was nothing more nor less than a primitive xylophone, the wooden bars having been literally laid over a straw-strewn base) to the modern elaborate instrument with its resonators and movable wheeled structure.

It is practically impossible to state categorically the range of the xylophone. It may vary from the two and a half octaves of the glockenspiel as in the simplest table model, to a four-octave contraption suitable for the dazzling displays of light-music solo virtuoso players. The instrument has, however, evolved in the process through the impinging on it of another and very important instrument, the MARIMBA.

The standard orchestral xylophone is a simple dry-to-clattery-sounding instrument, with straight, non-resonating wooden bars, high in pitch though in fact an octave less high than the glockenspiel. The xylophone can therefore generally be taken to sound an octave higher than written; at the same time, in determining this pitch factor the question of timbre has to be taken into account and this can be incredibly confusing. In the case of the lower register the overtones can even be so much stronger than the fundamental that one can be misled over what note is actually being played.

Until recently, however, the xylophone was the only member of its family recognized by symphonic composers, and although long known to be capable of virtuoso accomplishments, it was still rarely exploited except in such illustrative solos as Britten's *Young Person's Guide*, designed specifically to show off its potential. Normally xylophone solos are simple in character and modest in technical requirements, the colour of the instrument being usually the end in itself. Its first appearance in the symphony was in Mahler's Sixth.

However, with the researches of composers such as Orff in Germany and the Messiaen–Boulez school in France three members of the xylophone family (xylophone, marimba and especially the xylorimba) have begun to be exploited from every angle, while Puccini's *Turandot* provides an inspired use of a rare member of the family, the bass xylophone. This sounds an octave lower than the xylophone and Puccini, unusually for this kind of instrument, notates it in the bass clef. Today it is normally, if not quite correctly, replaced by the ubiquitous xylorimba. Orff uses further additional fringe instruments in *Antigonae* such as **trogxylophones**, soprano, tenor and bass no less, and, following his lead, Hartmann writes fantastically elaborate parts for marimba on two staves in his later symphonies. Here (as with the glockenspiel) the use of several sticks in each hand is a clear extension of technique. Different kinds of sticks (rubber, hardwood, felt, etc.) exist for all these instruments, but are not often prescribed by composers as this comes into the province of interpretation.

In *Duke Bluebeard's Castle* Bartók writes for a *xilofono a tastiera*, which is none other than a keyboard xylo. In practice, there being no longer any such thing, the passages in the opera are normally given to two players using conventional hammers.

It is not usual to find xylophone passages laid out on two staves so as to show how they should be distributed between the hands, though Ravel did so in the 'Laideronette' movement in *Ma Mère l'Oye*; no doubt at the time it was considered particularly exacting.

The name of the xylophone is international, only occasionally the characteristic 'x' being changed to an 's' or 'z' for some scores using Italian terminology: *silofono, zilofono*, etc. Schoenberg in *Gurrelieder* calls it a **Holzharmonika** but adds the conventional *xylophon* in brackets.

The instrument naturally comes into its own in music descriptive of wood or bones (skeletons, etc.) as in Saint-Saëns's *Danse Macabre* of 1874, which was such a pioneering use of the xylophone that the score contains a note explaining what it is (*de bois et paille* – like Strauss's in *Salome*), and stating that it could be obtained from the publishers. Bartók's *Wooden Prince* and Walton's *Belshazzar's Feast* ('Praise Ye

the God of Wood') give further obviously appropriate uses, while the solo at the opening of Janáček's *Jenufa*, descriptive of the turning of the mill wheel, is a famous atmospheric stroke of genius.

Xylorimba, *see* MARIMBA

Zimbalon (It.), *see* CIMBALOM

ZINKE

These, known equally as *zinke* or **cornetti**, are wind instruments made of wood covered with leather yet blown with a mouthpiece, so that they are to some extent hybrid with links to both woodwind and brass.

They were used by composers from Monteverdi to Bach and are not to be confused with cornets, though they had a similar range. For this reason, nevertheless, many cornetto parts are actually sometimes played, however anachronistically, on cornets or small trumpets for practical reasons. It has been said, however, that of present-day instruments clarinets and oboes played in unison give the nearest approximation to the quality of cornetti. There has been no post-baroque use of zinke/cornetto family except for the bass member, which is the SERPENT.

ZITHER

One would hardly have reckoned the zither an orchestral member but then the same is broadly true of the CIMBALOM and other such popular instruments that have become accredited through their use as local colour. Thus too, if to a lesser extent, the zither finds its way into the symphonic world mainly through the great Johann Strauss, for there are substantial solos in his popular waltz *Tales from the Vienna Woods*, though Villa Lobos has also included a part for it in his *Amazonas* where he calls it **cytharra**.

The zither is written at pitch on two staves as in piano or harp notation. It is a flat box-like instrument not unlike a cimbalom, though without the legs, and is plucked with the fingers of one hand as well as with a plectrum held in the other. According to the textbooks

the bottom note is: 🎼 (the

tuning of the lowest string) but Strauss writes happily down to the D below the stave. His uppermost note is B above the treble clef, which is consistent with

the tuning of the top string .

As with the cimbalom or bagpipes, a special artist is usually engaged and will often appear dressed in national (e.g. Tyrolean) costume, though it must be admitted that Strauss's score disappointingly includes *ossia* lines for a small ensemble drawn from the orchestral strings.

Zymbal (Ger.), *see* CYMBALS, 1